CCNA:
Fast Pass

CCNA™:
Fast Pass

Todd Lammle

San Francisco • London

SYBEX®

Associate Publisher: Neil Edde
Acquisitions Editor: Maureen Adams
Developmental Editor: Jeff Kellum
Production Editor: Elizabeth Campbell
Technical Editor: David Groth
Copyeditor: Rebecca Rider
Compositor: Scott Benoit
Graphic Illustrator: Tony Jonick
CD Coordinator: Dan Mummert
CD Technician: Kevin Ly
Proofreaders: Laurie O'Connell, Nancy Riddiough
Indexer: Nancy Guenther
Book Designer: Bill Gibson
Cover Design and Illustration: Richard Miller, Calyx Design

Library of Congress Card Number: 2003113690

ISBN: 0-7821-4309-1

Acknowledgments

I need to thank Neil Edde, Maureen Adams, Jeff Kellum, and Elizabeth Campbell for trying to keep my path straight and focused. This is no easy task for you and I applaud your patience and dedication to our vision.

Thanks also to the Sybex CD team for the super testing engine, Scott Benoit, who laid out these pages, David Groth, for his technical take on things, and Rebecca Rider whose eagle eye caught any grammar or spelling issues before they made it into the book.

Contents at a Glance

Contents

Introduction

Cisco's Cisco Certified Network Administrator (CCNA) certification provides a way to distinguish those brilliant and talented enough to become Cisco administrators from those who just might be, umm—well, better suited to another occupation. It's basically Cisco's version of separating the wheat from the chaff. The main reason that it's a really good thing to be the proud possessor of Cisco's certifications is that they give you a serious edge over the poor, wretched, unfortunate, and noncertified masses. Having one or more of these little beauties just screams, "I'm a wiz—I'm your living-breathing IT answer—hire me, not that hopeless, bungling *uncertified* quack you just interviewed!" In addition, any prospective employer worth his or her salt who's seeking solidly skilled, trained, experienced administrators knows to look for a job candidate with a CCNA certification. Okay, it's true. Being certified in something doesn't necessarily preclude hands-on experience. But people who have experience combined with certifications are well sought out, even in the toughest economies. It's simply, "have certs, will travel." They make you special.

Be forewarned, however—these certifications are not easy to get a hold of. You should know that the new Cisco 640-801 CCNA exam is downright harsh! You've just got to be prepared—no cruising with this one. If you want to seriously increase your odds of passing, meet two of your new best friends: this book and the CCNA: *Cisco Certified Network Associate Study Guide Fourth Edition (640-801)*, written by yours truly (Sybex, 2004). These two references are what you need to prepare for the new and nasty CCNA exam. Both of these valuable resources will also serve to further your understanding of a whole bunch of the vital knowledge and skills you need to become a successful Cisco administrator.

How Is This Book Organized?

This book is organized according to the official objectives list prepared by Cisco for the CCNA exam. The chapters correspond to the four broad categories: Planning and Design, Implementation and Operation, Troubleshooting, and Technology.

Within each chapter, the individual exam objectives are each addressed. Each section of a chapter covers one exam objective. For each objective, I first present the critical information and then follow it with several Exam Essentials. Additionally, each chapter ends with a section of Review Questions. Here is a closer look at each of these components:

Exam Objectives   The individual exam objective sections present detailed information that is relevant to the CCNA exam. This is the place to start if you're unfamiliar with or uncertain of the technical issues related to the objective.

Exam Essentials   Here I give you a short list of topics that you should explore fully before you take the test. These Exam Essentials sum up the key information you should take out of the exam objective section.

Review Questions   This section comes at the end of every chapter. It provides 10 questions that should help you gauge your mastery of the chapter.

Cisco Certified Network Associate (CCNA) Certification

The CCNA certification was the first in the new line of Cisco certifications, and was the precursor to all current Cisco certifications. With the new certification programs, Cisco has created a stepping-stone approach to CCIE certification. Now you can become a CCNA for the meager cost of this book, plus $125 for the test. You don't have to stop there—you can choose to continue with your studies and achieve a higher certification, the Cisco Certified Network Professional (CCNP). Someone with a CCNP has all the skills and knowledge he or she needs to attempt the CCIE lab. However, because no textbook can take the place of practical experience, I'll discuss what else you need to be ready for the CCIE lab shortly.

Why Become a CCNA?

Cisco, not unlike Microsoft or Novell, has created the certification process to give administrators a set of skills and to equip prospective employers with a way to measure skills or match certain criteria. Becoming a CCNA can be the initial step of a successful journey toward a new, highly rewarding, and sustainable career.

The CCNA program was created to provide a solid introduction not only to the Cisco Internetwork Operating System (IOS) and Cisco hardware, but also to internetworking in general, making it helpful to you in areas that are not exclusively Cisco's. At this point in the certification process, it's not unrealistic to imagine that future network managers—even those without Cisco equipment—could easily require Cisco certifications for their job applicants.

If you make it through the CCNA and are still interested in Cisco and internetworking, you're headed down a path to certain success.

What Skills Do You Need to Become a CCNA?

To meet the CCNA certification skill level, you must understand or be able to do the following:

- Install, configure, and operate simple-routed local area networks (LAN), routed wide area networks (WAN), and switched LAN networks.

- Understand and be able to configure Internet Protocol (IP), Interior Gateway Routing Protocol (IGRP), Enhanced IGRP (EIGRP), Open Shortest Path First (OSPF), ISDN, PPP, Frame Relay, IP Routing Information Protocol (RIP), virtual LANs (VLANs), Ethernet, and access lists.

- Install and/or configure a network.

- Optimize WANs through Internet-access solutions that reduce bandwidth and WAN costs, using features such as filtering with access lists, and dial-on-demand routing (DDR).

How Do You Become a CCNA?

The first step to becoming CCNA involves passing one little test (exam 640-801 CCNA) and—poof!—you're a CCNA. (Don't you wish it were that easy?) True, it's just one test, but you still must possess enough knowledge to understand (and read between the lines—trust me) what the test writers are saying.

However, Cisco has announced two tests that you can take in order to become a CCNA that may be easier then taking one longer exam. These tests are:

- 640-811 ICND
- 641-821 INTRO

> You spend more money if you take these two exams instead of the 640-801 exam, but it may be easier to break up the exam into two smaller exams. That's a personal choice. Understand that this book prepares you to pass the 640-801 exam, although you probably could pass both of the smaller exams using it as well.

I can't stress this enough—it's critical that you have some hands-on experience with Cisco routers. If you can get a hold of some 2500 routers, you're set. But if you can't, I've worked hard to provide many configuration examples throughout this book to help network administrators (or people who want to become network administrators) learn what they need to know to pass the CCNA exam.

One way to get the hands-on router experience you'll need in the real world is to attend one of the seminars offered by GlobalNet Training Solutions, Inc., which I own and run. The seminars are either 5 or 11 days long and will teach you everything you need to become a CCNA (or even a CCNP and CCSP). Each student gets hands-on experience by configuring at least three routers and two switches. See www.globalnettraining.com for more information.

> For hands-on training with Todd Lammle, please see www.globalnettraining .com. Also, check www.routersim.com for a full Cisco router simulator.

Where Do You Take the Exams?

You may take the CCNA exam at any of the more than 800 Prometric Authorized Testing Centers around the world; contact them at www.2test.com, or call 800-204-EXAM (3926). You can also register and take the exams at a Pearson VUE authorized center. You can contact them at www.vue.com or call (877) 404-EXAM (3926).

To register for a Cisco Certified Network Associate exam, follow these steps:

1. Determine the number of the exam you want to take. (The CCNA exam number is 640-801.)

2. Register with the nearest Prometric Registration Center or Pearson VUE testing center. At this point, you will be asked to pay in advance for the exam. At the time of this writing, the exams are $125 each and must be taken within one year of payment. You can schedule exams up to six weeks in advance or as late as the same day you want to take it—but if you fail a Cisco exam, you must wait 72 hours before you will be allowed to retake the exam. If something comes up and you need to cancel or reschedule your exam appointment, contact Prometric or Pearson VUE at least 24 hours in advance.

3. When you schedule the exam, you'll get instructions regarding all appointment and cancellation procedures, the ID requirements, and information about the testing-center location.

Tips for Taking Your CCNA Exam

The CCNA test contains around 50 questions (maybe more), to be completed in around 90 minutes (possibly less). These numbers are subject to change; every exam is unique. You must get a score of about 85 percent to pass this exam, but again, each exam can be different.

Many questions on the exam have answer choices that at first glance look identical—especially the syntax questions! Remember to read through the choices carefully, because close doesn't cut it. If you get commands in the wrong order or forget one measly character, you'll get the question wrong.

Also, never forget that the right answer is the Cisco answer. In many cases, more than one appropriate answer is presented, but the *correct* answer is the one that Cisco recommends. On the exam, if more than one answer is correct, the question always tells you to pick one, two, or three options, never to "choose all that apply."

The CCNA 640-801 exam includes the following test formats:

- Multiple-choice single answer
- Multiple-choice multiple answer
- Drag-and-drop
- Fill-in-the-blank
- Router simulations

Here are some general tips for exam success:

- Arrive early at the exam center so that you can relax and review your study materials.
- Read the questions *carefully*. Don't jump to conclusions. Make sure you're clear about *exactly* what each question asks.
- When answering multiple-choice questions that you're not sure about, use the process of elimination to get rid of the obviously incorrect answers first. Doing this greatly improves your odds if you need to make an educated guess.
- You can no longer move forward and backward through the Cisco exams, so double-check your answer before clicking Next since you can't change your mind.

After you complete an exam, you'll get immediate, online notification of your pass or fail status, a printed Examination Score Report that indicates your pass or fail status, and your exam results by section. (The test administrator will give you the printed score report.) Test scores are automatically forwarded to Cisco within five working days after you take the test, so you don't need to send your score to them. If you pass the exam, you'll receive confirmation from Cisco, typically within two to four weeks.

How to Contact the Author

You can reach Todd Lammle through GlobalNet Training Solutions, Inc. (www.globalnettraining .com), his training and systems integration company in Dallas, Texas—or through his software company (www.routersim.com) in Denver, Colorado, which creates both Cisco and Microsoft software simulation programs.

The CCNA Exam Objectives

Cisco has posted four categories that each contain specific objectives. As I mentioned earlier, these exam objectives form the outline for this book. Here are Cisco's objectives for the CCNA:

Planning & Designing

Design a simple LAN using Cisco Technology.

Design an IP addressing scheme to meet design requirements.

Select an appropriate routing protocol based on user requirements.

Design a simple internetwork using Cisco technology.

Develop an access list to meet user specifications.

Choose WAN services to meet customer requirements.

Implementation & Operation

Configure routing protocols given user requirements.

Configure IP addresses, subnet masks, and gateway addresses on routers and hosts.

Configure a router for additional administrative functionality.

Configure a switch with VLANS and inter-switch communication.

Implement a LAN.

Customize a switch configuration to meet specified network requirements.

Manage system image and device configuration files.

Perform an initial configuration on a router.

Perform an initial configuration on a switch.

Implement access lists.

Implement simple WAN protocols.

Troubleshooting

Utilize the OSI model as a guide for systematic network troubleshooting.

Perform LAN and VLAN troubleshooting.

Troubleshoot routing protocols.

Troubleshoot IP addressing and host configuration.

Troubleshoot a device as part of a working network.

Troubleshoot an access list.

Perform simple WAN troubleshooting.

Technology

Describe network communications using layered models.

Describe the Spanning Tree process.

Compare and contrast key characteristics of LAN environments.

Evaluate the characteristics of routing protocols.

Evaluate TCP/IP communication process and its associated protocols.

Describe the components of network devices.

Evaluate rules for packet control.

Evaluate key characteristics of WANs.

Chapter

1

Planning & Designing

CISCO CCNA EXAM GUIDELINES COVERED IN THIS CHAPTER:

- ✓ **1.1 Design a simple LAN using Cisco Technology**
- ✓ **1.2 Design an IP addressing scheme to meet design requirements**
- ✓ **1.3 Select an appropriate routing protocol based on user requirements**
- ✓ **1.4 Design a simple internetwork using Cisco technology**
- ✓ **1.5 Develop an access list to meet user specifications**
- ✓ **1.6 Choose WAN services to meet customer requirements**

A large part of the CCNA exam deals with not just the configuration, but the work that comes before you actually log into the router for setup and troubleshooting. This chapter addresses those issues. We will discuss the process of designing networks, and making decisions about issues such as which devices, IP addressing, and routing protocols to choose. Let's face it, if you don't have a handle on these decisions, how can you even order equipment?

Let's get started by looking first at a simple LAN and choosing which technologies to include.

1.1 Designing a Simple LAN Using Cisco Technology

You can substitute a number of interchangeable terms for local area network (LAN), depending on the context (these terms will be covered in more detail later in the chapter). They include the following:

- Broadcast domain, which is used in the context of Layer 2 vs. Layer 1 segmentation

- Subnet or network, which are used in the context of IP networking

- Data Link (Layer 2 from the OSI model)

- Virtual LAN (VLAN), which is used in the context of creating broadcast domains in switched Ethernet environments

Why discuss a simple LAN? Well, it is the basis of every internetwork. An *internetwork* is a collection of connected LANs. You can create an individual LAN using a variety of devices and techniques, including switches, routers, and hubs. These devices connect the hosts on the LAN to each other, and they connect the LAN to the other LANs, forming the internetwork.

The number of networks and the necessity of networking have grown exponentially over the last 15 years—and understandably so. They've had to evolve at light speed just to keep up with huge increases in basic mission-critical user needs like sharing data and printers, as well as more advanced demands like video conferencing. Unless everyone who needs to share network resources is located in the same office area (an increasingly uncommon situation), it is a challenge to connect the relevant and sometimes numerous networks so that all users can share the networks' wealth.

It's likely that at some point, you'll have to break up one large network into a number of smaller ones because user response has dwindled to a trickle as networks grew and grew and LAN traffic congestion reached overwhelming proportions. Congestion is a really big problem. Some possible causes of LAN traffic congestion are:

- Too many hosts in a broadcast domain
- Excessive Broadcasts
- Multicasting
- Low or insufficient bandwidth

You can help solve the congestion issue by breaking up a larger network into a number of smaller networks. This is known as *network segmentation*. Network segmentation is accomplished using routers, switches, and bridges.

Routers

You use *routers* to connect networks and route packets of data from one network to another. Cisco became the de facto standard of routers because of their high-quality router products, their great selection, and their fantastic customer service.

Routers, by default, break up a *broadcast domain*, which is the set of all the devices on a network segment that hear all the broadcasts sent on that segment. Breaking up a broadcast domain is important because when a host or server sends a network broadcast, every device on the network must read and process that broadcast—that is, unless you've got a router. When the router's interface receives this broadcast, it can respond by basically saying, "Thanks, but no thanks"; it can then discard the broadcast without forwarding it on to other networks.

Even though routers are known for breaking up broadcast domains by default, it's important to remember that they also break up collision domains as well.

Here are two ways that using routers in your network can reduce congestion:

- They don't forward broadcasts by default (switches and bridges do)
- They can filter the network based on Layer 3 information (that is, based on IP address); switches and bridges cannot.

Switches

Conversely, LAN switches aren't used to create internetworks—they're employed to add functionality to a LAN. The main purpose of a *switch* is to make a LAN work better—to optimize its performance—by providing more bandwidth for the LAN's users. And switches don't forward packets to other networks like routers do; instead, they only forward frames from one port to another within the switched network. Switches cannot forward frames between networks; they can only carry frames to routers to be forwarded to other networks by the router.

Switches and switching technologies are covered in more detail in Chapter 4, section 4.3, Compare and contrast key characteristics of LAN environments.

By default, switches break up collision domains. *Collision domain* is an Ethernet term used to describe the following network scenario. One particular device sends a packet on a network segment, forcing every other device on that segment to pay attention to it. At the same time, a different device tries to transmit, which leads to a collision, after which both devices must retransmit, one at a time. Not good—very inefficient! You'll typically find this situation in a hub environment where each host segment connects to a hub that represents only one collision domain and only one broadcast domain. By contrast, each and every port on a switch represents its own collision domain.

Switches create separate collision domains, but only one broadcast domain. Routers create separate broadcast domains.

Bridges

The term *bridging* was introduced before routers and hubs were implemented, so it's pretty common to hear people referring to bridges as *switches*. That's because bridges and switches basically do the same thing—they break up collision domains on a LAN. So what this means is that a switch is basically just a multiple port bridge with more brainpower, right? Well, pretty much, but there are differences. Switches do provide this function, but they do so with greatly enhanced management ability and features. Plus, most of the time, bridges only have two or four ports. Yes, you can get your hands on a bridge with up to 16 ports, but that's nothing compared to the hundreds available on some switches!

You should use a bridge in a network where you want to reduce collisions within broadcast domains and increase the number of collision domains in your network. In this situation, bridges provide more bandwidth for users.

The Router, Switch, and Bridge Working Together

Now it's time to see how the router, switch, and bridge operate together. Figure 1.1 shows how a network looks with all of these internetwork devices in place.

Remember that the router breaks up broadcast domains for every LAN interface, but it also breaks up collision domains as well.

FIGURE 1.1   Internetworking devices

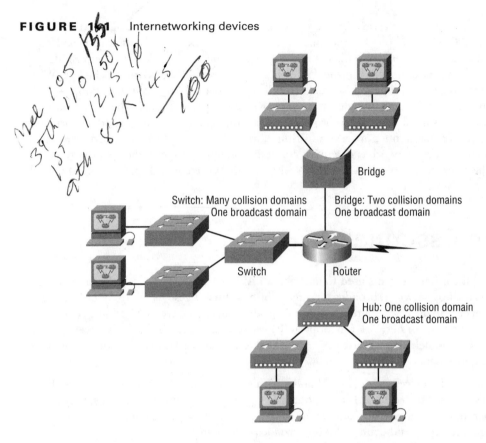

When you look at Figure 1.1, do you notice that the router is at center stage and that it connects each physical network? In this situation, I had to use this layout because of the older technologies involved——bridges and hubs. But once you have only switches in your network, things can change a lot! In the new network, you could place the LAN switches at the center of the network world and use the routers to connect only the logical networks together. If you've implemented this kind of setup, you've created virtual LANs (VLANs).

Okay, now refer back to Figure 1.1: In the top network, I used a bridge to connect the hubs to a router. The bridge breaks up collision domains, but all the hosts connected to both hubs are still crammed into the same broadcast domain. Also, this bridge only creates two collision domains, so each device connected to a hub is in the same collision domain as every other device connected to that same hub. This is actually pretty lame, but it's still better than having one collision domain for all your hosts!

Although bridges are used to segment networks, they will not isolate broadcast or multicast packets.

Notice something else: the three interconnected hubs at the bottom of the figure also connect to the router. This creates one humongous collision domain and one humongous broadcast domain—a messy situation, true. This makes the bridged network look much better indeed!

The best network connected to the router is the LAN switch network on the left. Why? Because, each port on that switch breaks up collision domains. But it's not all good—all the devices are still in the same broadcast domain. Remember why this can be a bad thing? Because all devices must listen to all broadcasts transmitted, and if your broadcast domains are too large, the users must process additional, and sometimes excessive, broadcasts.

Obviously, the best network is one that's correctly configured to meet the business requirements of the company it serves. LAN switches with routers, when correctly placed in the network, are the best network design.

Exam Essentials

Understand the different terms used to describe a LAN.   A LAN is basically the same thing as a VLAN, subnet or network, broadcast domain, or data link. These terms all describe roughly the same concept in different contexts. A broadcast domain is used when describing segmenting with routers, a subnet or network functions in IP networking, a data link defines Layer 2 boundaries of the OSI model, and you use a VLAN when you create broadcast domains in switched Ethernet environments.

Understand which devices create a LAN and which separate and connect LANs.   Switches and bridges are used to create LANs. Although they do separate collision domains, they do not create separate LANs (a collision domain and a LAN are not the same concept). Routers are used to separate LANs and connect LANs (broadcast domains).

1.2 Designing an IP Addressing Scheme to Meet Design Requirements

An *IP address* is a numeric identifier that is assigned to each machine on an IP network, and it designates the specific location of a device on that network. An IP address is a software address, not a hardware address—the latter is hardcoded on a network interface card (NIC) and is used for finding hosts on a local network. IP addressing was designed to allow a host on one network to communicate with a host on a different network, regardless of the type of LANs the hosts are participating in.

There are many items to consider when you go to design an IP addressing scheme because IP addressing is, well, a large topic. However, some aspects, when considered at design time, can save you significant maintenance time over the life of an internetwork. Here, I'll introduce you to some basic terminology and the hierarchical IP address system; you'll also look at private IP addresses and network address translation (NAT).

IP Terminology

The following are several important terms vital to your understanding of the Internet Protocol (IP):

Bit   A bit is one digit; either a 1 or a 0.

Byte   A byte is 7 or 8 bits, depending on whether parity is used. For the rest of this section, always assume a byte is 8 bits.

Octet   An octet, made up of 8 bits, is just an ordinary 8-bit binary number. In this chapter, the terms *byte* and *octet* are completely interchangeable.

Network address   The network address is the designation used in routing to send packets to a remote network—for example, 10.0.0.0, 172.16.0.0, and 192.168.10.0.

Broadcast address   This type of address is used by applications and hosts to send information to all nodes on a network. Examples include 255.255.255.255, which is all networks, all nodes; 172.16.255.255, which is all subnets and hosts on network 172.16.0.0; and 10.255.255.255, which broadcasts to all subnets and hosts on network 10.0.0.0.

The Hierarchical IP Addressing Scheme

An IP address consists of 32 bits of information. These bits are divided into four sections, referred to as octets or bytes, and each contains 1 byte (8 bits). You can depict an IP address using one of three methods:

- Dotted-decimal, as in 172.16.30.56

- Binary, as in 10101100.00010000.00011110.00111000

- Hexadecimal (hex for short), as in AC.10.1E.38

All these examples represent the same IP address. Hex isn't used as often as dotted-decimal or binary when IP addressing is being discussed, *but* you still might find an IP address stored in hex in some programs. The Windows Registry is a good example of a program that stores a machine's IP address in hex.

The 32-bit IP address is a structured or hierarchical address, as opposed to a flat or nonhierarchical address. Although you can use either type of addressing scheme, I'd advise that you use hierarchical addressing. The advantage of using a hierarchical address is that it can handle a large number of addresses, namely 4.3 billion (a 32-bit address space with two possible values for each position—either 0 or 1—gives you 2^{32}, or 4,294,967,296). The disadvantage of the flat addressing scheme and the reason it's not used for IP addressing relates to routing. If every address were unique, all routers on the Internet would need to store the address of every machine on the Internet. This would make efficient routing impossible, even if only a fraction of the possible addresses were used.

You can solve this problem by using a two- or three-level hierarchical addressing scheme that is structured by network and host, or network, subnet, and host.

This two- or three-level scheme is comparable to a telephone number. In a phone number, the first section, the area code, designates a very large area. The second section, the prefix, narrows the scope to a local calling area. The final segment, the customer number, zooms in on the specific connection. IP addresses use the same type of layered structure. Rather than all 32 bits being treated as a unique identifier, as would be the case in flat addressing, a part of the address is designated as the network address, and the other part is designated as either the subnet and host, or just the host address.

Network Addressing

The *network address* (also called *network number*) uniquely identifies each network. Every machine on the same network shares that network address as part of its IP address. In the IP address 172.16.30.56, for example, 172.16 is the network address.

The node address is assigned to, and uniquely identifies, each machine on a network. This part of the address must be unique because it identifies a particular machine—an individual— as opposed to a network, which is a group. This number can also be referred to as a *host address*. In the sample IP address 172.16.30.56, 30.56 is the node address.

The designers of the Internet decided to create classes of networks based on network size. For the small number of networks that possess a very large number of nodes, they created the Class A network. At the other extreme is the Class C network, which is reserved for the numerous networks with a small number of nodes. The class distinction for networks between very large and very small is predictably called the Class B network.

How you should subdivide an IP address into a network and node address is determined by the class designation of your network. Figure 1.2 summarizes the three classes of networks—a subject I'll explain in much greater detail throughout this section.

FIGURE 1.2   Summary of the three classes of networks

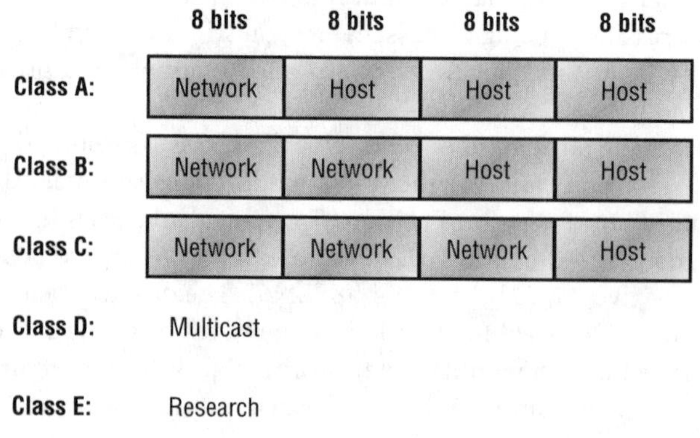

To ensure efficient routing, Internet designers defined a mandate for the leading-bits section of the address for each different network class. For example, since a router knows that a Class A network address always starts with a 0, the router might be able to speed a packet on its way after reading only the first bit of its address. This is where the address schemes define the difference between a Class A, Class B, and Class C address.

Class A Addresses

The designers of the IP address scheme said that the first bit of the first byte in a Class A network address must always be off, or 0. This means a Class A address must be between 0 and 127 inclusively. For example, consider the following network address:

0xxxxxxx

If you turn off the other 7 bits and then turn them back on, you'll find your Class A range of network addresses:

00000000 = 0
01111111 = 127

So, a Class A network is defined in the first octet between 0 and 127, and it can't be less or more, because that would make it illegal. (I'll talk about illegal addresses in a minute.)

In a Class A network address, the first byte is assigned to the network address, and the three remaining bytes are used for the node addresses. Thus, the Class A format is as follows:

network.node.node.node

For example, in the IP address 49.22.102.70, the 49 is the network address, and 22.102.70 is the node address. Every machine on this particular network would have the distinctive network address of 49.

Class A network addresses are one byte long, with the first bit of that byte reserved and the seven remaining bits available for manipulation (addressing). As a result, the maximum number of Class A networks that can be created is 128. Why? Because each of the seven bit positions can either be a 0 or a 1, thus 2^7 or 128.

To complicate matters further, the network address of all zeros (0000 0000) is reserved to designate the default route. Additionally, the address 127, which is reserved for diagnostics, can't be used either, which means that you can really only use the numbers 1 to 126 to designate Class A network addresses. This means that the actual number of usable Class A network addresses is 128 minus 2, or 126.

Each Class A address has three bytes (24-bit positions) for the node address of a machine. This means there are 2^{24}—or 16,777,216—unique combinations and, therefore, precisely that many possible unique node addresses for each Class A network. Because node addresses with the two patterns of all 0s and all 1s are reserved, the actual maximum usable number of nodes for a Class A network is 2^{24} minus 2, which equals 16,777,214. Either way, that's a huge number of hosts on a network segment!

Class B Addresses

In a Class B network, the request for comments (RFCs) state that the first bit of the first byte must always be turned on, but the second bit must always be turned off. If you turn the other six bits all off and then all on, you will find the range for a Class B network:

```
10000000 = 128
10111111 = 191
```

As you can see, this means that a Class B network is defined when the first byte is configured from 128 to 191.

In a Class B network address, the first two bytes are assigned to the network address, and the remaining two bytes are used for node addresses:

network.network.node.node

For example, in the IP address 172.16.30.56, the network address is 172.16, and the node address is 30.56.

Since a network address is two bytes (8 bits each), you would assume that there'd be 2^{16} unique combinations. But as with Class A addresses, the IP designers decided that all Class B network addresses should start with the binary digit 1, then 0 (two reserved bits). This leaves 14 bit positions to manipulate, and therefore there are only 16,384 (that is, 2^{14}) unique Class B network addresses.

A Class B address uses two bytes for node addresses. This means that there are 2^{16} minus the two reserved patterns (all 0s and all 1s), for a total of 65,534 possible node addresses for each Class B network.

Class C Addresses

For Class C networks, the RFCs define the first 2 bits of the first octet as always turned on, but the third bit can never be on. You can follow the same process as in the previous classes and convert from binary to decimal to find the range. Here's the range for a Class C network:

```
11000000 = 192
11011111 = 223
```

So, if you see an IP address that starts at 192 and goes to 223, you'll know it is a Class C IP address.

The first three bytes of a Class C network address are dedicated to the network portion of the address, with only one measly byte remaining for the node address. The format is

network.network.network.node

For example, if the IP address is 192.168.100.102, the network address is 192.168.100, and the node address is 102.

In a Class C network address, the first three bit positions are always the binary 110. So, here is the calculation you would use to figure out the number of possible Class C networks: 3 bytes, or 24 bits, minus 3 reserved positions, leaves 21 positions. Hence, there are 2^{21}, or 2,097,152, possible Class C networks.

Each unique Class C network has one byte to use for node addresses. This leads to 2^8 or 256, minus the 2 reserved patterns of all 0s and all 1s, for a total of 254 node addresses for each Class C network.

Network Addresses: Special Purpose

Some IP addresses are reserved for special purposes, so network administrators can't ever assign these addresses to nodes. Table 1.1 lists the members of this exclusive little club and why they're included in it.

TABLE 1.1   Reserved IP Addresses

Address	Function
Network address of all 0s	Interpreted to mean "this network or segment."
Network address of all 1s	Interpreted to mean "all networks."
Network 127.0.0.0	Reserved for loopback tests. This address designates the local node and allows that node to send a test packet to itself without generating network traffic.
Node address of all 0s	Interpreted to mean "network address" or any host on a specified network.
Node address of all 1s	Interpreted to mean "all nodes" on the specified network; for example, 128.2.255.255 means all nodes on network 128.2 (which is a Class B address).
Entire IP address set to all 0s	Used by Cisco routers to designate the default route. This address could also mean "any network."
Entire IP address set to all 1s (same as 255.255.255.255)	Broadcast to all nodes on the current network; sometimes called an all 1s broadcast or a limited broadcast.

Private IP Addresses

The people who created the IP addressing scheme also eventually created *private IP addresses*. These addresses can be used on a private network, but they're not routable through the public Internet. This not only creates a measure of much-needed security, but it also conveniently saves valuable IP address space.

If every host on every network had to have real routable IP addresses, we would have run out of IP addresses to hand out years ago. But by using private IP addresses, Internet service providers

(ISPs), corporations, and home users only need a relatively tiny group of real, bona fide IP addresses to connect their networks to the Internet. This means using the reserved IP address space is really economical because they can use private IP addresses on their inside networks and get along just fine, and they only have to pay for the outside IP addresses.

The reserved private addresses are listed in Table 1.2.

TABLE 1.2   Reserved IP Address Space

Address Class	Reserved Address Space
Class A	10.0.0.0 through 10.255.255.255
Class B	172.16.0.0 through 172.31.255.255
Class C	192.168.0.0 through 192.168.255.255

To accomplish this task, the ISP and the corporation—the end user, no matter who they are—need to use NAT, which basically takes a private IP address and converts it for use on the Internet. Many people can use the same real IP address to transmit out onto the Internet. Doing things this way saves megatons of address space—good for us all! Now let's discuss NAT in more detail.

Network Address Translation (NAT)

No matter whether your network is of the home or corporate type—if it uses the private IP addresses that I just talked about, you have to translate your private inside addresses to a public address by using NAT if you want to connect to the Internet. The main idea is to conserve Internet global address space, but it also increases network security by hiding internal IP addresses from external networks. In NAT terminology, the *inside network* is the set of networks that are subject to translation. The *outside network* refers to all other addresses—usually those located on the Internet. However, just to help confuse you, it's important to understand that you can translate packets coming into the private network, as well.

NAT operates on a Cisco router—generally only connecting two networks together—and translates your private (inside local) addresses within the internal network into public (inside global) addresses before any packets are forwarded to another network. This functionality gives you the option of configuring NAT so that it will only advertise one address for your entire network to the outside world. Doing this effectively hides the internal network from the whole world really well, which gives you some much-needed additional security.

Here are three different flavors of NAT:

Static NAT   Designed to allow one-to-one mapping between local and global addresses. This flavor requires you to have one real Internet IP address for every host on your network.

Dynamic NAT   Designed to map an unregistered IP address to a registered IP address from out of a pool of registered IP addresses. You don't have to configure your router to map an inside to an outside address statically as you would in static NAT, but you do have to have enough real IP addresses for everyone who wants to send packets to and from the Internet.

NAT Overload   This is the most popular type of NAT configuration. Overloading is a form of dynamic NAT that maps multiple unregistered IP addresses to a single registered IP address (many-to-one) by using different ports. Therefore, it's also known as *port address translation (PAT)*. By using PAT (NAT Overload), you can have thousands of users connect to the Internet using only one real global IP address—pretty slick! NAT Overload is the reason we have not run out of valid IP address on the Internet.

Exam Essentials

Understand the three different classes of the IP address, and their associated network sizes. The Class A address range in the first octet is 1–126, with 24 bits used for host addressing; the Class B address range in the first octet is 128–191, with 16 bits used for host addressing; and the Class C range is 192–223 with only 8 bits used for host addressing.

Understand private IP addresses and NAT   Private IP addresses are just like any other IP address, except they are not routable on the public Internet. The Class A private address range is 10.0.0.0–10.255.255.255; the Class B range is 172.16.0.0–172.31.255.255, and the Class C range is 192.168.0.0–192.168.255.255. By using NAT, you can use these private IP addresses on your internal networks.

1.3 Selecting an Appropriate Routing Protocol Based on User Requirements

Many factors may influence your decision as to which routing protocol is best in any given situation. Proprietary vs. open protocols, scalability, routed protocol support, ease of administration, and speed of convergence are all issues that immediately come to mind. Here, I will review IP routing basics and then show you each of three categories of routing protocol covered on the CCNA: distance vector, hybrid, and link state. We will also discuss routing protocols in each of these categories, and their characteristics. First, let's get some routing basics out of the way.

Routing Basics

The term *routing* is used for taking a packet from one device and sending it through the network to another device on a different network. Routers don't care about hosts—they only care about networks and the best path to each. The logical network address of the destination host is used to get packets to a network through a routed network; then the hardware address of the host is used to deliver the packet from a router to the correct destination host.

In dynamic routing, a protocol on one router communicates with the same protocol running on neighbor routers. The routers then update each other on all the networks they know about and place this information into the routing table. If a change occurs in the network, the dynamic routing protocols automatically inform all routers about the event. If static routing is used, the administrator is responsible for updating all changes by hand into all routers. Typically, in a large network, a combination of both static and dynamic routing is used. You need to know about static and dynamic routing as well as administrative distances, so let's talk about these here.

Static Routing

Static routing occurs when you manually add routes in each router's routing table. There are pros and cons to static routing, but that's true for all routing processes.

Things that are good about static routing include the following:

- No overhead on the router CPU

- No bandwidth usage between routers

- Security (because the administrator can only allow routing to certain networks)

Here are a few things that aren't so good about static routing:

- The administrator must really understand the internetwork and how each router is connected in order to configure routes correctly.

- If a network is added to the internetwork, the administrator has to add a route to it on all routers—by hand.

Static routing just won't work for you in large networks because just maintaining it would be a full-time job.

Dynamic Routing

Dynamic routing occurs when protocols are used to find and update routing tables on routers. True, this is easier than using static or default routing, but it'll cost you in terms of router CPU processes and bandwidth on the network links. A routing protocol defines the set of rules used by a router when it communicates between neighbor routers.

Two types of routing protocols are used in internetworks: interior gateway protocols (IGPs) and exterior gateway protocols (EGPs).

IGPs are used to exchange routing information with routers in the same *autonomous system (AS)*. An AS is a collection of networks under a common administrative domain, which basically means that all routers sharing the same routing table information are in the same AS.

EGPs are used to communicate between ASes. An example of an EGP is the Border Gateway Protocol (BGP).

Administrative Distances

The *administrative distance (AD)* is used to rate the trustworthiness of routing information received on a router from a neighbor router. An administrative distance is an integer from 0 to 255, where 0 is the most trusted and 255 means no traffic will be passed via this route.

If a router receives two updates listing the same remote network, the first thing the router checks is the AD. If one of the advertised routes has a lower AD than the other, then the route with the lowest AD will be placed in the routing table.

If both advertised routes to the same network have the same AD, then routing protocol metrics (such as hop count or bandwidth of the lines) will be used to find the best path to the remote network. The advertised route with the lowest metric will be placed in the routing table, but if both advertised routes have the same AD as well as the same metrics, then the routing protocol will load-balance to the remote network.

Table 1.3 shows the default administrative distances that a Cisco router uses to decide which route to use to a remote network:

TABLE 1.3   Default Administrative Distances

Route Source	Default AD
Connected interface	0
Static route	1
Enhanced Interior Gateway Routing Protocol (EIGRP)	90
Interior Gateway Routing Protocol (IGRP)	100
Open Shortest Path First (OSPF) protocol	110
Routing Information Protocol (RIP)	120
External EIGRP	170
Unknown	255 (this route will never be used)

If a network is directly connected, the router always uses the interface connected to the network. If an administrator configures a static route, the router believes that route over any other learned routes. You can change the administrative distance of static routes, but, by default, they have an AD of 1.

If you have a static route, a RIP-advertised route, and an IGRP-advertised route listing the same network, then by default, the router always uses the static route unless you change the AD of the static route.

Distance-Vector Routing Protocols (RIP and IGRP)

The *distance-vector routing* protocols find the best path to a remote network by judging distance. Each time a packet goes through a router, that's called a *hop*. The route with the least number of hops to the network is determined to be the best route. The vector indicates the direction to the remote network. RIP and IGRP are distance-vector routing protocols.

The distance-vector routing algorithm passes complete routing tables to neighboring routers that then combine the received routing table with their own routing tables to complete the inter-network map. This is called routing by rumor, because a router receiving an update from a neighbor router and believes the information about remote networks without actually finding out for itself.

RIP uses only hop count to determine the best path to an internetwork. If RIP finds more than one link to the same remote network with the same hop count, it will automatically per-form a round-robin load balancing. RIP can perform load balancing for up to six equal-cost links.

It's important to understand what a distance-vector routing protocol does when it starts up. In Figure 1.3, the four routers start off with only their directly connected networks in the routing table. After a distance-vector routing protocol starts on each router, the routing tables are updated with all the route information gathered from neighbor routers.

FIGURE 1.3   The internetwork with distance-vector routing

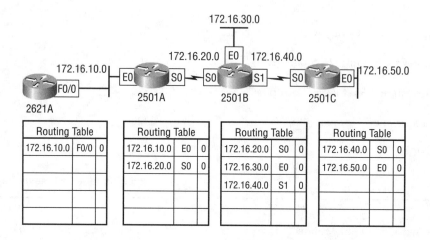

As you can see from Figure 1.3, each router has only the directly connected networks in each routing table. Each router sends its complete routing table out to each active interface. The routing table of each router includes the network number, exit interface, and hop count to the network.

In Figure 1.4, the routing tables are complete because they include information about all the networks in the internetwork. They are considered *converged*. When the routers are converging, no data is passed, which is why fast convergence time is a serious plus. In fact, that's one of the problems with RIP—its slow convergence time.

FIGURE 1.4   Converged routing tables

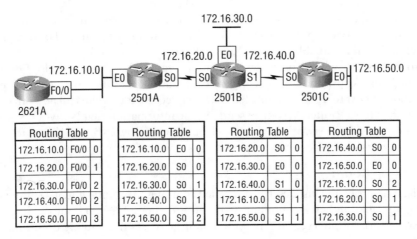

The routing table in each router keeps information regarding the remote network number, the interface to which the router will send packets to reach that network, and the hop count or metric to the network.

Routing Loops

Distance-vector routing protocols keep track of any changes to the internetwork by broadcasting periodic routing updates to all active interfaces. This broadcast includes the complete routing table, which works just fine, but it's expensive in terms of CPU process and link bandwidth. Also if a network outage happens, real problems can occur, and the slow convergence of distance-vector routing protocols can result in inconsistent routing tables and routing loops.

Routing loops can occur because every router isn't updated simultaneously, or even close to it. Here's an example—let's say that the interface to Network 5 in Figure 1.5 fails. All routers know about Network 5 from Router E. Router A, in its tables, has a path to Network 5 through Router B.

FIGURE 1.5   Routing loop example

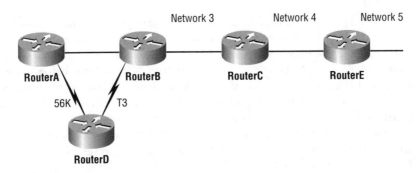

When Network 5 fails, Router E tells Router C. This causes Router C to stop routing to Network 5 through Router E. But Routers A, B, and D don't know about Network 5 yet, so they keep sending out update information. Router C will eventually send out its update and cause B to stop routing to Network 5, but Routers A and D are still not updated. To them, it appears that Network 5 is still available through Router B with a metric of 3.

The problem occurs when Router A sends out its regular 30-second "Hello, I'm still here—these are the links I know about" message, which includes the ability to reach Network 5 and an explanation of how to do so. Routers B and D then receive the wonderful news that Network 5 can be reached from Router A, so they send out the information that Network 5 is available. Any packet destined for Network 5 will go to Router A, to Router B, and then back to Router A. This is a *routing loop*—how do you stop it?

Maximum Hop Count

The routing loop problem I just described is called counting to infinity, and it's caused by gossip and wrong information being communicated and propagated throughout the internetwork. Without some form of intervention, the hop count increases indefinitely each time a packet passes through a router.

One way of solving this problem is to define a maximum hop count. Distance vector (RIP) permits a hop count of up to 15, so anything that requires 16 hops is deemed unreachable. In other words, after a loop of 15 hops, Network 5 will be considered down. Thus, the maximum hop count will keep packets from going around the loop forever. Though this is a workable solution, it won't remove the routing loop itself. Packets will still go into the loop, but instead of traveling on unchecked, they'll just whirl around for 16 bounces and then die.

Split Horizon

Another solution to the routing loop problem is called *split horizon*. This reduces incorrect routing information and routing overhead in a distance-vector network by enforcing the rule that information cannot be sent back in the direction from which it was received.

In other words, the routing protocol differentiates which interface a network route was learned on, and once it determines this, it won't advertise the route back out of that same interface. This would have prevented Router A from sending the updated information it received from Router B back to Router B.

Route Poisoning

Another way to avoid problems caused by inconsistent updates and stop network loops is *route poisoning*. For example, when Network 5 goes down, Router E initiates route poisoning by entering a table entry for Network 5 as 16, or unreachable (sometimes referred to as *infinite*).

By poisoning the route to Network 5, Router C prevents itself from being susceptible to incorrect updates about the route to Network 5. When Router C receives a route poisoning from Router E, it sends an update, called a *poison reverse*, back to Router E. This ensures that all routes on the segment have received the poisoned route information.

Route poisoning and split horizon create a much more resilient and dependable distance-vector network than you'd have without them, and they serve you well in preventing network loops. But we're not done yet—this isn't all you need to know about loop prevention in distance-vector networks, so read on.

Holddowns

A *holddown* prevents regular update messages from reinstating a route that is going up and down (called *flapping*). Typically, this happens on a serial link that's losing connectivity and then coming back up. If there wasn't a way to stabilize this, the network would never converge and that one flapping interface could bring the entire network down!

Holddowns prevent routes from changing too rapidly by allowing time for either the downed route to come back up, or the network to stabilize somewhat before changing to the next best route. These also tell routers to restrict, for a specific time period, any changes that might affect recently removed routes. This prevents inoperative routes from being prematurely restored to other routers' tables.

When a router receives an update from a neighbor that indicates that a previously accessible network isn't working and is inaccessible, the holddown timer starts. If a new update arrives from a neighbor with a better metric than the original network entry, the holddown is removed and data is passed. But if an update is received from a neighbor router before the holddown timer expires and it has an equal or lower metric than the previous route, the update is ignored and the holddown timer keeps ticking. This allows more time for the network to stabilize before it tries to converge.

Holddowns use triggered updates that reset the holddown timer to alert the neighbor routers of a change in the network. Unlike update messages from neighbor routers, triggered updates create a new routing table that is sent immediately to neighbor routers because a change was detected in the internetwork.

There are three instances when triggered updates will reset the holddown timer:

- The holddown timer expires.
- Another update is received with a better metric.
- A flush timer expires.

Routing Information Protocol (RIP)

RIP is a true distance-vector routing protocol. It sends the complete routing table out to all active interfaces every 30 seconds. RIP only uses hop count to determine the best way to a remote network, but it has a maximum allowable hop count of 15 by default, meaning that 16 is deemed unreachable. RIP works well in small networks, but it's inefficient on large networks with slow wide area network (WAN) links or on networks with a large number of routers installed.

RIP version 1 uses only *classful routing*, which means that all devices in the network must use the same subnet mask. This is because RIP version 1 doesn't send updates with subnet mask information in tow. RIP version 2 provides something called *prefix routing*, and does send subnet mask information with the route updates; this is called *classless routing*. I'm not going there though. I'm only going to talk about RIP version 1 because that's what the CCNA objectives require.

If you want to learn more about classless routing (or other Cisco topics), read my *CCNA: Cisco Certified Network Associate Study Guide, 4th Edition* (Sybex 2003).

RIP uses three different kinds of timers to regulate its performance:

Route update timer   Sets the interval (typically 30 seconds) between periodic routing updates in which the router sends a complete copy of its routing table out to all neighbors.

Route invalid timer   Determines the length of time that must elapse (180 seconds) before a router determines that a route has become invalid. It comes to this conclusion if it hasn't heard any updates about a particular route for that period. When that happens, the router sends out updates to all its neighbors letting them know that the route is invalid.

Route flush timer   Sets the time between a route becoming invalid and its removal from the routing table (240 seconds). Before it's removed from the table, the router notifies its neighbors of that route's impending demise. The value of the route invalid timer must be less than that of the route flush timer. This gives the router enough time to tell its neighbors about the invalid route before the routing table is updated.

Interior Gateway Routing Protocol (IGRP)

IGRP is a Cisco-proprietary distance-vector routing protocol. This means that all your routers must be Cisco routers if you want to use IGRP in your network. Cisco created this routing protocol to overcome the problems associated with RIP.

IGRP has a maximum hop count of 255 with a default of 100. This is helpful in larger networks and solves the problem of 15 hops being the maximum possible in a RIP network.

IGRP also uses a different metric from RIP. IGRP uses bandwidth and delay of the line by default as a metric for determining the best route to an internetwork. This is called a *composite metric*. Reliability, load, and maximum transmission unit (MTU) can also be used, although not by default.

Here is a list of the differences between IGRP and RIP:

- IGRP can be used in large internetworks.
- IGRP uses an AS number for activation.
- IGRP performs a full route table update every 90 seconds.
- IGRP uses bandwidth and delay of the line as a metric (lowest composite metric).

To control performance, IGRP includes the following timers with default settings:

Update timers   These specify how frequently routing-update messages should be sent. The default is 90 seconds.

Invalid timers   These specify how long a router should wait before declaring a route invalid if it doesn't receive a specific update about it. The default is three times the update period.

Holddown timers   These specify the holddown period. The default is three times the update timer period plus 10 seconds.

Flush timers   These indicate how much time should pass before a route should be flushed from the routing table. The default is seven times the routing update period. If the update timer is 90 seconds by default, then $7 \times 90 = 630$ seconds elapse before a route will be flushed from the route table.

Hybrid Routing Protocols or EIGRP

EIGRP is a classless, enhanced distance-vector protocol that gives us a real edge over another Cisco proprietary protocol, IGRP. That's basically why it's called Enhanced IGRP. Like IGRP, EIGRP uses the concept of an autonomous system to describe the set of contiguous routers that run the same routing protocol and share routing information. Unlike IGRP, EIGRP includes the subnet mask in its route updates. And as you now know, the advertisement of subnet information allows you to use Variable Length Subnet Masking (VLSM) and summarization when you design your networks!

EIGRP is sometimes referred to as a hybrid routing protocol because it has characteristics of both distance-vector and link-state protocols. For example, EIGRP doesn't send link-state packets as OSPF does; instead, it sends traditional distance-vector updates containing information about networks plus the cost of reaching them from the perspective of the advertising router. And EIGRP has link-state characteristics as well—it synchronizes routing tables between neighbors at startup, and then it sends specific updates only when topology changes occur.

A number of powerful features make EIGRP stand out from IGRP and other protocols. The main ones are listed here:

- Support for IP, IPX, and AppleTalk via protocol-dependent modules
- Efficient neighbor discovery
- Communication via Reliable Transport Protocol (RTP)
- Best path selection via the diffusing update algorithm (DUAL)
- Support for multiple autonomous systems (AS)
- Support for Variable Length Subnet Masking (VLSM) and summarization

Let's take a closer look at each of these technologies and how they work.

Protocol-Dependent Modules

One of the most interesting features of EIGRP is that it provides routing support for multiple Network layer protocols: IP, IPX, and AppleTalk. The only other routing protocol that comes close and supports multiple network layer protocols is Intermediate System-to-Intermediate System (IS-IS), but it only supports IP and Connectionless Network Service (CLNS).

EIGRP supports different Network layer protocols through the use of protocol-dependent modules (PDMs). Each EIGRP PDM maintains a separate series of tables containing the routing information that applies to a specific protocol. What this means to you is there will be IP/EIGRP tables, IPX/EIGRP tables, and AppleTalk/EIGRP tables.

Neighbor Discovery

Before EIGRP routers are willing to exchange routes with each other, they must become neighbors. There are three conditions that must be met for neighborship establishment:

- Hello or ACK (acknowledgment) received
- AS numbers match
- Identical metrics (K values)

Link-state protocols tend to use Hello messages to establish neighbors because they normally do not send out periodic route updates, and some sort of mechanism has to help neighbors realize when a new peer has moved in, or when an old one has left or gone down. To maintain the neighborship relationship, EIGRP routers must also continue receiving Hellos from their neighbors.

EIGRP routers that belong to different ASes don't automatically share routing information and they don't become neighbors. This behavior can be a real benefit when you use it in larger networks to reduce the amount of route information propagated through a specific AS. The only catch is that you might have to take care of redistribution between the different ASes manually.

The only time EIGRP advertises its entire routing table is when it discovers a new neighbor and forms an adjacency with it through the exchange of Hello packets. When this happens, both neighbors advertise their entire routing tables to one another. After each has learned its neighbor's routes, only changes to the routing table are propagated from then on.

When EIGRP routers receive their neighbors' updates, they store them in a local topology table. This table contains all known routes from all known neighbors, and serves as the raw material from which the best routes are selected and placed into the routing table.

Reliable Transport Protocol (RTP)

EIGRP uses a proprietary protocol, *RTP*, to manage the communication of messages between EIGRP-speaking routers. And as the name suggests, reliability is a key concern of this protocol. Cisco has designed a mechanism that leverages multicasts and unicasts to deliver updates quickly, and to track the receipt of the data.

When EIGRP sends multicast traffic, it uses the Class D address 224.0.0.10. As I said, each EIGRP router is aware of who its neighbors are, and for each multicast it sends out, it maintains a list of the neighbors who have replied. If EIGRP doesn't get a reply from a neighbor, it will switch to using unicasts to resend the same data. If it still doesn't get a reply after 16 unicast attempts, the neighbor is declared dead. People often refer to this process as *reliable multicast*.

Routers keep track of the information they send by assigning a sequence number to each packet. With this technique, it's possible for them to detect the arrival of old, redundant, or out of sequence information.

Being able to do these things is highly important because EIGRP is a quiet protocol. It depends upon its ability to synchronize routing databases at startup and then maintain the consistency of databases over time by only communicating any changes. So the permanent loss of any packets, or the out-of-order execution of packets can result in corruption of the routing database.

Diffusing Update Algorithm (DUAL)

EIGRP uses the *diffusing update algorithm (DUAL)* to select and maintain the best path to each remote network. This algorithm allows for the following:

- Backup route determination if one is available
- Support of VLSMs
- Dynamic route recoveries
- Querying neighbors for unknown alternate routes
- Sending out queries for an alternate route if no route can be found

DUAL provides EIGRP with possibly the fastest route convergence time among all protocols. The key to EIGRP's speedy convergence is twofold: first, EIGRP routers maintain a copy of all of their neighbors' routes, which they use to calculate their own cost to each remote network. If the best path goes down, it may be as simple as examining the contents of the topology table to select the best replacement route. Secondly, if there isn't a good alternative in the local topology table, EIGRP routers very quickly ask their neighbors for help finding one—they aren't afraid to ask directions! Relying on other routers, and leveraging the information they provide accounts for the "diffusing" character of DUAL.

As I said, the whole idea of the Hello messages is to enable the rapid detection of new or dead neighbors. RTP answers this call by providing a reliable mechanism for conveying and sequencing messages. Building upon this solid foundation, DUAL is responsible for selecting and maintaining information about the best paths.

Multiple AS

EIGRP uses autonomous system numbers (ASNs) to identify the collection of routers that share route information. Only routers that have the same ASN share routes. In large networks, you can easily end up with really complicated topology and route tables, and that can markedly slow convergence during diffusing computation operations.

So what's an administrator to do to mitigate the impact of managing really big networks? Well, it's possible to divide the network into multiple distinct EIGRP AS. Each AS is populated by a contiguous series of routers, and route information can be shared among the different AS via redistribution.

The use of redistribution within EIGRP leads us to another interesting feature. Normally, the administrative distance of EIGRP routes is 90, but this is true only for what are known as *internal EIGRP routes*. These are routes originated within a specific autonomous system by EIGRP routers that are members of the same autonomous system. The other type of route is called an *external EIGRP route* and it has an administrative distance of 170, which is not so good. These routes appear within EIGRP route tables courtesy of either manual or automatic redistribution, and they represent networks that originated outside of the EIGRP autonomous system. It doesn't matter if the routes originated from another EIGRP autonomous system or from another routing protocol like OSPF—they're all considered external routes when they are redistributed within EIGRP.

VLSM Support and Summarization

As one of the more sophisticated classless routing protocols, EIGRP supports the use of VLSMs. This support is really important because it allows address space to be conserved through the use of subnet masks that more closely fit the host requirements—like using 30-bit subnet masks for point-to-point networks. Because the subnet mask is propagated with every route update, EIGRP also supports the use of discontinuous subnets, something that gives you a lot more flexibility when you are designing your network's IP address plan. What's a discontinuous subnet? It's one that has two classful networks connected together by a different class of networks. Figure 1.6 displays a typical discontinuous network.

FIGURE 1.6   Discontiguous network

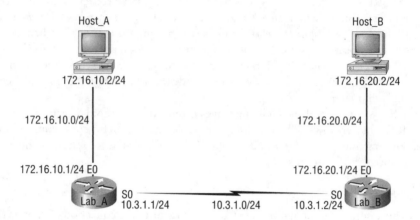

In this figure, the subnets 172.16.10.0 and 172.16.20.0 are connected with a 10.3.1.0 network. Each router thinks it has the entire 172.16.0.0 class B network by default.

EIGRP also supports the manual creation of summaries at any and all EIGRP routers, which can substantially reduce the size of the route table. However, EIGRP automatically summarizes networks at their classful boundaries. Figure 1.7 shows how an EIGRP network would see the network plus the boundaries that it would auto summarize.

FIGURE 1.7   EIGRP Auto Summarization

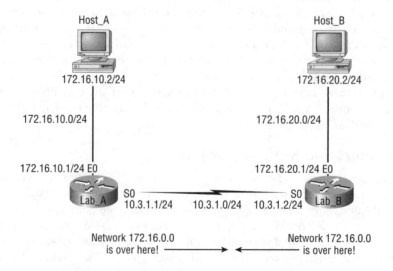

Obviously, this would never work by default!

Link State (OSPF)

In *link-state protocols*, also called *shortest path first protocols*, the routers each create three separate tables. One of these tables keeps track of directly attached neighbors, one determines the topology of the entire internetwork, and one is used as the routing table. Link-state routers know more about the internetwork than any distance-vector routing protocol. OSPF is an IP routing protocol that is completely link state. Link state protocols send updates containing the state of their own link to all other routers on the network.

OSPF is an open standards routing protocol that's been implemented by a wide variety of network vendors, including Cisco. If you have multiple routers, and not all of them are Cisco (what?!) then you can't use EIGRP, now can you? So your remaining options are basically RIP, RIPv2, or OSPF. If it's a large network, then really, your only options are OSPF, or something called *route redistribution*—a translation service between routing protocols.

OSPF works by using the *Dijkstra algorithm*. First, a shortest path first tree is constructed, and then the routing table is populated with the resulting best paths. OSPF converges quickly, although perhaps not as quickly as EIGRP, and it supports multiple, equal-cost routes to the same destination. But unlike EIGRP, it only supports IP routing—not really a negative to using OSPF, if you ask me!

OSPF is the first link-state routing protocol that most people are introduced to, so it's useful to see how it compares to more traditional distance-vector protocols like RIPv1. Table 1.4 compares these two protocols.

TABLE 1.4   Comparing OSPF and RIP

Characteristic	OSPF	RIPv1
Type of protocol	Link-state	Distance-vector
Classless support	Yes	No
VLSM support	Yes	No
Auto summarization	No	Yes
Manual summarization	Yes	No
Route propagation	Multicast on change	Periodic broadcast
Path metric	Bandwidth	Hops
Hop count limit	None	15
Convergence	Fast	Slow

TABLE 1.4   Comparing OSPF and RIP *(continued)*

Characteristic	OSPF	RIPv1
Peer authentication	Yes	No
Hierarchical network	Yes (using areas)	No (flat only)
Route computation	Dijkstra	Bellman-Ford

OSPF has many features beyond the few I've listed in Table 1.4, and all of them contribute to a fast, scalable, and robust protocol that can be actively deployed in thousands of production networks.

OSPF is supposed to be designed in a hierarchical fashion, which basically means that you can separate the larger internetwork into smaller internetworks called *areas*. This is the best design for OSPF.

The reasons for creating OSPF in a hierarchical design are as follows:

- To decrease routing overhead
- To speed up convergence
- To confine network instability to single areas of the network

This does not make configuring OSPF easier.

Figure 1.8 shows a typical OSPF simple design:

FIGURE 1.8   OSPF design example

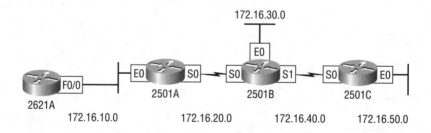

Notice how each router connects to the backbone—called area 0, or the backbone area. OSPF must have an area 0, and all routers should connect to this area if at all possible, but routers that connect other areas within an AS together are called *area border routers (ABRs)*. Still, at least one interface must be in area 0.

OSPF runs inside an AS, but it can also connect multiple AS together. The router that connects these AS together is called an *autonomous system boundary router (ASBR)*. Ideally, you would create other areas of networks to help keep route updates to a minimum, and to keep problems from propagating throughout the network.

Exam Essentials

Understand the differences between distance-vector, link state, and hybrid routing protocols.   Each technology has its own characteristics and methods for sharing routing information between routers. Be prepared to identify problems and solutions common to all distance-vector routing protocols.

Know what type of routing protocol RIP, IGRP, EIGRP, and OSPF are, and know their properties.   Rip and IGRP are distance-vector routing protocols, EIGRP is a hybrid, and OSPF is link state. IGRP and EIGRP are Cisco proprietary, RIP and OSPF are industry standard.

1.4 Designing a Simple Internetwork Using Cisco Technology

As I already mentioned, an internetwork is simply a collection of connected networks. In this section, I will show you one method of creating a simple internetwork by connecting multiple virtual LANs (VLANs).

Introduction to VLANs

Layer 2 switched networks are typically designed as a flat networks from a broadcast perspective, as you can see from Figure 1.9. Every broadcast packet that is transmitted is seen by every device on the network, regardless of whether the device needs to receive that data or not.

FIGURE 1.9   Flat network structure

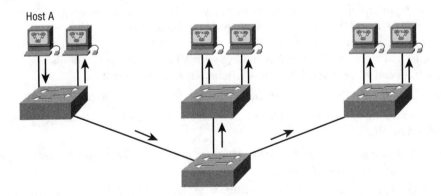

By default, routers allow broadcasts only within the originating network, but switches forward broadcasts to all segments. The reason it's called a flat network is because it's one broadcast domain, not because its design is physically flat.

In Figure 1.9, you can see Host A sending a broadcast and all ports on all switches forwarding this broadcast, except the port that originally received it. Now look at Figure 1.10, which shows a switched network. It shows Host A sending a frame with Host D as its destination, and as you can see, that frame is only forwarded out the port where Host D is located. This is a huge improvement over the old hub networks, unless having one collision domain by default is what you really want.

FIGURE 1.10   The benefit of a switched network

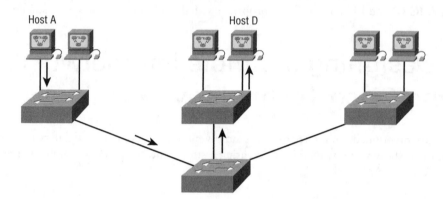

You already know that the largest benefit gained by having a Layer 2 switched network is that it creates individual collision domain segments for each device plugged into the switch. This scenario frees you from the Ethernet distance constraints, so now you can build larger networks. But with each new advance, you often encounter new issues—the larger the number of users and devices, the more broadcasts and packets each switch must handle.

And here's another benefit—security! This one's a real problem because within the typical Layer 2 switched internetwork, all users can see all devices by default. In addition, you can't stop devices from broadcasting, nor users from trying to respond to broadcasts. Your security options are dismally limited to placing passwords on the servers and other devices.

But not if you create a virtual LAN (VLAN), my friend! Yes, indeed, you can solve many of the problems associated with layer-2 switching with VLANs—as you'll soon see!

Here are several ways that VLANs simplify network management:

- The VLAN can group several broadcast domains into multiple logical subnets.

- You can accomplish network additions, moves, and changes by configuring a port into the appropriate VLAN.

- You can place a group of users who need high security into a VLAN so that no users outside of the VLAN can communicate with them.

- As a logical grouping of users by function, VLANs can be considered independent from their physical or geographic locations.

- VLANs can enhance network security.

- VLANs increase the number of broadcast domains while decreasing their size.

Broadcast Control

Broadcasts occur in every protocol, but how often they occur depends upon three things:

- The type of protocol
- The application(s) running on the internetwork
- How these services are used

Since switches have become more cost-effective lately, many companies are replacing their flat hub networks with a pure switched network and VLAN environment. All devices in a VLAN are members of the same broadcast domain and receive all broadcasts. The broadcasts, by default, are filtered from all ports on a switch that are not members of the same VLAN. This is great because it offers all the benefits you gain with a switched design without the serious anguish you would experience if all your users were in the same broadcast domain!

Security

It seems that there's always a catch, though, so let's get back to those security issues. A flat internetwork's security used to be tackled by connecting hubs and switches together with routers—so, basically, it was the router's job to maintain security. This arrangement was pretty ineffective for several reasons:

- First, anyone connecting to the physical network could access the network resources located on that physical LAN.
- Secondly, all anyone had to do to observe any and all traffic happening in that network was simply plug a network analyzer into the hub. And in that same vein, users could join a workgroup by just plugging their workstations into the existing hub.

So basically, this was non-security!

This is why VLANs are so cool. By building them and creating multiple broadcast groups, administrators can now have control over each port and user! The days where users could just plug their workstations into any switch port and gain access to network resources are history because the administrator now has control over each port and whatever resources that port can access.

Also, because you can create VLANs in accordance with the network resources a user requires, you can configure switches to inform a network management station of any unauthorized access to network resources. And if you need inter-VLAN communication, you can implement restrictions on a router to achieve it. You can also place restrictions on hardware addresses, protocols, and applications—now we're talking security!

VLANs and Switches

Layer 2 switches only read frames for filtering—they don't look at the Network layer protocol. Also, by default, switches forward all broadcasts, but if you create and implement VLANs, you're essentially creating smaller broadcast domains at Layer 2.

This means that broadcasts sent out from a node in one VLAN won't be forwarded to ports configured to be in a different VLAN. So by assigning switch ports or users to VLAN groups on a switch or group of connected switches (called a *switch fabric*), you gain the flexibility to add only the users you want into that broadcast domain regardless of their physical location! This setup can also work to block broadcast storms caused by a faulty NIC as well as prevent an application from propagating the storms throughout the entire internetwork. Those evils can still happen on the VLAN where the problem originated, but the disease will be quarantined to only that ailing VLAN.

Another advantage of segmenting with VLANs is that when a single VLAN gets too big, you can create multiple VLANs to keep the broadcasts from consuming too much bandwidth—the fewer users in a VLAN, the fewer users are affected by broadcasts. This is all well and good, but you must keep network services in mind and understand how the users connect to these services when you create your VLAN. It's a good idea to try and keep all services, except for the e-mail and Internet access that everyone needs, local to all users when possible.

To understand how a VLAN works within a switch, begin by looking at a traditional network. Figure 1.11 shows how a network can be created by connecting physical LANs using hubs to routers.

FIGURE 1.11   Physical LANs connected to routers

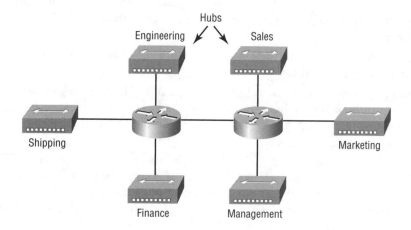

Here you can see that each network was attached with a hub port to the router (each segment also had its own logical network number, although this is not obvious from the figure). Each node attached to a particular physical network had to match that network number in order to be able to communicate on the internetwork. Notice that each department had its own LAN, so if you needed to add new users to Sales, for example, you would just plug them into the Sales LAN and they would have automatically been part of the Sales collision and broadcast domain. This design really did work well for many years.

But there was one major flaw: what happened if the hub for Sales was full and you needed to add another user to the Sales LAN? Or, what would you have done if there was no more physical space in the location where the Sales team was located for this new employee?

Well, as an example, let's say that there happens to be plenty of room in the Finance section of the building. That new Sales team member will have to sit on the same side of the building as the Finance people, and we'll plug the poor soul into the hub for Finance. Doing this obviously makes that the new user part of the Finance LAN, which is bad for many reasons. First and foremost, you now have a security issue because this new user is a member of the Finance broadcast domain and can therefore see all the same servers and network services that all of the Finance folks can. Secondly, for this user to access the Sales network services they need to get the job done, they would need to go through the router to login to the Sales server—not exactly efficient!

Now take a look at what a switch accomplishes. Figure 1.12 demonstrates how switches remove the physical boundary to solve our problem.

FIGURE 1.12   Using switches to remove physical boundaries

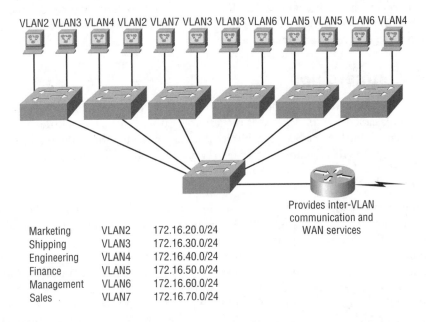

Marketing	VLAN2	172.16.20.0/24
Shipping	VLAN3	172.16.30.0/24
Engineering	VLAN4	172.16.40.0/24
Finance	VLAN5	172.16.50.0/24
Management	VLAN6	172.16.60.0/24
Sales	VLAN7	172.16.70.0/24

Figure 1.12 shows how six VLANs (numbered 2–7) were used to create a broadcast domain for each department. Each switch port was then administratively assigned a VLAN membership, depending on the host and which broadcast domain it must be in.

So now, if I need to add another user to the Sales VLAN (VLAN 7), I can just assign the port I need to VLAN 7, regardless of where the new Sales team member is physically located—nice! This illustrates one of the sweetest advantages to designing your network with VLANs over the old collapsed backbone design. Now, cleanly and simply, each host that needs to be in the Sales VLAN is merely assigned to VLAN 7.

Notice that I started assigning VLANs with VLAN number 2. The number is irrelevant, but you might be wondering what happened to VLAN 1. That VLAN is an administrative VLAN, and even though it can be used for a workgroup, Cisco recommends that you use it for administrative purposes only. You can't delete or change the name of VLAN 1, and by default, all ports on a switch are members of VLAN 1 until you change them.

Each VLAN is considered a broadcast domain, so it must also have its own subnet number, as shown in Figure 1.12. And if you're also using IPX, then you must assign each VLAN its own IPX network number.

Now let's get back to that "because of switches, we don't need routers anymore" misconception. In Figure 1.12, notice that there are seven VLANs or broadcast domains, counting VLAN 1. The nodes within each VLAN can communicate with each other, but not with anything in a different VLAN, because the nodes in any given VLAN "think" that they're actually in a collapsed backbone, as in Figure 1.11.

And what handy little tool do you need to enable the hosts in Figure 1.11 to communicate to a node or host on a different network? You guessed it—a router! Those nodes must go through a router, or some other Layer 3 device, just like when they were configured for VLAN communication (as shown in Figure 1.12). It's the same as if you are trying to connect different physical networks. Communication between VLANs must go through a Layer 3 device, so don't expect routers to disappear anytime soon!

VLAN Memberships

VLANs are usually created by an administrator who then assigns switch ports to each VLAN. Such a VLAN is called a *static VLAN*. If the administrator wants to do a little more work up front and assign all the host devices' hardware addresses into a database, they can configure the switches to assign VLANs dynamically whenever a host is plugged into a switch.

Static VLANs

In most implementations, you will usually use static. This type of VLAN is also the most secure. The switch port to which you assign a VLAN association always maintains that association until you manually change that port assignment.

This type of VLAN configuration is comparatively easy to set up and monitor, and it works well in a network where the movement of users within the network is controlled. Although it can be helpful to use network management software to configure the ports, it's not mandatory.

In Figure 1.12, each switch port was configured with a VLAN membership by an administrator based on which VLAN the host needed to be a member of—the device's actual physical location doesn't matter. The broadcast domain the hosts will become a member of is an administrative choice. Remember that each host must also have the correct IP address information. For example, each host in VLAN 2 must be configured into the 172.16.20.0/24 network. It is also important to remember that if you plug a host into a switch, you must verify the VLAN membership of that port. If the membership is different than what that host needs, the host will not be able to reach the needed network services, such as a workgroup server.

Dynamic VLANs

A *dynamic VLAN* determines a node's VLAN assignment automatically. Using intelligent management software, you can enable hardware (media access control [MAC]) addresses, protocols, or even applications to create dynamic VLANs; it's up to you. For example, suppose MAC addresses have been entered into a centralized VLAN management application. If a node is then attached to an unassigned switch port, the VLAN management database can look up the hardware address and assign and configure the switch port to the correct VLAN. This is very cool—it makes management and configuration easier because if a user moves, the switch will assign them to the correct VLAN automatically. However, you have to do a lot more work initially to set up the database.

Cisco administrators can use the VLAN Management Policy Server (VMPS) service to set up a database of MAC addresses that can be used for dynamic assignment of VLANs. A VMPS database maps MAC addresses to VLANs.

Identifying VLANs

As frames are switched throughout the internetwork, switches must be able to keep track of all the different types and understand what to do with them depending on their hardware addresses and the type of link they are traversing.

Here are two different types of links in a switched environment:

Access links   This type of link is only part of one VLAN, and it's referred to as the native VLAN of the port. Any device attached to an access link is unaware of a VLAN membership—the device just assumes it's part of a broadcast domain, but it does not understand the physical network.

Switches remove any VLAN information from the frame before it's sent to an access-link device. Access-link devices cannot communicate with devices outside their VLAN unless the packet is routed through a router.

Trunk links   Trunks can carry multiple VLANs and originally gained their name after the telephone system trunks that carry multiple telephone conversations.

A trunk link is a 100- or 1000Mbps point-to-point link between two switches, between a switch and router, or between a switch and server. These links carry the traffic of multiple VLANs— from 1 to 1005 at a time. You can't run them on 10Mbps links.

Trunking allows you to make a single port part of multiple VLANs at the same time. This can be a real advantage. For instance, you can actually set things up to have a server in two broadcast domains simultaneously so that your users won't have to cross a Layer 3 device (router) to log in and access it. Another benefit to trunking is apparent when you're connecting switches. Trunk links can carry some or all VLAN information across the link, but if the links between your switches aren't trunked, only VLAN 1 information will be switched across the link by default. This is why all VLANs are configured on a trunked link unless an administrator is clearing them by hand.

When you create trunk links, you have to have some way to indicate which VLAN a particular packet belongs to as it crosses between switches. The solution to this problem is to tag the frames with VLAN information. I will cover this next.

Frame Tagging

You can also create your VLANs to span more than one connected switch. This flexible, power-packed capability is probably the main advantage of implementing VLANs.

However, this can get kind of complicated—even for a switch—so you need to make sure that each switch can keep track of all the users and frames as they travel the switch fabric and VLANs. (Remember, a *switch fabric* is a group of switches that share the same VLAN information.) This is where *frame tagging* comes in. This frame identification method uniquely assigns a user-defined ID to each frame—sometimes people refer to this ID as a *VLAN ID* or *color*.

Here's how this ID works: each switch that the frame reaches must first identify the VLAN ID from the frame tag, then it looks at the information in the filter table to find out what to do with the frame. If the frame reaches a switch that has another trunked link, the frame will be forwarded out the trunk-link port.

Once the frame reaches an exit to an access link, the switch removes the VLAN ID so that the destination device can receive the frames without having to understand their VLAN identification.

VLAN Identification Methods

So, you now know that VLAN identification is what switches use to keep track of all those frames as they're traversing a switch fabric. VLAN identification also enables switches to identify which frames belong to which VLANs.

There are two ways of creating a trunk link that are covered by the CCNA exam. One is Cisco proprietary, the other is an IEEE standard. They are:

Inter-Switch Link (ISL)   This is proprietary to Cisco switches, and it's used for Fast Ethernet and Gigabit Ethernet links only. ISL routing can be used on a switch port, router interfaces, and server interface cards to trunk a server.

ISL lets you explicitly tag VLAN information onto an Ethernet frame. This tagging information allows VLANs to be multiplexed over a trunk link through an external encapsulation method, which allows the switch to identify the VLAN membership of a frame over the trunked link.

By running ISL, you can interconnect multiple switches and still maintain VLAN information as traffic travels between switches on trunk links. ISL functions at Layer 2 by encapsulating a data frame with a new header and cyclic redundancy check (CRC). In addition, since ISL is an external tagging process, the original frame isn't altered—it's only encapsulated with a new 26-byte ISL header. It also adds a second 4-byte frame check sequence (FCS) field at the end of the frame. Because the frame has been encapsulated by ISL with information, only ISL-aware devices can read it. These frames can be up to a whopping 1522 bytes long!

On multi-VLAN (trunk) ports, each frame is tagged as it enters the switch. ISL NICs allow servers to send and receive frames tagged with multiple VLANs so that they can traverse multiple VLANs without going through a router. This is good because it reduces latency. ISL makes it easy for users to access servers quickly and efficiently without having to go through a router every time they need to communicate with a resource. This technology can also be used with probes and certain network analyzers, and administrators can use it to include file servers in multiple VLANs simultaneously.

ISL VLAN information is added to a frame only if the frame is forwarded out a port configured as a trunk link. The ISL encapsulation is removed from the frame if the frame is forwarded out an access link—this is a really important ISL fact, so make a mental note, and don't forget it!

IEEE 802.1Q   Created by the IEEE as a standard method of frame tagging, this actually inserts a field into the frame to identify the VLAN. If you're trunking between a Cisco switched link and a different brand of switch, you have to use 802.1Q for the trunk to work.

VLAN Trunking Protocol (VTP)

Cisco created this one too, but this time it isn't proprietary. The basic goals of VTP are to manage all configured VLANs across a switched internetwork and to maintain consistency throughout that network. VTP allows an administrator to add, delete, and rename VLANs— information that is then propagated to all switches in the network.

Here's a list of some of the benefits VTP has to offer:

- Consistent VLAN configuration across all switches in the network
- VLAN trunking over mixed networks, like Ethernet to ATM LANE or even FDDI
- Accurate tracking and monitoring of VLANs
- Dynamic reporting of added VLANs to all switches
- Plug-and-play VLAN adding

Very cool—yes, but before you can get VTP to manage your VLANs across the network, you have to create a VTP server. All servers that need to share VLAN information must use the same domain name, and a switch can only be in one domain at a time. This means that a switch can only share VTP domain information with other switches if they're configured into the same VTP domain. You can use a VTP domain if you have more than one switch connected in a network, but if you've got all your switches in only one VLAN, you don't need to use VTP. VTP information is sent between switches via a trunk port.

Switches advertise VTP management domain information, as well as a configuration revision number and all known VLANs with any specific parameters. There's also something called *VTP transparent mode*; in it, you can configure switches to forward VTP information through trunk ports, but not to accept information updates or update their VTP databases.

If you find yourself having problems with users adding switches to your VTP domain, you can include passwords, but don't forget that every switch must be set up with the same password—this can get ugly.

Switches detect the additional VLANs within a VTP advertisement and then prepare to receive information on their trunk ports with the newly defined VLAN in tow. This information would be either VLAN ID, 802.10 SAID fields, or LANE information. Updates are sent out as revision numbers that are the notification plus 1. Any time a switch sees a higher revision number, it knows the information that it's receiving is more current, and it will overwrite the current database with that new information.

VTP Modes of Operation

There are three different modes of operation within a VTP domain. Figure 1.13 shows you all three:

FIGURE 1.13   VTP modes

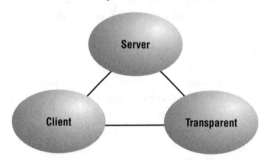

Server configuration: Saved in NVRAM

Client configuration: Not saved in NVRAM   Transparent configuration: Saved in NVRAM

Server   This is the default for all Catalyst switches. You need at least one server in your VTP domain to propagate VLAN information throughout the domain. The switch must be in server mode to be able to create, add, or delete VLANs in a VTP domain. You must also change VTP information in server mode, and any change you make to a switch in server mode will be advertised to the entire VTP domain.

Client   In client mode, switches receive information from VTP servers; they also send and receive updates, but they can't make any changes. Plus, none of the ports on a client switch can be added to a new VLAN before the VTP server notifies the client switch of the new VLAN. Here's a hint: if you want a switch to become a server, first make it a client so that it receives all the correct VLAN information, then change it to a server—much easier!

Transparent   Switches in transparent mode don't participate in the VTP domain, but they'll still forward VTP advertisements through any configured trunk links. These switches can't add and delete VLANs because they keep their own database—one they do not share with other switches. Transparent mode is really only considered locally significant.

VTP Pruning

VTP provides a way for you to preserve bandwidth by configuring it to reduce the amount of broadcasts, multicasts, and other unicast packets. This is called *pruning*. VTP pruning only sends broadcasts to trunk links that truly must have the information. Here's an example: if Switch A doesn't have any ports configured for VLAN 5, and a broadcast is sent throughout VLAN 5, that broadcast would not traverse the trunk link to this Switch A. By default, VTP pruning is disabled on all switches.

When you enable pruning on a VTP server, you enable it for the entire domain. By default, VLANs 2 through 1005 are pruning-eligible, but VLAN 1 can never prune because it's an administrative VLAN.

Exam Essentials

Remember the benefits of VLANs.   There are several benefits of VLANs:

- You can achieve network adds, moves, and changes by configuring a port into the appropriate VLAN.
- You can put a group of users needing high security into a VLAN so that no users outside of the VLAN can communicate with them.
- As a logical grouping of users by function, VLANs can be considered independent from their physical or geographic locations.
- VLANs can enhance network security.
- VLANs increase the number of broadcast domains while decreasing their size.

Understand the term "frame tagging."   Frame tagging refers to VLAN identification; this is what switches use to keep track of all those frames as they're traversing a switch fabric. It's how switches identify which frames belong to which VLANs.

Understand the ISL VLAN identification method.   Inter-Switch Link (ISL) is what you use to explicitly tag VLAN information onto an Ethernet frame. This tagging information allows VLANs to be multiplexed over a trunk link through an external encapsulation method, which allows the switch to identify the VLAN membership of a frame over the link. ISL is a Cisco-proprietary frame-tagging method that can only be used with Cisco switches.

Understand the 802.1Q VLAN identification method.   This is a nonproprietary IEEE method of frame tagging. If you're trunking between a Cisco switched link and a different brand of switch, you have to use 802.1Q for the trunk to work.

1.5 Developing an Access List to Meet User Specifications

Contributing mightily to the efficiency and operation of your network, access lists give network managers a huge amount of control over traffic flow throughout the enterprise. With access lists, managers can gather basic statistics on packet flow and implement security policies. Sensitive devices can also be protected from unauthorized access.

Access lists can be used to permit or deny packets moving through the router, permit or deny Telnet (VTY—also known as Virtual Teletype) access to or from a router, and create dial-on-demand interesting traffic that triggers dialing to a remote location.

There are two main types of access lists:

Standard access lists   These use only the source IP address in an IP packet as the condition test. All decisions are made based on this source IP address, which means that standard access lists basically permit or deny an entire suite of protocols. They don't distinguish between any of the many types of IP traffic such as World Wide Web (WWW), Telnet, User Datagram Protocol (UDP), and so on.

Extended access lists   Extended access lists can evaluate many of the other fields in the Layer 3 and Layer 4 header of an IP packet. They can evaluate source and destination IP addresses, the protocol field in the Network layer header, and the port number at the Transport layer header. This gives extended access lists the ability to make much more granular decisions when they are controlling traffic.

Once you create an access list, it's not really going to do anything until you apply it. Yes, this type of list is there on the router, but it's inactive until you tell that router what to do with it. To use an access list as a packet filter, you need to apply it to an interface on the router where you want the traffic filtered. You've also got to specify which direction of traffic you want the access list applied to. There's a good reason for this—you may want different controls in place for traffic leaving your enterprise destined for the Internet than you'd want for traffic coming into your enterprise from the Internet. So, by specifying the direction of traffic, you can—and frequently, you'll need to—use different access lists for inbound and outbound traffic on a single interface.

Inbound access lists   When an access list is applied to inbound packets on an interface, those packets are processed through the access list before being routed to the outbound interface. Any packets that are denied won't be routed because they're discarded before the routing process is invoked.

Outbound access lists   When an access list is applied to outbound packets on an interface, those packets are routed to the outbound interface and then processed through the access list before they are queued.

You should follow some general access list guidelines when you create and implement access lists on a router:

- You can only assign one access list per interface, per protocol, or per direction. This means that when creating IP access lists, you can only have one inbound access list and one out-bound access list per interface.

When you consider the implications of the implicit deny at the end of any access list, it makes sense that you can't have multiple access lists applied on the same interface in the same direction. This is because any packets that don't match some condition in the first access list are denied, and no packets are left over to compare against a second access list.

- Organize your access lists so that the more specific tests are at the top.
- Any time a new entry is added to the access list, it will be placed at the bottom of the list.
- You cannot remove one line from an access list. If you try to do this, you will remove the entire list. It is best to copy the access list to a text editor before removing the list, and to edit it there.
- Unless your access list ends with a `permit any` command, all packets will be discarded if they do not meet any of the lists' tests. Every list should have at least one permit statement, or it will deny all traffic.
- Create access lists and then apply them to an interface. Any access list applied to an interface without an access list present will not filter traffic.
- Access lists are designed to filter traffic going through the router. They will not filter traffic that has originated from the router.
- Place IP standard access lists as close to the destination as possible.
- Place IP extended access lists as close to the source as possible.

Exam Essentials

Understand the differences between standard and extended access lists.   Standard access lists make decisions based on source IP address only. Extended access lists can look at source and destination information at Layers 3 and 4, as well as protocol type information.

Know the rules for creating and applying access lists.   Access lists are directional—you can only have one access list per direction (inbound or outbound) on an interface. The implicit deny means that any packet not matching any line of an access list will be denied; it is as if every access list ends with a "deny all" function.

1.6 Choose WAN Services to Meet Customer Requirements

For the CCNA, we are concerned with the following WAN services:

- High-Level Data Link Control (HDLC) protocol
- Point-to-Point Protocol (PPP)
- Frame Relay
- Integrated Services Digital Network (ISDN)

Although there are certainly other options available in the real world, in this section, we will consider each of these technologies and appropriate times in which each would be used.

High-Level Data-Link Control (HDLC) Protocol

HDLC is a popular ISO-standard, bit-oriented Data Link layer protocol. It specifies an encapsulation method for data on synchronous serial data links using frame characters and checksums. HDLC is a point-to-point protocol used on leased lines. No authentication can be used with HDLC.

In byte-oriented protocols, control information is encoded using entire bytes. On the other hand, bit-oriented protocols may use single bits to represent control information. Bit-oriented protocols include SDLC, LLC, HDLC, TCP, IP, and so on.

HDLC is the default encapsulation used by Cisco routers over synchronous serial links. Cisco's HDLC is proprietary—it won't communicate with any other vendor's HDLC implementation. But don't give Cisco grief for it; *everyone's* HDLC implementation is proprietary. Figure 1.14 shows the Cisco HDLC format.

FIGURE 1.14   Cisco HDLC frame format

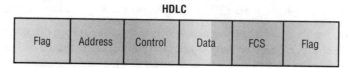

Cisco HDLC

| Flag | Address | Control | Proprietary | Data | FCS | Flag |

• Each vendor's HDLC has a proprietary data field to support multiprotocol environments.

HDLC

| Flag | Address | Control | Data | FCS | Flag |

• Supports only single-protocol environments.

As you can see in the figure, the reason that every vendor has a proprietary HDLC encapsulation method is that each vendor has a different way for the HDLC protocol to encapsulate multiple Network layer protocols. If the vendors didn't have a way for HDLC to communicate the different Layer 3 protocols, then HDLC would only be able to carry one protocol. This proprietary header is placed in the data field of the HDLC encapsulation.

Let's say you only have one Cisco router, and you needed to connect to, say, a Bay router because your other Cisco router is on order—what would you do? You couldn't use the default HDLC serial encapsulation—it wouldn't work. Instead, you would use something like PPP; an ISO-standard way of identifying the upper-layer protocols.

Point-to-Point Protocol (PPP)

PPP is a data-link protocol that you can use over either asynchronous serial (dial-up) or synchronous serial (ISDN) media. It uses the Link Control Protocol (LCP) to build and maintain data-link connections.

The basic purpose of PPP is to transport Layer 3 packets across a Data Link layer point-to-point link. Figure 1.15 shows the protocol stack compared to the OSI reference model.

FIGURE 1.15   Point-to-point protocol stack

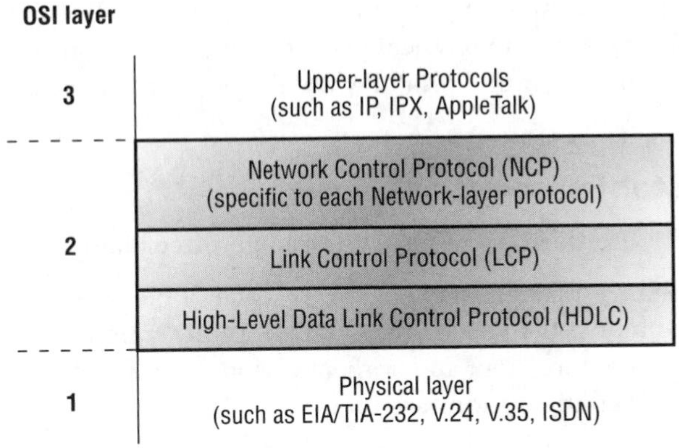

OSI layer

3	Upper-layer Protocols (such as IP, IPX, AppleTalk)
	Network Control Protocol (NCP) (specific to each Network-layer protocol)
2	Link Control Protocol (LCP)
	High-Level Data Link Control Protocol (HDLC)
1	Physical layer (such as EIA/TIA-232, V.24, V.35, ISDN)

PPP contains four main components:

EIA/TIA-232-C   A Physical layer international standard for serial communication.

HDLC   A method for encapsulating datagrams over serial links.

LCP   A method of establishing, configuring, maintaining, and terminating the point-to-point connection. (We'll talk more about LCP in just a moment).

NCP   A method of establishing and configuring different Network layer protocols. The Network Control Protocol (NCP) is designed to allow the simultaneous use of multiple Network layer protocols. Some examples of protocols here are Internet Protocol Control Protocol (IPCP) and Internetwork Packet Exchange Control Protocol (IPXCP).

Know that the PPP stack is specified at the Physical and Data Link layers only. NCP is used to allow communication of multiple Network layer protocols by encapsulating the protocols across a PPP data link.

Remember that if you have a Cisco router and a non-Cisco router connected with a serial connection, you must configure PPP or another encapsulation method, like Frame Relay, because the HDLC default won't work.

LCP Configuration Options

LCP offers different PPP encapsulation options like these:

Authentication   This option tells the calling side of the link to send information that can identify the user. The two methods are Password Authentication Protocol (PAP) and Challenge Handshake Authentication Protocol (CHAP).

Compression   This is used to increase the throughput of PPP connections by compressing the data or payload prior to transmission. PPP decompresses the data frame on the receiving end.

Error detection   PPP uses Quality and Magic Number options to ensure a reliable, loop-free data link.

Multilink   Starting in IOS version 11.1, multilink is supported on PPP links with Cisco routers. This option allows several separate physical paths to appear to be one logical path at Layer 3. For example, two T1s running multilink PPP would appear as a single 3Mbps path to a Layer 3 routing protocol.

PPP Session Establishment

When PPP connections are started, the links go through three phases of session establishment:

Link-establishment phase   LCP packets are sent by each PPP device to configure and test the link. These packets contain a field called the Configuration Option that allows each device to see the size of the data, compression, and authentication. If no Configuration Option field is present, then the default configurations are used.

Authentication phase   If required, either CHAP or PAP can be used to authenticate a link. Authentication takes place before Network layer protocol information is read.

Network layer protocol phase   PPP uses NCP to allow multiple Network layer protocols to be encapsulated and sent over a PPP data link.

PPP Authentication Methods

There are two methods of authentication that can be used with PPP links, either PAP or CHAP.

PAP   PAP is the less secure of the two methods. Passwords are sent in clear text, and PAP is only performed upon the initial link establishment. When the PPP link is first established, the remote node sends the username and password back to the sending router until authentication is acknowledged. That's it.

CHAP   CHAP is used at the initial startup of a link and at periodic checkups on the link to make sure the router is still communicating with the same host.

After PPP finishes its initial phase, the local router sends a challenge request to the remote device. The remote device sends a value calculated using a one-way hash function called MD5. The local router checks this hash value to make sure it matches. If the values don't match, the link is immediately terminated.

PPP Callback

PPP can be configured to callback after successful authentication. This feature can be a good thing for you based upon access charges, for accounting records, or for a variety of other reasons.

With callback enabled, a calling router (client) will contact a remote router (server) and authenticate as described above in the PPP Authentication Methods section. Both routers must be configured for the callback feature. Once authentication is completed, the remote router (server) will terminate the connection and then reinitiate a connection to the calling router (client) from the remote router (server).

Frame Relay

Frame Relay has become one of the most popular WAN services deployed over the past decade. There are good reasons for this, and they all begin with the almighty bottom line. Frame Relay technology is often a real bargain compared to other alternatives, and very few network designs ignore the cost factor!

Frame Relay has at its roots a technology called X.25. In many ways, Frame Relay incorporates the components of X.25 that are relevant to today's reliable and relatively "clean" telecommunications networks, and it leaves out the error correction components that aren't needed anymore. It's substantially more complex than the simple leased-line networks we discussed when we were exploring HDLC and PPP earlier. These leased-line networks are easy to conceptualize—just picture a really slick, high-tech pair of cans and a piece of string between them and you're good to go! Not so with Frame Relay. It can be significantly more complex and versatile, which is why it's often represented as a cloud in networking graphics. I'll get to that in a minute—for right now, I'm going to introduce Frame Relay in concept and show you how it differs from simpler leased-line technologies.

As part of your introduction to this technology, you'll get almost an encyclopedia of all the new terminology you'll need to get a grip on the basics of Frame Relay. After that, I'll guide you through some simple Frame Relay implementations.

Introduction to Frame Relay Technology

The section title, "Introduction to Frame Relay Technology," means what it says—this is only an introduction! As a CCNA, you need to understand the basics of this technology and be able to configure it in simple scenarios. So again, I'm just introducing Frame Relay here—this technology gets much deeper than what is covered here.

For more information on Frame Relay, look for *CCNP: Building Cisco Remote Access Networks Study Guide* (Sybex, 2004)

Frame Relay is a packet-switched technology. From everything you've learned so far, just telling you that should make you immediately realize several things about it:

- You won't be using the encapsulation HDLC or encapsulation PPP commands to configure it.

- Frame Relay doesn't work like a "point-to-point" leased line (although it can be made to look like one).

- Frame relay will in many cases be less expensive than a leased line, but there are some sacrifices made in order to gain that savings.

Here's an example of how packet switching versus leased line networks work to help you understand:

Let's say that you have a router in Miami and one in Denver that you want to connect. With a leased line, you pay a telecommunications company to provide a T1 line between them for you. Basically this means they'll provide the T1 and install a piece of equipment in each of your facilities that represents the demarcation point. You would plug this into your channel service unit/data service unit (CSU/DSU) and into your routers, select HDLC or PPP encapsulation, and continue to configure and troubleshoot the connection.

When buying a technology like this, you can expect the telco (telephone company) to provide you with a full T1 between your two sites. You can transmit at 1.544Mbps (full capacity) continuously if you want, and the telco has to deliver the packets. This is kind of like buying every seat to every showing of your favorite movie—you can see it whenever you want, as many times as you want—it's always available to you because, well, you paid for it.

So what happens if you skip a few showings at the theater? Do you get a refund just because you failed to show up? Nope! Likewise, if you choose to transmit at less than 1.544Mbps continuously, you don't get to enjoy any cost savings on a leased line. You're paying for the full T1 whether you use it or not. Yes, the infrastructure is always there for you, but you're going to pay for that availability whether you use it or not!

Let's go back to that connection between Miami and Denver. Suppose you had a way to get a connection that looked like a T1, and acted like a T1, but allowed you to pay for whatever portion of that T1 you actually used, without charging you for data you could've sent but didn't. Sound like a deal? That's essentially what packet-switched networks do.

This works because it is quite possible that your telecommunications company has hundreds, even thousands of customers who have locations in both Miami and Denver. Most likely, they've installed a significant amount of infrastructure in both cities, as well as at many sites in between. So if you buy a T1 from Miami to Denver, they have to carve you out a T1 from Miami to Denver, and reserve it for you all the time, just like in our movie theater analogy. However, if you're willing to share their infrastructure with some of their other customers, you get to save some serious cash.

Sometimes you'll find that you're transmitting at full T1 speeds, but other times you'll be transmitting hardly any bits at all. You may average only 25 percent of a full T1 over time. Well, if the telco has 1000 customers in Miami, each customer only averages 25 percent of a full T1, and these customers agree to share the telco's infrastructure (Frame Relay), the telco does not need 1000 T1s in Miami. Statistically, they can get away with a lot fewer than that because they only need enough to meet the peak demand of all their customers combined. Since probability says that all their customers will never need full capacity simultaneously, the telco needs fewer T1 lines than if each customer had their very own leased-line. Fewer T1 lines equals less infrastructure equals big money saved—voila!

This concept is called *oversubscription*. The telco sells the same infrastructure to a whole bunch of customers at a discount knowing that it's highly unlikely that there will come a time where all their customers need simultaneous access. Telcos have been doing this for years with voice networks—ever gotten an all circuits busy message on Mother's Day? They're pretty good at installing just enough but not too much. With Frame Relay, many customers share the telco's backbone frame network, and since the customers agree to share this infrastructure (oversubscription), they get a better price than if they each opted for dedicated leased lines. It's this win-win concept that amounts to huge savings for both customer and provider, and that is what makes Frame Relay so popular.

Frame Relay Technology in Action

Let's take a preliminary look at how Frame Relay technology works. Figure 1.16 is labeled with the various terms used to describe different parts of a Frame Relay network.

FIGURE 1.16   Frame Relay technology and terms

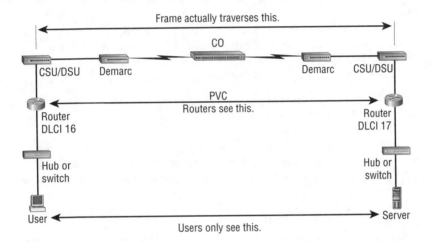

The basic idea behind Frame Relay networks is to allow users to communicate between two data terminal equipment (DTE) devices (routers here) through data communication equipment (DCE) devices. The users shouldn't see the difference between connecting to and gathering resources from a local server and a server at a remote site connected with Frame Relay other than a potential change in speed. Figure 1.16 illustrates everything that must happen in order for two DTE devices to communicate. Here is how the process works:

1. The user's network host sends a frame out on the LAN. The hardware address of the router (default gateway) will be in the header of the frame.

2. The router picks up the frame, extracts the packet, and discards the frame. It then looks at the destination IP address within the packet and checks to see whether it knows how to get to the destination network by looking into the routing table.

3. The router then forwards the data out the interface that it thinks can find the remote network. (If it can't find the network in its routing table, it'll just discard the packet.) Here, this will be a serial interface encapsulated with Frame Relay. The router puts the packet onto the Frame Relay network encapsulated within a Frame Relay frame.

4. The channel service unit/data service unit (CSU/DSU) receives the digital signal and encodes it into the type of digital signaling that the switch at the packet switching exchange (PSE) can understand. The PSE receives the digital signal and extracts the ones and zeros from the line.

5. The CSU/DSU is connected to a demarcation (demarc) installed by the service provider, and its location is the service provider's first point of responsibility (last point on the receiving end). The demarc is typically just an RJ-45 jack installed close to the router and CSU/DSU.

6. The demarc is typically a twisted-pair cable that connects to the local loop. The local loop connects to the closest central office (CO), sometimes called a *point of presence (POP)*. The local loop can connect using various physical mediums, but twisted-pair or fiber is common.

7. The CO receives the frame and sends it through the Frame Relay "cloud" to its destination. This cloud can be dozens of switching offices—or more!

8. Once the frame reaches the switching office closest to the destination office, it's sent through the local loop. The frame is received at the demarc, and is then sent to the CSU/DSU. Finally, the router extracts the packet, or datagram, from the frame and puts the packet in a new LAN frame to be delivered to the destination host. The frame on the LAN will have the final destination hardware address in the header. This was found in the router's Address Resolution Protocol (ARP) cache, or an ARP broadcast was performed. Whew!

The user and server do not need to know, nor should they know, everything that happens as the frame makes its way across the Frame Relay network. The remote server should be as easy to use as a locally connected resource.

There are several things that make the Frame Relay circuit different from a leased line. With a leased line, you typically specify the bandwidth you desire (T1, fractional T1, DS3, etc.). But with Frame Relay, you specify both an access rate (port speed) and a committed information rate (CIR). I'll talk about this next.

Committed Information Rate (CIR)

Frame Relay provides a packet-switched network to many different customers at the same time; this is very cool because it spreads the cost of the frame relay switches, telecommunications carrier trunk lines, etc. among many customers. But remember, Frame Relay is based on the assumption that all customers will never need to transmit constant data all at the same time.

Frame Relay works by providing a portion of dedicated bandwidth to each user, and also by allowing the user to exceed their guaranteed bandwidth if resources on the telco network are available. So basically, Frame Relay providers allow customers to buy a lower amount of bandwidth than what they really use. There are two separate bandwidth specifications with Frame Relay:

Access rate The maximum speed at which the Frame Relay interface can transmit.

CIR The maximum bandwidth of data guaranteed to be delivered.

If these two values are set to identical values, the Frame Relay connection is pretty much just like a leased line. But they can also be set to different values. Here's an example:

Let's say that you buy an access rate of T1 (1.544Mbps) and a CIR of 256Kbps. By doing this, you get the first 256Kbps of traffic you send guaranteed to be delivered. Anything beyond that is called a *burst*, which is a transmission that exceeds your guaranteed 256Kbps and can be any amount up to the T1 access rate. In a perfect world this always works beautifully—but remember that little word *guarantee*—as in the guaranteed rate of 256Kbps, to be exact? This means that any burst of data you send that exceeds your guaranteed 256Kbps rate will be delivered on something called a "best effort" basis of delivery. Or maybe not. If your telco's equipment doesn't have the capacity to deliver at the time you transmitted, then your frames will be discarded, and the DTE will be notified. Timing is everything—you can scream data out at six times (T1) your guaranteed rate of 256Kbps, *only if* your telco has the capacity available on their equipment at that moment! Remember that oversubscription we talked about? Well, here it is in action!

The CIR is the rate, in bits per second, at which the Frame Relay switch agrees to transfer data.

So the moral of the story is to choose—and choose carefully—a CIR based on realistic, anticipated traffic rates. Some Frame Relay providers allow you to purchase a CIR of zero. You can use a zero CIR to save money if retransmitting packets is acceptable to you. Doing that is a real crapshoot, though, because it means that every packet you send is eligible to be discarded in the provider's network!

Frame Relay Encapsulation Types

When configuring Frame Relay on Cisco routers, you need to specify it as an encapsulation on serial interfaces. As I said, you can't use HDLC or PPP with Frame Relay. When you configure Frame Relay, you specify an encapsulation of Frame Relay (as shown in the following code snippet). But unlike HDLC or PPP, with Frame Relay you have two encapsulation types: Cisco and the Internet Engineering Task Force (IETF). The following router output shows these two different encapsulation methods when choosing Frame Relay on your Cisco router:

```
RouterA(config)#int s0
RouterA(config-if)#encapsulation frame-relay ?
 ietf Use RFC1490 encapsulation
 <cr>
```

The default encapsulation is Cisco unless you manually type in IETF, and Cisco is the type used when you are connecting two Cisco devices. You'd want to opt for the IETF-type encapsulation if you needed to connect a Cisco device to a non-Cisco device with Frame Relay. Whichever you choose, make sure that the Frame Relay encapsulation is the same on both ends.

Virtual Circuits

Frame Relay operates using virtual circuits, as opposed to the real circuits that leased lines use. These virtual circuits are what connect the thousands of devices attached to the provider's "cloud" to each other. If you refer back to the Miami and Denver analogy that I introduced earlier, you will want these routers to connect to each other; that is, you will want a circuit between them. Frame Relay provides a virtual circuit to be established between your two DTE devices, which makes them look like they're connected via a circuit, when in reality they are dumping their frames into a large, shared infrastructure. *You never see the complexity of what is happening inside the cloud because you have a virtual circuit.*

There are two types of virtual circuits: permanent and switched. Permanent virtual circuits (PVCs) are by far the most common type in use today. What permanent means in this context is that the telco creates the mappings inside their gear, and as long as you pay the bill, there they stay. Switched virtual circuits (SVCs) are more like a phone call. The virtual circuit (VC) is established when data needs to be transmitted, then is taken down when data transfer is complete.

Data Link Connection Identifiers (DLCI)

Frame Relay PVCs are identified to DTE end devices using DLCIs. A Frame Relay service provider, such as the telephone company, typically assigns DLCI values, which are used on Frame Relay interfaces to distinguish between different VCs. Because many VCs can be terminated on one multipoint Frame Relay interface, many DLCIs are often affiliated with it.

Okay—to clarify this, let's say you have a central headquarters (HQ) with three branch offices. If you were to connect each branch office to HQ using a T1, you would need three serial interfaces on your router at HQ, one for each T1. Simple, huh? Well, suppose you use Frame Relay PVCs. You could have a T1 at each branch connected to a service provider, and only a *single* T1 at HQ. There would be three PVCs on the single T1 at HQ, one going to each branch. Even though there's only a single interface and a single CSU/DSU, the three PVCs function as three separate circuits. Remember what I said about saving big money? How much for two additional T1 interfaces and a pair of CSU/DSUs? Answer: $$$$$$$! So, just go ahead and ask for a percentage of the savings in your bonus.

Although some Frame Relay services can give the DLCI global significance, most only give the DLCI local significance. *Local significance* means that the DLCI really only identifies the PVC between your router and the first Frame Relay switch in the provider's network. That Frame Relay switch doesn't make forwarding decisions for your frame based on the DLCI on either end of your PVC; instead, the decisions are based upon some other hardcoded route in the provider's switch. DLCIs are important to you for keeping track of "is the PVC to Austin or to Cheyenne on this T1?" They're not used by the telco to "find" the other end of your PVC.

If you still need convincing that DLCIs are usually only locally significant, consider this: the DLCI is represented as a 10-bit field—that is, decimal values between 0 and 1023. I've worked with some small telcos, but none with only 1024 users—and that doesn't discount for the reserved DLCI values!

DLCI numbers, used to identify a PVC, are typically assigned by the provider and start at 16. You configure a DLCI number to be applied to an interface like this:

```
RouterA(config-if)#frame-relay interface-dlci ?
 <16-1007> Define a DLCI as part of the current
       subinterface
RouterA(config-if)#frame-relay interface-dlci 16
```

Local Management Interface (LMI)

LMI is a signaling standard used to transmit messages between your router and the first Frame Relay switch to which it's connected. It allows information to be passed about the operation and status of the VC between the provider's network and the DTE (your router). It communicates information about these things:

Keepalives   Verify data is flowing.

Multicasting   Provides a local DLCI PVC.

Multicast addressing   Provides global significance.

Status of virtual circuits   Provides DLCI status.

Remember, LMI isn't communication between your routers—it's communication between your router and the nearest Frame Relay switch. So it's entirely possible that the router on one end of a PVC is actively receiving LMI, but the router on the other end of the PVC isn't. Of course, PVCs won't work with one end down. I just said this to illustrates the local nature of LMI communications.

There are three different types of LMI message formats. The different kinds depend on the type and configuration of the telco's switching gear. It's imperative to configure your router for the correct one, which should be provided by the telco.

Beginning with Cisco IOS version 11.2, the LMI type is autosensed. This enables the interface to determine the LMI type supported by the switch without user configuration.

If you're not going to use the autosense feature, you'll need to check with your Frame Relay provider to find out which type to use instead. On Cisco equipment, the default type is Cisco, but you may need to change to American National Standards Institute (ANSI) or Q.933A depending on what your service provider tells you. The three different LMI types are depicted in the following router output:

```
RouterA(config-if)#frame-relay lmi-type ?
 cisco
 ansi
 q933a
```

This demonstrates that all three standard LMI signaling formats are supported. Here's a description of each:

Cisco   LMI defined by the Gang of Four (default).

ANSI   Annex D defined by ANSI standard T1.617.

ITU-T (Q933a)   Annex A defined by Q.933.

Routers receive LMI information from the service provider's Frame Relay switch on a frame-encapsulated interface and update the virtual circuit status to one of three different states:

Active state   Everything is up, and routers can exchange information.

Inactive state   The router's interface is up and working with a connection to the switching office, but the remote router is not working.

Deleted state   No LMI information is being received on the interface from the switch. It could be a mapping problem or a line failure.

Frame Relay Congestion Control

Remember back to our talk about CIR? From that, you know that the lower your CIR is set, the greater the risk that your data will become toast. But Toasted Data Syndrome could be easily avoided if you just had one key piece of information—when/when not to transmit that burst! So to get this information, you need to ask the following questions:

- Is there any way to find out when your telco's shared infrastructure is free and clear or crammed and clogged?

- If there is, how do you accomplish that?

In this section, I'm going to talk about how the Frame Relay switch notifies the DTE of congestion problems and address these very important questions.

There's a two-byte address field in the Frame Relay header—the first 10 bits are used for the DLCI, the remaining six are used for congestion management. Here are the three congestion messages and their meanings:

Discard Eligibility (DE)   As you know, when you burst (transmit packets beyond the CIR of a PVC), any packets exceeding the CIR are eligible to be discarded if the provider's network is congested. Because of this, the excess bits are marked with a DE bit in the Frame Relay header. If the providers network is congested, the Frame Relay switch discards the packets with the DE bit set first. So if your bandwidth is configured with a CIR of zero, the DE will always be on.

Forward-Explicit Congestion Notification (FECN)   When the Frame Relay network recognizes congestion in the cloud, the switch will set the FECN bit to 1 in a Frame Relay packet header. This indicates to the destination DCE that the path just traversed is congested.

Backward-Explicit Congestion Notification (BECN)   When the switch detects congestion in the Frame Relay network, it'll set the BECN bit in a Frame Relay packet that's destined for the source router. This notifies the router that congestion is being encountered ahead.

Cisco routers do not necessarily take action on this congestion information unless you tell them to. For further information on this, search for "Frame Relay Traffic Shaping" on Cisco's website.

Integrated Services Digital Network (ISDN)

ISDN is a digital service that is designed to run over existing telephone networks. ISDN can support both data and voice—a telecommuter's dream. But ISDN applications require bandwidth. Typical ISDN applications and implementations include high-speed image applications (such as Group IV facsimile), high-speed file transfer, videoconferencing, and multiple links into homes of telecommuters.

ISDN is actually a set of communication protocols proposed by telephone companies that allows them to carry a group of digital services that simultaneously convey data, text, voice, music, graphics, and video to end users; it was designed to achieve this over the telephone systems already in place. ISDN is referenced by a suite of ITU-T standards that encompass the OSI model's Physical, Data Link, and Network layers.

The ISDN standards define the hardware and call-setup schemes for end-to-end digital connectivity.

PPP is typically used with ISDN to provide data encapsulation, link integrity, and authentication. So don't think of ISDN as a replacement for PPP, HDLC, or Frame Relay, because it's really an underlying infrastructure that any of these could use. As I said, PPP is the most common encapsulation across ISDN connections.

These are the benefits of ISDN:

- It can carry voice, video, and data simultaneously.

- Call setup is faster than with a modem.

- Data rates are faster than on a modem connection.

- Full-time connectivity across the ISDN is spoofed by the Cisco IOS routers using dial-on-demand routing (DDR).

- Small office and home office sites can be economically supported with ISDN Basic Rate Interface (BRI) services.

- ISDN can be used as a backup service for a leased-line connection between the remote and central offices.

- Modem racking and cabling can be eliminated by integration of digital modem cards on Cisco IOS Network Access Server (NAS).

Integrated Services Digital Network (ISDN) Connections

ISDN BRI is made up of two B (Bearer) channels of 64k each, and one D (Data) channel of 16k for signaling and clocking.

ISDN BRI routers come with either a U interface or something known as an S/T interface. The difference between the two is that the U interface is already a two-wire ISDN convention that can plug right into the ISDN local loop. Conversely, the S/T interface is a four-wire interface that basically needs an adapter—a Network Termination type 1 (NT 1)— to convert from a four-wire to the two-wire ISDN specification.

The U interface has a built-in NT 1 device. If your service provider uses an NT 1 device, then you need to buy a router that has an S/T interface. Most Cisco router BRI interfaces are marked with a U or an S/T. When in doubt, ask Cisco or the salesperson.

ISDN Terminals

Devices connecting to the ISDN network are known as terminal equipment (TE) and network termination (NT) equipment. There are two types of each:

TE1   A terminal equipment type 1 (TE1) device refers to those terminals that understand ISDN standards and can plug right into an ISDN network.

TE2   A terminal equipment type 2 (TE2) device refers to those terminals that predate ISDN standards. To use a TE2, you have to use a terminal adapter (TA) to be able to plug into an ISDN network. An example of a TE2 device would be a serial interface on a router or a standard PC.

NT1   The network termination 1 (NT1) device implements the ISDN Physical layer specifications and connects the user devices to the ISDN network by converting the network from a four-wire to the two-wire network used by ISDN. Basically, I'll call this a "U" reference point that connects into the telco. I'll talk about reference points next.

NT2   The network termination 2 (NT2) device is typically a provider's equipment, like a switch or private branch exchange (PBX). It also provides Data Link and Network layer implementation. It's very rare to find these on a customer's premises.

TA   A terminal adapter (TA) converts TE2 non-ISDN signaling to signaling that's used by the ISDN switch. It connects into an NT1 device for conversion into a two-wire ISDN network.

ISDN Reference Points

Reference points are a series of specifications that define the connection among the various pieces of equipment used in an ISDN network. ISDN has four reference points that define logical interfaces:

R   The R reference point defines the point between non-ISDN equipment (TE2) and a TA.

S   The S reference point defines the point between the customer router and an NT2. This reference point enables calls between the different customer equipment.

T   The T reference point defines the point between NT1 and NT2 devices. S and T reference points are electrically the same and can perform the same function; because of this, they're sometimes referred to as the *S/T reference point*.

U   The U reference point defines the point between NT1 devices and line-termination equipment in a carrier network. (This is only in North America, where the NT1 function isn't provided by the carrier network.)

ISDN Protocols

ISDN protocols are defined by the International Telecommunication Union (ITU), and there are several series of protocols dealing with diverse issues:

- Protocols beginning with the letter *E* deal with using ISDN on the existing telephone network.
- Protocols beginning with the letter *I* deal with concepts, aspects, and services.
- Protocols beginning with the letter *Q* cover switching and signaling. These are the protocols I use to connect to an ISDN network and troubleshoot it. The Q.921 protocol describes the ISDN Data Link process of the Link Access Procedure on the D channel (LAPD). The Q.931 specifies the OSI reference model Layer 3 functions.

ISDN Switch Types

We can credit AT&T and Nortel for the majority of the ISDN switches in place today, but other companies also make them.

In Table 1.5, in the Keyword column, you'll find the right keyword to use along with the isdn switch-type command to configure a router for the variety of switches to which it's going to connect. If you don't know which switch your provider uses at their central office, call them to find out.

TABLE 1.5   ISDN Switch Types

Switch Type	Keyword
AT&T basic rate switch	basic-5ess
Nortel DMS-100 basic rate switch	basic-dms100
National ISDN-1 switch	basic-ni
AT&T 4ESS (ISDN Primary Rate Interface [PRI] only)	primary-4ess
AT&T 5ESS (ISDN PRI only)	primary-5ess
Nortel DMS-100 (ISDN PRI only)	primary-dms100

Basic Rate Interface (BRI)

ISDN BRI service, also known as 2B+1D, provides two B channels and one D channel. The BRI B-channel service operates at 64Kbps and carries data, whereas the BRI D-channel service operates at 16Kbps and usually carries control and signaling information. The total bandwidth for ISDN BRI is then 144k (64 + 64 + 16 = 144).

The D-channel signaling protocol spans the OSI reference model's Physical, Data Link, and Network layers. The D channel carries signaling information to set up and control calls. You can also use this channel for other functions like an alarm system for a building, or anything else that doesn't need much bandwidth since it's only giving you a whopping 16k. D channels work with LAPD at the Data Link layer for reliable connections.

When configuring ISDN BRI, you'll need to obtain service profile identifiers (SPIDs), and you should have one SPID for each B channel. SPIDs can be thought of as the telephone number of each B channel. The ISDN device gives the SPID to the ISDN switch, which then allows the device to access the network for BRI or PRI service. Without a SPID, many ISDN switches don't allow an ISDN device to place a call on the network.

To set up a BRI call, the following four events must take place:

1.   The D channel between the router and the local ISDN switch comes up.

2.   The ISDN switch uses the SS7 signaling technique to set up a path to a remote switch.

3.   The remote switch sets up the D-channel link to the remote router.

4.   The B channels are then connected end-to-end.

Primary Rate Interface (PRI)

In North America and Japan, the ISDN PRI service (also known as 23B+D1) delivers 23 64Kbps B channels and one 64Kbps D channel, for a total bit rate of up to 1.544Mbps.

In Europe, Australia, and other parts of the world, ISDN provides 30 64Kbps B channels and one 64Kbps D channel, for a total bit rate of up to 2.048Mbps.

Exam Essentials

Remember the default serial encapsulation on Cisco routers.   Cisco routers use a proprietary High-Level Data Link Control (HDLC) encapsulation on all their serial links by default.

Understand what the LMI is in Frame Relay.   The LMI is a signaling standard between a router and a frame relay switch. The LMI is responsible for managing and maintaining status between these devices. This standard also provides transmission keepalives to ensure that the PVC does not shut down because of inactivity.

Understand the different Frame Relay encapsulations.   Cisco uses two different Frame Relay encapsulation methods on their routers. Cisco is the default, and it means that the router is connected to a Cisco Frame Relay switch; Internet Engineering Task Force (IETF), the second, means your router is connecting to anything but a Cisco Frame Relay switch.

Remember what the CIR is in Frame Relay.   The CIR is the rate, in bits per second, at which the Frame Relay switch agrees to transfer data.

Remember the PPP Data Link layer protocols.   The three Data Link layer protocols are the Network Control Protocol (NCP), which defines the Network layer protocols; the Link Control Protocol (LCP), a method of establishing, configuring, maintaining, and terminating the point-to-point connection; and the High-Level Data Link Control (HDLC), the MAC layer protocol that encapsulates the packets.

Review Questions

1. What is the address range of a class C network address?

   A. 0–127

   B. 1–126

   C. 128–191

   D. 192–223

2. What is the result of using a hierarchical addressing scheme?

   A. Increased number of addresses

   B. Decreased amount of routers needed

   C. Increased memory usage on routers

   D. No routing tables needed on routers

3. What is the result of segmenting a network with a bridge (switch)? (Choose all that apply.)

   A. It increases the number of collision domains.

   B. It decreases the number of collision domains.

   C. It increases the number of broadcast domains.

   D. It decreases the number of broadcast domains.

   E. It makes smaller collision domains.

   F. It makes larger collision domains.

4. Which of the following is a characteristic of having a network segment on a switch?

   A. The segment is many collision domains.

   B. The segment can translate from one media to a different media.

   C. All devices on a segment are part of a different broadcast domain.

   D. One device per segment can concurrently send frames to the switch.

5. What is the default administrative distance for IGRP?

   A. 90

   B. 100

   C. 120

   D. 220

6. What does split horizon do?

    A. Ensures that information about a route will not be sent back in the direction from which the original update came.

    B. It splits the traffic when you have a large bus (horizon) physical network.

    C. It holds the regular updates from broadcasting to a downed link.

    D. It prevents regular update messages from reinstating a route that has gone down.

7. What does poison reverse do?

    A. It sends back the protocol received from a router as a poison pill, which stops the regular updates.

    B. It ensures that information received from a router can't be sent back to the originating router.

    C. It prevents regular update messages from reinstating a route that has just come up.

    D. It describes when a router sets the metric for a downed link to infinity.

8. Which of the following are used by default by EIGRP to calculate the best path to a destination network? (Choose all that apply.)

    A. Bandwidth

    B. Load

    C. Delay

    D. Reliability

9. What are benefits of using a link-state routing protocol? (Choose all that apply.)

    A. It uses the Hello protocol to establish adjacencies.

    B. It uses several components to calculate the metric of a route.

    C. It sends updates only when changes occur in the network.

    D. It is always a better solution to implement than a distance-vector protocol.

10. The LMI is responsible for which of the following?

    A. For keeping routers up and running with less memory overhead

    B. For telling the switch what type of router is running on each end

    C. For broadcasting IP routing protocol information

    D. For transmission keepalives to ensure that the PVC does not shut down because of inactivity

Answers to Review Questions

1. D. The address range of a class C network is 192–223.

2. A. The designers created a hierarchical addressing scheme when they created the IP address so that more addresses would be available to each network.

3. A, E . Bridges break up collision domains, which would increase the number of collision domains in a network and also make smaller collision domains.

4. D. Only one device on a network segment connected to a switch can send frames to the switch. A switch cannot translate from one media type to another on the same segment.

5. B. IGRP's default administrative distance is 100; RIP's default administrative distance is 120.

6. A. A split horizon will not advertise a route back to the same router from which it learned the route.

7. D. A poison reverse is used to communicate to a router that the link is down and that the hop count to that network is set to infinity or unreachable.

8. A, C . Bandwidth and delay are the only parameters used by default to calculate the metric of a route. Reliability and load are legitimate parameters that may also be used in the metric calculation, but they are not used by default.

9. A, C. Link-state routing protocols use the Hello protocol to establish adjacency, they update neighbors only when changes occur, and they send only the changed information and not the entire routing table. Using several components to calculate metrics is not an advantage of link-state protocols. Some distance-vector protocols, such as IGRP, use multiple components to calculate routes whereas some link-state protocols, like OSPF, use only one. It is also not always true that it is better to use a link-state protocol. RIP and IGRP are well suited for small environments, are easy to configure, and have relatively low overhead.

10. D. The LMI provides keepalives between the router and the frame switch to verify that the link and connection are still active.

Chapter 2

Implementation & Operation

CISCO CCNA EXAM OBJECTIVES COVERED IN THIS CHAPTER:

- ✓ 2.1 Configure routing protocols given user requirements
- ✓ 2.2 Configure IP addresses, subnet masks, and gateway addresses on routers and hosts
- ✓ 2.3 Configure a router for additional administrative functionality
- ✓ 2.4 Configure a switch with VLANS and inter-switch communication
- ✓ 2.5 Implement a LAN
- ✓ 2.6 Customize a switch configuration to meet specified network requirements
- ✓ 2.7 Manage system image and device configuration files
- ✓ 2.8 Perform an initial configuration on a router
- ✓ 2.9 Perform an initial configuration on a switch
- ✓ 2.10 Implement access lists
- ✓ 2.11 Implement simple WAN protocols

All right, this is the big one! Of all the chapters, this is the largest and likely where you will spend the most time. We will discuss the implementation of all of the technologies on the CCNA, everything from IP address, routing protocols, and VLANs to IOS image maintenance, access lists, and WANs. We will cover a lot of CLI (command line interface) stuff here, so get ready to type!

2.1 Configure Routing Protocols Given User Requirements

In this section, I am going to review the process of configuring a router to actually, well, route. As you will recall, you have several ways to route IP traffic between routers. Let's begin by reviewing static and default routing, then go on to configure Routing Information Protocol (RIP), Interior Gateway Routing Protocol (IGRP), Enhanced Interior Gateway Routing Protocol (EIGRP), and finally, Open Shortest Path First (OSPF).

To get started, I'll outline the configuration I will use throughout this section to illustrate the use of each of these routing protocols. I'll begin by configuring three routers with basic IP addressing and other configuration commands.

Preliminary Configuration

Figure 2.1 shows three routers: Lab_A, Lab_B, and Lab_C. Remember, by default, these routers only know about networks that are directly connected to them.

FIGURE 2.1 IP routing example with more routers

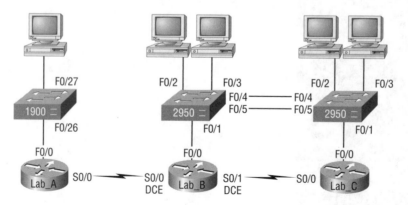

Okay—Figure 2.1 shows the three 2600 routers connected via a wide area network (WAN). Each router also has an Ethernet network connected. The idea is that each router must know about all five networks. The networks I'll use to configure the network are listed on the figure as well.

The first step is to configure each router with the correct IP address information. Table 2.1 shows the IP address scheme I'm going to use to configure the network. After I go over how the network is configured, I'll show you how to configure IP routing. Each network in the following table has a default class C 24-bit subnet mask (255.255.255.0).

TABLE 2.1   Network Addressing for the IP Network

Router	Network Address	Interface	Address
Lab_A	192.168.10.0	fa0/0	192.168.10.1
Lab_A	192.168.20.0	s0/0	192.168.20.1
Lab_B	192.168.20.0	s0/0	192.168.20.2
Lab_B	192.168.40.0	S0/1	192.168.40.1
Lab_B	192.168.30.0	Fa0/0	192.168.30.1
Lab_C	192.168.40.0	s0/0	192.168.40.2
Lab_C	192.168.50.0	Fa0/0	192.168.50.1

Router configuration is a really a pretty straightforward process since you just need to add IP addresses to your interfaces and then perform a no shutdown on those interfaces. It will get a tad bit more complex later on, but first, let's configure the IP addresses in the network.

Lab_A Configuration

To configure the Lab_A router, you just need to add an IP address to interface FastEthernet 0/0 as well as the Serial 0/0. Configuring the hostnames of each router will make identification easier. And why not set the interface descriptions, banner, and router passwords too? You really should get in the habit of configuring these commands on every router.

Here is how I did that:

```
Router>en
Router#config t
Router(config)#hostname Lab_A
Lab_A(config)#enable secret todd
Lab_A(config)#interface fa0/0
```

```
Lab_A(config-if)#ip address 192.168.10.1 255.255.255.0
Lab_A(config-if)#description Lab_A LAN Connection
Lab_A(config-if)#no shut
Lab_A(config-if)#interface serial 0/0
Lab_A(config-if)#ip address 192.168.20.1 255.255.255.0
Lab_A(config-if)#description WAN Connection to Lab_B
Lab_A(config-if)#no shut
Lab_A(config-if)#exit
Lab_A(config)#line console 0
Lab_A(config-line)#password todd
Lab_A(config-line)#login
Lab_A(config-line)#line aux 0
Lab_A(config-line)#password todd
Lab_A(config-line)#login
Lab_A(config-line)#line vty 0 4
Lab_A(config-line)#password todd
Lab_A(config-line)#login
Lab_A(config-line)#exit
Lab_A(config)#banner motd #
This is the Lab_A router
#
Lab_A(config-line)#^z
Lab_A#copy running-config startup-config
Destination filename [startup-config]? Enter
Lab_A#
```

To view the IP routing tables created on a Cisco router, use the privileged mode command show ip route. The command output follows momentarily. Notice that only the configured, directly connected networks are shown in the routing table. This means the router only knows how to get to networks 192.168.10.0 and 192.168.20.0.

```
Lab_A#sh ip route
Codes: C - connected, S - static, I - IGRP, R - RIP,
  M - mobile, B – BGP D - EIGRP, EX - EIGRP external, O -
  OSPF, IA - OSPF inter area N1 - OSPF NSSternal type
  1, N2 - OSPF NSSA external type 2 E1 - OSPF external
  type 1, E2 - OSPF external type 2, E – EGP i - IS-IS,
  L1 - IS-IS level-1, L2 - IS-IS level-2, * - candidate
  default, U - per-user static route, o - ODR, P -
  periodic downloaded static route, T - traffic
  engineered route
```

```
Gateway of last resort is not set

C     192.168.10.0/24 is directly connected, FastEthernet0/0
C     192.168.20.0/24 is directly connected, Serial 0/0
Lab_A#
```

Did you notice the C? When you see it, it means that the network is directly connected. The codes for each type of connection are listed at the top of the show ip route command with their abbreviations.

In the interest of brevity, the codes will be cut in the rest of this chapter.

Lab_B Configuration

It's now time to configure the next router. To configure Lab_B, you have three interfaces to deal with: FastEthernet 0/0, Serial 0/0 and Serial 0/1. Both serial interfaces are data communication equipment (DCE). What that means to you is that you'll have to add the clock rate command to each interface. And make sure you don't forget to add your passwords, interface descriptions, and banner to the router configuration!

```
Router>en
Router#config t
Router(config)#hostname Lab_B
Lab_B(config)#enable secret todd
Lab_B(config)#interface fa0/0
Lab_B(config-if)#ip address 192.168.30.1 255.255.255.0
Lab_B(config-if)#description Lab_B LAN Connection
Lab_B(config-if)#no shut
Lab_B(config-if)#interface serial 0/0
Lab_B(config-if)#ip address 192.168.20.2 255.255.255.0
Lab_B(config-if)#description WAN Connection to Lab_A
Lab_B(config-if)#clock rate 64000
Lab_B(config-if)#no shut
Lab_B(config-if)#interface serial 0/1
Lab_B(config-if)#ip address 192.168.40.1 255.255.255.0
Lab_B(config-if)#description WAN Connection to Lab_C
Lab_B(config-if)#clock rate 64000
Lab_B(config-if)#no shut
Lab_B(config-if)#exit
Lab_B(config)#line console 0
Lab_B(config-line)#password todd
```

```
Lab_B(config-line)#login
Lab_B(config-line)#line aux 0
Lab_B(config-line)#password todd
Lab_B(config-line)#login
Lab_B(config-line)#line vty 0 4
Lab_B(config-line)#password todd
Lab_B(config-line)#login
Lab_B(config-line)#exit
Lab_B(config)#banner motd #
This is the Lab_B router
#
Lab_B(config-line)#^z
Lab_B#copy running-config startup-config
Destination filename [startup-config]? Enter
Lab_B#
```

These commands configured Serial 0/0 into network 192.168.20.0, Serial 0/1 into network 192.168.40.0, and FastEthernet 0/0 into network 192.168.30.0. The show ip route command displays the following:

```
Lab_B#sh ip route
[output cut]
Gateway of last resort is not set

C       192.168.20.0/24 is directly connected, Serial0/0
C       192.168.40.0/24 is directly connected, Serial0/1
C       192.168.30.0 is directly connected FastEthernet 0/0
Lab_B#
```

Notice that router Lab_B knows how to get to networks 192.168.20.0, 192.168.30.0, and 172.16.40.0. Router Lab_A and Router Lab_B can now communicate because they're connected on the same WAN.

Lab_C Configuration

The configuration of Lab_C is the same as the other two routers. Make sure you remember to add passwords, interface descriptions, and your banner to the router configuration:

```
Router>en
Router#config t
Router(config)#hostname Lab_C
Lab_C(config)#enable secret todd
Lab_C(config)#interface fa0/0
```

```
Lab_C(config-if)#ip address 192.168.50.1 255.255.255.0
Lab_C(config-if)#description Lab_C LAN Connection
Lab_C(config-if)#no shut
Lab_C(config-if)#interface serial 0/0
Lab_C(config-if)#ip address 192.168.40.2 255.255.255.0
Lab_C(config-if)#description WAN Connection to Lab_B
Lab_C(config-if)#no shut
Lab_C(config-if)#exit
Lab_C(config)#line console 0
Lab_C(config-line)#password todd
Lab_C(config-line)#login
Lab_C(config-line)#line aux 0
Lab_C(config-line)#password todd
Lab_C(config-line)#login
Lab_C(config-line)#line vty 0 4
Lab_C(config-line)#password todd
Lab_C(config-line)#login
Lab_C(config-line)#exit
Lab_C(config)#banner motd #
This is the Lab_C router
#
Lab_C(config-line)# ^z
Lab_C#copy running-config startup-config
Destination filename [startup-config]? Enter
Lab_C#
```

The output of the following show ip route command displays the directly connected networks of 192.168.50.0 and 192.168.40.0.

```
Lab_C#sh ip route
[output cut]
Gateway of last resort is not set



C       192.168.50.0/24 is directly connected, FastEthernet0/0
C       192.168.40.0/24 is directly connected, Serial0/0
lab_C#
```

Routers Lab_A and Lab_B can communicate because they're on
Lab_B and Lab_C can also communicate because they're connected
Router Lab_A can't communicate with the Lab_C router because it do
work 172.16.40.0 and 192.168.50.0—at least not yet.

Configuring IP Routing in Your Network

Okay—cool. Your network is good to go—right? After all, it's been correctly configured with IP addressing! But wait... how does a router send packets to remote networks? They can only send packets by looking at the routing table to find out how to get to the remote networks. Your configured routers only have information about directly connected networks in each routing table. And what happens when a router receives a packet with a network that isn't listed in the routing table? It doesn't send a broadcast looking for the remote network—the router just discards it. Period.

So you're not exactly ready to rock yet after all. But no worries—you still have several ways to configure the routing tables to include all the networks in your little internetwork so that packets will be forwarded. However, what's best for one network isn't necessarily what's best for another. Understanding the different types of routing will really help you come up with the best solution for your specific environment and business requirements.

Once again, the different types of routing you'll configure in this section are as follows:

- Static routing
- Default routing
- Dynamic routing

I'm going to start off by describing and implementing static routing on your network because if you can implement static routing, *and* make it work, it means you have a solid understanding of the internetwork! So let's get started...

Here's the command you use to add a static route to a routing table:

```
ip route [destination_network] [mask] [next-hop_address
  or exitinterface] [administrative_distance] [permanent]
```

This list describes each command in the string:

ip route   The command used to create the static route.

destination network   The network you're placing in the routing table.

mask   The subnet mask being used on the network.

next-hop address   The address of the next-hop router that will receive the packet and forward it to the remote network. This is a router interface that's on a directly connected network. You must be able to ping the router interface before you add the route. If you type in the wrong next-hop address, or the interface to that router is down, the static route shows up in the router's configuration, but not in the routing table.

exitinterface   You can use this in place of the next-hop address if you want, but it's got to be on a point-to-point link, like a WAN. This command won't work on a LAN like Ethernet.

administrative_distance   By default, static routes have an administrative distance of 1. You can change the default value by adding an administrative weight at the end of the command. This is a subject I'll talk a lot more about later in the chapter when I get to the section dynamic routing.

permanent   If the interface is shut down or the router can't communicate to the next-hop router, the route is automatically discarded from the routing table. Choosing the permanent option keeps the entry in the routing table no matter what happens.

To help you understand how static routes work, I'll demonstrate the configuration on the internetwork shown previously in Figure 2.1.

Lab_A

Each routing table automatically includes directly connected networks. To be able to route to all networks in the internetwork, the routing table must include information that describes where these other networks are located and how to get there.

The Lab_A router is connected to networks 192.168.10.0 and 192.168.20.0. For the Lab_A router to be able to route to all networks, the following networks have to be configured in its routing table:

- 192.168.30.0
- 192.168.40.0
- 192.168.50.0

The following router output shows the configuration of static routes on the Lab_A router and the routing table after the configuration. For the Lab_A router to find the remote networks, you must place an entry in the routing table that describes the network, the mask, and where to send the packets. Notice that each static route sends the packets to 192.168.20.2, which is the Lab_A router's next hop.

```
Lab_A(config)#ip route 192.168.30.0 255.255.255.0
  192.168.20.2
Lab_A(config)#ip route 192.168.40.0 255.255.255.0
  192.168.20.2
Lab_A(config)#ip route 192.168.50.0 255.255.255.0
  192.168.20.2
```

After the router is configured, you can type show running-config and show ip route to see the static routes. Remember that if the routes don't appear in the routing table, it's because the router cannot communicate with the next-hop address you configured. Remember—you can use the **permanent** parameter to keep the route in the routing table even if you can't contact the next-hop device.

```
Lab_A#sh ip route
[output cut]S      192.168.50.0 [1/0] via 192.168.20.2
S      192.168.40.0 [1/0] via 192.168.20.2
S      192.168.30.0 [1/0] via 192.168.20.2
C      192.168.20.0 is directly connected, Serial 0/0
C      192.168.10.0 is directly connected, FastEthernet0/0
Lab_A#
```

The S in the routing table entries means that the network is a static entry. The [1/0] is the administrative distance and metric (which I'll talk about soon) to the remote network. Here it's 0 indicating that it's directly connected.

The Lab_A router now has all the information it needs to communicate with the other remote networks. However, if the Lab_B and Lab_C routers are not configured with all the same information, the packets will be discarded at Lab_B and at Lab_C. You need to fix this.

Lab_B

- The Lab_B router is connected to the networks 192.168.20.0, 192.168.30.0, and 192.168.40.0. You must configure the following static routes on the Lab_B router:
- 192.168.10.0
- 192.168.50.0

Here's the configuration for the Lab_B router.

```
Lab_B(config)#ip route 192.168.10.0 255.255.255.0
  192.168.20.1
Lab_B(config)#ip route 192.168.50.0 255.255.255.0
  192.168.40.2
```

Okay—by next looking at the routing table, you can see that the Lab_B router now understands how to find each network.

```
Lab_B#sh ip route
[output cut]
S        192.168.50.0 [1/0] via 192.168.40.2
C        192.168.40.0 is directly connected, Serial0/1
C        192.168.30.0 is directly connected, FastEthernet 0/0
C        192.168.20.0 is directly connected, Serial0/0
S        192.168.10.0 [1/0] via 192.168.20.1
Lab_B#
```

The Lab_B router now has a complete routing table. As soon as the other routers in the internetwork have the same routing table, Lab_B can communicate to all remote networks.

Lab_C

The Lab_C router is directly connected to networks 192.168.40.0 and 192.168.50.0. You need to add three routes: 192.168.30.0, 192.168.20.0, and 192.168.10.0.

```
Lab_C(config)#ip route 192.168.30.0 255.255.255.0
192.168.40.1
Lab_C(config)#ip route 192.168.20.0 255.255.255.0
  172.16.40.1
Lab_C(config)#ip route 192.168.10.0 255.255.255.0
192.168.40.1
```

The following output shows the routing table on the Lab_C router.

```
Lab_C#sh ip route
[output cut]
C       192.168.50.0 is directly connected, FastEthernet0/0
C       192.168.40.0 is directly connected, Serial0/0
S       192.168.30.0 [1/0] via 192.168.40.1
S       192.168.20.0 [1/0[ via 192.168.40.1
S       192.168.10.0 [1/0] via 192.168.40.1
Lab_C#
```

Lab_C now shows all the networks in the internetwork and can communicate with all routers and networks.

Now all the routers have the correct routing table, and all the routers and hosts should be able to communicate without a problem. But if you add even one more network or another router to the internetwork, you'll have to update all routers' routing tables by hand. As I said, this isn't a problem at all if you've got a small network, but it's way too time-consuming a task if you're dealing with a large internetwork.

Verifying Your Configuration

Once you have configured all the routers' routing tables, you need to verify them. The best way to do this, besides using the show ip route command, is with the Ping program. By pinging from routers Lab_A and Lab_C, you can test the whole internetwork end-to-end. Really, the best test would be to use the Telnet program from one host to another, but for now, ping is king!

Here is the output of a ping to network 192.168.50.0 from the Lab_A router:

```
Lab_A#ping 192.168.50.1
Type escape sequence to abort.
Sending 5, 100-byte ICMP Echos to 172.16.50.1, timeout is
  2 seconds:
.!!!!
Success rate is 80 percent (4/5), round-trip min/avg/max
  = 64/66/68 ms
Lab_A#
```

Notice that the first response is a period. This is because the first ping times out waiting for the Address Resolution Protocol (ARP) request and response. Once the ARP has found the hardware address of the default gateway, the IP-to-Ethernet mapping will be in the ARP cache and will stay in the router's cache for four hours. Any other IP connectivity to the next-hop router won't time out, because no ARP broadcasts have to be performed.

From Router Lab_C, a ping to 192.168.10.0 will test for good IP connectivity. Here is the router output:

```
Lab_C#ping 192.168.10.1
Type escape sequence to abort.
Sending 5, 100-byte ICMP Echos to 172.16.10.1, timeout
  is 2 seconds:
!!!!!
Success rate is 100 percent (5/5), round-trip min/avg/max
  = 64/67/72 ms
```

Since you can ping from end-to-end without a problem, your static route configuration was a success! Let's do it again, this time with 50 routers—not!

Default Routing

You use default routing to send packets with a remote destination network not in the routing table to the next-hop router. You can only use default routing on *stub networks*—those with only one exit port out of the network.

In the internetworking example used in the previous section, the only routers that are considered to be in a stub network are Lab_A and Lab_C. If you tried to put a default route on router Lab_B, packets wouldn't be forwarded to the correct networks because they have more than one interface routing to other routers. Even though router Lab_C has two connections, it doesn't have a router on the 192.168.50.0 network that needs packets sent to it. Lab_C will only send packets to 192.168.40.1, which is the Serial 0/0 interface of Lab_B. Router Lab_A will only send packets to the 192.168.20.2 interface of Lab_A.

To configure a default route, you use wildcards in the network address and mask locations of a static route. In fact, you can just think of a default route as a static route that uses wildcards instead of network and mask information. In this section, you'll create a default route on the Lab_C router.

Router Lab_C is directly connected to networks 192.168.40.0 and 192.168.50.0. The routing table needs to know about networks 192.168.10.0, 192.168.20.0, and 192.168.30.0.

To configure the router to route to the other three networks, I placed three static routes in the routing table. By using a default route, you can create just one static route entry instead. First, you must delete the existing static routes from the router, and then you should add the default route.

```
Lab_C(config)#no ip route 192.168.10.0 255.255.255.0
  192.168.40.1
Lab_C(config)#no ip route 192.168.20.0 255.255.255.0
  192.168.40.1
```

```
Lab_C(config)#no ip route 192.168.30.0 255.255.255.0
192.168.40.1
Lab_C(config)#ip route 0.0.0.0 0.0.0.0 192.168.40.1
```

Okay—if you look at the routing table now, you'll see only the two directly connected networks, plus an S*, which indicates that this entry is a candidate for a default route.

```
Lab_C#sh ip route
[output cut]
Gateway of last resort is 192.168.40.1 to network 0.0.0.0

C       192.168.50.0 is directly connected, FastEthernet0/0
C       192.168.40.0 is directly connected, Serial0/0
S*      0.0.0.0/0 [1/0] via 192.168.40.1
Lab_C#
```

Notice also in the routing table that the gateway of last resort is now set. Even so, there's one more command you must be aware of when using default routes: the ip classless command.

All Cisco routers are classful routers, meaning they expect a default subnet mask on each interface of the router. When a router receives a packet for a destination subnet that's not in the routing table, it drops the packet by default. If you're using default routing, you've got to use the ip classless command because no remote subnets will be in the routing table.

Since I have version 12.x of the Internetwork Operating System (IOS) on my routers, the ip classless command is on by default. If you're using default routing and this command isn't in your configuration, you'd need to add it if you had subnetted networks on your routers (which you don't at this time). The command is shown here:

```
Lab_C(config)#ip classless
```

Notice that it's a global configuration mode command. The interesting part of the ip classless command is that default routing sometimes works without it, but sometimes it doesn't. So just to be on the safe side, you should always turn on the ip classless command when you use default routing.

Configuring RIP Routing

Configuring RIP is actually simpler than configuring static or default routing. To configure RIP routing, just turn on the protocol with the **router rip** command and tell the RIP routing protocol which networks to advertise. That's it. Let's configure your three-router internetwork (shown again in Figure 2.2) with RIP routing and practice that.

FIGURE 2.2   IP RIP routing example

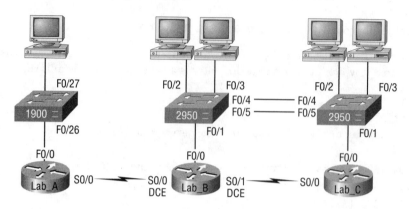

Lab_A

RIP has an administrative distance of 120. Static routes have an administrative distance of 1 by default and, since you currently have static routes configured, the routing tables won't be propagated with RIP information. So, the first thing you need to do is delete the static routes off of each router.

You can do this with the `no ip route` command. Notice that in the following Lab_A router output, you must type the whole `ip route` command to delete the entry.

```
Lab_A(config)#no ip route 192.168.30.0 255.255.255.0
  192.168.20.2
Lab_A(config)#no ip route 192.168.40.0 255.255.255.0
  192.168.20.2
Lab_A(config)#no ip route 192.168.50.0 255.255.255.0
  192.168.20.2
```

Once you have deleted the static routes from the configuration, you can add the RIP routing protocol by using the `router rip` command and the `network` command. The `network` command tells the routing protocol which network to advertise.

Look at the next router configuration. Note the fact that you've got to type in every directly connected network that you want RIP to advertise. But you're going to leave out networks 30, 40, and 50 because it's RIP's job to find them and populate the routing table.

```
Lab_A(config)#router rip
Lab_A(config-router)#network 192.168.10.0
Lab_A(config-router)#network 192.168.20.0
Lab_A(config-router)#^Z
Lab_A#
```

That's it. Just a couple commands, and you're done—it sure makes your job a lot easier than when you were using static routes, doesn't it? However, keep in mind the extra router CPU process and bandwidth that you're consuming.

RIP and IGRP use the classful address when they configure the network address. Because of this, all subnet masks must be the same on all devices in the network classful routing). To clarify this, say you're using a class B network address of 172.16.0.0/24 with subnets 172.16.10.0, 172.16.20.0, and 172.16.30.0. In this case, you'd only type in the classful network address of 172.16.0.0 and let RIP find the subnets and place them in the routing table.

    Understand that RIP is configured with classful routing network addresses!

Lab_B

To configure RIP on the Lab_B router, you need to remove the two static routes you added from the earlier example. Once you make sure no routes are in the routing table with a better administrative distance than 120, you can add RIP. The Lab_B router has three directly connected networks and you want RIP to advertise them all, so you will add three network statements.

Again, if you don't remove the static routes, the RIP routes will never be found in the routing table even though RIP will still be running in the background causing a bunch of CPU processing on the routers and gobbling up precious bandwidth! So, let's get rid of them, then add in RIP.

```
Lab_B#config t
Enter configuration commands, one per line. End with CNTL/Z.
Lab_B(config)#no ip route 192.168.10.0 255.255.255.0
  192.168.20.1
Lab_B(config)#no ip route 192.168.50.0 255.255.255.0
  192.168.40.2
Lab_B(config)#router rip
Lab_B(config-router)#network 192.168.20.0
Lab_B(config-router)#network 192.168.30.0
Lab_B(config-router)#network 192.168.40.0
Lab_B(config-router)#^Z
Lab_B#
```

It doesn't get much easier than this.

Lab_C

You've already removed the static routes on the Lab_C router because you placed a default route on it. So now all you need here is remove the default route from the Lab_C router. Once it's dust, you can turn on RIP routing for the two directly connected routes:

```
Lab_C#config t
Enter configuration commands, one per line. End with CNTL/Z.
Lab_C(config)#no ip route 0.0.0.0 0.0.0.0 192.168.40.1
Lab_C(config)#router rip
```

```
Lab_C(config-router)#network 192.168.40.0
Lab_C(config-router)#network 192.168.50.0
Lab_C(config-router)#^Z
Lab_C#
```

It's important to remember why you're doing this. Directly connected routes have an administrative distance of 0, static routes have an administrative distance of 1, and RIP has an administrative distance of 120. I call RIP the "gossip protocol" because it reminds me of junior high school, where if you hear a rumor (advertised route), it just has to be true without exception. That pretty much sums up how RIP behaves on an internetwork—rumor mill as protocol!

Verifying the RIP Routing Tables

Each routing table should now have the routers' directly connected routes as well as RIP-injected routes received from neighboring routers.

This output shows the contents of the Lab_A routing table:

```
Lab_A#sh ip route
[output cut]

R    192.168.50.0 [120/2] via 192.168.20.2, 00:00:23, Serial0/0
R    192.168.40.0 [120/1] via 192.168.20.2, 00:00:23, Serial0/0
R    192.168.30.0 [120/1] via 192.168.20.2, 00:00:23, Serial0/0
C    192.168.20.0 is directly connected, Serial0/0
C    192.168.10.0 is directly connected, FastEthernet0/0
Lab_A#
```

Looking at this, you can see that the routing table has the same entries that it had when you were using static routes—except for that R, that is. This means that networks were added dynamically using RIP. The [120/1] is the administrative distance of the route (120) along with the number of hops to that remote network (1).

This output displays Lab_B's routing table:

```
Lab_B#sh ip route
[output cut]

R  192.168.50.0 [120/2] via 172.16.40.2, 00:00:11, Serial0/1
C  192.168.40.0 is directly connected, Serial0/1
C  192.168.30.0 is directly connected, FastEthernet0/0
C  192.168.20.0 is directly connected, Serial0/0
R  192.168.10.0 [120/1] via 172.16.20.1, 00:00:21, Serial0/0
Lab_B#
```

Again notice that the same networks are in the routing table here and they weren't added manually.

Let's check out Lab_C's routing table:

```
Lab_C#sh ip route
[output cut]
Gateway of last resort is not set

C  192.168.50.0 is directly connected, FastEthernet0/0
C  192.168.40.0 is directly connected, Serial0/0
R  192.168.30.0 [120/1] via 192.168.40.1, 00:00:04, Serial0/0
R  192.168.20.0 [120/1] via 192.168.40.1, 00:00:26, Serial0/
R  192.168.10.0 [120/1] via 192.168.40.1, 00:00:04, Serial0/0
Lab_C#
```

So while yes, it's true—RIP has worked really well in our little internetwork, it's not the solution for every enterprise. That's because this technique has a maximum hop count of only 15 (16 is deemed unreachable), and it performs full routing-table updates every 30 seconds, both things that can wreak havoc in a larger internetwork.

RIP Problem!

I have one more thing I want to show you about RIP routing tables and the parameters used to advertise remote networks. Notice, as an example, that the following routing table shows [120/15] in the 192.168.10.0 network metric. This means that the administrative distance is 120, the default for RIP, but the hop count is 15. Remember that each time a router receives an update from another router, it increments the hop count by one for each route.

```
Lab_C#sh ip route
[output cut]
Gateway of last resort is not set

C  192.168.50.0 is directly connected, FastEthernet0/0
C  192.168.40.0 is directly connected, Serial0/0
R  192.168.30.0 [120/1] via 192.168.40.1, 00:00:04, Serial0/0
R  192.168.20.0 [120/1] via 192.168.40.1, 00:00:26, Serial0/
R  192.168.10.0 [120/15] via 192.168.40.1, 00:00:04, Serial0/0
Lab_C#
```

So this [120/15] is really bad because the next router that receives the table from router Lab_C will just discard the route to network 192.168.10.0, because the hop count would then be 16, which is invalid. I know that you don't have another router connected to the right of Lab_ C in this example, but hopefully you get my point here.

Holding Down RIP Propagations

You probably don't want your RIP network advertised everywhere on your LAN and WAN— you can't gain a whole lot by advertising your RIP network to the Internet, now can you?

No worries—you can stop unwanted RIP updates from propagating across your LANs and WANs a few different ways. The easiest one is by using the `passive-interface` command. This command prevents RIP update broadcasts from being sent out a defined interface, but that same interface can still receive RIP updates.

Here's an example of how to configure a `passive-interface` on a router:

```
Lab_A#config t
Lab_A(config)#router rip
Lab_A(config-router)#network 192.168.10.0
Lab_A(config-router)#passive-interface serial 0/0
```

This command stops RIP updates from being propagated out serial interface 0/0, but serial interface 0/0 can still receive RIP updates.

Configuring IGRP Routing

The command you use to configure IGRP is the same as the one you use to configure RIP routing, with one important difference: you use an autonomous system (AS) number. All routers within an AS must use the same AS number or they won't communicate with routing information. Here's how to turn on IGRP routing:

```
Lab_A#config t
Lab_A(config)#router igrp 10
Lab_A(config-router)#network 192.168.10.0
```

Notice that the configuration in these router commands is as simple as it was in RIP routing except that IGRP uses an AS number. This number advertises only to the specific routers with which you want to share routing information.

> You absolutely *must* remember that you type a classful network number in when you configure IGRP!

IGRP can load-balance up to six unequal links. RIP networks must have the same hop count to load-balance, whereas IGRP uses bandwidth to determine how to load-balance. To load-balance over unequal-cost links, you must use the `variance` command, which controls the load balancing between the best metric and the worst acceptable metric.

> Load balancing and traffic sharing are covered more in depth in the *CCNP: Building Scaleable Cisco Internetworks Study Guide*, by Carl Timm and Wade Edwards (Sybex, 2004).

Configuring IGRP is pretty straightforward and not much different from configuring RIP. However, you do need to decide on an AS number before you configure your routers. Remember that all routers in your internetwork must use the same AS number if you want them to share routing information.

In the sample internetwork I've been using throughout this chapter, you'll use AS 10 to configure the routers.

Okay, let's configure your internetwork with IGRP routing.

Lab_A

The AS number, as shown in the following router output, can be any number from 1 to 65535. A router can be a member of as many ASes as you need it to be.

```
Lab_A#config t
Enter configuration commands, one per line. End with CNTL/Z.
Lab_A(config)#router igrp ?
  <1-65535>  Autonomous system number

Lab_A(config)#router igrp 10
Lab_A(config-router)#netw 192.168.10.0
Lab_A(config-router)#netw 192.168.20.0
Lab_A(config-router)#^Z
Lab_A#
```

The router igrp command turns IGRP routing on in the router. As with RIP, you still need to add the network numbers you want to advertise. IGRP uses classful routing, which means that subnet mask information isn't sent along with the routing protocol updates.

> If you're using the 172.16.0.0/24 network, know that if you did type in the subnet 172.16.10.0, the router would accept it and then change the configuration to a classful entry of 172.16.0.0. But don't do that—at least not on the exam! The exam system is definitely not so forgiving and it will simply mark your answer wrong if you type the wrong network number. I cannot stress this enough: think classful if you are using subnets!

Lab_B

To configure the Lab_B router, all you need to do is turn on IGRP routing using AS 10 and then add the network numbers, as shown here:

```
Lab_B#config t
Enter configuration commands, one per line. End with CNTL/Z.
Lab_B(config)#router igrp 10
```

```
Lab_B(config-router)#netw 192.168.20.0
Lab_B(config-router)#netw 192.168.30.0
Lab_B(config-router)#netw 192.168.40.0
Lab_B(config-router)#^Z
Lab_B#
```

Lab_C

To configure Lab_C, once again you need to turn on IGRP using AS 10:

```
Lab_C#config t
Enter configuration commands, one per line. End with CNTL/Z.
Lab_C(config)#router igrp 10
Lab_C(config-router)#netw 192.168.40.0
Lab_C(config-router)#netw 192.168.50.0
Lab_C(config-router)#^Z
Lab_C#
```

Verifying the IGRP Routing Tables

Once the routers are configured, you need to verify the configuration with the show ip route command.

In all of the router outputs coming up, notice that the only routes to networks are either directly connected or IGRP-injected routes. Since you didn't turn off RIP, it's still running in the background, munching router CPU cycles and bandwidth. What's more, the routing tables will never use a RIP-found route because IGRP has a better administrative distance than RIP does.

Check out this output from the Lab_A router. Notice that all routes are in the routing table:

```
Lab_A#sh ip route
[output cut]
I       192.168.50.0 [100/170420] via 192.168.20.2, Serial0/0
I       192.168.40.0 [100/160260] via 192.168.20.2, Serial0/0
I       192.168.30.0 [100/158360] via 192.168.20.2, Serial0/0
C       192.168.20.0 is directly connected Serial0/0
C       192.168.10.0 is directly connected, FastEthernet0/0
```

The I means IGRP-injected routes. The 100 in [100/160360] is the administrative distance of IGRP. The 160360 is the composite metric. The lower the composite metric, the better the route.

Remember that the composite metric is calculated by using the bandwidth and delay of the line by default. The delay of the line can also be referred to as the cumulative interface delay.

This is Lab_B's routing table:

```
Lab_B#sh ip route
[output cut]
I       192.168.50.0 [100/8576] via 192.168.40.2, 00:01:11, Serial0/1
C       192.168.40.0 is directly connected, Serial0/1
C       192.168.30.0 is directly connected, FastEthernet0/0
C       192.168.20.0 is directly connected, Serial0/0
I       192.168.10.0 [100/158350] via 192.168.20.1, 00:00:36, Serial0/0
Lab_B#
```

And here's Lab_C's routing table:

```
Lab_C#sh ip route
[output cut]
C       192.168.50.0 is directly connected, FastEthernet 0/0
C       192.168.40.0 is directly connected, Serial0/0
I       192.168.30.0 [100/143723] via 192.168.40.1, 00:00:42, Serial0/0
I       192.168.20.0 [100/152365] via 192.168.40.1, 00:00;52, Serial0/0
I       192.168.10.0 [100/158350] via 192.168.20.1, 00:00:36, Serial0/0
Lab_C#
```

Configuring EIGRP

Although EIGRP can be configured for IP, IPX, and AppleTalk, as a future Cisco Certified Network Associate, you really only need to focus on configuring IP.

You can enter EIGRP commands from two modes: router configuration mode and interface configuration mode. *Router configuration mode* enables the protocol, determines which networks will run EIGRP, and sets global characteristics. *Interface configuration mode* allows customization of summaries, metrics, timers, and bandwidth. This book, like the CCNA objectives, focus on the global characteristics only.

To start an EIGRP session on a router, use the `router eigrp` command followed by the AS number of your network. Then enter the network numbers connected to the router using the `network` command followed by the network number.

Let's look at an example of enabling EIGRP for AS 20 on a router connected to two networks, with the network numbers being 10.3.1.0/24 and 172.16.10.0/24:

```
Router#config t
Router(config)#router eigrp 20
Router(config-router)#network 172.16.0.0
Router(config-router)#network 10.0.0.0
```

Remember, as with IGRP, you use the classful network address, which has subnet and host bits turned off.

Say you need to stop EIGRP from working on a specific interface, like a BRI interface, or a serial connection to the Internet. To do that, you need to flag the interface as passive. The following command shows you how to make interface Serial 0/1 a passive interface:

```
Router(config)#router eigrp 20
Router(config-router)#passive-interface serial 0/1
```

Doing this prohibits the interface from sending or receiving Hello packets, and as a result, stops it from forming adjacencies. This means it won't send or receive route information on this interface.

> The impact of the `passive-interface` command depends upon the routing protocol under which the command is issued. For example, on an interface running RIP, the `passive-interface` command prohibits the sending of route updates but allows their receipt. Thus, a RIP router with a passive interface will still learns about the networks advertised by other routers. This is different from EIGRP, where a `passive-interface` will neither send nor receive updates.

OK, let's configure that same network that you configured in the last section with RIP and IGRP. It doesn't matter that RIP and IGRP are already running—unless you're worried about bandwidth consumption and CPU cycles, of course, because EIGRP has an administrative distance of 90. (Remember that IGRP is 100 and RIP is 120, so only EIGRP routes will populate the routing tables, even if all three routing protocols are enabled.)

Figure 2.3 shows the network that you've been working with—the same one you're going to use to configure with EIGRP:

FIGURE 2.3   Our Internetwork example

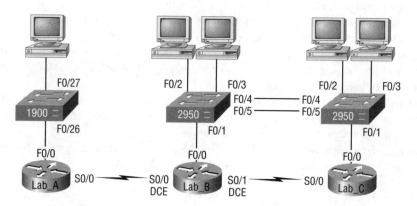

It's actually really easy to add EIGRP to your internetwork. I'll be using the same commands as I did with IGRP, only I'll add the "e".

Lab_A

The AS number, as shown in the following router output, can be any number from 1 to 65535. A router can be a member of as many ASes as you want it to be, but for this book's purposes, you're just going to configure a single AS:

```
Lab_A#config t
Enter configuration commands, one per line. End with CNTL/Z.
Lab_A(config)#router eigrp ?
  <1-65535>  Autonomous system number

Lab_A(config)#router eigrp 10
Lab_A(config-router)#netw 192.168.10.0
Lab_A(config-router)#netw 192.168.20.0
Lab_A(config-router)#^Z
Lab_A#
```

The `router eigrp [as]` command turns EIGRP routing on in the router. As with RIP and IGRP, you still need to add the network numbers you want to advertise. But unlike IGRP, EIGRP uses classless routing, which I'm sure you remember means that the subnet mask information is sent along with routing protocol updates.

Lab_B

To configure the Lab_B router, all you need to do is turn on EIGRP routing using AS 10 and then add the network numbers like this:

```
Lab_B#config t
Enter configuration commands, one per line. End with CNTL/Z.
Lab_B(config)#router eigrp 10
Lab_B(config-router)#netw 192.168.20.0
Lab_B(config-router)#netw 192.168.30.0
Lab_B(config-router)#netw 192.168.40.0
Lab_B(config-router)#^Z
Lab_B#
```

Lab_C

And to configure Lab_C, all you need to do is to again turn on EIGRP using AS 10:

```
Lab_C#config t
Enter configuration commands, one per line. End with CNTL/Z.
Lab_C(config)#router eigrp 10
```

```
Lab_C(config-router)#netw 192.168.40.0
Lab_C(config-router)#netw 192.168.50.0
Lab_C(config-router)#^Z
Lab_C#
```

That's it—really! Most routing protocols are pretty simple to set up, and EIGRP is no exception. That's only for the basic configuration, of course! Okay—now take a look at your configuration with all three routing protocols configured on Lab_B:

```
!
router eigrp 10
 network 192.168.20.0
 network 192.168.30.0
 network 192.168.40.0
!
router rip
 network 192.168.20.0
 network 192.168.30.0
 network 192.168.40.0
!
router igrp 10
 network 192.168.20.0
 network 192.168.30.0
 network 192.168.40.0
!
```

Seems pretty harmless, but remember, only EIGRP routes are going to wind up in the routing table because it has the lowest administrative distance. So by having RIP and IGRP running in the background, you're not only using more memory and CPU cycles on the router, you're sucking up precious bandwidth across all your links! This can be nasty, so it's something you need to keep in mind.

Configuring OSPF

Configuring basic OSPF isn't as simple as RIP, IGRP, and EIGRP, and it can get really complex once the many options that are allowed within OSPF are factored in. But no worries—you're only interested in the basic single area OSPF configuration for the CCNA. The following sections describe how to configure single area OSPF.

These two elements are the basic elements of OSPF configuration:

- Enabling OSPF
- Configuring OSPF areas

Enabling OSPF

The easiest, and also least scalable way to configure OSPF is to just use a single area. Doing this requires a minimum of two commands.

Here is the command you use to activate the OSPF routing process:

```
Lab_A(config)#router ospf ?
<1-65535>
```

A value in the range 1–65535 identifies the OSPF Process ID. It's a unique number on this router that groups a series of OSPF configuration commands under a specific running process. Different OSPF routers don't have to use the same Process ID in order to communicate. It's purely a local value that essentially has little meaning.

You can have more than one OSPF process running simultaneously on the same router if you want, but this isn't the same as running multi-area OSPF. The second process maintains an entirely separate copy of its topology table and manages its communications independently of the first process. And because the CCNA objectives only cover single area OSPF with each router running a single OSPF process, that's what I'm going to focus on.

Configuring OSPF Areas

After identifying the OSPF process, you need to identify the interfaces that you want to activate OSPF communications on, as well as the area in which each resides. This also configures the networks you're going to advertise to others. OSPF uses wildcards in the configuration. Okay—so here's an OSPF basic configuration example for you:

```
Lab_A#config t
Lab_A(config)#router ospf 1
Lab_A(config-router)#network 10.0.0.0 0.255.255.255
  area ?
  <0-4294967295>  OSPF area ID as a decimal value
  A.B.C.D          OSPF area ID in IP address format
Lab_A(config-router)#network 10.0.0.0 0.255.255.255
  area 0
```

Remember, the OSPF process ID number is irrelevant. It can be the same on every router on the network, or it can be different—it doesn't matter. It's locally significant and just enables the OSPF routing on the router.

The arguments of the network command are the network number (10.0.0.0) and the wildcard mask (0.255.255.255). The combination of these two numbers identifies the interfaces that OSPF operates on and will also be included in its OSPF Link State Advertisements (LSAs). OSPF will use this command to find any interface on the router that's configured in the 10.0.0.0 network, and it will place that interface into area 0.

And now for a quick review of wildcards—a 0 octet in the wildcard mask indicates that the corresponding octet in the network must match exactly. On the other hand, a 255 indicates that you don't care what the corresponding octet is in the network number. A network and wildcard mask combination of 1.1.1.1 0.0.0.0 would match 1.1.1.1 only, and nothing else. This is really useful if you want to activate OSPF on a specific interface in a very clear and simple way. If you insist on matching a range of networks, the network and wildcard mask combination of 1.1.0.0 0.0.255.255 would match anything in the range 1.1.0.0–1.1.255.255. Because of this, it's simpler and safer to stick to using wildcard masks of 0.0.0.0 and identifying each OSPF interface individually.

The final argument is the area number. It indicates the area to which the interfaces identified in the network and wildcard mask portion belong. Remember that OSPF routers only become neighbors if their interfaces share a network that's configured to belong to the same area number. The format of the area number is either a decimal value from the range 1–4294967295, or a value represented in standard dotted-decimal notation. For example, Area 0.0.0.0 is a legitimate area, and is identical to area 0.

Okay—now it's time for some fun! Let's configure your internetwork with OSPF using just area 0. Before you do that, you've got to remove IGRP and EIGRP first because OSPF has an administrative distance of 110. (IGRP is 100 and EIGRP is 90—but you already knew that, right!?) And while you're at it, remove RIP too, just because you should.

There are a bunch of different ways to configure OSPF and as I said, the most simple and the easiest is to use the wildcard mask of 0.0.0.0. However, I want to demonstrate that you can configure each router differently with OSPF and still come up with the same result. This is one reason why OSPF is more fun than other routing protocols—it gives everybody a lot more ways to mess things up!

Lab_A

So here's the Lab_A router's configuration:

```
Lab_A#config t
Enter configuration commands, one per line.  End with CNTL/Z.
Lab_A(config)#no router eigrp 10
Lab_A(config)#no router igrp 10
Lab_A(config)#no router rip
Lab_A(config)#router ospf 132
Lab_A(config-router)#network 192.168.10.1 0.0.0.0 area 0
Lab_A(config-router)#network 192.168.20.1 0.0.0.0 area 0
Lab_A(config-router)#^Z
Lab_A#
```

Hmmmm—it seems we have a few things to discuss here. First, I removed EIGRP, IGRP, and RIP, then I added OSPF. So why did I use OSPF 132? It really doesn't matter—the number is irrelevant.

The two network commands are pretty straightforward. I typed in the IP address of each interface and used the wildcard mask of 0.0.0.0, which makes things match each octet exactly. Now, let's go on to Lab_B, where you're going to use a different configuration.

Lab_B

The Lab_B router is directly connected to networks 20, 30, and 40. Instead of typing in each interface, I can use one network command and still make it work:

```
Lab_B#config t
Enter configuration commands, one per line.  End with CNTL/Z.
Lab_B(config)#no router eigrp 10
Lab_B(config)#no router igrp 10
Lab_B(config)#no router rip
Lab_B(config)#router ospf 1
Lab_B(config-router)#network 192.168.0.0 0.0.255.255 area0
                                                         ^
% Invalid input detected at '^' marker.

Lab_B(config-router)#network 192.168.0.0 0.0.255.255 area 0
Lab_B(config-router)#^Z
Lab_B#
```

Okay—other than my little typo, where I forgot to place a space between the area command and the area number, this is a fast, efficient configuration.

I first disabled the other routing protocols. Then, I turned on OSPF routing process 1 and added the network command 192.168.0.0 with a wildcard of 0.0.255.255. What this just said is, "find any interface that starts with 192.168, and place those interfaces into area 0"—quick and easy—slick!

Lab_C

Let's give the Lab_C router that's directly connected to networks 40 and 50 some attention:

```
Lab_C#config t
Enter configuration commands, one per line.  End with CNTL/Z.
Lab_C(config)#no router eigrp 10
Lab_C(config)#no router igrp
% Incomplete command.

Lab_C(config)#no router igrp 10
Lab_C(config)#no router rip
Lab_C(config)#router ospf 64999
```

```
Lab_C(config-router)#network 192.168.40.0 0.0.0.255 area 0
Lab_C(config-router)#network 192.168.50.0 0.0.0.255 area 0
Lab_C(config-router)#^Z
Lab_C#
```

Cool—now that you've configured all the routers with OSPF, what should you do next? ...Miller Time? Sorry—not yet. It's that verification thing again. You still have to make sure that OSPF is really working.

Loopback Interfaces

Configuring loopback interfaces when using the OSPF routing protocol is important, and Cisco suggests using them whenever you configure OSPF on a router.

Loopback interfaces are logical interfaces, which means they are not real router interfaces. You can use them for diagnostic purposes as well as OSPF configuration. The reason you want to configure a loopback interface on a router is because if you don't, the highest IP address on a router becomes that router's Router ID (RID). The RID is used to advertise the routes as well as elect the designated router (DR) and backup designated router (BDR).

Let's say that you are not using loopback interfaces and your serial interface of your router is the RID of the router because it has the highest IP address of active interfaces. If this interface goes down, then a re-election must occur on who is going to be the DR and BDR on the network. Not necessarily a bid deal; however, what happens if this is a flapping link (going up/down)? If this is the case, the routers will not converge because the election is never completed. This is obviously a problem with OSPF. Loopback interfaces solve this problem because they never go down and the RID of the router never changes.

Configuring Loopback Interfaces

Configuring loopback interfaces rocks mostly because it's the easiest part of OSPF configuration, and all you need is a break about now—right? So hang on—you're in home stretch!

Okay—first, let's see what the RID is on the Lab_A router with the show ip ospf command:

```
Lab_A#sh ip ospf
 Routing Process "ospf 132" with ID 192.168.20.1
[output cut]
```

You can see that the RID is 192.168.20.1, or the Serial 0/0 interface of the router. So let's configure a loopback interface using a completely different IP addressing scheme:

```
Lab_A#config t
Enter configuration commands, one per line.  End with CNTL/Z.
Lab_A(config)#int loopback 0
Lab_A(config-if)#ip address 172.16.10.1 255.255.255.0
Lab_A(config-if)#^Z
Lab_A#
```

The IP scheme really doesn't matter here, but each router has to be in a separate subnet. Let's configure Lab_B now:

```
Lab_B#config t
Enter configuration commands, one per line.  End with CNTL/Z.
Lab_B(config)#int lo0
Lab_B(config-if)#ip address 172.16.20.1 255.255.255.0
Lab_B(config-if)#no shut
Lab_B(config-if)#^Z
Lab_B#
```

Here is the configuration of the loopback interface on Lab_C:

```
Lab_C#config t
Enter configuration commands, one per line.  End with CNTL/Z.
Lab_C(config)#int lo0
Lab_C(config-if)#ip address 172.16.30.1 255.255.255.0
Lab_C(config-if)#no shut
Lab_C(config-if)#^Z
Lab_C#
```

The only question left to answer is if you want to advertise the loopback interfaces under OSPF. There are pros and cons to using an address that won't be advertised versus using an address that will be. Using an unadvertised address saves on real IP address space, but the address won't appear in the OSPF table, so you can't ping it. So basically, what you're faced with here is a choice that equals a trade-off between the ease of debugging the network, and conservation of address space—what to do? A really tight strategy is to use a private IP address scheme as I did. Do this, and all will be good.

Verifying Loopbacks and RIDs

To verify your loopback addresses, use the show running-config—it's the easiest way to do it:

```
Lab_C#show running-config
!
hostname Lab_C
!
interface Loopback0
 ip address 172.16.30.1 255.255.255.0
!
```

And to verify the new RIDs of each router, you can use either the show ip ospf interface command, the show ip ospf database, or just the show ip ospf command, like this:

```
Lab_C#sho ip ospf database
            OSPF Router with ID (172.16.30.1) (Process ID 64999)
                Router Link States (Area 0)
Link ID          ADV Router      Age   Seq# Checksum Link count
172.16.10.1      172.16.10.1     689   0x80000002 0xB404  3
172.16.20.1      172.16.20.1     139   0x8000000A 0x4AB1  5
172.16.30.1      172.16.30.1     138   0x80000002 0x2B14  3
```

The show ip ospf database shows the RID in the first line of output. The show ip ospf interface also displays this information, but you have to dig for it a little more:

```
Lab_C#show ip ospf interface
FastEthernet0/0 is up, line protocol is up
  Internet Address 192.168.50.1/24, Area 0
  Process ID 64999, Router ID 172.16.30.1, Network Type BROADCAST, Cost: 10
  Transmit Delay is 1 sec, State DR, Priority 1
  Designated Router (ID) 172.16.30.1, Interface address 192.168.50.1
  No backup designated router on this network
[output cut]
```

The show ip ospf command shows the RID in the first line of output:

```
Lab_C#show ip ospf
Routing Process "ospf 64999" with ID 172.16.30.1 and Domain ID 0.0.253.231
  [output cut]
```

An important thing to keep in mind is that the new RIDs didn't show up after I set the loopback interface on each router until I rebooted the routers!

Exam Essentials

Understand how to configure RIP routing.   To configure RIP routing, you must first be in global configuration mode:

```
enable
config t
```

Then you type the following command:

```
router rip
```

Then you add all directly connected networks, but make sure you use the classful address. For example, if you have network 10.1.1.0 directly connected to your network, the command would be as follows:

```
network 10.0.0.0
```

Be able to configure IGRP routing.   IGRP is configured mostly like RIP, but with just one major difference: you must configure the autonomous system (AS). Here is an example:

```
router igrp 10
```

This put your router into AS 10. The router will not accept any routes except from AS 10. Like RIP, you configure only classful networks with IGRP.

```
network 10.0.0.0
```

Know how to configure EIGRP.   Basic configuration is very similar to IGRP; however, EIGRP has several additional features such as passive interface and summarization.

Be able to configure single area OSPF.   A minimal single area configuration involves only two commands: `router ospf process-id` *and* `network x.x.x.x y.y.y.y area Z.`

2.2 Configuring IP Addresses, Subnet Masks, and Gateway Addresses on Routers and Hosts

In the last section, I reviewed not only routing protocol configuration but also basic router configuration including configuring IP addresses, subnet masks, and gateway addresses. So I must be done with this section already, right? Well, not hardly. You see, Cisco does not just expect you to be able to *configure* subnet masking and all the fun that goes with it, but also expects you to be able to *implement* IP addressing strategies from classful addresses. In this section, you won't see a lot of Cisco command line syntax. Instead, you'll have to review the mechanics of traditional subnetting as well as Variable Length Subnet Masks (VLSMs). Let's get started!

Configuring Subnet Masks

Most people in IT know how to find the valid host ranges used in a Class A, Class B, or Class C network address by turning the host bits all off and then all on. This is very good, but here's the catch: you are only defining one network. What happens if you wanted to take one network address and create six networks from it? You would have to do something called *subnetting*, because that's what allows you to take one larger network and break it into a bunch of smaller networks.

There are loads of reasons why you should use subnetting. Some of the benefits include the following:

Reduced network traffic   We all appreciate less traffic of any kind. Networks are no different. Without trusty routers, packet traffic could grind the entire network down to a near standstill. With routers, most traffic stays on the local network; only packets destined for other networks pass through the router. Routers create broadcast domains. The smaller the broadcast domains you create, the less network traffic you'll have on that network segment.

Optimized network performance   This is a result of reduced network traffic.

Simplified management   It's easier to identify and isolate network problems in a group of smaller connected networks than within one gigantic network.

Facilitated spanning of large geographical distances   Because WAN links are considerably slower and more expensive than LAN links, a single large network that spans long distances can create problems. Connecting multiple smaller networks makes the system more efficient.

In the following sections, I'm going to cover how to create subnets and discuss subnet masks. Then, I am going to move on to discuss subnetting a network address. This is the good partÖready?

How to Create Subnets

To create subnetworks, take bits from the host portion of the IP address and reserve them to define the subnet address. This means you'll have fewer bits for hosts, so the more subnets you have, the fewer bits are available for defining hosts.

Later in this section, you'll learn how to create subnets, starting with Class C addresses, but before you actually implement subnetting, you need to determine your current requirements as well as plan for future conditions. Follow these steps:

1. Determine the number of required network IDs:
    - One for each subnet
    - One for each wide area network connection

2. Determine the number of required host IDs per subnet:
    - One for each TCP/IP host
    - One for each router interface

3. Based on the above requirement, create the following:
    - One subnet mask for your entire network
    - A unique subnet ID for each physical segment
    - A range of host IDs for each subnet

Subnet Masks

For the subnet address scheme to work, every machine on the network must know which part of the host address will be used as the subnet address. You accomplish this by assigning a subnet mask to each machine. A *subnet mask* is a 32-bit value that allows the recipient of IP packets to distinguish the network ID portion of the IP address from the host ID portion of the IP address.

The network administrator creates a 32-bit subnet mask composed of 1s and 0s. The 1s in the subnet mask represent the positions that refer to the network or subnet addresses.

Not all networks need subnets, meaning they use the default subnet mask. This is basically the same as saying that a network doesn't have a subnet address. Table 2.2 shows the default subnet masks for Classes A, B, and C. These default masks cannot change. In other words, you can't make a Class B subnet mask read 255.0.0.0. If you try, the host will read that address as invalid and usually won't even let you type it in. For a Class A network, you can't change the first byte in a subnet mask; it must read 255.0.0.0 at a minimum. Similarly, you can't assign 255.255.255.255, because this is all 1s—a broadcast address. A Class B address must start with 255.255.0.0, and a Class C has to start with 255.255.255.0.

TABLE 2.2   Default Subnet Mask

Class	Format	Default Subnet Mask
A	network.node.node.node	255.0.0.0
B	network.network.node.node	255.255.0.0
C	network.network.network.node	255.255.255.0

Classless Inter-Domain Routing (CIDR)

Classless Inter-Domain Routing (CIDR) is basically the method that Internet service providers (ISPs) use to allocate an amount of addresses to a company, a home, or a customer. ISPs provide addresses in a certain block size—something I'll be going into in greater detail later.

When you receive a block of addresses from an ISP, what you get will look something like this: 192.168.10.32/28. What this tells you is what your subnet mask is. The slash notation (/) tells you how many bits are turned on (1s). Obviously, the maximum can only be /32 because a byte is 8 bits and there are four bytes in an IP address: (4 × 8 = 32). However, keep in mind that the largest subnet mask available (regardless of the class of address) can only be a /30 because you've got to keep at least 2 bits for host bits.

Take for example a Class A default subnet mask, which is 255.0.0.0. This means that the first byte of the subnet mask is all ones (1s) or 11111111. When referring to a slash notation, you need to count all the 1s bits to figure out your mask. The 255.0.0.0 is considered a /8 because it has 8 bits that are 1s, that is, turned on.

A Class B default mask would be 255.255.0.0, which is a /16 because 16 bits are 1s: 11111111.11111111.00000000.00000000.

Table 2.3 lists every available subnet mask and its equivalent CIDR slash notation.

TABLE 2.3 CIDR Values

Subnet Mask	CIDR Value
255.0.0.0	/8
255.128.0.0	/9
255.192.0.0	/10
255.224.0.0	/11
255.240.0.0	/12
255.248.0.0	/13
255.252.0.0	/14
255.254.0.0	/15
255.255.0.0	/16
255.255.128.0	/17
255.255.192.0	/18
255.255.224.0	/19
255.255.240.0	/20
255.255.248.0	/21
255.255.252.0	/22
255.255.254.0	/23
255.255.255.0	/24
255.255.255.128	/25
255.255.255.192	/26
255.255.255.224	/27
255.255.255.240	/28

TABLE 2.3 CIDR Values *(continued)*

Subnet Mask	CIDR Value
255.255.255.248	/29
255.255.255.252	/30

No, you cannot configure a Cisco router using this slash format. Wouldn't that be nice?

Subnetting Class C Addresses

You can subnet a network in many different ways. The right way is the way that works best for you. First I'll show you how to use the binary method, and then I'll show you an easier way to do the same thing.

In a Class C address, only 8 bits are available for defining the hosts. Remember that subnet bits start at the left and go to the right, without skipping bits. This means that the only Class C subnet masks can be the following:

```
Binary      Decimal  Shorthand
-------------------------------------------------------------
10000000 = 128     /25   (Not valid on the Cisco exams!)
11000000 = 192     /26
11100000 = 224     /27
11110000 = 240     /28
11111000 = 248     /29
11111100 = 252     /30
11111110 = 254     /31   (Not valid)
```

The Request for Comments (RFCs) say that you can't have only 1 bit for subnetting, since that would mean that the subnet bit would always be either off or on, which is illegal. So, the first subnet mask you can legally use is 192, and the last one is 252 because you need at least 2 bits for defining hosts.

In production, you can use 1 bit for assigning subnets. This is called *subnet-zero*. But know that Cisco doesn't consider subnet-zero valid on any of their certification exams!

In the following sections, you are going to look at the binary way of subnetting, then you'll move into the new, improved, easy-to-understand and implement subnetting method!

The Binary Method: Subnetting a Class C Address

In this section, I'm going to teach you how to subnet a Class C address using the binary method. I'll start by using the first subnet mask available with a Class C address, which borrows 2 bits for subnetting. For this example, I'll be using 255.255.255.192. To review the binary translation of 192:

192 = 11000000

Here, the 1s represent the subnet bits, and the 0s represent the host bits available in each subnet. 192 provides 2 bits for subnetting and 6 bits for defining the hosts in each subnet.

What are the subnets? Since the subnet bits can't be both off or on at the same time, the only two valid subnets are these:

01000000 = 64 (all host bits off)

10000000 = 128 (all host bits off)

The valid hosts would be defined as the numbers between the subnets, minus the all-host-bits-off and all-host-bits-on numbers.

To find the hosts, first find your subnet by turning all the host bits off, and then turn all the host bits on to find your broadcast address for the subnet. The valid hosts must be between those two numbers. Table 2.4 shows the 64 subnet, valid host range, and broadcast address. Table 2.5 shows the 128 subnet, valid host range, and broadcast address. (The subnet and host bits equal one byte.)

TABLE 2.4   Subnet 64

Subnet	Host	Meaning
01	000000 = 64	The network (Do this first.)
01	000001 = 65	The first valid host
01	111110 = 126	The last valid host
01	111111 = 127	The broadcast address (Do this second.)

TABLE 2.5   Subnet 128

Subnet	Host	Meaning
10	000000 = 128	The subnet address
10	000001 = 129	The first valid host

TABLE 2.5   Subnet 128 *(continued)*

Subnet	Host	Meaning
10	111110 = 190	The last valid host
10	111111 = 191	The broadcast address

Hopefully, you understand what I am trying to show you. The example I presented only used 2 subnet bits, so what if you had to subnet using 9, 10, or even 20 subnet bits? Try that with the binary method and see how long it takes you.

In the following section, I'm going to teach you an alternate method of subnetting that makes it easier to subnet larger numbers in no time.

> Since the Cisco CCNA exam gives you just over a minute for each question, it's really important to know how much time you'll spend on a subnetting question. That's why committing as much as possible to memory is vital. Using the binary method can take you way too long and you could fail the exam even if you know the material!

The Fast Way: Subnetting a Class C Address

When you've chosen a possible subnet mask for your network and need to determine the number of subnets, valid hosts, and broadcast addresses of a subnet that the mask provides, all you need to do is answer five simple questions:

- How many subnets does the chosen subnet mask produce?
- How many valid hosts per subnet are available?
- What are the valid subnets?
- What's the broadcast address of each subnet?
- What are the valid hosts in each subnet?

At this point it's important that you both understand and have memorized your powers of 2. Here's how you get the answers to those five big questions:

How many subnets?

$2^x - 2$ = number of subnets. x is the number of masked bits, or the 1s. For example, in 11000000, the number of ones gives us $2^2 - 2$ subnets. In this example, there are 2 subnets.

How many hosts per subnet? $2^y - 2$ = number of hosts per subnet. y is the number of unmasked bits, or the 0s. For example, in 11000000, the number of zeros gives us $2^6 - 2$ hosts. In this example, there are 62 hosts per subnet.

What are the valid subnets?   *256 – subnet mask = block size*, or *base number*. For example, 256 – 192 = 64. 64 is the first subnet. The next subnet would be the base number plus itself, or

64 + 64 = 128 (the second subnet). You keep adding the base number to itself until you reach the value of the subnet mask, which is not a valid subnet because all subnet bits would be turned on (1s).

What's the broadcast address for each subnet?   The broadcast address is all host bits turned on, which is the number immediately preceding the next subnet.

What are the valid hosts?   Valid hosts are the numbers between the subnets, minus all 0s and all 1s.

I know, this can truly seem confusing. But it really isn't as hard as it seems to be at first—just hang in there! Why not try a few and see for yourself?

Subnetting Practice Examples: Class C Addresses

Here's your opportunity to practice subnetting Class C addresses using the method I just described. You're going to start with the first Class C subnet mask and work through every subnet that you can using a Class C address. When you're done, I'll show you how easy this is with Class A and B networks too!

Practice Example #1C: 255.255.255.192 (/26)

Let's use the Class C subnet mask from the preceding example, 255.255.255.192, to see how much simpler this method is than writing out the binary numbers. You're going to subnet the network address 192.168.10.0 and subnet mask 255.255.255.192.

192.168.10.0 = Network address

255.255.255.192 = Subnet mask

Now, let's answer the big five:

- *How many subnets?* Since 192 is 2 bits on (**11**000000), the answer would be $2^2 - 2 = 2$. (The minus 2 (− 2) is the subnet bits all on or all off, which are not valid by default.)
- *How many hosts per subnet?* We have 6 host bits off (11**000000**), so the equation would be $2^6 - 2 = 62$ hosts.
- *What are the valid subnets?* 256 − 192 = 64, which is the first subnet and our base number or block size. Keep adding the block size to itself until you reach the subnet mask. 64 + 64 = 128. 128 + 64 = 192, which is invalid because it is the subnet mask (all subnet bits turned on). Your two valid subnets are then 64 and 128.

- *What's the broadcast address for each subnet?* The number right before the value of the next subnet is all host bits turned on and equals the broadcast address.

- *What are the valid hosts?* These are the numbers between the subnet and broadcast address. The easiest way to find the hosts is to write out the subnet address and the broadcast address. This way the valid hosts are obvious. The following table shows the 64 and 128 subnets, the valid host ranges of each, and the broadcast address of both subnets:

	64	128
The subnets (do this first)	64	128
Our first host (perform host addressing last)	65	129
Our last host	126	190
The broadcast address (do this second)	127	191

See? You really did come up with the same answers as when you did it the binary way, and this way is so much easier because you never have to do any binary-to-decimal conversions! About now, you might be thinking that it's not easier than the first method I showed you. And I'll admit, for the first subnet with only two subnet bits—you're right, it isn't that much easier. But remember, you're going after the gold: being able to subnet in your head. And to do that, you need one thing: practice!

Practice Example #2C: 255.255.255.224 (/27)

This time, you'll subnet the network address 192.168.10.0 and subnet mask 255.255.255.224.

192.168.10.0 = Network address

255.255.255.224 = Subnet mask

- *How many subnets?* 224 is 11100000, so your equation would be $2^3 - 2 = 6$.

- *How many hosts?* $2^5 - 2 = 30$.

- *What are the valid subnets?* 256 − 224 = 32, 32 + 32 = 64, 64 + 32 = 96, 96 + 32 = 128, 128 + 32 = 160, 160 + 32 = 192, and 192 + 32 = 224, which is invalid because it is your subnet mask (all subnet bits on). Therefore, your subnets are 32, 64, 96, 128, 160, and 192.

- *What's the broadcast address for each subnet (always the number right before the next subnet)?*

- *What are the valid hosts (the numbers between the subnet number and the broadcast address)?*

To answer questions 4 and 5, first just write out the subnets, then write out the broadcast addresses—the number right before the next subnet. Lastly, fill in the host addresses.

The following table gives you all the subnets for the 255.255.255.224 Class C subnet mask:

The subnet address	32	64	96	128	160	192
The first valid host	33	65	97	129	161	193
The last valid host	62	94	126	158	190	222
The broadcast address	63	95	127	159	191	223

Subnetting in Your Head: Class C Addresses

It really is possible to subnet in your head. Even if you don't believe me, I'll show you how. And it's not all that hard either—take the following example, for instance:

192.168.10.33 = Node address

255.255.255.224 = Subnet mask

First, determine the subnet and broadcast address of the preceding IP address. You can do this by answering question 3 of the big five questions: $256 - 224 = 32$. $32 + 32 = 64$. The address falls between the two subnets and must be part of the 192.168.10.32 subnet. The next subnet is 64, so the broadcast address is 63. (Remember that the broadcast address of a subnet is always the number right before the next subnet.) The valid host range is 33–62. This is too easy! No, it's not?

Okay, then let's try another one. We'll subnet another Class C address:

192.168.10.33 = Node address

255.255.255.240 = Subnet mask

What subnet and broadcast address is the preceding IP address a member of? $256 - 240 = 16$. $16 + 16 = 32$. $32 + 16 = 48$. And bingo—the host address is between the 32 and 48 subnets. The subnet is 192.168.10.32, and the broadcast address is 47. Therefore, the valid host range is 33–46.

Okay, you need to do more, just to make sure you have this down.

You have a node address of 192.168.10.174 with a mask of 255.255.255.240. What is the valid host range?

The mask is 240, so you'd do a $256 - 240 = 16$. This is our block size. Just keep adding 16 until you pass the host address of 174: 16, 32, 48, 64, 80, 96, 112, 128, 144, 160, 176. The host address of 174 is between 160 and 176, so the subnet is 160. The broadcast address is 175, so the valid host range is 161–174. That was a tough one.

One more—just for fun. This is the easiest one of all Class C subnetting:

192.168.10.17 = Node address

255.255.255.252 = Subnet mask

What subnet and broadcast address is the preceding IP address a member of? 256 – 252 = 4, 8, 12, 16, 20. You've got it! The host address is between the 16 and 20 subnets. The subnet is 192.168.10.16, and the broadcast address is 19. The valid host range is 17–18.

Now that you're all over Class C subnetting, let's move on to Class B subnetting.

Subnetting Class B Addresses

Before you dive into this, take a look at all the possible Class B subnet masks first. Notice that you have a lot more possible subnets than you do with a Class C network address:

```
255.255.128.0  (/17)      255.255.255.0    (/24)
255.255.192.0  (/18)      255.255.255.128  (/25)
255.255.224.0  (/19)      255.255.255.192  (/26)
255.255.240.0  (/20)      255.255.255.224  (/27)
255.255.248.0  (/21)      255.255.255.240  (/28)
255.255.252.0  (/22)      255.255.255.248  (/29)
255.255.254.0  (/23)      255.255.255.252  (/30)
```

You know the Class B network address has 16 bits available for host addressing. This means you can use up to 14 bits for subnetting because you have to leave at least 2 bits for host addressing.

> By the way, do you notice anything interesting about that list of subnet values—a pattern, maybe? Ah ha! That's exactly why I recommend that you memorize the binary-to-decimal numbers. Since subnet mask bits start on the left, move to the right, and can't skip bits, the numbers are always the same regardless of the class of address. Memorize this pattern.

The process of subnetting a Class B network is pretty much the same as it is for a Class C, except that you just have more host bits. Use the same subnet numbers for the third octet with Class B that you used for the fourth octet with Class C, but add a zero to the network portion and a 255 to the broadcast section in the fourth octet. The following table shows you a host range of two subnets used in a Class B subnet:

First subnet	16.0	32.0
Second subnet	16.255	32.255

Just add the valid hosts between the numbers, and you're set!

Subnetting Practice Examples: Class B Addresses

This section gives you an opportunity to practice subnetting Class B addresses.

Practice Example #1B: 255.255.240.0 (/20)

> 172.16.0.0 = Network address
>
> 255.255.240.0 = Subnet address

- *Subnets?* $2^4 - 2 = 14$.
- *Hosts?* $2^{12} - 2 = 4094$.
- *Valid subnets?* $256 - 240 = 16, 32, 48$, and so on, up to 224. Notice that these are the same numbers as a Class C 240 mask.
- *Broadcast address for each subnet?*
- *Valid hosts?*

The following table shows the first three subnets, valid hosts, and broadcast addresses in a Class B 255.255.240.0 mask:

Subnet	16.0	32.0	48.0	etc.
First host	16.1	32.1	48.1	...
Last host	31.254	47.254	63.254	...
Broadcast	31.255	47.255	63.255	...

Practice Example #2B: 255.255.255.0 (/24)

Contrary to popular belief, 255.255.255.0 used with a Class B network address is not called a Class B network with a Class C subnet mask. It's amazing how many people see this mask used in a Class B network and think it's a Class C subnet mask. This is a Class B subnet mask with 8 bits of subnetting—it's considerably different from a Class C mask. Subnetting this address is fairly simple:

> 172.16.0.0 = Network address
>
> 255.255.255.0 = Subnet address

- *Subnets?* $2^8 - 2 = 254$.
- *Hosts?* $2^8 - 2 = 254$.
- *Valid subnets?* $256 - 255 = 1, 2, 3$, and so on, all the way to 254.
- *Broadcast address for each subnet?*
- *Valid hosts?*

The following table shows the first three subnets and the last one, valid hosts, and broadcast addresses in a Class B 255.255.255.0 mask:

Subnet	1.0	2.0	3.0	...	254.0
First host	1.1	2.1	3.1	...	254.1
Last host	1.254	2.254	3.254	...	254.254
Broadcast	1.255	2.255	3.255	...	254.255

Practice Example #3B: 255.255.255.128 (/25)

Oh no! This one's got to be illegal, right? What type of mask is it? (Don't you wish it were illegal?) Well, it's a drag, but it's not illegal. It is one of the hardest subnet masks you can play with, though. And worse, it actually is a really good subnet to use in production, because it creates over 500 subnets with 126 hosts for each subnet—a nice mixture. So, don't skip over it! (Cisco thinks it's nice too!)

172.16.0.0 = Network address

255.255.255.128 = Subnet address

- *Subnets?* $2^9 - 2 = 510$.

- *Hosts?* $2^7 - 2 = 126$.

- *Valid subnets?* Okay, now for the tricky part. $256 - 255 = 1, 2, 3$, and so on, for the third octet. But you can't forget the one subnet bit used in the fourth octet. Remember when I showed you how to figure one subnet bit with a Class C mask? You figure this the same way. (Now you know why I showed you the 1-bit subnet mask in the Class C section—to make this part easier.) You actually get two subnets for each fourth octet value, hence the 510 subnets. For example, if the third octet is showing subnet 3, the two subnets would actually be 3.0 and 3.128.

- *Broadcast address for each subnet?*

- *Valid hosts?*

The following table shows how you can create subnets, valid hosts, and broadcast addresses using the Class B 255.255.255.128 subnet mask (the first seven subnets are shown, and then the last subnet):

Subnet	0.128	1.0	1.128	2.0	2.128	3.0	3.128	...	255.0
First host	0.129	1.1	1.129	2.1	2.129	3.1	3.129	...	255.1
Last host	0.254	1.126	1.254	2.126	2.254	3.126	3.254	...	255.126
Broadcast	0.255	1.127	1.255	2.127	2.255	3.127	3.255	...	255.127

Subnetting in Your Head: Class B Addresses

You're probably wondering if I am nuts about now. Subnet Class B addresses in your heads? If you think easier equals crazy, then, yes, I'm a few sails short, but it's actually easier than writing it out—I'm not kidding! Let me show you how:

Question: What subnet and broadcast address is the IP address 172.16.10.33 255.255.255.224 a member of?

Answer: $256 - 224 = 32$. $32 + 32 = 64$. Bingo: 33 is between 32 and 64. However, remember that the third octet is considered part of the subnet, so the answer would be the 10.32 subnet. The broadcast is 10.63, since 10.64 is the next subnet.

Question: What subnet and broadcast address is the IP address 172.16.90.66 255.255.255.192 a member of?

Answer: $256 - 192 = 64$. $64 + 64 = 128$. The subnet is 172.16.90.64. The broadcast must be 172.16.90.127, since 90.128 is the next subnet.

Question: What subnet and broadcast address is the IP address 172.16.50.97 255.255.255.224 a member of?

Answer: 256 – 224 = 32, 64, 96, 128. The subnet is 172.16.50.96, and the broadcast must be 172.16.50.127 since 50.128 is the next subnet.

Question: What subnet and broadcast address is the IP address 172.16.10.10 255.255.255.192 a member of?

Answer: 256 – 192 = 64. This address must be in the 172.16.10.0 subnet, and the broadcast must be 172.16.10.63.

Question: What subnet and broadcast address is the IP address 172.16.10.10 255.255.255.252 a member of?

Answer: 256 – 252 = 4. The subnet is 172.16.10.8, with a broadcast of 172.16.10.11.

Subnetting Class A Addresses

Class A subnetting is not performed any differently from subnetting Classes B and C, but there are 24 bits to play with instead of the 16 in a Class B address and the 8 bits in a Class C address.

Let's start by listing all the Class A subnets:

255.128.0.0	(/9)	255.255.240.0	(/20)
255.192.0.0	(/10)	255.255.248.0	(/21)
255.224.0.0	(/11)	255.255.252.0	(/22)
255.240.0.0	(/12)	255.255.254.0	(/23)
255.248.0.0	(/13)	255.255.255.0	(/24)
255.252.0.0	(/14)	255.255.255.128	(/25)
255.254.0.0	(/15)	255.255.255.192	(/26)
255.255.0.0	(/16)	255.255.255.224	(/27)
255.255.128.0	(/17)	255.255.255.240	(/28)
255.255.192.0	(/18)	255.255.255.248	(/29)
255.255.224.0	(/19)	255.255.255.252	(/30)

That's it. You must leave at least 2 bits for defining hosts. I hope you can see the pattern by now.

Variable Length Subnet Masks (VLSMs)

You could easily devote an entire section to VLSMs, but instead, I'm going to show you a simple way to take one network and create many networks using subnet masks of different lengths on different types of network designs. This is called *VLSM networking*, and it brings up another subject: classful and classless networking.

Neither RIPv1 nor IGRP routing protocols has a field for subnet information, so the subnet information gets dropped. What this means is that if a router running RIP has a subnet mask of a certain value, it assumes that *all* interfaces within the classful address space have the same subnet mask. This is called *classful routing*, and RIP and IGRP are both considered classful routing protocols. If you mix and match subnet mask lengths in a network running RIP or IGRP, that network just won't work!

Classless routing protocols, however, do support the advertisement of subnet information. Therefore, you can use VLSM with routing protocols such as RIPv2, EIGRP, or OSPF. The benefit of this type of network is that you save a bunch of IP address space with it.

As the name suggests, with VLSMs you can have different subnet masks for different subnets. Look at Figure 2.4 to see an example of why VLSM networks are so beneficial.

FIGURE 2.4 Typical Classful Network

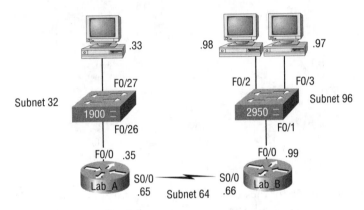

In this figure, you'll notice that you have two routers; each has a LAN, and they are connected together with a WAN serial link. In a typical classful network design (RIP or IGRP routing protocols), you could subnet a network as follows:

192.168.10.0 = Network

255.255.255.224 = Mask

Your subnets would be (you know this part, right?) 32, 64, 96, 128, 160, and 192. You can then assign three subnets to your three networks. But how many hosts are available on each network? Well, as you should be well aware of by now, each subnet provides 30 hosts. This means that each LAN has 30 valid hosts, but the point-to-point WAN link also has 30 valid hosts. All hosts and router interfaces have the same subnet mask—again, this is called classful routing.

The only problem here is that the link between the two routers never uses more then two valid hosts! That wastes valuable IP address space, and it's the very reason I'm going to talk about VLSM network design. Following our discussion of VLSM design, we will look at how to implement VLSM networks.

VLSM Design

It's time to jump into how to design and implement VLSM networks. First, take a look at a classful network, and then redesign the IP address scheme to work with VLSM. Check out Figure 2.5. It has a network with 14 subnets running only classful addressing.

To figure out how many networks you have, count the router interfaces in Figure 2.5. Each interface is its own subnet or network. The WAN links between two routers are one subnet, and each router must have a valid host address on that configured subnet for the two routers to be able to communicate with each other.

FIGURE 2.5   Fourteen subnets with no VLSM applied

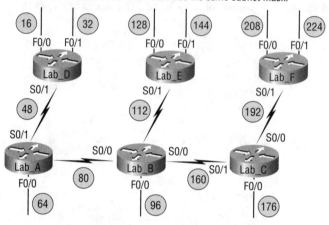

The only IP subnet option for the network design in Figure 2.5 is to use the 255.255.255.240 mask, because this gives you 14 subnets, each with 14 hosts. In Figure 2.5, the circled numbers are the subnets assigned a router interface.

However, the WAN links are point-to-point, and use only two IP addresses. So you're basically wasting 12 valid host addresses per WAN link! Take a look at Figure 2.6.

FIGURE 2.6   Fourteen subnets with VLSM applied

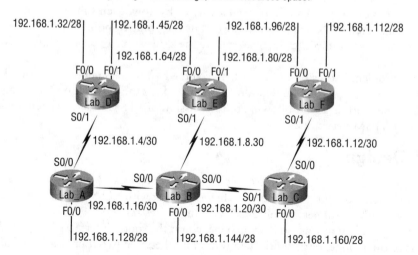

Remember, you can use different size masks on each interface. If you do that, you get 2 hosts per WAN interface and 14 hosts per LAN interface—nice! It makes a huge difference—not only can you get more hosts on a LAN, you still have room to add more WANs and LANs on the same network.

In Figure 2.6, each LAN has a /28 or 255.255.255.240 mask, which provides each LAN with 14 hosts, but each WAN uses the /30 or 255.255.255.252 mask. Are you wondering why the subnets are listed as they are and why the WAN links are subnets 4, 8, 12, 16, and 20, and the LANs start at subnet 32, and work in blocks of 16 up to subnet 160? Good! You're on the right track! The rest of this section explains how all this came to be.

Implementing VLSM Networks

To create VLSMs quickly and efficiently, you need to understand how block sizes and charts work together to create the VLSM masks. Table 2.6 shows you the block sizes used when creating VLSMs with Class C networks. For example, if you need 25 hosts, then you'll need a block size of 32. If you need 11 hosts, you'll use a block size of 16. Need 40 hosts? Then you'll need a block of 64. You just cannot make up block sizes—they've got to be the block sizes shown in Table 2.6. So memorize the block sizes in this table—it's easy. They're the same numbers we used with subnetting!

TABLE 2.6   Block Sizes

Prefix	Mask	Hosts	Block Size
/26	192	62	64
/27	224	30	32
/28	240	14	16
/29	248	6	8
/30	252	2	4

The next step is to create a VLSM table. Figure 2.7 shows you the table used in creating a VLSM network. The reason you use this table is so you don't accidentally overlap networks.

FIGURE 2.7   The VLSM table

Variable Length Subnet Masks Worksheet

Subnet	Mask	Subnets	Hosts	Block
/26	192	2	62	64
/27	224	6	30	32
/28	240	14	14	16
/29	248	30	6	8
/30	252	62	2	4

Class C Network   192.168.10.0

Network	Hosts	Block	Subnet	Mask
A				
B				
C				
D				
E				
F				
G				
H				
I				
J				
K				
L				
M				

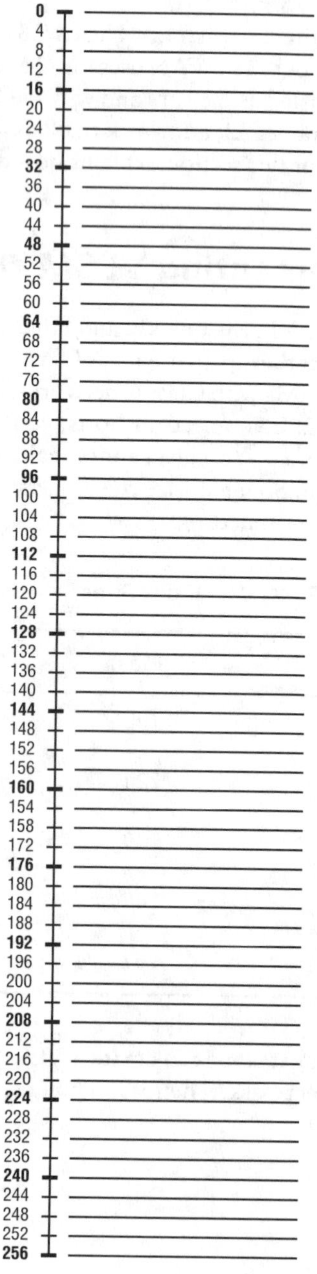

You'll find the sheet shown in Figure 2.7 to be very valuable because it lists every block size you can use for a network address. All you have to do is fill in the chart in the lower-left corner, then add them to the chart on the right.

So let's take what you've learned so far about your block sizes and VLSM table and create a VLSM using a Class C network address, 192.168.10.0, for the network in Figure 2.6. Then, fill out the VLSM table, as shown in Figure 2.7.

In Figure 2.8, you have four WAN links and four LANs connected together.

FIGURE 2.8   A VLSM network, example one

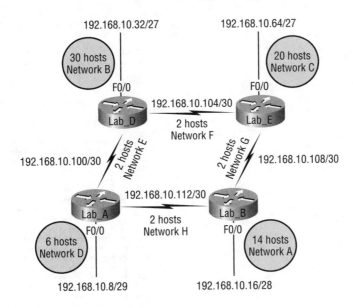

You need to create a VLSM network that allows you to save address space. Looks like you have two block sizes of 32, a block size of 16, and a block size of 8, and your WANs each have a block size of 4. Take a look and see how I filled out your VLSM chart in Figure 2.9.

You still have plenty of room for growth with this VLSM network design. You never could be this efficient in the use of addresses with one subnet mask.

FIGURE 2.9 VLSM table, example one

Variable Length Subnet Masks Worksheet

Subnet	Mask	Subnets	Hosts	Block
/26	192	2	62	64
/27	224	6	30	32
/28	240	14	14	16
/29	248	30	6	8
/30	252	62	2	4

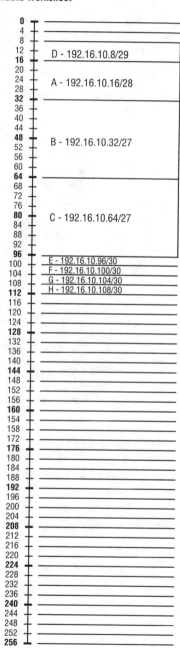

Class C Network 192.168.10.0

Network	Hosts	Block	Subnet	Mask
A	12	16	/28	240
B	20	32	/27	224
C	25	32	/27	224
D	4	8	/29	248
E	2	4	/30	252
F	2	4	/30	252
G	2	4	/30	252
H	2	4	/30	252

Let's do another one. Figure 2.10 shows a network with 11 networks, two block sizes of 64, two of 32, four of 16, and three of 4.

FIGURE 2.10   VLSM network, example two

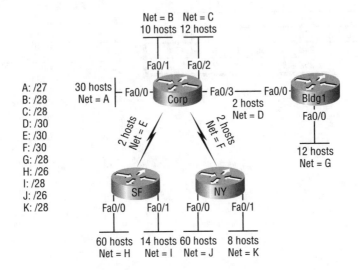

First, create your VLSM table and use your block size chart to fill in the table with the subnets you need. Figure 2.11 shows a possible solution.

Notice that I filled in this entire chart and only have room for one more block size of 4! Only with a VLSM network can you provide this type of address space savings.

Keep in mind that it doesn't matter where you start your block sizes as long as you always count from zero. For example, if you had a block size of 16, you must start at 0 and count from there—0, 16, 32, 48, and so on. You can't start a block size of 16 from, say, 40 or anything other than increments of 16.

Here's another example. If you had block sizes of 32, you must start at zero like this: 0, 32, 64, 96, and so on. Just remember that you don't get to start wherever you want, you must always start counting from zero. In the answer in Figure 2.11, I started at 64 and 128, with my two block sizes of 64. I didn't have a lot of choice, because my options are 0, 64, 128, and 192. However, I added the block size of 32, 16, 8, and 4 wherever I wanted just as long as they were in the correct increments for that block size.

It's important to note that I used subnet-zero in my network design. Although I use this in production and it does work, it is important to remember that Cisco still does not consider subnet-zero valid on their exams—yet.

FIGURE 2.11 VLSM table, example two

Variable Length Subnet Masks Worksheet

Subnet	Mask	Subnets	Hosts	Block
/26	192	2	62	64
/27	224	6	30	32
/28	240	14	14	16
/29	248	30	6	8
/30	252	62	2	4

Class C Network   192.168.10.0

Network	Hosts	Block	Subnet	Mask
A	30	32	32	224
B	10	16	0	240
C	12	16	16	240
D	2	4	244	252
E	2	4	248	252
F	2	4	252	252
G	12	16	208	240
H	60	64	64	192
I	14	16	192	240
J	60	64	128	192
K	8	16	224	240
L				
M				

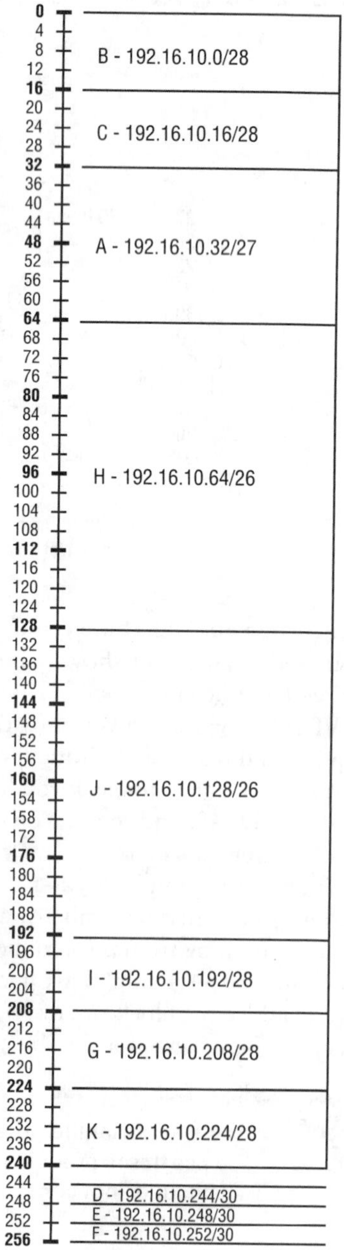

```
0
4
8       B - 192.16.10.0/28
12
16
20
24      C - 192.16.10.16/28
28
32
36
40
44
48      A - 192.16.10.32/27
52
56
60
64
68
72
76
80
84
88
92
96      H - 192.16.10.64/26
100
104
108
112
116
120
124
128
132
136
140
144
148
152
156
160
154     J - 192.16.10.128/26
158
172
176
180
184
188
192
196
200     I - 192.16.10.192/28
204
208
212
216     G - 192.16.10.208/28
220
224
228
232     K - 192.16.10.224/28
236
240
244
248     D - 192.16.10.244/30
252     E - 192.16.10.248/30
256     F - 192.16.10.252/30
```

Exam Essentials

Remember the steps you need to follow to subnet in your head.   Understand how IP addressing and subnetting work. First, determine your block size by using the 256-subnet mask math. Then count your subnets and determine the broadcast address of each subnet—it is always the number right before the next subnet. Your valid hosts are the numbers between the subnet address and the broadcast address.

Understand the various block sizes.   This is an important part of understanding IP addressing and subnetting. The valid block sizes are always 4, 8, 16, 32, 64, 128, and so on. You can determine your block size by using the 256-subnet mask math.

2.3 Configuring a Router for Additional Administrative Functionality

Do you ever wish you could change the functionality of a router? I'm not talking configuration issues like turning on a routing protocol or adding a static route, I'm talking about changing the way the router works. Well, in a limited way, you can change some of the default functions on a router. No setting will allow your router to say, fly, or print genuine currency, but you can change certain default functions. A word of warning here—defaults are set with certain well-intentioned reasons. With that in mind, let's take a look at how to modify the default administrative functions on a Cisco router.

All Cisco routers have a 16-bit software register that's written into nonvolatile random access memory (NVRAM). In this section, we are going to look at how you can use this register to change default functionality on the router. By default, the configuration register is set to load the Cisco IOS from flash memory and to look for and load the startup-config file from NVRAM. You can configure several other options as well. I'll begin by explaining the configuration register; later I'll show you how to change it and what this can be used to accomplish.

Understanding the Configuration Register Bits

The 16 bits of the configuration register are read from 15 to 0, from left to right. The default configuration setting on Cisco routers is 0x2102. This means that bits 13, 8, and 1 are on, as shown in Table 2.7. Notice that each set of 4 bits is read in binary with a value of 1, 2, 4, and 8, from right to left.

T A B L E   2 . 7   The Configuration Register Bit Numbers

Configuration Register		2					1			0			2	
Bit number	15 14	13	12	11 10	9	8	7	6	5	4	3	2 1	0		

TABLE 2.7 The Configuration Register Bit Numbers *(continued)*

Configuration Register			2				1			0			2		
Binary	0	0	1	0	0	0	0	1	0	0	0	0	0	0	1	0

Add the prefix 0x to the configuration register address. The 0x means that the digits that follow are in hexadecimal.

Table 2.8 lists the software configuration bit meanings. Notice that bit 6 can be used to ignore the NVRAM contents. This bit is used for password recovery—something I'll go over with you soon in the "Recovering Passwords" section.

TABLE 2.8 Software Configuration Meanings

Bit	Hex	Description
0–3	0x0000–0x000F	Boot field (see Table 2.9).
6	0x0040	Ignore NVRAM contents.
7	0x0080	OEM bit enabled.
8	0x101	Break disabled.
10	0x0400	IP broadcast with all zeros.
11–12	0x0800–0x1000	Console line speed.
13	0x2000	Boot default read-only memory (ROM) software if network boot fails.
14	0x4000	IP broadcasts do not have net numbers.
15	0x8000	Enable diagnostic messages and ignore NVM contents.

The boot field, which consists of bits 0–3 in the configuration register, controls the router boot sequence. Table 2.9 describes the boot field bits.

TABLE 2.9   The Boot Field (Configuration Register Bits 00–03)

Boot Field	Meaning	Use
00	ROM monitor mode	To boot to ROM monitor mode, set the configuration register to 2100. You must manually boot the router with the b command. The router will show the rommon> prompt.
01	Boot image from ROM	To boot an IOS image stored in ROM, set the configuration register to 2101. The router will show the router(boot)> prompt.
02–F	Specifies a default boot filename	Any value from 2102 through 210F tells the router to use the boot commands specified in NVRAM.

Remember that in hex, the scheme is 0–9 and A–F (A = 10, B = 11, C = 12, D = 13, E = 14, and F = 15). This means that a 210F setting for the configuration register is actually 210(15), or 1111 in binary.

Checking the Current Configuration Register Value

You can see the current value of the configuration register by using the show version command (sh version or show ver for short), as demonstrated here:

```
Router#sh version
Cisco Internetwork Operating System Software
IOS (tm) C2600 Software (C2600-I-M), Version 12.1(8)T3,
  RELEASE SOFTWARE (fc1)
[output cut]
Configuration register is 0x2102
```

The last information given from this command is the value of the configuration register. In this example, the value is 0x2102—the default setting. The configuration register setting of 0x2102 tells the router to look in NVRAM for the boot sequence.

Notice the show version command also provides the IOS version, and in the preceding example, it shows the IOS version as 12.1(8)T3.

The show version command displays system hardware configuration information, software version, and the names and sources of configuration files and boot images on a router.

Changing the Configuration Register

You can change the configuration register value to modify how the router boots and runs like this:

1. Force the system into the ROM monitor mode.
2. Select a boot source and default boot filename.
3. Enable or disable the Break function.
4. Control broadcast addresses.
5. Set the console terminal baud rate.
6. Load operating software from ROM.
7. Enable booting from a Trivial File Transfer Protocol (TFTP) server.

Before you change the configuration register, make sure you know the current configuration register value. Use the show version command to get this information.

You can also change the configuration register by using the config-register command. Here's an example: the following commands tell the router to boot a small IOS from ROM monitor mode and then show the current configuration register value:

```
Router(config)#config-register 0x101
Router(config)#^Z
Router#sh ver
[output cut]
Configuration register is 0x2102 (will be 0x0101 at next
   reload)
```

Notice that the show version command shows the current configuration register value, as well as what it will be when the router reboots. Any change to the configuration register won't take effect until the router reloads. The 0x0101 will load the IOS from ROM the next time the router is rebooted. You may see it listed as 0x101, which is basically the same thing; it can be written either way.

Recovering Passwords

If you're locked out of a router because you forgot the password, you can change the configuration register to help you get back on your feet. As I said earlier, bit 6 in the configuration register is used to tell the router whether to use the contents of NVRAM to load a router configuration.

The default configuration register value is 0x2102, meaning bit 6 is off. With the default setting, the router looks for and loads a router configuration stored in NVRAM (startup-config). To recover a password, you need to turn on bit 6. Doing this tells the router to ignore the NVRAM contents. The configuration register value to turn on bit 6 is 0x2142.

Here are the main steps to password recovery:

1. Boot the router and interrupt the boot sequence by performing a break.

2. Change the configuration register to turn on bit 6 (with the value 0x2142).

3. Reload the router and enter privileged mode.

I'm going to cover these steps in more detail, and I'll show you the commands you can use to restore access to 2600 and 2500 series routers.

Interrupting the Router Boot Sequence

Your first step in password recovery is to boot the router and perform a break. You usually do this by pressing the Ctrl+Break key combination when you are using HyperTerminal.

 WARNING   The Windows NT or 2000 default HyperTerminal program won't perform the break. You've got to upgrade the HyperTerminal program or use Windows 95/98 instead.

Okay—after you've performed a break, you should see something like this:

```
System Bootstrap, Version 11.3(2)XA4, RELEASE SOFTWARE (fc1)
Copyright (c) 1999 by cisco Systems, Inc.
TAC:Home:SW:IOS:Specials for info
PC = 0xfff0a530, Vector = 0x500, SP = 0x680127b0
C2600 platform with 32768 Kbytes of main memory
PC = 0xfff0a530, Vector = 0x500, SP = 0x80004374
monitor: command "boot" aborted due to user interrupt
rommon 1 >
```

Notice the line "boot" aborted due to user interrupt. At this point, you will be at the rommon 1> prompt on some routers.

Changing the Configuration Register

As I explained earlier, you can change the configuration register by using the config-register command. To turn on bit 6, use the configuration register value 0x2142. Let's take a look at how to do this on the 2500 and 2600 series routers.

Remember that if you change the configuration register to 0x2142, then the startup-config will be bypassed and the router will load into setup mode.

Cisco 2600 Series Commands

To change the bit value on a Cisco 2600 series router, you just enter the command at the rommon 1> prompt:

```
rommon 1 > confreg 0x2142
You must reset or power cycle for new config to take effect
```

Cisco 2500 Series Commands

To change the configuration register on a 2500 series router, type **o** after creating a break sequence on the router. This brings up a menu of configuration register option settings. To change the configuration register, enter the command **o/r**, followed by the new register value. Here's an example of turning on bit 6 on a 2501 router:

```
System Bootstrap, Version 11.0(10c), SOFTWARE
Copyright (c) 1986-1996 by cisco Systems
2500 processor with 14336 Kbytes of main memory
Abort at 0x1098FEC (PC)
>o
Configuration register = 0x2102 at last boot
Bit#    Configuration register option settings:
15      Diagnostic mode disabled
14      IP broadcasts do not have network numbers
13      Boot default ROM software if network boot fails
12-11   Console speed is 9600 baud
10      IP broadcasts with ones
08      Break disabled
07      OEM disabled
06      Ignore configuration disabled
03-00   Boot file is cisco2-2500 (or 'boot system' command)
>o/r 0x2142
```

Notice that the last entry in the router output is 03-00. This tells the router what the IOS boot file is. By default, the router will use the first file found in the flash memory, so if you want to boot a different file name, you can either change the configuration register or use the boot system *ios_name* command. Another way is to load an IOS image from a TFTP host by using the command boot system *tftp ios_name ip_address*.

Reloading the Router and Entering Privileged Mode

All right, you have interrupted the book sequence and have changed the configuration register. Next, you'll reload the router with the configuration register set to ignore the startup configuration and you'll be able to gain access to privileged mode without, ahem, any inconvenient passwords. At this point, you need to reset the router like this:

- From the 2600 series router, type **reset**.

- From the 2500 series router, type **I** (for initialize).

The router will reload and ask if you want to use setup mode (because no startup-config is used). Answer No to entering setup mode, press Enter to go into user mode, and then type **enable** to go into privileged mode. You will not be required to enter a password; it is just as if you had no startup-config at all!

Viewing and Changing the Configuration

Now you're past the point where you would need to enter the user mode and privileged mode passwords in a router. Next, you can copy the startup-config file to the running-config file:

```
copy startup-config running-config
```

or use the shortcut:

```
copy start run
```

The configuration is now running in RAM, and you're in privileged mode, which means that you can now view and change the configuration. Just to recap, you got here without any passwords, and you are now in privileged mode on a router that has a running configuration, but you do not have the passwords to get here! Do you understand now why you should lock up your routers and control physical access to them? But you can't view the enable secret setting for the password; however, you can change it. To change the password, do this:

```
config t
enable secret todd
```

Resetting the Configuration Register and Reloading the Router

After you're finished changing passwords, you need to reset the configuration register and reload the router. To do this, set the configuration register back to the default value using the `config-register` command:

```
config t
config-register 0x2102
```

Finally, save the new configuration with a `copy running-config startup-config` and reload the router.

Exam Essentials

Understand how to check the value of the current configuration register setting.   You can check the current configuration register setting by using the `show version` command.

Know the various configuration register commands and settings.   The 0x2102 setting is the default on all Cisco routers and tells the router to look in NVRAM for the boot sequence. 0x2101 tells the router to boot from ROM, and 0x2142 tells the router not to load the startup-config in NVRAM to provide password recovery.

2.4 Configure a Switch With VLANS and Inter-switch Communication

What fun would Ethernet switching be without VLANs? Big flat networks, broadcasts everywhere, why you might as well just have a bunch of hubs!

Well okay, switches are a huge improvement over hubs whether you use VLANs or not. However, in many environments the use of VLANs on layer 2 switches can add significant benefit in the area of administration and security. Certainly, understanding the application and configuration of VLAN technology on switches is necessary both for the exam and the real world.

In this section, you will start by looking at how you would need to configure a switch to use VLANs. Then you will learn about the ways to connect multiple switches that are using VLANs. You will also look at trunk ports that can carry multiple VLANs between switches, issues with routing between VLANs, and a Cisco technology called VTP (VLAN Trunking Protocol) that can reduce the administrative overhead of running many switches with VLANs.

Configuring a Switch with VLANs

Configuring VLANs is actually pretty easy. Figuring out which users you want in each VLAN is not. It's super time consuming, but once you've decided on the number of VLANs you want to create, and once you've established the users you want to belong to each one, it's time to bring your first VLAN into existence. To configure VLANs on a Catalyst 1900 switch, use the vlan [vlan#] name [vlan name] command. I'm going to demonstrate how to configure VLANs on the 1900 switch by creating three VLANs for three different departments (VLAN 1 is the native and administrative VLAN):

```
>en
#config t
Enter configuration commands, one per line.  End with CNTL/Z
(config)#hostname 1900
1900(config)#vlan 2 name sales
1900(config)#vlan 3 name marketing
1900(config)#vlan 4 name mis
1900(config)#exit
```

After you create the VLANs that you want, you can use the show vlan command to see them, but notice that by default, all ports on the switch are in VLAN 1. To change the VLAN associated with a port, you need to go to each interface and tell it which VLAN to be a part of.

Remember that a created VLAN is unused until it is assigned to a switch port or ports, and that all ports are always in VLAN 1 unless set otherwise.

Verifying VLAN Configuration

Once the VLANs are created, verify your configuration with the show vlan command (sh vlan for short):

```
1900#sh vlan
```

VLAN	Name	Status	Ports
1	default	Enabled	1-12, AUI, A, B
2	sales	Enabled	
3	marketing	Enabled	
4	mis	Enabled	
1002	fddi-default	Suspended	
1003	token-ring-defau	Suspended	
1004	fddinet-default	Suspended	
1005	trnet-default	Suspended	

```
[output cut]
```

Creating VLANs for the 2950 Switch

Creating VLANs for the 2950 switch is very different. You configure them in what is called a *VLAN database*. Here's how:

```
Switch#vlan database
Switch(vlan)#?
VLAN database editing buffer manipulation commands:
  abort  Exit mode without applying the changes
  apply  Apply current changes and bump revision number
  exit   Apply changes, bump revision number, and exit mode
  no     Negate a command or set its defaults
  reset  Abandon current changes and reread current database
  show   Show database information
  vlan   Add, delete, or modify values associated with a single VLAN
  vtp    Perform VTP administrative functions.
Switch(vlan)#
```

Notice that to create VLANs on the 2950 you have to enter the VLAN database through privileged mode—not configuration mode! Here's an example of creating three VLANs on the 2950 switch. (I left the Sales VLAN out of this configuration):

```
Switch(vlan)#vlan 1 name Sales
A default VLAN may not have its name changed.
Switch(vlan)#vlan 2 name Marketing
VLAN 2 modified:
    Name: Marketing
Switch(vlan)#vlan 3 name Accouting
VLAN 3 added:
    Name: Accouting
Switch(vlan)#Vlan 4 name Shipping
VLAN 4 added:
    Name: Shipping
Switch(vlan)#apply
APPLY completed.
Switch(vlan)#control+c
Switch#
```

Notice that you have to apply the changes with the `apply` command or the changes won't take effect. Also, in the fist line where I tried to change VLAN 1, I received an error. That's because it's the default VLAN, so you can't change it. It's the native VLAN of all switches by default, and Cisco recommends that you use this as your administrative VLAN. *Native VLAN* basically means that any packets that aren't specifically assigned to a different VLAN are sent down the native VLAN.

To see the VLAN database, use the `show vlan` command or the `show vlan brief` command, as shown here:

```
Switch#sh vlan brief

VLAN Name                      Status    Ports
---- ------------------------- --------- -------------------------
1    default                   active    Fa0/1, Fa0/2, Fa0/3, Fa0/4
                                         Fa0/7, Fa0/8, Fa0/9, Fa0/10
                                         Fa0/11, Fa0/12

2    Marketing                 active
3    Accounting                active
4    Shipping                  active
21   VLAN0021                  active
22   VLAN0022                  active
51   VLAN0051                  active
52   VLAN0052                  active
1002 fddi-default              active
1003 token-ring-default        active
1004 fddinet-default           active
1005 trnet-default             active
Switch#
```

Okay—now that you can see the VLANs created, you can assign switch ports to specific ones. Each port can only be part of one VLAN. With the trunking I mentioned earlier, you can make a port available to more than one VLAN at a time. I'm going to cover that with you in a minute.

Assigning Switch Ports to VLANs

You can configure each port on a 1900 switch to be in a VLAN by using the `vlan-membership` command, and you can only configure VLANs one port at a time. There's no command available with the 1900 switch that lets you assign more than one port to a VLAN at a time.

Remember that you can configure either static memberships or dynamic memberships on a port. Even so, I'm only going to cover the static flavor in this book.

In the following example, I configure interface 2 to VLAN 2, interface 4 to VLAN 3, and interface 5 to VLAN 4:

```
1900#config t
Enter configuration commands, one per line.  End with CNTL/Z
1900(config)#int e0/2
1900(config-if)#vlan-membership ?
  dynamic  Set VLAN membership type as dynamic
```

```
     static   Set VLAN membership type as static
1900(config-if)#vlan-membership static ?
  <1-1005>   ISL VLAN index
1900(config-if)#vlan-membership static 2
1900(config-if)#int e0/4
1900(config-if)#vlan-membership static 3
1900(config-if)#int e0/5
1900(config-if)#vlan-membership static 4
1900(config-if)#exit
1900(config)#exit
```

Now, type **show vlan** again to see the ports assigned to each VLAN:

```
1900#sh vlan
```

```
VLAN Name              Status      Ports
--------------------------------------
1    default           Enabled     1, 3, 6-12, AUI, A, B
2    sales             Enabled     2
3    marketing         Enabled     4
4    mis               Enabled     5
1002 fddi-default      Suspended
1003 token-ring-defau  Suspended
1004 fddinet-default   Suspended
1005 trnet-default     Suspended
--------------------------------------
[output cut]
```

And of course it's really different for the 2950:

```
Switch(config-if)#int f0/2
Switch(config-if)#switchport access vlan 2
Switch(config-if)#int f0/3
Switch(config-if)#switchport access vlan 3
Switch(config-if)#int f0/4
Switch(config-if)#switchport access vlan 4
Switch(config-if)#
```

If you want to verify your configuration, just use the show vlan or show vlan brief command like this:

Switch#**sh vlan brief**

VLAN	Name	Status	Ports
1	default	active	Fa0/1, Fa0/7, Fa0/8, Fa0/9
			Fa0/10, Fa0/11, Fa0/12
2	Marketing	active	Fa0/2
3	Accounting	active	Fa0/3
4	Shipping	active	Fa0/4

That's it—your ready to rock with your VLANs. Well, sort of, because if you plugged devices into each VLAN port, they can only talk to other devices in the same VLAN. You want to enable inter-VLAN communication and I'm going to show you how to do that, but first, you need to learn about trunking.

Configuring Inter-Switch Communication: Trunk Ports

The 1900 switch only runs the Dynamic Inter-Switch Link (DISL) encapsulation method. To configure trunking on a FastEthernet port, use the interface command trunk [parameter].

This switch output shows the trunk configuration on interface 26 as set to trunk on:

```
1900#config t
Enter configuration commands, one per line.  End with CNTL/Z
1900(config)#int f0/26
1900(config-if)#trunk ?
  auto        Set DISL state to AUTO
  desirable   Set DISL state to DESIRABLE
  nonegotiate Set DISL state to NONEGOTIATE
  off         Set DISL state to OFF
  on          Set DISL state to ON

1900(config-if)#trunk on
```

Here's a list that describes the different options available when setting a trunk interface.

Auto   The interface becomes trunked only if the connected device is set to on or desirable.

Desirable   If a connected device is either on, desirable, or auto, it negotiates to become a trunk port.

Nonegotiate   The interface becomes a permanent Inter-Switch Link (ISL) trunk port and will not negotiate with any attached device.

Off   The interface is disabled from running trunking and tries to convert any attached device to be on-trunk as well.

On   The interface becomes a permanent ISL trunk port. It can negotiate with a connected device to convert the link to trunk mode.

On the 2950, you use the `switchport` command:

```
Switch#config t
Enter configuration commands, one per line.  End with CNTL/Z.
Switch(config)#int f0/12
Switch(config-if)#switchport mode trunk
Switch(config-if)#^Z
Switch#
```

To disable trunking on an interface, use the `switchport mode access` command. You can verify your configuration with the `show running-config` command:

```
[output cut]
!
interface FastEthernet0/2
 switchport access vlan 2
 no ip address
!
interface FastEthernet0/3
 switchport access vlan 3
 no ip address
!
interface FastEthernet0/4
 switchport access vlan 4
 no ip address
!
interface FastEthernet0/12
 switchport mode trunk
 no ip address
!
[output cut]
```

Nice—you're looking tight. So now, let's get really stylin' by connecting a router to our network and configuring inter-VLAN communication!

Configuring Inter-Switch Communication: Inter-VLAN Routing

By default, only hosts that are members of the same VLAN can communicate. To change this and get inter-VLAN communication to be possible, you need a router or a Layer 3 switch. We're going to take the router approach and use one to connect to both a 1900 and a 2950 switch to make inter-VLAN communication happen.

To support ISL or 802.1Q routing on a FastEthernet interface, the router's interface is divided into logical interfaces—one for each VLAN. These are called *subinterfaces*.

It's important to understand that you can't provide trunking between the 1900 and 2950 switch by default because the 1900 switch only supports ISL routing and the 2950 switch only supports 802.1Q routing. And these two trunking methods aren't compatible by default. What's more, it's really weird that Cisco doesn't support ISL on their 2950 switch since ISL is a Cisco proprietary frame tagging method—bizarre, huh!

Anyway, from a FastEthernet or Gigabit Ethernet interface, you can set the interface to trunk with the `encapsulation` command. For a connection to a 1900 trunk port (ISL), use the following command:

```
2600#config t
2600(config)#int f0/0.1
2600(config-subif)#encapsulation isl vlan#
```

This configuration chooses a subinterface, then sets the encapsulation used for a particular VLAN. The subinterface number is locally significant only, so it doesn't matter at all what the subinterface numbers are configured on the router. Most of the time, I'll configure a subinterface with the same number as the VLAN I want to route. It's easy to remember that way, and since the subinterface number is only used for administrative purposes, it's good to remember it.

For a router trunk connection to a 2950 switch (802.1q), use this command:

```
2600(config)#int f0/0.1
2600(config-subif)#encapsulation dotlq vlan#
```

It's important to understand that each VLAN is a separate subnet. True, I know—they don't *have* to be. But it really is a good idea to configure your VLANs as separate subnets, so just do that. After I show you how to configure VTP, then you can go through the switches in your internetwork and configure inter-VLAN routing on the Lab_C router.

Configuring Inter-Switch Communication: VTP

Both the Catalyst 1900 and 2950 switches—actually all switches—are configured to be VTP servers by default. To configure VTP, first you have to configure the domain name you want to use. And of course, once you configure the VTP information on a switch, you need to verify it.

Configuring the Domain

When you create the VTP domain, you get a whole bunch of options, like setting the domain name, password, operating mode, and pruning capabilities of the switch. Use the vtp global configuration mode command to set all this information. In the following example, I set the switch to a vtp server, the VTP domain to Lammle, and the VTP password to todd:

```
1900(config)#vtp ?
  client       VTP client
  domain       Set VTP domain name
  password     Set VTP password
  pruning      VTP pruning
  server       VTP server
  transparent  VTP transparent
  trap         VTP trap
1900(config)#vtp server
1900(config)#vtp domain lammle
1900(config)#vtp password todd
```

After you configure the VTP information, you can verify it with the show vtp command.

```
1900#sh vtp
    VTP version: 1
    Configuration revision: 0
    Maximum VLANs supported locally: 1005
    Number of existing VLANs: 5
    VTP domain name       : lammle
    VTP password          : todd
    VTP operating mode    : Server
    VTP pruning mode      : Disabled
    VTP traps generation  : Enabled
    Configuration last modified by: 0.0.0.0 at 00-00-0000 00:00:00
1900#
```

The preceding switch output shows the VTP domain, the VTP password, and the switch's mode.

To configure VTP on the 2950 switch, you again configure the domain name you want to use first. And again, once you configure the VTP information on a switch, you need to verify it. You use the vtp global configuration mode command to set this information. In the following example, I'll set the switch to a VTP server, (which it already is by default), and then set the VTP domain to routersim:

```
Switch(config)#vtp mode ?
     client      Set the device to client mode.
     server      Set the device to server mode.
     transparent Set the device to transparent mode

Switch(config)#vtp mode server
     Device mode already VTP SERVER.

Switch(config)#vtp domain ?
     WORD   The ascii name for the VTP administrative domain.

Switch(config)#vtp domain routersim
     Changing VTP domain name from NULL to routersim
Switch(config)#
```

Verifying the VTP Configuration

After you configure the VTP information, you can verify it with the show vtp command:

```
SwitchA#sh vtp ?
  counters  VTP statistics
  status    VTP domain status

SwitchA#sh vtp status
VTP Version                   : 2
Configuration Revision        : 1
Maximum VLANs supported locally : 64
Number of existing VLANs      : 7
VTP Operating Mode            : Server
VTP Domain Name               : routersim
VTP Pruning Mode              : Disabled
VTP V2 Mode                   : Disabled
VTP Traps Generation          : Disabled
MD5 digest                    : 0x4C 0x60 0xA6 0x5D 0xD7 0x41 0x8C 0x37
Configuration last modified by 172.16.10.1 at 3-1-94 06:40:09
Local updater ID is 172.16.10.1 on interface Vl1 (lowest numbered VLAN interface
found)
```

Configuring the Switching in Our Sample Internetwork

Okay—you've configured the routers in your internetwork throughout this chapter, and now it's time to get to those switches. Figure 2.12 shows the network that you've been configuring so far:

FIGURE 2.12 Your internetwork

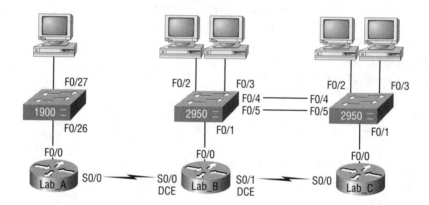

Your internetwork has two 2950s interconnected and they're ripe for you to configure VLANs! Name the 2950 connected to the Lab_C router, 2950C, and the 2950 connected to the Lab_B router, 2950B.

For your management VLAN (VLAN1), use the 172.16.10.0/24 network, with the fa0/0 interface of Lab_B being the router port you'll use to configure inter-VLAN routing. Each switch must have an IP address in the 172.16.10.0 subnet configured to be able to communicate.

You'll also create two more VLANs: VLAN2 will have the subnet 172.16.20.0/24 and VLAN 3 will have the subnet 172.16.30.0/24.

Start by adding hostnames, passwords, banner, interface description, and IP addresses to each switch:

```
Switch>en
Switch#config t
Enter configuration commands, one per line.  End with CNTL/Z.
Switch(config)#hostname 2950C
2950C(config)#enable secret todd
2950C(config)#line con 0
2950C(config-line)#login
2950C(config-line)#password console
2950C(config-line)#line vty 0 15
2950C(config-line)#login
2950C(config-line)#password telnet
2950C(config-line)#banner motd #
```

```
Enter TEXT message.  End with the character '#'.
This is my 2950C switch
#
2950C(config)#int f0/1
2950C(config-if)#description Connection to router
2950C(config-if)#interface f0/4
2950C(config-if)#description Connection to 2950B
2950C(config-if)#int f0/5
2950C(config-if)#description 2nd connection to 2950B
2950C(config-if)#int vlan1
2950C(config-if)#ip address 172.16.10.2 255.255.255.0
2950C(config-if)#no shut
2950C(config-if)#exit
2950C(config)#ip default-gateway 172.16.10.1
2950C(config)#^Z
2950C#copy run start
Destination filename [startup-config]? (return)
Building configuration...
[OK]
2950C#
```

That should do if for the 2950C switch. Let's continue on with the 2950B switch:

```
Switch>en
Switch#config t
Enter configuration commands, one per line.  End with CNTL/Z.
Switch(config)#hostname 2950B
2950B(config)#enable secret todd
2950B(config)#line con 0
2950B(config-line)#login
2950B(config-line)#password console
2950B(config-line)#line vty 0 15
2950B(config-line)#login
2950B(config-line)#password telnet
2950B(config-line)#banner motd #
Enter TEXT message.  End with the character '#'.
This is my 2950B switch
#
2950B(config)#
2950B(config)#int f0/4
2950B(config-if)#desc connection to 2950C
2950B(config-if)#int f0/5
```

```
2950B(config-if)#desc 2nd connection to 2950C
2950B(config-if)#int vlan 1
2950B(config-if)#ip address 172.16.10.3 255.255.255.0
2950B(config-if)#no shut
2950B(config-if)#exit
2950B(config)#ip default-gateway 172.16.10.1
2950B(config)#exit
2950B#copy run start
Destination filename [startup-config]? (return)
Building configuration...
[OK]
2950B#
2950B#ping 172.16.10.2

Type escape sequence to abort.
Sending 5, 100-byte ICMP Echos to 172.16.10.2, timeout is 2 seconds:
.!!!!
Success rate is 80 percent (4/5), round-trip min/avg/max = 1/3/4 ms
2950B#
```

Now that the two switches are configured with all the basic administrative information and they can ping each other, set the trunking on the ports connecting each switch together. I'm going to set trunking up on the port connecting to the router too:

```
2950B#config t
2950B(config)#int f0/1
2950B(config-if)#switchport mode trunk
2950B(config-if)#int f0/4
2950B(config-if)#switchport mode trunk
2950B(config-if)#int fa0/5
2950B(config-if)#switchport mode trunk
2950B(config-if)#


2950C#config t
Enter configuration commands, one per line.  End with CNTL/Z.
2950C(config)#int fa0/4
2950C(config-if)#switchport mode trunk
2950C(config-if)#int fa0/5
2950C(config-if)#switchport mode trunk
2950C(config-if)#
```

You can verify your trunk information on each switch with the show interface trunk command:

```
2950B#sh int trunk

Port      Mode      Encapsulation  Status      Native vlan
Fa0/1     on        802.1q         trunking    1
Fa0/4     on        802.1q         trunking    1
Fa0/5     on        802.1q         trunking    1
[output cut]
```

Sweet—now you've configured both switches with administrative information, set the trunk ports, and verified it all. So what's next? If you were thinking that you haven't configured the VTP information, set the VLANs, or assigned ports to the VLANs, you're totally right! On the 2950C switch, set the VTP information and then create two VLANs, as I have done here:

```
2950C#config t
Enter configuration commands, one per line.  End with CNTL/Z.
2950C(config)#vtp mode server
Device mode already VTP SERVER.
2950C(config)#vtp domain RouterSim
2950C(config)#^z
2950C#vlan database
2950C(vlan)#vlan 2 name Sales
VLAN 2 added:
    Name: Sales
2950C(vlan)#vlan 3 name Marketing
VLAN 3 added:
    Name: Marketing
2950C(vlan)#apply
APPLY completed.
2950C(vlan)#
```

In the preceding configuration, the VTP information has to be set before you can create your VLANs. If you don't set this, you'll be sorry because you could easily end up with a problem with the VTP database. You can verify that your changes took effect by using the show vlan brief command:

```
2950C#sh vlan brief

VLAN Name                  Status      Ports
---- -------------------   ---------   ----------------------------
1    default               active      Fa0/1, Fa0/2, Fa0/3, Fa0/4
                                        Fa0/7, Fa0/8, Fa0/11, Fa0/12
```

```
2    Sales                 active
3    Marketing             active
[output cut]
```

Almost there, gang—there's one more configuration on the 2950C switch—setting the interfaces to the VLAN memberships. Interface fa0/2 will be in VLAN 2, and int fa0/3 will be in VLAN3. Remember that all ports are in VLAN 1 unless set otherwise.

```
2950C#config t
2950C(config)#int fa0/2
2950C(config-if)#switchport access vlan 2
2950C(config-if)#int fa0/3
2950C(config-if)#switchport access vlan 3
```

Let's verify your VLAN information on the 2950C switch:

```
2950C#sh vlan brief
```

```
VLAN Name                     Status    Ports
---- ------------------------  --------- ----------------------------
1    default                   active    Fa0/1, Fa0/4, Fa0/5, Fa0/6
                                         Fa0/7, Fa0/8, Fa0/9, Fa0/10
2    Sales                     active    Fa0/2
3    Marketing                 active    Fa0/3
```

You still have to configure the 2950B switch with VTP information and assign the ports. Remember that the purpose of setting the VTP information is to ensure that all switches share the same VLAN database. This means you only set your VLANs once and all switches will build their VLAN databases from the VTP server. 2950B is a VTP client.

```
2950B#config t
Enter configuration commands, one per line.  End with CNTL/Z.
2950B(config)#vtp mode cleint
Device mode set to VTP CLIENT.
2950B(config)#vtp domain RouterSim
2950B(config)#^z
2950B#
```

Let's check and make sure your 2950B switch has received the VLAN information from the VTP server (2950C):

```
2950B#sh vlan brief
```

VLAN	Name	Status	Ports
1	default	active	Fa0/1, Fa0/2, Fa0/3, Fa0/4
			Fa0/7, Fa0/8, Fa0/11, Fa0/12
2	Sales	active	
3	Marketing	active	

[output cut]

Yes, from this you can tell that the 2950B switch knows about the VLANs. You still need to set the VLAN memberships and then move onto the router configuraiton.

```
2950B#config
2950B(config)#int fa0/2
2950B(config-if)#switchport access vlan 2
2950B(config-if)#int fa0/3
2950B(config-if)#switchport access vlan 3
```

And let's verify your VLAN information on the 2950B switch:

```
2950B#sh vlan brief
```

VLAN	Name	Status	Ports
1	default	active	Fa0/1, Fa0/4, Fa0/5, Fa0/6
			Fa0/7, Fa0/8, Fa0/9, Fa0/10
2	Sales	active	Fa0/2
3	Marketing	active	Fa0/3

All right—woohoo! You have now completely configured both switches, and you've verified that it's all good. The hosts can now only communicate with hosts that are members of the same VLAN, right? Right. So this means that only the hosts in ports fa0/2 can communicate with each other; this is also true for the hosts in ports fa0/3. Are you down with that? *No way*, not you. You want it all, and if you want to have all your hosts talking, you need a router or Layer 3 switch to make that happen. In this example, you're going to use the Lab_B router to configure inter-VLAN communication. Here's how:

```
Router>enable
Router#config t
Enter configuration commands, one per line.  End with CNTL/Z.
Router(config)#hostname Trunkrouter
Trunkrouter(config)#int f0/0
Trunkrouter(config-if)#no ip address
```

```
Trunkrouter(config-if)#no shutdown
Trunkrouter(config-if)#int f0/0.1
```

Configuring IP routing on a LAN subinterface is only allowed if that subinterface is already configured as part of an IEEE 802.10, IEEE 802.1Q, or ISL VLAN, as shown here:

```
Trunkrouter(config-subif)#encapsulation dot1q 1
Trunkrouter(config-subif)#ip address 172.16.10.1 255.255.255.0
Trunkrouter(config-subif)#int f0/0.2
Trunkrouter(config-subif)#encap dot1q 2
Trunkrouter(config-subif)#ip address 172.16.20.1 255.255.255.0
Trunkrouter(config-subif)#int f0/0.3
Trunkrouter(config-subif)#encap dot1q 3
Trunkrouter(config-subif)#ip address 172.16.30.1 255.255.255.0
Trunkrouter(config-subif)#exit
```

When configuring this router, I created three subinterface—one for each VLAN. Remember that the subinterface number isn't really important except for administration, but I did match it to each VLAN number so it's easy to remember. Also, notice that when I tried to set an IP address on the first subinterface, it wouldn't let me go there until I set the encapsulation type. Let's check out your router configuration now:

```
Trunkrouter#show run
!
interface FastEthernet0/0
 no ip address
 no ip directed-broadcast
!
interface FastEthernet0/0.1
 encapsulation dot1Q 1
 ip address 172.16.10.1 255.255.255.0
 no ip directed-broadcast
!
interface FastEthernet0/0.2
 encapsulation dot1Q 2
 ip address 172.16.20.1 255.255.255.0
 no ip directed-broadcast
!
interface FastEthernet0/0.3
 encapsulation dot1Q 3
 ip address 172.16.30.1 255.255.255.0
 no ip directed-broadcast
!
```

This looks good—all of your hosts should now be able to communicate freely.

Exam Essentials

Know how to check a switch port's VLAN assignment when you are plugging in a new host. If you plug a new host into a switch, then you must verify the VLAN membership of that port. If the membership is different than what is needed for that host, the host will not be able to reach the needed network services, such as a workgroup server.

Understand that VLAN configuration is more than just assigning a port to a VLAN. Trunk links must be considered and configured, as well as VTP configurations on individual switches. We looked at two examples of ways to configure VLAN port assignments on different switch models.

2.5 Implement a LAN

Wow, implementing a LAN. That could be a series of books, not a single exam objective! However, you are preparing for the CCNA, so let's take a deeper look at what you need to implement a LAN.

A LAN is a collection of interconnected and intercommunicating hosts. It implies a single network or subnet; multiple networks are called *internetworks*. So, you can take routing out of a single LAN. Now, for the CCNA, the LAN means Ethernet. You can ignore other technologies. So what are you left with? Switching and the technologies that go along with it; VLANs, VTP, ISL, cut-through, FragmentFree, and so on. However, I have covered these elsewhere in this book. What do I have left to discuss?

Ah, I have forgotten Layer 1, the Physical layer. What fun are a bunch of switches without cabling? Are you ready to abandon cable for the world of wireless? Not hardly. In most installations, the LAN remains tied to its cable plant, and understanding and maintaining Ethernet LANs at Layer 1 is a required skill for any network engineer. In this section, you will look at Layer 1 of the Ethernet LAN and its support. I will discuss how to create straight-through and crossover cables. I will also show you how to make another type of cable, a rolled cable that you can use to establish a serial connection to a router.

 If you are studying for your CCNA exam, you better know your Ethernet cabling types!

Straight-Through Cable

The straight-through Ethernet cable is used to connect

- The host to the switch or hub
- The router to the switch or hub

Four wires are used in the straight-through cable to connect Ethernet devices. You can create this type relatively easily. Figure 2.13 shows the four wires used in a straight-through Ethernet cable.

FIGURE 2.13   Straight-through Ethernet cable

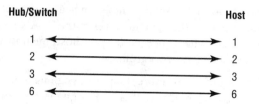

Notice that only pins 1, 2, 3, and 6 are used. Just connect 1 to 1, 2 to 2, 3 to 3, and 6 to 6, and you'll be up and networking in no time—however, remember that by doing so, you make this an Ethernet-only cable and therefore, it won't work with Voice, Token Ring, ISDN, and so on.

Crossover Cable

Crossover Ethernet cable can be used to connect the following:

- Switch to switch
- Hub to hub
- Host to host
- Router direct to host
- Switch to Hub

The same four wires are used in this cable as you used in the straight-through cable, but you just connect different pins together. Figure 2.14 shows how the four wires are used in a crossover Ethernet cable.

FIGURE 2.14   Crossover Ethernet cable

Notice that instead of connecting 1 to 1, 2 to 2, and so on, here you connect pins 1 to 3, and 2 to 6 on each side of the cable.

Rolled Cable

Although a rolled cable isn't used to connect any Ethernet connections together, you can use a rolled Ethernet cable to connect a host to a router console serial communication (com) port.

If you have a Cisco router or switch, you'd use this rolled cable to connect your PC running HyperTerminal to the Cisco hardware. Eight wires are used in this cable to connect serial devices, although all eight are not used to send information, as is the case in Ethernet networking. Figure 2.15 shows the eight wires used in a rolled cable.

FIGURE 2.15   Rolled Ethernet cable

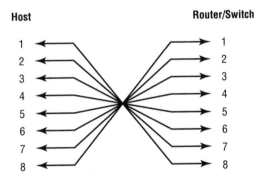

Rolled cables are probably the easiest cables to make, because you just cut the end off on one side of a straight-through cable and reverse the end.

Once you have the correct cable connected from your PC to the Cisco router or switch, you can start HyperTerminal to create a console connection and configure the device. Set the configuration as follows:

1. Open HyperTerminal and enter a name for the connection. It is irrelevant what you name it, but I always just use "Cisco." Then click OK.

2. Choose the communications port—either COM1 or COM2, whichever is open on your PC.

3. Now set the port settings. The default values (2400bps and no flow control) will not work; you must set the port settings as shown in Figure 2.16.

FIGURE 2.16 Port settings for a rolled cable connection

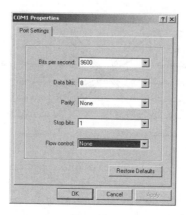

Notice the bit rate is now set to 9600 and the flow control is set to none. At this point, you can click OK and press the Enter key, and you should be connected to your Cisco device console port.

Exam Essentials

Remember the types of Ethernet cabling and when you would use them. The three types of cables that can be created from an Ethernet cable are straight-through (to connect a PC or a router's Ethernet interface to a hub or switch), crossover (to connect hub to hub, hub to switch, switch to switch, or PC to PC), and rolled (for a console connection from a PC to a router or switch).

Understand how to connect a console cable from a PC to a router and start HyperTerminal. Take a rolled cable and connect it from the COM port of the host to the console port of a router. Start HyperTerminal and set the bits per second (bps) to 9600 and flow control to None.

2.6 Customize a Switch Configuration to Meet Specified Network Requirements

A frequently specified network requirement is redundancy. How many of you are buying things in pairs to increase availability? Well, while this is a good practice, deploying two of something doesn't necessarily mean just doing something twice. When you start to deploy redundant switches, for example, you frequently run into a spanning tree. In this section, you are going to learn about some of the specifics of the Spanning Tree Protocol (STP). You were introduced to VLAN configuration earlier in Section 2.4, and you'll look at remaining aspects of switch configuration in Section 2.9 later in this chapter. For now, you need to review STP and how it may require you to customize switch configuration.

It's important to see how a spanning tree works in an internetwork, partly because it really helps you better understand the spanning tree protocol. So in the upcoming section, I'll give you a chance to observe what you've learned as it takes place in a live network.

Check it out: in Figure 2.17, you can assume that all five switches have the same priority of 32,768. Now study the MAC address of each switch. By looking at the priority and MAC addresses of each device, you should be able to determine the root bridge.

FIGURE 2.17   Spanning tree example

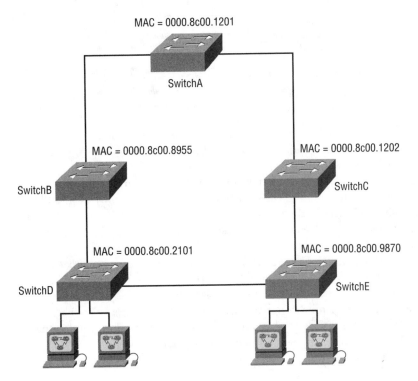

Once you've established which switch has got to be the root bridge, look at the figure again and try to figure out which is the root port on each of the switches. (Hint: Root ports are always designated ports, which means they are always in forwarding mode.) Okay, next try to establish which of the ports will be in blocking mode.

Figure 2.18 has the answers for each of the port states for each switch.

FIGURE 2.18 Spanning tree example answers

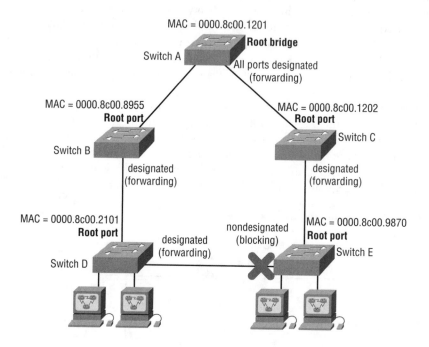

Since Switch A has the lowest MAC address, and all five switches use the default priority, Switch A gets to be the root bridge. And remember this: a root bridge always has every port in forwarding mode (designated ports).

To determine the root ports on Switch B and Switch C, just follow the connection to the root bridge. Each direct connection to the root bridge will be a root port, so it will become designated. On Switches D and E, the ports connected to Switches B and C are Switches D and E's closest ports to the root bridge (lowest cost), so those ports are root ports and are in forwarding mode (designated).

Take another look at the Figure 2.18. Can you tell which of the ports between Switch D and E must be shut down so a network loop doesn't occur? Let's work it out: since the connection from Switches D and E to Switches B and C are root ports, those can't be shut down. Next, the bridge ID is used to determine designated and nondesignated ports; so, because Switch D has the lowest (best) bridge ID, Switch E's port to Switch D will become nondesignated (blocking), and Switch D's connection to Switch E will be designated (forwarding).

If you have fewer than six switches in your internetwork, then depending on the number of users in your network, you'd usually just let STP do its job and not worry about it.

If you have fewer than 6 switches in your network, you probably don't need to worry too much about spanning tree. But if you have dozens of switches and hundreds of users, it's time to pay attention to how STP is running. That's because if you don't set the root switch in this larger switched network, your STP may never converge between switches—a nasty situation that could bring your network down.

Exam Essentials

Understand how to determine which switch will be the root bridge.   Assuming the priority is equal, the switch with the lowest MAC address will become the root bridge.

2.7 Manage System Image and Device Configuration Files

On most Cisco devices, you are primarily concerned with two files: the operating system and the configuration. The operating system, or system image, is generally stored in flash memory. The configuration is generally stored in NVRAM. Managing these files consists simply of backing them up and updating them on a device.

Backing Up and Restoring the System Image File

Before you upgrade or restore a Cisco IOS, you really should copy the existing file to a TFTP host as a backup, just in case the new image crashes and burns.

You can use any TFTP host to accomplish this. By default, the flash memory in a router is used to store the Cisco IOS. In the following section, I'll describe how to check the amount of flash memory, how to copy the Cisco IOS from flash memory to a TFTP host, and how to copy the IOS from a TFTP host to flash memory.

However, before you back up an IOS image to a network server, you've got to do these three things:

- Make sure you can access the network server.
- Ensure the network server has adequate space for the code image.
- Verify the file naming and path requirement.

Verifying Flash Memory

Before you attempt to upgrade the Cisco IOS on your router with a new IOS file, it's a really good idea to verify that your flash memory has enough room to hold the new image. You can verify the amount of flash memory and the file or files being stored in flash memory by using the show flash command (sh flash for short):

```
Router#sh flash
System flash directory:
File  Length   Name/status
  1   8121000  c2500-js-l.112-18.bin
[8121064 bytes used, 8656152 available, 16777216 total]
16384K bytes of processor board System flash (Read ONLY)
Router#
```

Notice that the filename in this example is c2500-js-l.112-18.bin. The name of the file is platform-specific and is derived as follows:

- c2500 is the platform.
- j indicates that the file is an enterprise image.
- s indicates the file contains extended capabilities.
- l indicates that the file can be moved from flash memory if need be and it is not compressed.
- 112-18 is the revision number. In this case, it refers to release 11.2(18).
- .bin indicates that the Cisco IOS is a binary executable file.

The last line in the router output shows that the flash is 16,384KB (or 16MB). So if the new file that you want to use is, say, 10MB in size, you know that there's plenty of room for it. Once you've verified that flash memory can hold the IOS you want to copy, you're free to continue with your backup operation.

Backing Up the Cisco IOS

To back up the Cisco IOS to a TFTP host, you use the copy flash tftp command. It's a straightforward command that requires only the source filename and the IP address of the TFTP host.

The key to success in this backup routine is to make sure that you've got good, solid connectivity to the TFTP host. Check this by pinging the device from the router console prompt like this:

```
Router#ping 192.168.0.120
Type escape sequence to abort.
Sending 5, 100-byte ICMP Echos to 192.168.0.120, timeout
  is 2 seconds:
!!!!!
Success rate is 100 percent (5/5), round-trip min/avg/max
  = 4/4/8 ms
```

Okay—so after you ping the TFTP host to make sure that IP is working, you can use the copy flash tftp command to copy the IOS to the TFTP host, as shown next. Look at the output—you can see that after you enter the command, the name of the file in flash memory is displayed.

This is very cool because it makes this easy for you. Just copy the filename and then paste it when you are prompted for the source filename:

```
Router#copy flash tftp
System flash directory:
File  Length    Name/status
   1  8121000  c2500-js-l.112-18.bin
[8121064 bytes used, 8656152 available, 16777216 total]
Address or name of remote host [255.255.255.255]?
  192.168.0.120
Source file name?c2500-js-l.112-18.bin
Destination file name [c2500-js-l.112-18.bin]?[Enter]
Verifying checksum for 'c2500-js-l.112-18.bin')file #1)
...OK
Copy '/c2500-js-l.112-18' from Flash to server
  as '/c2500-js-l.112-18'? [yes/no]y
!!!!!!!!!!!!!!!!!!!!!!!!!!!!!!!!!!!!!!!!!!!!!!!!!!!!!!!!!!!!
    !!!!!!!!!!!!!!!!!!!!! [output cut]
Upload to server done
Flash copy took 00:02:30 [hh:mm:ss]
Router#
```

In this example, the content of flash memory was copied successfully to the TFTP host. The address of the remote host is the IP address of the TFTP host, and the source filename is the file in flash memory.

The copy flash tftp command won't prompt you for the location of any file or ask you where to put the file. TFTP is just a "grab it and place it" program in this situation. This means that the TFTP host has to have a default directory specified, or it won't work!

Restoring or Upgrading the Cisco Router IOS

What happens if you need to restore the Cisco IOS to flash memory to replace an original file that has been damaged, or if you want to upgrade the IOS? No worries—you just download the file from a TFTP host to flash memory by using the copy tftp flash command. This command requires the IP address of the TFTP host and the name of the file you want to download.

But before you begin, make sure that the file you want to place in flash memory is in the default TFTP directory on your host. When you issue the command, TFTP won't ask you where the file is, so if the file you want to restore isn't in the default directory of the TFTP host, this just won't work.

WARNING   Copying the IOS from the TFTP host to flash memory requires a router reboot. So, instead of upgrading or restoring the IOS at 9 a.m. on Monday morning, you should probably wait until lunchtime, right?!

After you enter the `copy tftp flash` command, you'll see a message informing you that the router must reboot and run a ROM-based IOS image to perform this operation:

```
Router#copy tftp flash

            ****   NOTICE   ****
Flash load helper v1.0
This process will accept the copy options and then
terminate the current system image to use the ROM based
image for the copy. Routing functionality will not be
available during that time. If you are logged in via
telnet, this connection will terminate. Users with
console access can see the results of the copy operation.
           ---- ******** ----
Proceed? [confirm][Enter]
```

After you press Enter to confirm you truly understand that the router needs to reboot, you'll be presented with the following output. Once the router has used the TFTP host, it remembers the address, and just prompts you to press Enter:

```
System flash directory:
File  Length    Name/status
  1   8121000   /c2500-js-1.112-18
[8121064 bytes used, 8656152 available, 16777216 total]
Address or name of remote host [192.168.0.120]?[Enter]
```

The next prompt is for the name of the file you want to copy to flash memory. And remember—this file must be in your TFTP host's default directory:

```
Source file name?c2500-js56i-1.120-9.bin
Destination file name [c2500-js56i-1.120-9.bin]?[Enter]
Accessing file 'c2500-js56i-1.120-9.bin' on 192.168.0.120
...
Loading c2500-js56i-1.120-9.bin from 192.168.0.120
  (via Ethernet0): ! [OK]
```

After you tell the router the filename and where the file is, it asks you to confirm that you understand the contents of flash memory will be erased.

If you don't have enough room in flash memory to store both copies, or if the flash memory is new and no file has been written to flash memory before, the router will ask if it can erase the contents of the flash memory before writing the new file into flash memory.

You are prompted three times—yes, three times—just to make sure that you really want to proceed with erasing flash memory. If you haven't issued a copy run start command, you'll be prompted to do so because the router needs to reboot:

```
Erase flash device before writing? [confirm][Enter]
Flash contains files. Are you sure you want to erase?
  [confirm][Enter]

System configuration has been modified. Save? [yes/no]: y
Building configuration...
[OK]
Copy 'c2500-js56i-1.120-9.bin' from server
  as 'c2500-js56i-1.120-9.bin' into Flash WITH erase?
  [yes/no] y
```

After you say yes, yes, and yes again to erasing flash memory, the router must reboot to load a small IOS from ROM memory. You can't delete the flash file if it's being used.

Once this is done, the contents of flash memory are erased, and the file from the TFTP host is accessed and copied to flash memory:

```
%SYS-5-RELOAD: Reload requested
%FLH: c2500-js56i-1.120-9.bin from 192.168.0.120 to flash
...
System flash directory:
File  Length   Name/status
  1   8121000  /c2500-js-1.112-18
[8121064 bytes used, 8656152 available, 16777216 total]
Accessing file 'c2500-js56i-1.120-9.bin' on 192.168.0.120
...
Loading c2500-js56i-1.120-9.bin .from 192.168.0.120
  (via Ethernet0): ! [OK]

Erasing device... eeeeeeeeeeeeeeeeeeeeeeeeeeeeeeeeeeeeeeeeee
  eeeeeeeeeeeeeeeeeeeeeee
Loading c2500-js56i-1.120-9.bin from 192.168.0.120
  (via Ethernet0):
```

!!!
!!!!!!!!!!!!!!!!!!!!!!!!!!!!!!!!!!!! *[output cut]*

The row of **e** characters shows the contents of flash memory being erased. Each exclamation point (!) means that one UDP segment has been successfully transferred.

Once the copy is complete, you should receive this message:

```
[OK - 10935532/16777216 bytes]

Verifying checksum...  OK (0x2E3A)
Flash copy took 0:06:14 [hh:mm:ss]
%FLH: Re-booting system after download
```

After the file is loaded into flash memory and a checksum is performed, the router is rebooted to run the new IOS file.

> Cisco routers can become a TFTP-server for a router system image that's run in flash. The global configuration command is `tftp-server tftp:` *ios_name*.

Backing Up and Restoring the Device Configuration File

Any changes that you make to the router configuration are stored in the running-config file. If you don't enter a `copy run start` command after you make a change to running-config, that change goes poof if the router reboots or gets powered down. So, you probably want to make another backup of the configuration information just in case the router or switch completely dies on you. Even if your machine is healthy and happy, the backup is good to have for reference and documentation reasons. In the following sections, I'll describe how to copy the configuration of a router and switch to a TFTP host and how to restore that configuration.

Backing Up the Cisco Router Configuration

To copy the router's configuration from a router to a TFTP host, you can use either the `copy running-config tftp` or the `copy startup-config tftp` command. Either one will back up the router configuration that's currently running in dynamic RAM (DRAM), or that's stored in NVRAM.

Verifying the Current Configuration

To verify the configuration in DRAM, use the `show running-config` command (`sh run` for short) like this:

```
Router#sh run
Building configuration...
```

```
Current configuration:
!
version 12.0
```

The current configuration information indicates that the router is now running version 12.0 of the IOS.

Verifying the Stored Configuration

Okay—next, check the configuration stored in NVRAM. To see this, use the show startup-config command (sh start for short) like this:

```
Router#sh start
Using 366 out of 32762 bytes
!
version 11.2
```

The second line shows you how much room your backup configuration is using. Here, you can see that NVRAM is 32KB, and that only 366 bytes of it are used. Also notice that the version of configuration in NVRAM is 11.2. That's because I haven't yet copied running-config to startup-config since upgrading the router.

If you're not sure that the files are the same, and the running-config file is what you want to use, then use the copy running-config startup-config command. This will help you verify that both files are in fact the same. I'll go through this with you in the next section.

Copying the Current Configuration to NVRAM

By copying running-config to NVRAM as a backup, as shown in the following output, you're assured that your running-config will always be reloaded if the router gets rebooted. In the new IOS version 12.0, you're prompted for the filename you want to use. And because the version of IOS was 11.2 the last time a copy run start was performed, the router will tell you that it's going to replace that file with the new 12.0 version:

```
Router#copy run start
Destination filename [startup-config]?[Enter]
Warning: Attempting to overwrite an NVRAM configuration
  previously written by a different version of the system
  image.
Overwrite the previous NVRAM configuration?
  [confirm][Enter]
Building configuration...
[OK]
```

Now when you run show startup-config, the version shows 12.0:

```
Router#sh start
```

```
Using 487 out of 32762 bytes
!
version 12.0
```

Copying the Configuration to a TFTP Host

Once the file is copied to NVRAM, you can make a second backup to a TFTP host by using the copy running-config tftp command (copy run tftp for short), like this:

```
Router#copy run tftp
Address or name of remote host []?192.168.0.120
Destination filename [router-confg]?todd1-confg
!!
487 bytes copied in 12.236 secs (40 bytes/sec)
Router#
```

Notice that this took only two exclamation points (!!), which means only two UDP acknowledgments. In this example, I named the file todd1-confg because I had not set a hostname for the router. If you have a hostname already configured, the command automatically uses the hostname plus the extension -confg as the name of the file.

Restoring the Cisco Router Configuration

If you've changed your router's running-config and want to restore the configuration to the version in startup-config, the easiest way to do this is to use the copy startup-config running-config command (copy start run for short). You can also use the older Cisco command, config mem, to restore a configuration. Of course, this works only if you first copied running-config into NVRAM before making any changes!

So if you did copy the router's configuration to a TFTP host as a second backup, you can restore the configuration using the copy tftp running-config command (copy tftp run for short), or the copy tftp startup-config command (copy tftp start for short), as shown here:

```
Router#copy tftp run
Address or name of remote host []?192.168.0.120
Source filename []?todd1-confg
Destination filename [running-config]?[Enter]
Accessing tftp://192.168.0.120/todd1-confg...
Loading todd1-confg from 192.168.0.120 (via Ethernet0):
!!
[OK - 487/4096 bytes]
487 bytes copied in 5.400 secs (97 bytes/sec)
Router#
00:38:31: %SYS-5-CONFIG: Configured from
  tftp://192.168.0.120/todd1-confg
Router#
```

The configuration file is an ASCII text file, meaning that before you copy the config-uration stored on a TFTP host back to a router, you can make changes to the file with any text editor.

It is important to remember that when you copy or merge a configuration from a TFTP host to a router's RAM, the interfaces are shut down by default and you must manually go and enable each interface with the no shutdown command.

Erasing the Configuration

To delete the startup-config file on a Cisco router, use the command erase startup-config, like this:

```
Router#erase startup-config
Erasing the nvram filesystem will remove all files!
  Continue? [confirm][Enter]
[OK]
Erase of nvram: complete
Router#
```

This command deletes the contents of NVRAM on the router, so the next time the router boots, it'll run the setup mode.

Exam Essentials

Know how to back up an IOS image. By using the privileged-mode command copy flash tftp, you can back up a file from flash memory to a TFTP (network) host.

Know how to restore or upgrade an IOS image. By using the privileged-mode command copy tftp flash, you can restore or upgrade a file from a TFTP (network) server to flash memory.

Know how to prepare to back up an IOS image to a network server. In order to back up an IOS image to a network server, you must first make sure you can access the network server, ensure the network server has adequate space for the code image, and verify the file naming and path requirement.

Know how to save the configuration of a router. There are a couple ways to save the configuration of a router, but the most common, as well as the most tested, method is copy running-config startup-config.

Know how to erase the configuration of a router. To erase the configuration of a router, type the privileged-mode command **erase startup-config** and reload the router.

2.8 Perform an Initial Configuration on a Router

The Cisco IOS is the kernel of Cisco routers and most switches. What's a kernel? It's the basic, indispensable part of an operating system that allocates resources, and manages things like low-level hardware interfaces, security, and so on. Cisco has created something called CiscoFusion, which is supposed to make all Cisco devices run the same operating system. They don't, however, because Cisco has acquired devices that they haven't designed and built themselves. Almost all Cisco routers run the same IOS, in contrast to only about half of their switches—but that number is growing fast.

In this section, I'll give you a look at the Cisco IOS and how to configure a Cisco router step-by-step, using setup mode. In the next section, I'll show you how to do this using the command-line interface (CLI). I'm going to save Cisco switch configurations the next section.

Cisco Router IOS

The Cisco IOS was created to deliver network services and enable networked applications. It runs on most Cisco routers and on some Cisco Catalyst switches, like the Catalyst 2950.

These are some of the important things the Cisco router IOS software is responsible for:

- Carrying network protocols and functions
- Connecting high-speed traffic between devices
- Adding security to control access and stop unauthorized network use
- Providing scalability for ease of network growth and redundancy
- Supplying network reliability for connecting to network resources

You can access the Cisco IOS through the console port of a router, from a modem into the Aux port, or even through Telnet. Access to the IOS command line is called an EXEC session.

Connecting to a Cisco Router

You can connect to a Cisco router to configure it, verify its configuration, and check statistics. There are different ways to do this, but most often, the first place you would connect to is the console port. The *console port* is usually an RJ-45 connection located at the back of the router—by default, there's no password set.

You can also connect to a Cisco router through an auxiliary port, which is really the same thing as a console port, so it follows, you can use it as one. But this auxiliary port also allows you to configure modem commands so a modem can be connected to the router. This is a cool feature—it let's you to dial up a remote router and attach to the auxiliary port if the router is down and you need to configure it "out-of-band" ("out-of-the-network"). "In-band" means the opposite—you configure the network through the network.

The third way to connect to a Cisco router is through the program Telnet (in-band). Telnet is a terminal emulation program that acts as though it's a dumb terminal. You can use Telnet to connect to any active interface on a router like an Ethernet or serial port.

Figure 2.19 shows an illustration of a 2501 Cisco router. Pay special attention to all the different kinds of interfaces and connections.

FIGURE 2.19   A Cisco 2501 router

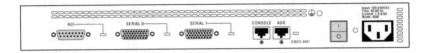

The 2501 router has two serial interfaces for WAN connection and one Attachment Unit Interface (AUI) connection for a 10Mbps Ethernet network connection. This router also has one console and one auxiliary connection via RJ-45 connectors.

A Cisco 2600 series router is a better router then those populating the 2500 series because it has a faster processor and can handle a lot more interfaces. Figure 2.20 shows a diagram of a Cisco 2600 modular router.

FIGURE 2.20   A Cisco 2600 router

Cisco 2610 router

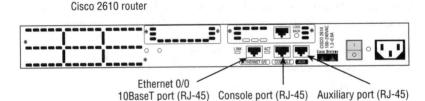

Ethernet 0/0
10BaseT port (RJ-45)   Console port (RJ-45)   Auxiliary port (RJ-45)

I prefer to use 2600 when I give you examples of configurations. This is because 2500 series machines just aren't capable of handling the demands of today's typical corporate network. You'll find 2600 or better in that kind of environment. The 2500 series still works great for home use, and when I do use them for an example, I'll point it out.

Bringing Up a Router

Okay—so let's get started! When you first bring up a Cisco router, it runs a power-on self-test (POST), and if that passes, it then looks for and loads the Cisco IOS from flash memory—if a file is present. In case you don't know, *flash memory* is an electronically erasable programmable read-only memory (EEPROM). The IOS then proceeds to load and then look for a valid configuration—the startup-config—that's stored by default in nonvolatile RAM, or NVRAM.

You'll be greeted with the following messages when you first boot or reload a router:

```
System Bootstrap, Version 12.2(13)T, RELEASE SOFTWARE (fc1)
Copyright (c) 2000 by cisco Systems, Inc.
C2600 platform with 32768 Kbytes of main memory
```

This is the first part. It's information about the bootstrap program which first runs the POST, and then tells the router how to load. By default the router will try to find the IOS in flash memory.

The next part, shown in the following code, shows us that the IOS is being decompressed into RAM. This step doesn't happen the same way for all routers. The output you're being shown is from my 2600 router that I just talked about. It's telling me that the IOS is being loaded into RAM. (The 2500 series router runs the IOS from flash memory—it doesn't load the IOS into RAM.)

```
program load complete, entry point: 0x80008000, size:
  0x43b7fc
Self decompressing the image :
###########################################################################
###########################################################################
###########################################################################
###########################################################################
###########################################################################
###########################################################################
################# [OK]
```

Okay, so after the IOS is decompressed into RAM, the IOS is then loaded and starts running the router, as shown in the following code. Notice the IOS version is stated as version 12.1(8).

```
Cisco Internetwork Operating System Software
IOS (tm) C2600 Software (C2600-I-M), Version 12.2(13),
  RELEASE SOFTWARE (fc1)
Copyright (c) 1986-2001 by cisco Systems, Inc.
Compiled Tue 17-Apr-01 04:55 by kellythw
Image text-base: 0x80008088, data-base: 0x8080853C
```

Once the IOS is loaded, the information learned from the POST is then displayed, as shown here:

```
cisco 2621 (MPC860) processor (revision 0x101) with
  26624K/6144K bytes of memory.
Processor board ID JAD050697JB (146699779)
M860 processor: part number 0, mask 49
Bridging software.
X.25 software, Version 3.0.0.
2 FastEthernet/IEEE 802.3 interface(s)
1 Serial network interface(s)
32K bytes of non-volatile configuration memory.
8192K bytes of processor board System flash (Read/Write)
```

Once the IOS is loaded and up and running, a valid configuration will be loaded from NVRAM. If there isn't one in NVRAM, the router goes into *setup mode*—a step-by-step process that helps you configure the router. You can also enter setup mode at any time from the command line by typing the command **setup** from something called privileged mode, which I'll get to in a minute. Setup mode only covers some very global commands, but it can be really helpful if you don't know how to configure certain protocols, like bridging or DECnet.

Setup Mode

You actually have two options when you are using setup mode: Basic Management and Extended Setup. Basic Management only gives you enough configurations to allow connectivity to the router, but Extended Setup gives you the power to configure some global parameters as well as interface configuration parameters:

```
    --- System Configuration Dialog ---
Would you like to enter the initial configuration dialog?
  [yes/no]: y


At any point you may enter a question mark '?' for help.
Use ctrl-c to abort configuration dialog at any prompt.
Default settings are in square brackets '[]'.
```

Notice the preceding two lines that say you can use Ctrl+C to abort configuration dialog at any prompt, and that the default settings are in square brackets ([]).

Basic Management setup configures only enough connectivity for managing the system. Because you can do so much more with Extended Setup, this mode asks you to configure each interface on the system.

```
Would you like to enter basic management setup?[yes/no]:n


First, would you like to see the current interface
  summary? [yes]: [Enter]
Any interface listed with OK? value "NO" does not have a
  valid configuration
```

Interface	IP-Address	OK?	Method	Status	Protocol
FastEthernet0/0	unassigned	NO	unset	up	up
FastEthernet0/1	unassigned	NO	unset	up	up

```
Configuring global parameters:
  Enter host name [Router]: Todd


The enable secret is a password used to protect access
```

```
to privileged EXEC and configuration modes. This
password, after entered, becomes encrypted in the
configuration. Enter enable secret: todd

The enable password is used when you do not specify an
enable secret password, with some older software
versions, and some boot images.
Enter enable password: todd
% Please choose a password that is different from the
  enable secret
Enter enable password: todd1
```

There's something I really want you to look at—did you notice that setup mode asks you to configure two enable passwords? You should know that you really only use the enable secret password. The enable password is for pre-10.3 IOS routers (really old routers). Even so, you've got to configure the password when in setup mode, and it has to be different. It will never be used if the enable secret is configured, though.

 The enable secret is encrypted, and the enable password is not.

The next password is for setting up Telnet sessions to the router. The reason setup mode has you configure a Telnet (VTY) password is because you can't telnet into a router by default if a password for the VTY lines hasn't been set.

```
The virtual terminal password is used to protect
access to the router over a network interface.
Enter virtual terminal password: todd
Configure SNMP Network Management? [yes]: [Enter]
 Community string [public]: [Enter]
Configure DECnet? [no]: [Enter]
Configure AppleTalk? [no]: [Enter]
Configure IP? [yes]: [Enter]
 Configure IGRP routing? [yes]:n
 Configure RIP routing? [no]: [Enter]
Configure bridging? [no]: [Enter]
Configure IPX? [no]: [Enter]
```

The preceding commands can help you configure a protocol if you're not sure which commands you need to configure. But if you use the CLI instead of setup mode, you'll have a lot more flexibility. I'll show you the CLI in the next section.

If you have an Async modem card installed in your router, you can have setup mode configure the modems for you:

```
Async lines accept incoming modems calls. If you will
have users dialing in via modems, configure these lines.
  Configure Async lines? [yes]:n
```

If your router has an ISDN BRI interface, you'll be prompted for the ISDN switch type to be configured. Take a look at the router output:

```
BRI interface needs isdn switch-type to be configured
Valid switch types are:
[0] none.........Only if you don't want to configure BRI
[1] basic-1tr6....1TR6 switch type for Germany
[2] basic-5ess....AT&T 5ESS switch type for the US/Canada
[3] basic-dms100..Northern DMS-100 switch type for
                  US/Canada
[4] basic-net3....NET3 switch type for UK and Europe
[5] basic-ni......National ISDN switch type
[6] basic-ts013...TS013 switch type for Australia
[7] ntt...........NTT switch type for Japan
[8] vn3...........VN3 and VN4 switch types for France
Choose ISDN BRI Switch Type [2]:2
```

The next section of the Extended Setup involves configuring the interfaces. You only have two Fast Ethernet interfaces on this router: FastEthernet 0/0 and FastEthernet 0/1.

```
Configuring interface parameters:

Do you want to configure FastEthernet0/0 interface?
  [yes]:[Enter]
 Use the 100 Base-TX (RJ-45) connector? [yes]:[Enter]
 Operate in full-duplex mode? [no]: y and [Enter]
 Configure IP on this interface? [yes]:[Enter]
  IP address for this interface: 1.1.1.1
  Subnet mask for this interface [255.0.0.0]: 255.255.0.0
  Class A network is 1.0.0.0, 16 subnet bits; mask is /16

Do you want to configure FastEthernet0/1 interface?
  [yes]:[Enter]
 Use the 100 Base-TX (RJ-45) connector? [yes]:[Enter]
 Operate in full-duplex mode? [no]:y and [Enter]
 Configure IP on this interface? [yes]:[Enter]
```

```
IP address for this interface: 2.2.2.2
Subnet mask for this interface [255.0.0.0]: 255.255.0.0
Class A network is 2.0.0.0, 16 subnet bits; mask is /16
```

I know this configuration is very basic, but it allows you to get a router up and running quickly. Notice the mask is displayed as /16, which means 16 out of 32 bits are being used.

The Extended Setup now shows the running configuration created:

```
The following configuration command script was created:

hostname Todd
enable secret 5 $1$BOwu$5FOm/EDdtRkQ4vy4a8qwC/
enable password todd1
line vty 0 4
password todd
snmp-server community public
!
no decnet routing
no appletalk routing
ip routing
no bridge 1
no ipx routing
!
interface FastEthernet0/0
media-type 100BaseX
full-duplex
ip address 1.1.1.1 255.255.0.0
no mop enabled
!
interface FastEthernet0/1
media-type 100BaseX
full-duplex
ip address 2.2.2.2 255.255.0.0
no mop enabled
dialer-list 1 protocol ip permit
dialer-list 1 protocol ipx permit
!
end


[0] Go to the IOS command prompt without saving this
    config.
[1] Return back to the setup without saving this config.
```

```
[2] Save this configuration to nvram and exit.

Enter your selection [2]:0
```

The most interesting part of the Extended Setup is the options you get at the end. You can go to CLI mode and discard the running-config (0); you can go back to setup to do it all over again (1), or you can save this configuration to NVRAM—something known as startup-config (2). This file would then be loaded every time the router is rebooted.

I'm going to choose 0 to go to the IOS—I'm not going to save the file I just created. Selecting 0 takes us directly to the CLI.

 You can exit setup mode at anytime by pressing Ctrl+C.

Command-Line Interface (CLI)

Because it's so much more flexible, the CLI truly is the best way to configure a router. I sometimes refer to the CLI as the "Cash Line Interface" because if you can create advanced configurations on Cisco routers and switches using the CLI, then you'll get the cash!

To use the CLI, just say No to entering the initial configuration dialog. After you do that, the router responds with messages that tell you all about the status of each and every one of the router's interfaces.

```
Would you like to enter the initial configuration dialog?
  [yes]:n
Would you like to terminate autoinstall? [yes]:[Enter]

Press RETURN to get started!

00:00:42: %LINK-3-UPDOWN: Interface FastEthernet0/0, changed
  state to up
00:00:42: %LINK-3-UPDOWN: Interface Serial0/0, changed
  state to down
00:00:42: %LINK-3-UPDOWN: Interface Serial0/1, changed
  state to down
00:00:42: %LINEPROTO-5-UPDOWN: Line protocol on Interface
  FastEthernet0/0, changed state to up
00:00:42: %LINEPROTO-5-UPDOWN: Line protocol on Interface
  Serial0/0, changed state to down
00:00:42: %LINEPROTO-5-UPDOWN: Line protocol on Interface
  Serial0/1, changed state to down
00:01:30: %LINEPROTO-5-UPDOWN: Line protocol on Interface
```

```
FastEthernet0/0, changed state to down
00:01:31: %LINK-5-CHANGED: Interface Serial0/0, changed
   state to administratively down
00:01:31: %LINK-5-CHANGED: Interface FastEthernet0/0, changed
   state to administratively down
00:01:31: %LINK-5-CHANGED: Interface Serial0/1, changed
   state to administratively down
00:01:32: %IP-5-WEBINST_KILL: Terminating DNS process
00:01:38: %SYS-5-RESTART: System restarted --
Cisco Internetwork Operating System Software
IOS (tm) 2600 Software (2600-BIN-M), Version 12.2(13),
   RELEASE SOFTWARE (fc1)
Copyright (c) 1986-2003 by cisco Systems, Inc.
Compiled Tue 04-Jan-03 19:23 by dschwart
```

Logging into the Router

After the interface status messages appear and you press Enter, the Router> prompt appears. This is called *user mode* and is mostly used to view statistics, but it's also a stepping-stone to logging into privileged mode. You can only view and change the configuration of a Cisco router in privileged mode, which you get into with the enable command.

```
Router>
Router>enable
Router#
```

You now end up with a Router# prompt, which indicates you're now in *privileged mode*, where you can both view and change the router's configuration. You can go back from privileged mode into user mode by using the disable command.

```
Router#disable
Router>
```

At this point, you can type **logout** to exit the console:

```
Router>logout
```

```
Router con0 is now available
Press RETURN to get started.
```

or you could just type **logout** or **exit** from the privileged-mode prompt to log out:

```
Router>en
Router#logout
```

```
Router con0 is now available
Press RETURN to get started.
```

Overview of Router Modes

To configure from a CLI, you can make global changes to the router by typing **configure terminal** (or **config t** for short), which puts you in global configuration mode and changes what's known as the running-config. A global command (commands run from global config) is one that is set once and affects the entire router.

You can type **config** from the privileged-mode prompt and then just press Enter to take the default of terminal.

```
Router#config
Configuring from terminal, memory, or network
   [terminal]? [Enter]
Enter configuration commands, one per line. End with
   CNTL/Z.
Router(config)#
```

At this point, you make changes that affect the router as a whole, hence the term *global configuration* mode.

To change the running-config—the current configuration running in DRAM—you use the `configure terminal` command, or just `config t`. To change the startup-config—the configuration stored in NVRAM—you use the `configure memory` command, or `config mem` for short. If you want to change a router configuration stored on a TFTP host, you use the `configure network` command, or just `config net`.

However, you need to understand that for a router to actually make a change to a configuration, it needs to put that configuration in RAM. So, if you actually type **config mem** or **config net**, you'll replace the current running-config with the config stored in NVRAM or a configuration stored on a TFTP host.

configure terminal, configure memory, and configure network are all considered commands that are used to configure information into RAM on a router; however, typically only the configure terminal command is used.

CLI Prompts

It's really important that you understand the different prompts you can find when configuring a router. Knowing these well helps you navigate and recognize where you are at any time within configuration mode. In this section, I'm going to demonstrate the prompts that are used on a Cisco router. (Always check your prompts before making any changes to a router's configuration!)

I'm not going into every different command offered. Doing that would be reaching beyond the scope of this exam. Instead, I'm going to describe all the different prompts you'll see for the CCNA exam. These commands are the ones you'll use most in real life—and the ones you'll need to know for the exam.

Interfaces

To make changes to an interface, you use the `interface` command from global configuration mode:

```
Router(config)#interface ?
 Async              Async interface
 BVI                Bridge-Group Virtual Interface
 CTunnel            CTunnel interface
 Dialer             Dialer interface
 FastEthernet       FastEthernet IEEE 802.3
 Group-Async        Async Group interface
 Lex                Lex interface
 Loopback           Loopback interface
 MFR                Multilink Frame Relay bundle interface
 Multilink          Multilink-group interface
 Null               Null interface
 Serial             Serial
 Tunnel             Tunnel interface
 Vif                PGM Multicast Host interface
 Virtual-Template   Virtual Template interface
 Virtual-TokenRing  Virtual TokenRing
 range              interface range command
```

```
Router(config)#interface fastethernet 0/0
Router(config-if)#
```

Did you notice the prompt changed to `Router(config-if)#`? This tells you that you're in interface configuration mode. And wouldn't it be nice if it also gave you an indication of what interface you were configuring? Well, at least for now we'll have to live without it because it doesn't. Could this be one of the reasons Cisco administrators make more money than Windows administrators? Or is it just that we're smarter and better looking? This hasn't been studied, but one thing is for sure: you really have to pay attention when configuring a router!

Subinterfaces

Subinterfaces allow you to create logical interfaces within the router. The prompt then changes to `Router(config-subif)#`.

```
Router(config)#int f0/0.?
 <0-4294967295> FastEthernet interface number
```

```
Router(config)#int f0/0.1
Router(config-subif)#
```

Line Commands

To configure user mode passwords, use the `line` command. The prompt then becomes `Router(config-line)#.`

```
Router#config t
Enter configuration commands, one per line. End with
  CNTL/Z.
Router(config)#line ?
  <0-70>   First Line number
  aux      Auxiliary line
  console  Primary terminal line
  tty      Terminal controller
  vty      Virtual terminal
  x/y      Slot/Port for Modems

2600A(config)#line
Router(config)#line console 0
Router(config-line)#
```

The `line console 0` command is known as a *major command* (also called a *global command*), and any command typed from the (`config-line`) prompt is known as a *subcommand*.

Routing Protocol Configurations

To configure routing protocols like RIP and IGRP, use the prompt (`config-router`)#:

```
Router#config t
Enter configuration commands, one per line. End with
  CNTL/Z.
Router(config)#router rip
Router(config-router)#
```

Editing and Help Features

You can use the Cisco advanced editing features to help you configure your router. If you type in a question mark (**?**) at any prompt, you'll be given the list of all the commands available from that prompt:

```
Router#?
Exec commands:
  access-enable   Create a temporary Access-List entry
```

```
access-profile  Apply user-profile to interface
access-template Create a temporary Access-List entry
bfe             For manual emergency modes setting
clear           Reset functions
clock           Manage the system clock
configure       Enter configuration mode
connect         Open a terminal connection
copy            Copy configuration or image data
debug           Debugging functions (see also 'undebug')
disable         Turn off privileged commands
disconnect      Disconnect an existing network connection
enable          Turn on privileged commands
erase           Erase flash or configuration memory
exit            Exit from the EXEC
help            Description of the interactive help system
lock            Lock the terminal
login           Log in as a particular user
logout          Exit from the EXEC
mrinfo          Request neighbor and version information
                from a multicast router
--More-
```

Plus, at this point, you can press the spacebar to get another page of information, or you can press Enter to go one command at a time. You can also press Q or any other key to quit and return to the prompt.

And here's a shortcut: to find commands that start with a certain letter, use the letter and the question mark (?) with no space between them:

```
Router#c?
clear clock configure connect copy
```

```
Router#c
```

See that? By typing **c?**, I received a response listing all the commands that start with *c*. Also notice that the Router# prompt that appeared with the command is still present. This can be helpful when you have long commands and need the next possible command. It would be pretty lame if you had to retype the entire command every time you used a question mark!

To find the next command in a string, type the first command and then a question mark:

```
Router#clock ?
 set Set the time and date
```

```
Router#clock set ?
 hh:mm:ss Current Time
Router#clock set 10:30:10 ?
 <1-31> Day of the month
 MONTH  Month of the year
Router#clock set 10:30:10 28 ?
 MONTH  Month of the year
Router#clock set 10:30:10 28 may ?
 <1993-2035> Year
Router#clock set 10:30:10 28 may 2003 ?
 <cr>
Router#
```

By typing the clock command, followed with a space and a question mark, you'll get a list of the next possible commands and what they do. Notice that you should just keep typing a command, a space, and then a question mark until <cr> (carriage return) is your only option.

If you are typing commands and receive this:

```
Router#clock set 10:30:10
% Incomplete command.
```

you'll know that the command string isn't yet done. Just press the Up arrow key to receive the last command entered, and then continue with the command by using your question mark.

And if you receive this error:

```
Router(config)#access-list 110 permit host 1.1.1.1
                                     ^
% Invalid input detected at '^' marker.
```

you've entered a command incorrectly. See that little caret (^)? It's a very helpful tool that marks the point where you have entered the command wrong.

Now if you receive this error:

```
Router#sh te
% Ambiguous command: "sh te"
```

it means you didn't enter all the keywords or values required by this command. Use the question mark to find the command you need:

```
Router#sh te?
WORD tech-support terminal
```

Table 2.10 shows the list of the enhanced editing commands available on a Cisco router.

TABLE 2.10   Enhanced Editing Commands

Command	Meaning
Ctrl+A	Moves your cursor to the beginning of the line
Ctrl+E	Moves your cursor to the end of the line
Esc+B	Moves back one word
Ctrl+F	Moves forward one character
Esc+F	Moves forward one word
Ctrl+D	Deletes a single character
Backspace	Deletes a single character
Ctrl+R	Redisplays a line
Ctrl+U	Erases a line
Ctrl+W	Erases a word
Ctrl+Z	Ends configuration mode and returns to EXEC
Tab	Finishes typing a command for you

Another cool editing feature I want to show you is the automatic scrolling of long lines. In the following example, the command typed had reached the right margin and automatically moved 11 spaces to the left. The dollar sign ($) indicates that the line has been scrolled to the left.

```
Router#config t
Enter configuration commands, one per line. End with CNTL/Z.
Router(config)#$110 permit host 171.10.10.10 0.0.0.0 host
```

You can review the router-command history with the commands shown in Table 2.11:

TABLE 2.11   Router-Command History

Command	Meaning
Ctrl+P or Up arrow	Shows last command entered
Ctrl+N or Down arrow	Shows previous commands entered

TABLE 2.11   Router-Command History *(continued)*

Command	Meaning
show history	Shows last 10 commands entered by default
show terminal	Shows terminal configurations and history buffer size
terminal history size	Changes buffer size (max 256)

The following example demonstrates the show history command and how to change the history size, as well as how to verify it with the show terminal command.

First, use the show history command to see the last 10 commands that were entered on the router:

```
Router#sh history
 en
 sh history
 show terminal
 sh cdp neig
 sh ver
 sh flash
 sh int fa0
 sh history
 sh int s0/0
 sh int s0/1
```

Now you use the show terminal command to verify the terminal history size:

```
Router#sh terminal
Line 0, Location: "", Type: ""
[output cut]
History is enabled, history size is 10.
Full user help is disabled
Allowed transports are lat pad v120 telnet mop rlogin
  nasi. Preferred is lat.
No output characters are padded
No special data dispatching characters
Group codes:   0
```

The terminal history size command, used from privileged mode, can change the size of the history buffer:

```
Router#terminal history size ?
 <0-256> Size of history buffer
Router#terminal history size 25
```

Verify the change with the show terminal command.

```
Router#sh terminal
Line 0, Location: "", Type: ""
[output cut]
Editing is enabled.
History is enabled, history size is 25.
Full user help is disabled
Allowed transports are lat pad v120 telnet mop rlogin
  nasi. Preferred is lat.
No output characters are padded
No special data dispatching characters
Group codes:  0
```

Gathering Basic Routing Information

The show version command provides basic configuration for the system hardware as well as the software version, the names and sources of configuration files, and the boot images:

```
Router#sh version
Cisco Internetwork Operating System Software
IOS (tm) C2600 Software (C2600-BIN-M), Version 12.2(13)T1,   RELEASE SOFTWARE
(fc1)
TAC Support: http://www.cisco.com/tac
Copyright (c) 1986-2003 by cisco Systems, Inc.
Compiled Sat 04-Jan-03 05:58 by ccai
Image text-base: 0x80008098, data-base: 0x80C4AD94
```

The preceding section of output describes the Cisco IOS running on the router. The following section describes the ROM used, which is used to boot the router.

```
ROM: System Bootstrap, Version 11.3(2)XA4, RELEASE SOFTWARE (fc1)
```

The next section shows how long the router has been running, how it was restarted (if you see a "system restarted by bus-error," that is a very bad thing), as well as where the Cisco IOS was loaded from, plus the IOS name. Flash is the default:

```
Router uptime is 1 week, 2 hours, 39 minutes
System returned to ROM by reload
System image file is "flash:c2600-bin-mz.122-13.T1.bin"
```

This next section displays the processor (a whopping 68030!), the amount of DRAM and flash memory, and the interfaces the POST test found on the router:

```
cisco 2621 (MPC860) processor (revision 0x101) with 27648K/5120K bytes of memory
Processor board ID JAB0402040J (2308906173)
```

```
M860 processor: part number 0, mask 49
Bridging software.
X.25 software, Version 3.0.0.
2 FastEthernet/IEEE 802.3 interface(s)
2 Serial network interface(s)
32K bytes of non-volatile configuration memory.
8192K bytes of processor board System flash (Read/Write)

Configuration register is 0x2102
```

The configuration register value is listed last.

Setting Passwords

There are five passwords used to secure your Cisco routers. Just as you learned earlier in the chapter, the first two passwords are used to set your enable password, which is used to secure privileged mode. This prompts a user for a password when the `enable` command is used. The other three are used to configure a password when user mode is accessed either through the console port, the auxiliary port, or via Telnet.

Enable Passwords

You set the enable passwords from global configuration mode like this:

```
Router(config)#enable ?
  last-resort Define enable action if no TACACS servers
              respond
  password    Assign the privileged level password
  secret      Assign the privileged level secret
  use-tacacs  Use TACACS to check enable passwords
```

There are four options available. Let's take a closer look at each:

Last-resort   Allows you to still enter the router if you set up authentication through a TACACS server and it's not available. However, this isn't used if the TACACS server is working.

Password   Sets the enable password on older, pre-10.3 systems and isn't ever used if an enable secret is set.

Secret   The newer, encrypted password that overrides the enable password if it's set.

Use-tacacs   Tells the router to authenticate through a TACACS server. This password is convenient if you have dozens or even hundreds of routers, because, well, would you like to face the fun of changing the password on 200 routers? If you go through the TACACS server, you only have to change the password once.

Here's an example of setting the enable passwords:

```
Router(config)#enable secret todd
Router(config)#enable password todd
```

The enable password you have chosen is the same as your
  enable secret. This is not recommended. Re-enter the
  enable password.

If you try and set the enable secret and enable passwords so they are the same, the router gives you a nice, polite warning to change the second password. If you don't have older legacy routers, don't even bother to use the enable password.

User mode passwords are assigned by using the `line` command:

```
Router(config)#line ?
  <0-70>   First Line number
  aux      Auxiliary line
  console  Primary terminal line
  tty      Terminal controller
  vty      Virtual terminal
  x/y      Slot/Port for Modems
```

Here are the lines you should be concerned about:

Aux   Sets the user mode password for the auxiliary port. It's usually used for configuring a modem on the router, but you can use it as a console as well.

Console   Sets a console user mode password.

Vty   Sets a Telnet password on the router. If this password isn't set, then Telnet can't be used by default.

To configure the user mode passwords, you configure the line you want and use either the `login` or `no login` command to tell the router to prompt for authentication. The next section provides a line-by-line example of each line configuration.

Auxiliary Password

To configure the auxiliary password, go into global configuration mode and type **line aux ?**. You can see that you only get a choice of 0–0. That's because there's only one port:

```
Router#config t
Enter configuration commands, one per line. End with CNTL/Z.
Router(config)#line aux ?
  <0-0> First Line number
Router(config)#line aux 0
Router(config-line)#login
Router(config-line)#password todd
```

It's important to remember the `login` command, or the auxiliary port won't prompt for authentication.

Okay—now watch what happens when I try and set the Aux on the "newer" IOS that Cisco has released:

```
2600A#config t
Enter configuration commands, one per line.  End with CNTL/Z.
2600A(config)#line aux 0
2600A(config-line)#login
% Login disabled on line 65, until 'password' is set
2600A(config-line)#
```

The reason Cisco has begun this process of not letting you set the "login" command before a password is set on a line, is because if you set the login command under a line, and then don't set a password, the line won't be usable. If you could do this, the router would prompt for a password that doesn't exist. So this is a good thing—a feature, not a hassle!

> **NOTE**   Definitely remember that although Cisco has the new "feature" on their routers starting in their newer IOS (12.2 and above), it's not in all their IOSs, and it is *not* on the Cisco CCNA exam!

Console Password

To set the console password, use the `line console 0` command. But look what happened when I tried to type `line console 0 ?` from the aux line configuration—I received an error. You can still type `line console 0` and it will accept it, but the help screens just don't work from that prompt. Type **exit** to get back one level and you'll find that your help screens now work. This is a "feature." Really.

```
Router(config-line)#line console ?
% Unrecognized command
Router(config-line)#exit
Router(config)#line console ?
  <0-0> First Line number
Router(config)#line console 0
Router(config-line)#login
Router(config-line)#password todd1
```

Since there's only one console port, I can only choose `line console 0`. You can set all your line passwords to the same password, but for security reasons, I'd recommend that you make them different.

You should know a few other important commands for the console port.

First, the `exec-timeout 0 0` command sets the timeout for the console EXEC session to zero, which basically means it is set so that it never times out. The default timeout is 10 minutes. (If you're feeling mischievous or vengeful, try this on people at work: Set it to 0 1. That will make the console time out in 1 second! To fix it, you have to continually press the Down arrow key while changing the timeout time with your free hand.)

Logging synchronous is a very cool command, and it should be a default command, but it's not. It's basically a pop-up killer that stops annoying console messages from popping up and disrupting the input you're trying to type. This makes your input messages oh-so-much easier to read.

Here's an example of how to configure both commands:

```
Router(config)#line con 0
Router(config-line)#exec-timeout ?
 <0-35791> Timeout in minutes
Router(config-line)#exec-timeout 0 ?
 <0-2147483> Timeout in seconds
 <cr>
Router(config-line)#exec-timeout 0 0
Router(config-line)#logging synchronous
```

Telnet Password

To set the user mode password for Telnet access into the router, use the line vty command. Routers that aren't running the Enterprise edition of the Cisco IOS default to five VTY lines— 0 through 4. But if you have the Enterprise edition, you'll have significantly more. The best way to find out how many lines you have is to use that question mark:

```
Router(config-line)#line vty 0 ?
 <1-4> Last Line Number
 <cr>
Router(config-line)#line vty 0 4
Router(config-line)#login
Router(config-line)#password todd2
```

 The Cisco CCNA exam only cares about lines 0 through 4 for the VTY lines. My routers actually have 70 lines, but no worries—I just demonstrated all you need for the CCNA exam.

So what happens if you try to telnet into a router that doesn't have a VTY password set? You'll receive an error stating that the connection is refused because, well, the password isn't set. You can get around this and tell the router to allow Telnet connections without a password by using the no login command:

```
Router(config-line)#line vty 0 4
Router(config-line)#no login
```

After your routers are configured with an IP address, you can use the Telnet program to configure and check your routers instead of having to use a console cable. You can use the Telnet program by typing **telnet** from any command prompt (DOS or Cisco).

If you can ping a router but are unable to telnet into it, the likely problem is that you didn't set the password on the VTY lines.

Encrypting Your Passwords

Because only the enable secret password is encrypted by default, you'll need to manually configure the user mode and enable passwords.

And notice that you can see all the passwords except the enable secret when you perform a show running-config on a router:

```
Router#sh running-config
[output cut]
!
enable secret 5 $1$rFbM$8.aXocHg6yHrM/zzeNkAT.
enable password todd1
!
[output cut]
line con 0
 password todd1
 login
line aux 0
 password todd
 login
line vty 0 4
 password todd2
 login

!
end

Router#
```

To manually encrypt your passwords, use the service password-encryption command. Here's how:

```
Router#config t
Enter configuration commands, one per line. End with CNTL/Z.
Router(config)#service password-encryption
```

```
Router(config)#^Z
Router#sh run
Building configuration...
[output cut]
!
enable secret 5 $1$rFbM$8.aXocHg6yHrM/zzeNkAT.
enable password 7 0835434A0D
!
[output cut]
!
line con 0
 password 7 111D160113
 login
line aux 0
 password 7 071B2E484A
 login
line vty 0 4
 password 7 0835434A0D
 login
line vty 5 197
 password 7 09463724B
 login
!
end
```

```
Router#config t
Router(config)#no service password-encryption
Router(config)#^Z
```

There you have it! The passwords are now be encrypted. You just encrypt the passwords, perform a show run, and then turn off the command. You can see that the enable password and the line passwords are all encrypted.

Banners

A good reason for having a banner is to add a security notice to users dialing into your inter-network. You can set a banner on a Cisco router so that when either a user logs into the router or an administrator telnets into the router, the banner will give them the information you want them to have. There are four different banners available:

```
Router(config)#banner ?
  LINE    c banner-text c, where 'c' is a delimiting
          character
```

```
exec      Set EXEC process creation banner
incoming  Set incoming terminal line banner
login     Set login banner
motd      Set Message of the Day banner
```

Message of the day (MOTD) is the most extensively used banner. It gives a message to every person dialing into or connecting to the router via Telnet, an auxiliary port, or through a console port:

```
Router(config)#banner motd ?
LINE c banner-text c, where 'c' is a delimiting character
Router(config)#banner motd #
Enter TEXT message. End with the character '#'.
$ Acme.com network, then you must disconnect immediately.
#
Router(config)#^Z
Router#
00:25:12: %SYS-5-CONFIG_I: Configured from console by
  console
Router#exit


Router con0 is now available

Press RETURN to get started.

If you are not authorized to be in Acme.com network, then
  you must disconnect immediately.


Router>
```

The preceding MOTD banner essentially tells anyone connecting to the router that if they're not on the guest list, they should get lost. The part to understand is the delimiting character—the thing that's used to tell the router when the message is done. You can use any character you want for it, but you can't use the delimiting character in the message itself. Also, once the message is complete, press Enter, then the delimiting character, then Enter again. It'll still work if you don't do that, but if you have more than one banner, they'll be combined as one message and put on a single line.

These are the other banners:

Exec banner   You can configure a line-activation (exec) banner to be displayed when an EXEC process (such as a line-activation or incoming connection to a VTY line) is created.

Incoming banner   You can configure a banner to be displayed on terminals connected to reverse Telnet lines. This banner is useful for providing instructions to users who use reverse Telnet.

Login banner   You can configure a login banner to be displayed on all connected terminals. This banner is displayed after the MOTD banner, but before the login prompts. The login banner can't be disabled on a per-line basis, so to globally disable it, you've got to delete it with the `no banner login` command.

Router Interfaces

Interface configuration is one of the most important router configurations, because without interfaces, a router is a totally useless thing. Plus, interface configurations must be exact to enable communication with other devices. Some of the configurations used to configure an interface are Network layer addresses, media type, bandwidth, and other administrator commands.

Different routers use different methods to choose the interfaces used on them. For instance, the following command shows a Cisco 2522 router with 10 serial interfaces, labeled 0 through 9:

```
Router(config)#int serial ?
 <0-9> Serial interface number
```

Now it's time to choose the interface you want to configure. Once you do that, you will be in interface configuration for that specific interface. The command to choose serial port 5, for example, would be as follows:

```
Router(config)#int serial 5
Router(config-if)#
```

The 2522 router has one Ethernet 10BaseT port, and typing **interface ethernet 0** can configure that interface:

```
Router(config)#int ethernet ?
 <0-0> Ethernet interface number
Router(config)#int ethernet 0
Router(config-if)#
```

The 2500 router, as previously demonstrated, is a fixed configuration router, which means that when you buy that model, you're stuck with that physical configuration.

To configure an interface, you always use the `interface type number` sequence, but the 2600, 3600, 4000, and 7000 series routers use a physical slot in the router, with a port number on the module plugged into that slot. So on a 2600 router, the configuration would be `interface type slot/port`:

```
Router(config)#int fastethernet ?
 <0-1> FastEthernet interface number
Router(config)#int fastethernet 0
% Incomplete command.
```

```
Router(config)#int fastethernet 0?
/
Router(config)#int fastethernet 0/?
 <0-1> FastEthernet interface number
```

Also, make note of the fact that you can't just type **int fastethernet 0**. You must type the full command—**type slot/port**, or **int fastethernet 0/0**, or **int fa 0/0**.

To set the type of connector used, use the media-type command. This is usually auto-detected:

```
Router(config)#int fa 0/0
Router(config-if)#media-type ?
 100BaseX Use RJ45 for -TX; SC FO for -FX
 MII      Use MII connector
```

Bringing Up an Interface

You can turn an interface off with the interface command shutdown, and turn it on with the no shutdown command. If an interface is shut down, it'll display administratively down when using the show interface command. Another way to check an interface's status is via the show running-config command. All interfaces are shut down by default.

```
Router#sh int ethernet0
Ethernet0 is administratively down, line protocol is down
[output cut]
```

Bring up the interface with the no shutdown command.

```
Router#config t
Enter configuration commands, one per line. End with
  CNTL/Z.
Router(config)#int ethernet0
Router(config-if)#no shutdown
Router(config-if)#^Z
00:57:08: %LINK-3-UPDOWN: Interface Ethernet0, changed
  state to up
00:57:09: %LINEPROTO-5-UPDOWN: Line protocol on Interface
  Ethernet0, changed state to up

Router#sh int ethernet0
Ethernet0 is up, line protocol is up
[output cut]
```

Configuring an IP Address on an Interface

Even though you don't have to use IP on your routers, it's most often what people use. To configure IP addresses on an interface, use the ip address command from interface configuration mode:

```
Router(config)#int e0
Router(config-if)#ip address 172.16.10.2 255.255.255.0
Router(config-if)#no shut
```

Don't forget to turn on an interface with the no shutdown command (no shut for short). Remember to look at the command show interface e0 to see if it's administratively shut down or not. Show running-config will also give you this information.

> The ip address *address mask* command starts the IP processing on the interface.

If you want to add a second subnet address to an interface, you have to use the secondary command. If you type another IP address and press Enter, it replaces the existing IP address and mask. This is definitely a most excellent feature of the Cisco IOS.

So, let's try it. To add a secondary IP address, just use the secondary command:

```
Router(config-if)#ip address 172.16.20.2 255.255.255.0
  secondary
Router(config-if)#^Z
```

You can verify that both addresses are configured on the interface with the show running-config command (sh run for short):

```
Router#sh run
Building configuration...
Current configuration:
[output cut]
!
interface Ethernet0
 ip address 172.16.20.2 255.255.255.0 secondary
 ip address 172.16.10.2 255.255.255.0
!
```

I really wouldn't recommend having multiple IP addresses on an interface because it's inefficient, but I showed you anyway, just in case you someday find yourself dealing with an MIS manager who's in love with really lame network design and makes you administrate it. And who knows? Maybe someone will ask you about it some day and you'll get to seem really smart because you know!

Serial Interface Commands

Before you jump in and configure a serial interface, you need to know a couple of things. First, the interface is usually attached to a channel service unit/data service unit (CSU/DSU) type of device that provides clocking for the line. If you have a back-to-back configuration (for example, one that's used in a lab environment), one end—the data communication equipment (DCE) end of the cable—must provide clocking. By default, Cisco routers are all data terminal equipment (DTE) devices, so you must tell an interface to provide clocking if you need it to act like a DCE device. You configure a DCE serial interface with the clock rate command:

```
Router#config t
Enter configuration commands, one per line. End with CNTL/Z.
Router(config)#int s0
Router(config-if)#clock rate ?
   Speed (bits per second)
 1200
 2400
 4800
 9600
 19200
 38400
 56000
 64000
 72000
 125000
 148000
 250000
 500000
 800000
 1000000
 1300000
 2000000
 4000000

   <300-4000000>  Choose clockrate from list above

Router(config-if)#clock rate 64000
%Error: This command applies only to DCE interfaces
Router(config-if)#int s1
Router(config-if)#clock rate 64000
```

It doesn't hurt anything to try and put a clock rate on an interface. Notice that the clock rate command is in bps.

The next command you need to get acquainted with is the bandwidth command. Every Cisco router ships with a default serial link bandwidth of T1 (1.544Mbps), but this has nothing to do with how data is transferred over a link. The bandwidth of a serial link is used by routing protocols such as IGRP, EIGRP, and OSPF to calculate the best cost (path) to a remote network. So if you're using RIP routing, then the bandwidth setting of a serial link is irrelevant, because RIP uses only hop count to determine that.

```
Router(config-if)#bandwidth ?
 <1-10000000> Bandwidth in kilobits

Router(config-if)#bandwidth 64
```

 Did you notice that, unlike the clock rate command, the bandwidth command is configured in kilobits?

Hostnames

You can set the identity of the router with the hostname command. This is only locally significant, which means it has no bearing on how the router performs name lookups or how the router works on the internetwork.

```
Router#config t
Enter configuration commands, one per line. End with
  CNTL/Z.
Router(config)#hostname Todd
Todd(config)#hostname Atlanta
Atlanta(config)#
```

Even though it's pretty tempting to configure the hostname after your own name, it's a better idea to name the router something pertinent to the location.

Descriptions

Setting descriptions on an interface is helpful to the administrator and, like the hostname, only locally significant. This is a helpful command because you can use it to keep track of circuit numbers, as is demonstrated in the following example:

```
Atlanta(config)#int e0
Atlanta(config-if)#description Sales Lan
Atlanta(config-if)#int s0
Atlanta(config-if)#desc Wan to Miami circuit:6fdda4321
```

You can view the description of an interface either with the show running-config command or the show interface command.

```
Atlanta#sh run
[cut]
interface Ethernet0
 description Sales Lan
 ip address 172.16.10.30 255.255.255.0
 no ip directed-broadcast
!
interface Serial0
 description Wan to Miami circuit:6fdda4321
 no ip address
 no ip directed-broadcast
 no ip mroute-cache
Atlanta#sh int e0
Ethernet0 is up, line protocol is up
 Hardware is Lance, address is 0010.7be8.25db (bia
  0010.7be8.25db)
 Description: Sales Lan
 [output cut]
Atlanta#sh int s0
Serial0 is up, line protocol is up
 Hardware is HD64570
 Description: Wan to Miami circuit:6fdda4321
[output cut]
Atlanta#
```

Viewing and Saving Configurations

If you run through setup mode, you'll be asked if you want to use the configuration you just created. If you say Yes, it will copy the configuration running in DRAM (known as the running-config) into NVRAM and name the file startup-config.

You can manually save the file from DRAM to NVRAM by using the copy running-config startup-config command. You can use the shortcut copy run start also:

```
Atlanta#copy run start
Destination filename [startup-config]?[Enter]
Warning: Attempting to overwrite an NVRAM configuration
  previously written by a different version of the system
  image.
```

```
Overwrite the previous NVRAM configuration?[confirm]
  [Enter]
Building configuration...
```

Notice that the message you received here tells you you're trying to write over the older startup-config. The IOS had been just upgraded to version 12.2, and the last time the file was saved, 11.3 was running. When you see a question with an answer in [], it means that if you just press Enter, you're choosing the default answer.

Also, when the command asked for the destination filename, the default answer was startup-config. The "feature" aspect of this command output is that you can't even type anything else in or you'll get an error!

```
Atlanta#copy run start
Destination filename [startup-config]?todd
%Error opening nvram:todd (No such file or directory)
Atlanta#
```

Okay, you're right—it's weird! Why on earth do they even ask if you can't change it at all? Well, since this "feature" was first introduced with the release of the 12.x IOS, we're all pretty sure it will turn out to be relevant and important some time in the future.

Anyway, you can view the files by typing **show running-config** or **show startup-config** from privileged mode. The sh run command, which is the shortcut for show running-config, tells you that you are viewing the current configuration:

```
Atlanta#sh run
Building configuration...

Current configuration:
!
version 12.0
service timestamps debug uptime
service timestamps log uptime
no service password-encryption
!
hostname Atlanta
ip subnet-zero
frame-relay switching
!
[output cut]
```

The sh start command—the shortcut for the show startup-config command—shows you the configuration that will be used the next time the router is reloaded. It also tells you how much NVRAM is being used to store the startup-config file:

```
Atlanta#sh start
Using 4850 out of 32762 bytes
!
version 12.0
service timestamps debug uptime
service timestamps log uptime
no service password-encryption
!
hostname Atlanta
!
!
ip subnet-zero
frame-relay switching
!
[output cut]
```

You can delete the startup-config file by using the erase startup-config command, after which you'll receive an error if you ever try to view the startup-config file.

```
Atlanta#erase startup-config
Erasing the nvram filesystem will remove all files!
  Continue? [confirm]
[OK]
Erase of nvram: complete
Atlanta#sh start
%% Non-volatile configuration memory is not present
Atlanta#reload
```

If you reload or power down and up the router after using the erase startup-config command, you'll be put into Setup mode because there's no configuration saved in NVRAM. You can press Ctrl+C to exit setup mode at any time. (The reload command can only be used from privileged mode.)

At this point, you shouldn't use Setup mode to configure your router. Setup mode was designed to help people who do not know how to use the CLI, and this no longer applies to you!

Verifying Your Configuration

Obviously, show running-config would be the best way to verify your configuration, and show startup-config would be the best way to verify the configuration that'll be used the next time the router is reloaded—right?

Well, once you take a look at the running-config, and if all appears well, you can verify your configuration with utilities like Ping and Telnet. Ping (Packet Internet Groper) is a program that uses Internet Control Message Protocol (ICMP) echo requests and replies. Ping sends a packet to a remote host, and if that host responds, you know that the host is alive. But you don't know if it's alive and also *well*—just because you can ping an NT server does not mean you can log in. Even so, Ping is an awesome starting point for troubleshooting an internetwork.

Did you know that you can ping with different protocols? You can test this by typing **ping ?** at either the router user-mode or privileged mode prompt:

```
Router#ping ?
WORD       Ping destination address or hostname
appletalk  Appletalk echo
decnet     DECnet echo
ip         IP echo
ipx        Novell/IPX echo
srb        srb echo
<cr>
```

If you want to find a neighbor's Network layer address, you either need to go to the router or switch itself, or you can type **show cdp entry * protocol** to get the Network layer addresses you need for pinging. (By the way, CDP stands for Cisco Discovery Protocol.)

Traceroute uses ICMP timeouts to track the path a packet takes through an internetwork, in contrast to Ping that just finds the host and responds, and Traceroute can also be used with multiple protocols.

```
Router#traceroute ?
WORD       Trace route to destination address or hostname
appletalk  AppleTalk Trace
clns       ISO CLNS Trace
ip         IP Trace
oldvines   Vines Trace (Cisco)
vines      Vines Trace (Banyan)
<cr>
```

Telnet is the best tool since it uses IP at the Network layer and TCP at the Transport layer to create a session with a remote host. If you can telnet into a device, your IP connectivity just has to be good. You can only telnet to devices that use IP addresses, and you can use Windows hosts or router prompts to telnet to a remote device.

```
Router#telnet ?
  WORD  IP address or hostname of a remote system
  <cr>
```

From the router prompt, you just type a hostname or IP address and it assumes you want to telnet—you don't need to type the actual command, `telnet`.

Verifying with the *show interface* Command

Another way to verify your configuration is by typing `show interface` commands, the first of which is `show interface ?`. Using this command reveals all the available interfaces to configure. The following output is from my 2600 routers:

```
Router#sh int ?
  Async               Async interface
  BVI                 Bridge-Group Virtual Interface
  CTunnel             CTunnel interface
  Dialer              Dialer interface
  FastEthernet        FastEthernet IEEE 802.3
  Loopback            Loopback interface
  MFR                 Multilink Frame Relay bundle interface
  Multilink           Multilink-group interface
  Null                Null interface
  Serial              Serial
  Tunnel              Tunnel interface
  Vif                 PGM Multicast Host interface
  Virtual-Template    Virtual Template interface
  Virtual-TokenRing   Virtual TokenRing
  accounting          Show interface accounting
  crb                 Show interface routing/bridging info
  dampening           Show interface dampening info
  description         Show interface description
  irb                 Show interface routing/bridging info
  mac-accounting      Show interface MAC accounting info
  mpls-exp            Show interface MPLS experimental accounting info
  precedence          Show interface precedence accounting info
  rate-limit          Show interface rate-limit info
  summary             Show interface summary
```

```
switching              Show interface switching
|                      Output modifiers
<cr>
```

The only "real" physical interfaces are FastEthernet and Serial; the rest are all logical interfaces. In addition, the newer IOS shows the "possible" show commands that you can use to verify your router interfaces—a very new feature from Cisco.

The next command is show interface fastethernet 0/0; it reveals the hardware address, logical address, and encapsulation method, as well as statistics on collisions:

```
Router#sh int fastethernet 0/0
FastEthernet0/0 is up, line protocol is up
  Hardware is AmdFE, address is 00b0.6483.2320 (bia 00b0.6483.2320)
  Description: connection to LAN 40
  Internet address is 192.168.1.33/27
  MTU 1500 bytes, BW 100000 Kbit, DLY 100 usec,
     reliability 255/255, txload 1/255, rxload 1/255
  Encapsulation ARPA, loopback not set
  Keepalive set (10 sec)
  Full-duplex, 100Mb/s, 100BaseTX/FX
  ARP type: ARPA, ARP Timeout 04:00:00
  Last input never, output 00:00:04, output hang never
  Last clearing of "show interface" counters never
  Input queue: 0/75/0/0 (size/max/drops/flushes); Total output drops: 0
  Queueing strategy: fifo
  Output queue: 0/40 (size/max)
  5 minute input rate 0 bits/sec, 0 packets/sec
  5 minute output rate 0 bits/sec, 0 packets/sec
     0 packets input, 0 bytes
     Received 0 broadcasts, 0 runts, 0 giants, 0 throttles
     0 input errors, 0 CRC, 0 frame, 0 overrun, 0 ignored
     0 watchdog
     0 input packets with dribble condition detected
     84639 packets output, 8551135 bytes, 0 underruns
     0 output errors, 0 collisions, 16 interface resets
     0 babbles, 0 late collision, 0 deferred
     0 lost carrier, 0 no carrier
     0 output buffer failures, 0 output buffers swapped out
```

The most important statistic of the show interface command is the output of the line and Data Link protocol status.

If the output reveals that FastEthernet 0/0 is up and the line protocol is up, then the interface is up and running.

```
Router#sh int fa0/0
FastEthernet0/0 is up, line protocol is up
```

The first parameter refers to the Physical layer, and it's up when it receives carrier detect. The second parameter refers to the Data Link layer, and it looks for keepalives from the connecting end. (Keepalives are used between devices to make sure connectivity has not dropped.)

```
Router#sh int s0/0
Serial0/0 is up, line protocol is down
```

If you see that the line is up but the protocol is down, as just shown, you are experiencing a clocking (keepalive) or framing problem. Check the keepalives on both ends to make sure that they match, that the clock rate is set if needed, and that the encapsulation type is the same on both ends. This up/down status would be considered a Data Link layer problem.

```
Router#sh int s0/0
Serial0/0 is down, line protocol is down
```

If you discover that both the line interface and the protocol are down, it's a cable or interface problem, which would be considered a Physical layer problem.

If one end is administratively shut down (as shown next), the remote end would present as down and down.

```
Router#sh int s0/0
Serial0/0 is administratively down, line protocol is down
```

To enable the interface, use the command no shutdown from interface configuration mode.

The next show interface serial 0/0 command demonstrates the serial line and the maximum transmission unit (MTU)—1500 bytes by default. It also shows the default bandwidth (BW) on all Cisco serial links—1.544Kbs. You use this to determine the bandwidth of the line for routing protocols like IGRP, EIGRP, and OSPF.

Another important configuration to notice is the keepalive, which is 10 seconds by default. Each router sends a keepalive message to its neighbor every 10 seconds, and if both routers aren't configured for the same keepalive time, it won't work.

You can clear the counters on the interface by typing the command clear counters.

```
Router#sh int s0/0
Serial0/0 is up, line protocol is up
 Hardware is HD64570
 MTU 1500 bytes, BW 1544 Kbit, DLY 20000 usec,
  reliability 255/255, txload 1/255, rxload 1/255
```

Encapsulation HDLC, loopback not set, keepalive set
  (10 sec)
Last input never, output never, output hang never
Last clearing of "show interface" counters never
Queueing strategy: fifo
Output queue 0/40, 0 drops; input queue 0/75, 0 drops
5 minute input rate 0 bits/sec, 0 packets/sec
5 minute output rate 0 bits/sec, 0 packets/sec
  0 packets input, 0 bytes, 0 no buffer
  Received 0 broadcasts, 0 runts, 0 giants, 0 throttles
  0 input errors, 0 CRC, 0 frame, 0 overrun, 0 ignored,
  0 abort
  0 packets output, 0 bytes, 0 underruns
  0 output errors, 0 collisions, 16 interface resets
  0 output buffer failures, 0 output buffers swapped out
  0 carrier transitions
  DCD=down DSR=down DTR=down RTS=down CTS=down

```
Router#clear counters ?
  Async              Async interface
  BVI                Bridge-Group Virtual Interface
  CTunnel            CTunnel interface
  Dialer             Dialer interface
  FastEthernet       FastEthernet IEEE 802.3
  Group-Async        Async Group interface
  Line               Terminal line
  Loopback           Loopback interface
  MFR                Multilink Frame Relay bundle interface
  Multilink          Multilink-group interface
  Null               Null interface
  Serial             Serial
  Tunnel             Tunnel interface
  Vif                PGM Multicast Host interface
  Virtual-Template   Virtual Template interface
  Virtual-TokenRing  Virtual TokenRing
  <cr>
```

```
Router#clear counters s0/0
Clear "show interface" counters on this interface
  [confirm][Enter]
```

```
Router#
00:17:35: %CLEAR-5-COUNTERS: Clear counter on interface
  Serial0 by console
Router#
```

Verifying with the *show ip interface* Command

The show ip interface command provides you with information regarding the Layer 3 configurations of a router's interfaces.

```
Router#sh ip interface
FastEthernet0/0 is up, line protocol is up
  Internet address is 1.1.1.1/24
  Broadcast address is 255.255.255.255
  Address determined by setup command
  MTU is 1500 bytes
  Helper address is not set
  Directed broadcast forwarding is disabled
  Outgoing access list is not set
  Inbound  access list is not set
  Proxy ARP is enabled
  Security level is default
  Split horizon is enabled
[output cut]
```

The status of the interface, the IP address and mask, and information on whether an access list is set on the interface as well as basic IP information is included in this output.

Using the *show ip interface brief* Command

This is probably one of the most helpful commands that you can ever use on a Cisco router. The show ip interface brief provides a quick overview of the routers interfaces including the logical address and status:

```
Router#sh ip int brief
Interface        IP-Address     OK? Method Status                   Protocol
FastEthernet0/0  192.168.1.33   YES manual up                       up

FastEthernet0/1  10.3.1.88      YES manual up                       up

Serial0/0        10.1.1.1       YES manual up                       up

Serial0/1        unassigned     YES NVRAM  administratively down down
```

Using the *show controllers* Command

The show controllers command displays information about the physical interface. It'll also give you the type of serial cable plugged into a serial port. Usually, this will only be a DTE cable that plugs into a type of DSU.

```
Router#sh controllers serial 0/0
HD unit 0, idb = 0x1229E4, driver structure at 0x127E70
buffer size 1524 HD unit 0, V.35 DTE cable
cpb = 0xE2, eda = 0x4140, cda = 0x4000

Router#sh controllers serial 0/1
HD unit 1, idb = 0x12C174, driver structure at 0x131600
buffer size 1524 HD unit 1, V.35 DCE cable
cpb = 0xE3, eda = 0x2940, cda = 0x2800
```

Notice that Serial 0/0 has a DTE cable, whereas the Serial 0/1 connection has a DCE cable. Serial 0/1 would have to provide clocking with the clock rate command. Serial 0/0 would get its clocking from the DSU.

Exam Essentials

Understand the sequence of what happens when you power on a router. When you first bring up a Cisco router, it will run a power-on self-test (POST), and if that passes, it will then look for and load the Cisco IOS from Flash memory, if a file is present. The IOS then proceeds to load and look for a valid configuration in NVRAM called the startup-config. If no file is present in NVRAM, the router will go into setup mode.

Know what setup mode provides. Setup mode automatically starts if a router boots and no startup-config is in NVRAM. You can also bring up setup mode by typing **setup** from the privileged mode. Setup provides a minimum amount of configuration in an easy format for someone who does not understand how to configure a Cisco router from the command line.

Understand the difference between user mode and privileged mode. User mode provides a command-line interface with very few available commands by default. User mode does not allow the configuration to be viewed or changed. Privileged mode allows a user to both view and change the configuration of a router. You can enter privileged mode by typing the command **enable** and entering the enable password or enable secret password, if set.

Understand what the command show version provides. The show version command provides basic configuration for the system hardware as well as the software version, the names and sources of configuration files, and the boot images.

Know how to set the hostname of a router.   The command sequence to set the hostname of a router is as follows:

```
enable
config t
hostname Todd
```

Know the difference between the enable password and enable secret password.   Both of these passwords are used to gain access to privilege mode; however, the enable secret is newer and encrypted by default. Also, if you set the enable password and then set the enable secret, only the enable secret will be used.

Know how to set the enable secret on a router.   To set the enable secret, you use the command `enable secret`. Do not use `enable secret password` *password*, or you will set your password to "password *password*". Here is an example:

```
enable
config t
enable secret todd
```

Know how to set the console password on a router.   To set the console password, use the following sequence:

```
enable
config t
line console 0
login
password todd
```

Be able to set the Telnet password on a router.   To set the Telnet password, use the following sequence:

```
enable
config t
line vty 0 4
login
password todd
```

Understand how to troubleshoot a serial link.   If you type `show interface serial 0` and see that it is "down, line protocol is down," this will be considered a Physical layer problem. If you see it as "up, line protocol is down," then you have a Data Link layer problem.

2.9 Perform an Initial Configuration on a Switch

The 1900 switch is the Cisco Catalyst switch family's low-end model. In fact, there are actually two different models associated with the Catalyst 1900 switch: the 1912 and the 1924. The 1912 switches have 12 10BaseT ports and the 1924 switches have 24 10BaseT ports. Each has two 100Mbps uplinks—either twisted-pair or fiber optic.

The 2950 comes in a bunch of flavors and runs 10Mbps all the way up to 1Gbps switched ports, with either twisted-pair or fiber. These switches have more intelligence to offer than a 1900 series switch does—they can provide basic data, video, and voice services. If you're faced with buying a switch of this type, you'll find yourself choosing one of the dozen models Cisco has available—all of which can be found on the Cisco website.

Okay—it's time to show you how to start up and configure both the Cisco Catalyst 1900 and the 2950 switches using the CLI. I'll teach you the basic configuration commands to use on each type of switch.

Here's a list of the basic tasks we'll be covering:

- Setting the passwords
- Setting the hostname
- Configuring the IP address and subnet mask
- Setting a description on the interfaces
- Erasing the switch configurations

1900 and 2950 Switch Startup

When the 1900 switch is first powered on, it runs through a POST. At first, all port LEDs are green, and if, upon completion, the POST determines that all ports are in good shape, all the LEDs blink, and then turn off. But if the POST finds a port that has failed, both the System LED and the port's LED turn amber. If you have a console cable connected to the switch, the menu in the following code appears after the POST. By pressing K, you get to use the CLI, and when you press M, you'll be allowed to configure the switch through a menu system. Pressing I allows you to configure the IP configuration of the switch, but you can also do this through the menu or CLI at any time, and once the IP configuration is set, the "I" selection no longer appears.

This is what the switch's output looks like on the console screen after the switch is powered up:

```
1 user(s) now active on Management Console.

        User Interface Menu
```

```
[M] Menus
[K] Command Line
[I] IP Configuration

Enter Selection:  K

        CLI session with the switch is open.
        To end the CLI session, enter [Exit].
>
```

When you power on a 2950 switch, it's just like a Cisco router—the switch comes up into setup mode. But unlike a router, the switch is actually usable in fresh-outta-the-box condition. Really—you can just plug the switch into your network and connect network segments together without any configuration! This is because switch ports are enabled by default, and you don't need an IP address on a switch to make it work in a network—that is, unless you want to manage the switch via the network or run VLANs on it. Here's the 2950 switch's initial output:

```
--- System Configuration Dialog ---
Would you like to enter the initial configuration dialog? [yes/no]: no

Press RETURN to get started!

00:04:53: %LINK-5-CHANGED: Interface Vlan1, changed state to administratively
down
00:04:54: %LINEPROTO-5-UPDOWN: Line protocol on Interface Vlan1, changed state
to down
Switch>
```

I'm going to complicate things by showing you how to configure this switch, which is really just like configuring a router.

Setting the Passwords

The first thing you're going to configure—that you always want to configure first on a switch—are the passwords. Why? Because it's *your* switch, and you don't want to share it with any unauthorized users! You can set both the user mode and privileged mode passwords just like you can for a router.

The login (user mode) password can be used to verify authorization on the switch, including accessing any line and the console. You can use the enable password to allow access to the switch so that the configuration can be viewed or changed. Again, this is the same as it is with any Cisco router.

But even though the 1900 switch uses a CLI running an IOS, the commands for the user mode and enable mode passwords are different than the ones you use for routers. Yes—true, you do use the command enable password, which is the same, but you choose different access levels. These are optional on a Cisco router but not on the 1900 switch. The 2950 is done exactly like a router though.

Setting the User Mode and Enable Mode Passwords

You use the same command to set the user mode password and enable mode password on the 1900 switch, but you do use different level commands to control the type of access that each password provides.

To configure the user mode and enable mode password, press K at the switch console output. You get into enable mode by using the enable command, then you enter global configuration mode by using the config t command.

Once you're in global configuration mode, you can set both the user mode and enable mode passwords by using the enable password command. The following output shows the configuration of both the user mode and enable mode passwords:

```
(config)#enable password ?
  level  Set exec level password
(config)#enable password level ?
  <1-15>  Level number
```

To enter the user mode password, use level number 1. To enter the enable mode password, use level mode 15. The password must be at least four characters, but no longer than eight. The following switch output shows the user mode password being set and denied because it's more than eight characters:

```
(config)#enable password level 1 toddlammle
Error: Invalid password length.
Password must be between 4 and 8 characters
```

This output is an example of how to set both the user mode and enable mode passwords on the 1900 switch:

```
(config)#enable password level 1 todd
(config)#enable password level 15 todd1
(config)#exit
#exit
CLI session with the switch is now closed.
Press any key to continue.
```

To set the user mode passwords for the 2950, I configured the lines just as I would on a router:

```
Switch>enable
Switch#config t
Enter configuration commands, one per line.  End with CNTL/Z.
```

```
Switch(config)#line ?
  <0-16>   First Line number
  console  Primary terminal line
  vty      Virtual terminal

Switch(config)#line vty ?
  <0-15>   First Line number

Switch(config)#line vty 0 15
Switch(config-line)#login
Switch(config-line)#password telnet
Switch(config-line)#line con 0
Switch(config-line)#login
Switch(config-line)#password todd
Switch(config-line)#exit
Switch(config)#exit
Switch#
```

Cool—you've just learned how to set the user mode passwords and the enable password on the 1900, but there's still is one more password that needs attention on each switch: the enable secret.

Setting the Enable Secret Password

The enable secret password is more secure, and it supersedes the enable password if you set it. So this means that if you have an enable secret set, you don't need to bother setting the enable mode password. You set the enable secret the same way you do on a router:

```
(config)#enable secret todd2
```

You can make the enable password and enable secret commands the same on the 1900 switch, but not on a router. And on the 2950, the enable password and enable secret must be different, as shown here:

```
Switch(config)#enable password todd
Switch(config)#enable secret todd
The enable secret you have chosen is the same as your enable password.
This is not recommended.  Re-enter the enable secret.

Switch(config)#enable secret todd1
Switch(config)#
```

Again, I didn't set the enable password because the enable secret will supersede it anyway.

Setting the Hostname

As it is with a router, the hostname on a switch is only locally significant. This means that it doesn't have any function on the network or with name resolution whatsoever. But it's still helpful to set a hostname on a switch so that you can identify the switch when connecting to it. A good rule of thumb is to name the switch after the location it is serving.

From the 1900 switch, just set the hostname like you would on a router:

```
#config t
Enter configuration commands, one per line.  End with CNTL/Z
(config)#hostname Todd1900
Todd1900(config)#
```

From the 2950, use the same command.

```
Switch(config)#hostname Todd2950
Todd2950(config)#
```

Setting IP Information

Remember—you don't have to set any IP configuration on the switch to make it work—you can just plug and play as you would on a hub if you want! But there are two reasons you probably do want to set the IP address information on the switch: so you can manage the switch via Telnet or other management software, or so you can configure the switch with different VLANs and other network functions, if you want to.

By default, no IP address or default gateway information is set. You would set both of these on a Layer 2 switch just as you would on any host. By using the command show ip (or sh ip), you can see the 1900's default IP configuration:

```
Todd1900#sh ip
IP Address: 0.0.0.0
Subnet Mask: 0.0.0.0
Default Gateway: 0.0.0.0
Management VLAN:  1
Domain name:
Name server 1: 0.0.0.0
Name server 2: 0.0.0.0
HTTP server : Enabled
HTTP port :  80
RIP : Enabled
```

Look at this output one more time—did you notice that no IP address, default gateway, or other IP parameters are configured? Good! You use the ip address command to set the IP configuration on a 1900 switch, and the ip default-gateway command to set the default gateway.

This output shows an example of how to set the IP address and default gateway:

```
Todd1900#config t
Enter configuration commands, one per line.  End with CNTL/Z
Todd1900(config)#ip address 172.16.10.16 255.255.255.0
Todd1900(config)#ip default-gateway 172.16.10.1
Todd1900(config)#
```

The IP address is configured differently on the 2950 switch than it is on the 1900, or on any router—you actually configure it under the VLAN1 interface! Remember that every port on every switch is a member of VLAN1 by default. This really confuses a lot of people—you'd think that you would set an IP address under a switch interface—but no, that's not where it goes. Remember that you set an IP address "for" the switch so you can manage the thing in-band (through the network). Check out this output:

```
Todd2950#config t
Enter configuration commands, one per line.  End with CNTL/Z.
Todd2950(config)#int vlan1
Todd2950(config-if)#ip address 172.16.10.17 255.255.255.0
Todd2950(config-if)#no shut
Todd2950(config-if)#exit
00:22:01: %LINK-3-UPDOWN: Interface Vlan1, changed state to up
00:22:02: %LINEPROTO-5-UPDOWN: Line protocol on Interface Vlan1, changed state
to up
Todd2950(config)#ip default-gateway 172.16.10.1
Todd2950(config)#
```

Notice that I set the IP address for the 2950 switch under the VLAN 1 interface. And notice that I also had to enable the interface with the no shutdown command. The default gateway command is deployed from global configuration mode.

Configuring Interface Descriptions

You can administratively set a name for each interface on the switches, and like the hostname, the descriptions are only locally significant.

For the 1900 and 2950 series switch, use the description command. You can't use spaces with this command on the 1900, but you can use underscores if you need to.

To set the descriptions, you've got to be in interface configuration mode first. So, from interface configuration mode, use the description command to describe each interface. Your descriptions can include more than one word, but remember—you can't use spaces. Here's an example—in it, I used underscores instead of spaces:

```
Todd1900#config t
Enter configuration commands, one per line.  End with CNTL/Z
```

```
Todd1900(config)#int e0/1
Todd1900(config-if)#description Finance_VLAN
Todd1900(config-if)#int f0/26
Todd1900(config-if)#description trunk_to_Building_4
Todd1900(config-if)#
```

I set descriptions on both a 10Mbps port and a 100Mbps port on the 1900 switch.

When you set descriptions on a 2950 switch, you get to use spaces:

```
Todd2950(config)#int fastEthernet 0/?
  <0-12>  FastEthernet interface number

Todd2950(config)#int fastEthernet 0/1
Todd2950(config-if)#description Sales Printer
Todd2950(config-if)#int f0/12
Todd2950(config-if)#description Connection to backbone
Todd2950(config-if)#^Z
Todd2950#
```

All of the ports on my 2950 switch are 10/100 ports. You can see by looking at this output that I set the interface descriptions on ports 0/1 and 0/12. Since both interfaces are FastEthernet (and not Ethernet), they must be 10/100.

Once you've got your descriptions neatly configured on each interface, you can take a look at them any time you want with either the show interface command or the show running-config command.

Erasing the Switch Configuration

As is true on routers, both the 1900 and 2950's configurations are stored in NVRAM. You don't get to check out the startup-config or the contents of NVRAM on the 1900—you can only look at the running-config. When you make a change to the switches' running-config, the switch automatically copies the configuration on itself over to NVRAM. This is a big difference from a router where you have to type copy running-config startup-config. You just can't do that on a 1900!

But the 2950 switch has a running-config and a startup-config. You save the configuration with the copy run start command, and you can erase the contents of NVRAM with the erase startup-config.

Check out the following 1900 switch output, and notice that there are two options: nvram and vtp. I want to delete the contents of NVRAM to restore the factory default settings, since that is where all configuration information is stored.

```
Todd1900#delete ?
  nvram  NVRAM configuration
  vtp    Reset VTP configuration to defaults
```

Todd190N#**delete nvram**
This command resets the switch with factory defaults. All system parameters
will revert to their default factory settings. All static and dynamic addresses
will be removed.
Reset system with factory defaults, [Y]es or [N]o? **Yes**

Notice the message the 1900 gave me when I used the delete nvram command—this shows
that once you say yes, the configuration is gone!

Now to delete the 2950, you just type **erase startup-config** from the privileged mode
prompt like this:

Todd2950#**erase startup-config**
Erasing the nvram filesystem will remove all files! Continue? [confirm] **[Enter]**
[OK]
Erase of nvram: complete
Todd2950#

Unlike the 1900, when you erase the configuration on the 2950, you have to reload the
switch before the running-config will actually be deleted.

Exam Essentials

Know how to set up an IP address and default gateway on the 1900 and 2950.   On the 1900,
you use the following commands:

```
Todd1900#config t
Enter configuration commands, one per line.  End with CNTL/Z
Todd1900(config)#ip address 172.16.10.16 255.255.255.0
Todd1900(config)#ip default-gateway 172.16.10.1
Todd1900(config)#
```

On the 2950, here is the example configuration:

```
Todd2950#config t
Enter configuration commands, one per line.  End with CNTL/Z.
Todd2950(config)#int vlan1
Todd2950(config-if)#ip address 172.16.10.17 255.255.255.0
Todd2950(config-if)#no shut
Todd2950(config-if)#exit
00:22:01: %LINK-3-UPDOWN: Interface Vlan1, changed state to up
00:22:02: %LINEPROTO-5-UPDOWN: Line protocol on Interface Vlan1, changed state
to up
Todd2950(config)#ip default-gateway 172.16.10.1
Todd2950(config)#
```

Know how to erase the configuration on the 1900 and 2950.   On the 1900, here is the example:

```
Todd1900#delete ?
  nvram  NVRAM configuration
  vtp    Reset VTP configuration to defaults
Todd190N#delete nvram
This command resets the switch with factory defaults. All system parameters
will revert to their default factory settings. All static and dynamic
addresses will be removed.
Reset system with factory defaults, [Y]es or [N]o? Yes
```

On the 2950, here is how to delete the configuration:

```
Todd2950#erase startup-config
Erasing the nvram filesystem will remove all files! Continue? [confirm]
[Enter]
[OK]
Erase of nvram: complete
Todd2950#
```

2.10 Implement Access Lists

To prepare you for the CCNA, I'll show you three types of access lists; standard IP access lists, extended IP access lists, and named access lists. You'll also see a technique for specifying ranges of addressing called wildcard masking that you can use with all three types of access list. For now, let's get started on standard access lists.

Standard IP Access Lists

Standard IP access lists filter network traffic by examining the source IP address in a packet. You create a standard IP access list by using the access-list numbers 1–99 or 1300–1999 (expanded range). Access list types are generally differentiated using a number. Based on the number used when the access list is created, the router knows which type of syntax to expect as the list is entered. By using numbers 1–99 or 1300–1999, you're telling the router that you want to create a standard IP access list so that the router will expect syntax specifying the source IP address in the conditional.

The following is an example of the many access-list number ranges that you can use to filter traffic on your network. The protocols for which you can specify access lists depend on your IOS version.

```
Lab_A(config)#access-list ?
  <1-99>       IP standard access list
```

```
<100-199>    IP extended access list
<1000-1099>  IPX SAP access list
<1100-1199>  Extended 48-bit MAC address access list
<1200-1299>  IPX summary address access list
<1300-1999>  IP standard access list (expanded range)
<200-299>    Protocol type-code access list
<2000-2699>  IP extended access list (expanded range)
<300-399>    DECnet access list
<600-699>    Appletalk access list
<700-799>    48-bit MAC address access list
<800-899>    IPX standard access list
<900-999>    IPX extended access list
```

 As you can see, you can create a bunch of different types of access lists. But for the CCNA, we'll focus exclusively on IP access lists.

Okay—let's take a look at the syntax you'd use when creating a standard access list. As I said, by using the access-list numbers between 1–99 or 1300–1999, you're telling the router that you want to create a standard IP access list.

```
Lab_A(config)#access-list 10 ?
  deny    Specify packets to reject
  permit  Specify packets to forward
```

After you choose the access-list number, you need to decide if you are creating a permit or deny statement. For this example, you will create a deny statement:

```
Lab_A(config)#access-list 10 deny ?
  Hostname or A.B.C.D  Address to match
  any                  Any source host
  host                 A single host address
```

The next step requires a more detailed explanation. There are three options available. You can use the any command to permit or deny any host or network, you can use an IP address to specify either a single host or a range of them, or you can use the host command to specify a specific host only. The any command is pretty obvious—any source address matches the statement, so every packet compared against this line matches. The host command is relatively simple. Here's an example that uses it:

```
Lab_A(config)#access-list 10 deny host 172.16.30.2
```

This tells the list to deny any packets from host 172.16.30.2. The default command is host. In other words, if you type **access-list 10 deny 172.16.30.2**, the router assumes you mean host 172.16.30.2.

But there's another way to specify either a specific host, or a range of hosts—you can use wildcard masking. In fact, to specify any range of hosts, you have to use wildcard masking in the access list. What's wildcard masking? Read onÖ InjêP

Wildcard Masking

Wildcard masks are used with access lists to specify an individual host, a network, or a certain range of a network or networks. To understand a wildcard mask, you need to understand what a block size is; *block sizes* are used to specify a range of addresses. Some of the different block sizes available are 64, 32, 16, 8, and 4.

When you need to specify a range of addresses, you choose the next-largest block size for your needs. For example, if you need to specify 34 networks, you need a block size of 64. If you want to specify 18 hosts, you need a block size of 32. If you only specify 2 networks, then a block size of 4 would work.

You use wildcards with the host or network address to tell the router a range of available addresses to filter. To specify a host, the address would look like this:

172.16.30.5 0.0.0.0

The four zeros represent each octet of the address. Whenever a zero is present, it means that octet in the address must match exactly. To specify that an octet can be any value, the value of 255 is used. As an example, here's how a /24 subnet is specified with a wildcard:

172.16.30.0 0.0.0.255

This tells the router to match up the first three octets exactly, but the fourth octet can be any value.

Now, that was the easy part. What if you want to specify only a small range of subnets? This is where the block sizes come in. You have to specify the range of values in a block size. In other words, you can't choose to specify 20 networks. You can only specify the exact amount as the block size value. For example, the range would either have to be 16 or 32, but not 20.

Let's say that you want to block access to part of network that is in the range from 172.16.8.0 through 172.16.15.0. That is a block size of 8. Your network number would be 172.16.8.0, and the wildcard would be 0.0.7.255. Whoa! What is that?!? The 7.255 is what the router uses to determine the block size. The network and wildcard tell the router to start at 172.16.8.0 and go up a block size of eight addresses to network 172.16.15.0.

Seriously—it really is easier than it looks. I could certainly go through the binary math for you, but no one needs that. All you have to do is remember that the wildcard is always one number less than the block size. So, in our example, the wildcard would be 7 since our block size is 8. If you used a block size of 16, the wildcard would be 15. Easy, huh?

But just in case, I'll go through some examples to help you nail it. The following example tells the router to match the first three octets exactly but that the fourth octet can be anything.

```
Lab_A(config)#access-list 10 deny 172.16.10.0 0.0.0.255
```

The next example tells the router to match the first two octets and that the last two octets can be any value.

```
Lab_A(config)#access-list 10 deny 172.16.0.0
   0.0.255.255
```

Try to figure out this next line:

```
Lab_A(config)#access-list 10 deny 172.16.16.0 0.0.3.255
```

The preceding configuration tells the router to start at network 172.16.16.0 and use a block size of 4. The range would then be 172.16.16.0 through 172.16.19.0.

The following example shows an access list starting at 172.16.16.0 and going up a block size of 8 to 172.16.23.0.

```
Lab_A(config)#access-list 10 deny 172.16.16.0 0.0.7.255
```

The next example starts at network 172.16.32.0 and goes up a block size of 32 to 172.16.63.0.

```
Lab_A(config)#access-list 10 deny 172.16.32.0
   0.0.31.255
```

The last example starts at network 172.16.64.0 and goes up a block size of 64 to 172.16.127.0.

```
Lab_A(config)#access-list 10 deny 172.16.64.0
   0.0.63.255
```

Here are two more things to keep in mind when working with block sizes and wildcards:

- Each block size must start at 0. For example, you can't say that you want a block size of 8 and then start at 12. You must use 0–7, 8–15, 16–23, and so on. For a block size of 32, the ranges are 0–31, 32–63, 64–95, and so on.
- The command any is the same thing as writing out the wildcard 0.0.0.0 255.255.255.255.

NOTE   Wildcard masking is a crucial skill to master when creating IP access lists. It's used identically when you are creating standard and extended IP access lists.

Standard Access List Example

In this section, you'll learn how to use a standard access list to stop specific users from gaining access to the finance department LAN.

In Figure 2.21, a router has three LAN connections and one WAN connection to the Internet. Users on the Sales LAN should not have access to the Finance LAN, but they should be able to access the Internet and the marketing department. The Marketing LAN needs to access the Finance LAN for application services.

FIGURE 2.21   IP access list example with three LANs and a WAN connection

On the Acme router, the following standard IP access list is configured:

```
Acme#config t
Acme(config)#access-list 10 deny 172.16.40.0 0.0.0.255
Acme(config)#access-list 10 permit any
```

It's very important to know that the any command is the same thing as saying the following using wildcard masking:

```
Acme(config)#access-list 10 permit 0.0.0.0
  255.255.255.255
```

Because the wildcard mask says that none of the octets are to be evaluated, every address matches the mask. So this is functionally the same as using the any keyword.

At this point, the access list is configured to deny source addresses from the Sales LAN access to the Finance LAN, and allow everyone else. But remember, no action will be taken until the access list is applied on an interface in a specific direction. But where should this access list be placed? If you place it as an incoming access list on E0, you might as well shut down the Ethernet interface because all of the Sales LAN devices will be denied access to all networks attached to the router. The best place to apply this access list is on the E1 interface as an outbound list.

```
Acme(config)#int e1
Acme(config-if)#ip access-group 10 out
```

This completely stops traffic from 172.16.40.0 from getting out Ethernet 1. It has no effect on the hosts from the Sales LAN accessing the Marketing LAN and the Internet, because traffic to those destinations doesn't go through interface E1.

Controlling VTY (Telnet) Access

You'll probably have a difficult time trying to stop users from telnetting to a large router because any active interface on a router is fair game for VTY access. You could try to create an extended IP access list that limits Telnet access to every IP address on the router, but if you did that, you'd have to apply it inbound on every interface, and that really wouldn't scale well to a large router with tens, even hundreds of interfaces, now would it? No worries—here's a much better solution. Use a standard IP access list to control access to the VTY lines.

Why does this work? Because when you apply an access to the VTY lines, you don't need to specify the Telnet protocol because access to the VTY implies terminal access. You also don't need to specify a destination address, since it really doesn't matter which interface address the user used as a target for the Telnet session. You really only need to control where the user is coming from—in other words, the source IP address. Nice!

To perform this function, follow these steps:

1. Create a standard IP access list that permits only the host or hosts you want to be able to telnet into the routers.

2. Apply the access list to the VTY line with the `access-class` command.

Here is an example of allowing only host 172.16.10.3 to telnet into a router:

```
Lab_A(config)#access-list 50 permit 172.16.10.3
Lab_A(config)#line vty 0 4
Lab_A(config-line)#access-class 50 in
```

Because of the implied deny any at the end of the list, the access list stops any host from telnetting into the router except the host 172.16.10.3, regardless of which individual IP address on the router is used as a target.

Extended Access Lists

In the standard IP access list example, notice how you had to block all access from the Sales LAN to Finance. What if you needed Sales to gain access to a certain server on the Finance LAN, but not to other network services for security reasons? With a standard IP access list, you can't allow users to get to one network service and not another. Said another way, when you need to make decisions based on both source and destination addresses, a standard access list won't allow you to do that since it only makes decisions based on source address. However, an *extended access list* will hook you up. That's because extended access lists allow you to specify source and destination address as well as the protocol and port number that identify the upper-layer protocol or application. By using extended access lists, you can effectively allow users access to a physical LAN and stop them from accessing either specific hosts, or even specific services on those hosts.

Extended Access List Example 1

Here's an example of an extended IP access list. The first command shows the access list numbers that are available. You'll use the extended access list range, 100–199. Be sure to notice that the range 2000–2699 is also available for extended IP access lists.

```
Lab_A(config)#access-list ?
  <1-99>         IP standard access list
  <100-199>      IP extended access list
  <1000-1099>    IPX SAP access list
  <1100-1199>    Extended 48-bit MAC address access list
  <1200-1299>    IPX summary address access list
  <1300-1999>    IP standard access list (expanded range)
  <200-299>      Protocol type-code access list
  <2000-2699>    IP extended access list (expanded range)
  <300-399>      DECnet access list
  <600-699>      Appletalk access list
  <700-799>      48-bit MAC address access list
  <800-899>      IPX standard access list
  <900-999>      IPX extended access list
```

At this point, you need to decide what type of list entry you are making. For this example, you'll choose a deny list entry.

```
Lab_A(config)#access-list 110 ?
  deny       Specify packet
  dynamic    Specify a DYNAMIC list of PERMITs or DENYs
  permit     Specify packets to forward
```

Once you choose the access list type, you then need to select a protocol field entry.

If you want to filter by Application layer protocol, you've got to choose the appropriate Layer 4 transport protocol here. For example, to filter Telnet or FTP, you'd choose TCP since both Telnet and FTP use TCP at the Transport layer. If you were to choose IP, you wouldn't be allowed to specify a specific application protocol later.

```
Lab_A(config)#access-list 110 deny ?
 <0-255>  An IP protocol number
 eigrp    Cisco's EIGRP routing protocol
 gre      Cisco's GRE tunneling
 icmp     Internet Control Message Protocol
 igmp     Internet Gateway Message Protocol
 igrp     Cisco's IGRP routing protocol
 ip       Any Internet Protocol
 ipinip   IP in IP tunneling
 nos      KA9Q NOS compatible IP over IP tunneling
 ospf     OSPF routing protocol
 tcp      Transmission Control Protocol
 udp      User Datagram Protocol
```

Okay—here, you choose to filter an Application layer protocol that uses TCP by selecting TCP as the protocol. You'll specify the specific TCP port later. Next, you are prompted for the source IP address of the host or network. You can choose the any command to allow any source address.

```
Lab_A(config)#access-list 110 deny tcp ?
 A.B.C.D  Source address
 any      Any source host
 host     A single source host
```

After you select the source address, choose the destination address:

```
Lab_A(config)#access-list 110 deny tcp any ?
 A.B.C.D Destination address
 any      Any destination host
 eq       Match only packets on a given port number
 gt       Match only packets with a greater port number
 host     A single destination host
 lt       Match only packets with a lower port number
 neq      Match only packets not on a given port number
 range    Match only packets in the range of port numbers
```

In the following example, any source IP address that has a destination IP address of 172.16.30.2 has been denied.

```
Lab_A(config)#access-list 110 deny tcp any host  172.16.30.2 ?
 eq            Match only packets on a given port number
 established  Match established connections
```

```
fragments       Check fragments
gt              Match only packets with a greater port
                number
log             Log matches against this entry
log-input       Log matches against this entry,including
                inputinterface
lt              Match only packets with a lower port
                number
neq             Match only packets not on a given port
                number
precedence      Match packets with given precedence value
range           Match only packets in the range of port
                numbers
tos             Match packets with given TOS value
<cr>
```

You can press Enter here and leave the access list as is. But if you do that, all TCP traffic to host 172.16.30.2 will be denied, regardless of destination port. You can be even more specific: once you have the host addresses in place, just specify the type of service you are denying. The following help screen shows you the available options. You can choose a port number or use the application or protocol name.

```
Lab_A(config)#access-list 110 deny tcp any host  172.16.30.2 eq ?
  <0-65535>     Port number
  bgp           Border Gateway Protocol (179)
  chargen       Character generator (19)
  cmd           Remote commands (rcmd, 514)
  daytime       Daytime (13)
  discard       Discard (9)
  domain        Domain Name Service (53)
  echo          Echo (7)
  exec          Exec (rsh, 512)
  finger        Finger (79)
  ftp           File Transfer Protocol (21)
  ftp-data      FTP data connections (20, 21)
  gopher        Gopher (70)
  hostname      NIC hostname server (101)
  ident         Ident Protocol (113)
  irc           Internet Relay Chat (194)
  klogin        Kerberos login (543)
  kshell        Kerberos shell (544)
```

login	Login (rlogin, 513)
lpd	Printer service (515)
nntp	Network News Transport Protocol (119)
pim-auto-RP	PIM Auto-RP
pop2	Post Office Protocol v2 (109)
pop3	Post Office Protocol v3 (110)
smtp	Simple Mail Transport Protocol (25)
sunrpc	Sun Remote Procedure Call (111)
syslog	Syslog (514)
tacacs	TAC Access Control System (49)
talk	Talk (517)
telnet	Telnet (23)
time	Time (37)
uucp	Unix-to-Unix Copy Program (540)
whois	Nicname (43)
www	World Wide Web (HTTP, 80)

At this point, let's block Telnet (port 23) to host 172.16.30.2 only. If the users want to FTP, fine, that's allowed. The log command is used to log messages every time the access list is hit. This can be an extremely cool way to monitor inappropriate access attempts.

```
Lab_A(config)#access-list 110 deny tcp any host
  172.16.30.2 eq 23 log
```

You need to keep in mind that the next line is an implicit **deny any** by default. If you apply this access list to an interface, you might as well just shut the interface down, since by default, an implicit **deny all** appears at the end of every access list. You've got to follow up the access list with the following command:

```
Lab_A(config)#access-list 110 permit ip any any
```

Remember, the 0.0.0.0 255.255.255.255 is the same command as any, so the command could look like this:

```
Lab_A(config)#access-list 110 permit ip 0.0.0.0
  255.255.255.255 0.0.0.0 255.255.255.255
```

Once the access list is created, you need to apply it to an interface. It's the same command as the IP standard list:

```
Lab_A(config-if)#ip access-group 110 in
```

or

```
Lab_A(config-if)#ip access-group 110 out
```

Extended Access List Example 2

Using Figure 2.21 from the IP standard access list example again, let's use the same network and deny access to a host at 172.16.30.5 on the Finance LAN for both Telnet and FTP services. All other services on this and all other hosts are acceptable for the sales and marketing departments to access.

First, create the following access list:

```
Acme#config t
Acme(config)#access-list 110 deny tcp any host
   172.16.30.5 eq 21
Acme(config)#access-list 110 deny tcp any host
   172.16.30.5 eq 23
Acme(config)#access-list 110 permit ip any any
```

The access-list 110 tells the router you are creating an extended IP Access list. The tcp is the protocol field in the Network layer header. If the list doesn't say tcp here, you cannot filter by port numbers 21 and 23, as is shown in the example. (These are FTP and Telnet, and they both use TCP for connection-oriented services.) The any command is the source, which means any IP address, and the host is the destination IP address.

After the list is created, it needs to be applied to the Ethernet 1 interface outbound. This applies the policy we created to all hosts and effectively blocks all FTP and Telnet access to 172.16.30.5 from outside the local LAN. If this list was created only to block access from the Sales LAN, then you'd have put this list closer to the source, or on Ethernet interface 0. Here, you'd apply the list to inbound traffic. Go ahead and apply the list to interface E1 and block all outside FTP and Telnet access to the host:

```
Acme(config-if)#ip access-group 110 out
```

Named Access Lists

As I said, using named access lists is just another way to create standard and extended access lists. In medium to large enterprises, managing access lists can become, well, a real hassle over time. For example, when you need to make a change to an access list, a frequent practice is to copy the access list to a text editor, change the number, edit the list, and then paste the new list back into the router. With this done, you can then simply change the access list number on the interface from the old to the new access list. There is never a time on the network where an access list isn't in place.

This works pretty well if it weren't for what I call "packrat" mentality. You start asking yourself questions like the following: what do I do with the old access list? Delete it? Or should I save it in case I find a problem with the new list and need to back out of the change? What happens is that over time, through this and countless other scenarios, you end up with a whole bunch of unapplied access lists building up on a router. What were they for? Are they important? Do you need them? All good questions.

This can also apply to access lists that are up and running. Let's say that you come into an existing network and are looking at access lists on a router. Suppose you find an access list 177 (extended) that is 33 lines long. This could cause you much needless existential questioning—what is it for? Why is it here? Instead, wouldn't an access list called, say, Finance LAN be more descriptive than one that's named 177?

Named access lists allow you to use names to both create and apply either standard or extended access lists. There is nothing new or different about these access lists aside from that you are able to refer to them in a way that makes sense to humans. However, there are some subtle changes to the syntax, so let's re-create the standard access list you created earlier for your test network in Figure 2.21 using a named access list:

```
Acme#config t
Enter configuration commands, one per line.  End with CNTL/Z.
Acme(config)#ip access-list ?
  extended  Extended Acc
  logging   Control access list logging
  standard  Standard Access List
```

Notice that I started by typing **ip access-list**, not **access-list**. This allows me to enter a named access list. Next, I'll need to specify that it's to be a standard access list:

```
Acme(config)#ip access-list standard ?
  <1-99>  Standard IP access-list number
  WORD    Access-list name
```

```
Acme(config)#ip access-list standard BlockSales
Acme(config-std-nacl)#
```

Okay—I've specified a standard access list, and then added a name—BlockSales. Notice that I could've used a number for a standard access list, but instead, I chose to use a descriptive name. Also, notice that after entering the name, I hit return, and the router prompt changed. I'm now in named-access-list configuration mode, and am ready to enter the named access list. Let's go ahead and enter the list:

```
Acme(config-std-nacl)#?
Standard Access List configuration commands:
  default  Set a command to its defaults
  deny     Specify packets to reject
  exit     Exit from access-list configuration mode
  no       Negate a command or set its defaults
  permit   Specify packets to forward
```

```
Acme(config-std-nacl)#deny 172.16.40.0 0.0.0.255
```

```
Acme(config-std-nacl)#permit any
Acme(config-std-nacl)#exit
Acme(config)#^Z
Acme#
```

Here, I entered the access list, and then exited out of configuration mode. Next, let's take a look at the running configuration to verify that the access list is indeed in the router:

```
Acme#show running-config
...
!
ip access-list standard BlockSales
 deny    172.16.40.0 0.0.0.255
 permit any
!
...
```

Okay—you can see that the BlockSales access list has truly been created and is in the running-config of the router. Next, I'll need to apply the access list to an interface:

```
Acme#config t
Enter configuration commands, one per line.   End with CNTL/Z.
Acme(config)#int el
Acme(config-if)#ip access-group BlockSales out
Acme(config-if)#^Z
Acme#
```

Done—woohoo! At this point, you've re-created the work done earlier using named access lists.

Exam Essentials

Understand the standard IP access list configuration command.   To configure a standard IP access list, use the access-list numbers 1–99 or 1300–1999 in global configuration mode. Choose permit or deny, then choose the source IP address you want to filter on using one of the three techniques covered earlier (using the host, or any keywords, or wildcard masking).

Understand the extended IP access list configuration command.   To configure an extended IP access list, use the access-list numbers 100–199 or 2000–2699 in global configuration mode. Choose permit or deny, the Network layer protocol, the source IP address you want to filter on, the destination address you want to filter on, and finally the Transport layer protocol (if selected).

2.11 Implement Simple WAN Protocols

What is a simple WAN protocol? Are Frame Relay and ISDN simple? Not hardly! Prevalent, popular, widespread, significant—they are all of these things. But simple? I don't think so. For our purposes, simple WAN protocols are those covered on the CCNA exam. Just as I limited our LAN discussions to Ethernet, in the WAN, the CCNA focuses on PPP, ISDN/DDR, and Frame Relay.

In this section, I will begin by showing you some of technologies you can use to cable up the WAN. You'll also look at configuration of PPP and Frame Relay, and then finish up with Dial on Demand Routing (DDR). DDR is a way to provide backup connections; in the examples in this section, you'll configure DDR across ISDN connections.

Cabling the Wide Area Network

You need to know a couple of things (well, okay, more than a couple, but I'll start with these) in order to connect your WAN. First, you've got to understand the WAN Physical layer implementation provided by Cisco, and next, you must be familiar with the various types of WAN serial connectors.

Cisco serial connections support almost any type of WAN service. The typical WAN connections are dedicated leased lines that use High-Level Data Link Control (HDLC), Point-to-Point Protocol (PPP), Integrated Services Digital Network (ISDN), and Frame Relay. Typical speeds run at anywhere from 2400bps to 45Mbps (T3).

HDLC, PPP, and Frame Relay can use the same Physical layer specifications, but ISDN has different pinouts and specifications at the Physical layer.

Serial Transmission

WAN serial connectors use *serial transmission* that takes place one bit at a time, over a single channel. Parallel transmission can pass at least 8 bits at a time, but all WANs use serial transmission.

Cisco routers use a proprietary 60-pin serial connector that you have to buy from them or a provider of Cisco equipment. The type of connector you have on the other end of the cable depends on your service provider or end-device requirements. The different ends available are as follows:

- EIA/TIA-232
- EIA/TIA-449
- V.35 (used to connect to a CSU/DSU)
- X.21 (used in X.25)
- EIA-530

Serial links are described in frequency or cycles-per-second (hertz). The amount of data that can be carried within these frequencies is called *bandwidth*. Bandwidth is the amount of data in bits-per-second that the serial channel can carry.

Data Terminal Equipment and Data Communication Equipment

Router interfaces are, by default, DTE, and they connect into DCE like CSU/DSU. The CSU/DSU then plugs into a demarcation location (demarc) and is the service provider's last responsibility. Most of the time, the demarc is a jack that has an RJ-45 female connector located in a telecommunications closet. You may have heard of demarcs if you've ever had the glorious experience of reporting a problem to your service provider—they'll always tell you it tests fine up to the demarc, and that the problem must be the customer premise equipment (CPE). In other words, it's your problem, not theirs.

The idea behind a WAN is that you should be able to connect two DTE networks through a DCE network. The DCE network includes the CSU/DSU, through the provider's wiring and switches, all the way to the CSU/DSU at the other end. The network's DCE device provides clocking to the DTE-connected interface (the router's serial interface).

 Terms such as EIA/TIA-232, V.35, X.21, and HSSI (High-Speed Serial Interface), describe the physical layer between the DTE (router) and DCE device (CSU/DSU).

Fixed and Modular Interfaces

Some of the routers Cisco sells have fixed interfaces and others are modular. The fixed routers, such as the 2500 series, have set interfaces that can't be changed. The 2501 router has two serial connections and one 10BaseT AUI interface. If you need to add a third serial interface, then you need to buy a new router—ouch! However, the 1600, 1700, 2600, 3600, and higher routers have modular interfaces that allow you to buy what you need now and add almost any type of interface you may need later. The 1600 and 1700 are limited and have both fixed and modular ports, but the 2600 and up provide many serials, FastEthernet, and even voice-module availability—now we're talking!

Now it's time to get into the various WAN protocols and nail those down so that you can get on with configuring your Cisco routers.

Configuring PPP on Cisco Routers

Configuring PPP encapsulation on an interface is a pretty straightforward process. Just use these commands:

```
Router#config t
Enter configuration commands, one per line. End with CNTL/Z.
Router(config)#int s0
```

```
Router(config-if)#encapsulation ppp
Router(config-if)#^Z
Router#
```

Of course, PPP encapsulation must be enabled on both interfaces connected to a serial line to work. You get several additional configuration options by using the help command.

After you configure your serial interface to support PPP encapsulation, you can then configure authentication using PPP between routers. First set the hostname of the router if it's not already set. Then set the username and password for the remote router connecting to your router.

```
Router#config t
Enter configuration commands, one per line. End with CNTL/Z.
Router(config)#hostname RouterA
RouterA(config)#username RouterB password cisco
```

When using the hostname command, remember that the username is the hostname of the remote router connecting to your router, and that it's case sensitive. Also, the password on both routers must be the same—a plain-text password that you can see with a show run command. You can encrypt the password by using the command service password-encryption. You've got to have a username and password configured for each remote system you plan to connect to. The remote routers must also be configured with usernames and passwords.

After you set the hostname, usernames, and passwords, choose the authentication type, either Challenge Handshake Authentication Protocol (CHAP) or Password Authentication Protocol (PAP):

```
RouterA#config t
Enter configuration commands, one per line. End with CNTL/Z.
RouterA(config)#int s0
RouterA(config-if)#ppp authentication chap
RouterA(config-if)#ppp authentication pap
RouterA(config-if)#^Z
RouterA#
```

If both methods are configured as shown here, then only the first method will be used during link negotiation—the second is a backup if the first method fails.

Frame Relay Implementation

There are a ton of Frame Relay commands and configuration options, but I'm going to zero in on the ones you really need for the CCNA. I'm going to start with one of the simplest—two routers with a single permanent virtual circuit (PVC) between them. Next, I'll show you a more complex configuration using subinterfaces and demonstrate some of the monitoring commands that you can use to verify the configuration.

Single Interface

Okay—let's get started by looking at a simple example. Suppose that you just want to connect two routers with a single PVC. Here's how that configuration would look:

```
RouterA#config t
Enter configuration commands, one per line.  End with CNTL/Z.
RouterA(config)#int s0/0
RouterA(config-if)#encapsulation frame-relay
RouterA(config-if)#ip address 172.16.20.1 255.255.255.0
RouterA(config-if)#frame-relay lmi-type ansi
RouterA(config-if)#frame-relay interface-dlci 101
RouterA(config-if)#^Z
RouterA#
```

The first step is to specify the encapsulation as frame relay. Notice that since I didn't specify a specific type, Cisco or Internet Engineering Task Force (IETF), the Cisco default type was used. If the other router were non-Cisco, I would've specified IETF. Next, I assigned an IP address to the interface, then specified the Local Management Interface (LMI) type of ANSI (the default was Cisco) based on information provided by the telecommunications provider. Finally, I added the Data Link Connection Identifier (DLCI) of 101 that indicates the PVC you wish to use—assuming there's only one PVC on this physical interface.

Okay—that's it! Well, it's a start at least. Assuming that both sides are configured correctly, the circuit will come up. Next, I'll give you a slightly more complex configuration example.

Subinterfaces

As I said, you can have multiple virtual circuits on a single serial interface and yet treat each as a separate interface. This is accomplished by creating subinterfaces. Think of a subinterface as a logical interface defined by the IOS software. Several subinterfaces will share a single hardware interface, yet for configuration purposes, they operate as if they were separate physical interfaces.

You define subinterfaces using the int s0.subinterface number command as shown in the following code. After you first set the encapsulation on the serial interface, you can then define the subinterfaces—generally one subinterface per PVC:

```
RouterA(config)#int s0
RouterA(config-if)#encapsulation frame-relay
RouterA(config-if)#int s0.?
  <0-4294967295>  Serial interface number
RouterA(config-if)#int s0.16 ?
  multipoint      Treat as a multipoint link
  point-to-point  Treat as a point-to-point link
RouterA(config-if)#int s0.16 point-to-point
```

You can define a nearly limitless number of subinterfaces on a given physical interface, keeping in mind that there are only 1000ish available DLCIs. In the preceding example, I chose to use subinterface 16 because that represents the DLCI number assigned to that PVC by the carrier. There are two types of subinterfaces:

Point-to-point   Used when a single virtual circuit connects one router to another. Each point-to-point subinterface requires its own subnet.

Multipoint   Used when the router is the center of a star of virtual circuits. Uses a single subnet for all routers' serial interfaces connected to the frame switch.

I'm going to show you an example of a production router running multiple subinterfaces next. In the following output, notice that the subinterface number matches the DLCI number. This isn't a requirement, but it helps with the administration of the interfaces. Also notice that there's no LMI type defined. This means they're running either the Cisco default, or using auto-detect (if running Cisco IOS version 11.2 or newer). This configuration was taken from one of my customers' production routers—used with their permission, of course! Notice that each interface is defined as a separate subnet, separate IPX network, and separate AppleTalk cable range. (IPX and AppleTalk configuration are beyond the scope of this exam):

```
interface Serial0
 no ip address
 no ip directed-broadcast
 encapsulation frame-relay
!
interface Serial0.102 point-to-point
 ip address 10.1.12.1 255.255.255.0
 no ip directed-broadcast
 appletalk cable-range 12-12 12.65
 appletalk zone wan2
 appletalk protocol eigrp
 no appletalk protocol rtmp
 ipx network 12
 frame-relay interface-dlci 102
!
interface Serial0.103 point-to-point
 ip address 10.1.13.1 255.255.255.0
 no ip directed-broadcast
 appletalk cable-range 13-13 13.174
 appletalk zone wan3
 appletalk protocol eigrp
 no appletalk protocol rtmp
 ipx network 13
```

```
 frame-relay interface-dlci 103
!
interface Serial0.104 point-to-point
 ip address 10.1.14.1 255.255.255.0
 no ip directed-broadcast
 appletalk cable-range 14-14 14.131
 appletalk zone wan4
 appletalk protocol eigrp
 no appletalk protocol rtmp
 ipx network 14
 frame-relay interface-dlci 104
!
interface Serial0.105 point-to-point
 ip address 10.1.15.1 255.255.255.0
 no ip directed-broadcast
 appletalk cable-range 15-15 15.184
 appletalk zone wan5
 appletalk protocol eigrp
 no appletalk protocol rtmp
 ipx network 15
 frame-relay interface-dlci 105
!
interface Serial0.106 point-to-point
 ip address 10.1.16.1 255.255.255.0
 no ip directed-broadcast
 appletalk cable-range 16-16 16.28
 appletalk zone wan6
 appletalk protocol eigrp
 no appletalk protocol rtmp
 ipx network 16
 frame-relay interface-dlci 106
!
interface Serial0.107 point-to-point
 ip address 10.1.17.1 255.255.255.0
 no ip directed-broadcast
 appletalk cable-range 17-17 17.223
 appletalk zone wan7
 appletalk protocol eigrp
 no appletalk protocol rtmp
```

```
 ipx network 17
 frame-relay interface-dlci 107
!
interface Serial0.108 point-to-point
 ip address 10.1.18.1 255.255.255.0
 no ip directed-broadcast
 appletalk cable-range 18-18 18.43
 appletalk zone wan8
 appletalk protocol eigrp
 no appletalk protocol rtmp
 ipx network 18
 frame-relay interface-dlci 108
```

Dial-on-Demand Routing (DDR)

You can use *dial-on-demand routing (DDR)* to allow two or more Cisco routers to dial an ISDN dial-up connection on an as-needed basis. DDR is only used for low-volume, periodic network connections using either a public switched telephone network (PSTN) or ISDN. This was designed to reduce WAN costs if you have to pay on a per-minute or per-packet basis.

DDR works when a packet received on an interface meets the requirements of an access list defined by an administrator, which defines interesting traffic. The following five steps give a basic description of how DDR works when an interesting packet is received in a router interface:

1. Route to the destination network is determined.

2. Interesting packets dictate a DDR call.

3. Dialer information is looked up.

4. Traffic is transmitted.

5. Call is terminated when no more traffic is being transmitted over a link and the idle-timeout period ends.

Configuring DDR

To configure legacy DDR, you need to perform three tasks:

1. Define static routes, which define how to get to the remote networks and what interface to use to get there.

2. Specify the traffic that is considered interesting to the router.

3. Configure the dialer information that will be used to dial the interface to get to the remote network.

Configuring Static Routes

To forward traffic across the ISDN link, you configure static routes in each of the routers. You certainly can configure dynamic routing protocols to run on your ISDN link, but then the link never drops. So the better choice would be static routes. Keep the following in mind when you are creating static routes:

- All participating routers must have static routes defining all routes of known networks.
- Default routing can be used if the network is a stub network.

Here's an example of static routing with ISDN:

```
RouterA(config)#ip route 172.16.50.0 255.255.255.0
  172.16.60.2
RouterA(config)#ip route 172.16.60.2 255.255.255.255 bri0
```

What this does is tell the router how to get to network 172.16.50.0 through 172.16.60.2. The second line tells the router how to get to 172.16.60.2.

Specifying Interesting Traffic

After setting the route tables in each router, you need to configure the router to determine what brings up the ISDN line. An administrator using the `dialer-list` global configuration command defines interesting packets.

The command to turn on all IP traffic is shown in this output:

```
804A(config)#dialer-list 1 protocol ip permit
804A(config)#int bri0
804A(config-if)#dialer-group 1
```

The `dialer-group` command sets the access list on the BRI interface. Extended access lists can be used with the `dialer-list` command to define interesting traffic to just certain applications. I'll cover that in a minute.

> If you use the `dialer-list` command, you must enter the `dialer-group` command on an interface before this will work!

Configuring the Dialer Information

There are five steps to configuring the dialer information:

1. Choose the interface.
2. Set the IP address.
3. Configure the encapsulation type.
4. Link interesting traffic to the interface.
5. Configure the number or numbers to dial.

Here's how to configure those five steps:

```
804A#config t
804A(config)#int bri0
804A(config-if)#ip address 172.16.60.1 255.255.255.0
804A(config-if)#no shut
804A(config-if)#encapsulation ppp
804A(config-if)#dialer-group 1
804A(config-if)#dialer string 8350661
```

Instead of the dialer string command, you can use a dialer map. It provides more security.

```
804A(config-if)#dialer map ip 172.16.60.2 name 804B
   8350661
```

You can use the dialer map command with the dialer-group command and its associated access list to initiate dialing. The dialer map command uses the IP address of the next hop router, the hostname of the remote router for authentication, and then the number to dial to get there.

The five basic Dialer Map steps that you must be aware of are:

1. Dialer
2. Map
3. Protocol
4. Next hop
5. Dial string

Remember, the dialer map command is used to associate an ISDN phone number with the next hop router address.

Take a look at the configuration of an 804 router:

```
804B#sh run
Building configuration...
Current configuration:
!
version 12.0
no service pad
service timestamps debug uptime
service timestamps log uptime
no service password-encryption
!
```

```
hostname 804B
!
ip subnet-zero
!
isdn switch-type basic-ni
!
interface Ethernet0
 ip address 172.16.50.10 255.255.255.0
 no ip directed-broadcast
!
interface BRI0
 ip address 172.16.60.2 255.255.255.0
 no ip directed-broadcast
 encapsulation ppp
 dialer idle-timeout 300
 dialer string 8358661
 dialer load-threshold 2 either
 dialer-group 1
 isdn switch-type basic-ni
 isdn spid1 0835866201 8358662
 isdn spid2 0835866401 8358664
 hold-queue 75 in
!
ip classless
ip route 172.16.30.0 255.255.255.0 172.16.60.1
ip route 172.16.60.1 255.255.255.255 BRI0
!
dialer-list 1 protocol ip permit
!
```

What can you determine by looking at this output? Well, first, the BRI interface is running the PPP encapsulation, and it has a timeout value of 300 seconds. The load-threshold command makes both BRI interfaces come up immediately—hey, I feel that if I am paying for both, I want them both up all the time! The one thing you really want to notice is the dialer-group 1 command. That number must match the dialer-list number. The hold-queue 75 in command tells the router that when it receives an interesting packet, it should queue up to 75 packets while it's waiting for the BRI to come up. If there are more than 75 packets queued before the link comes up, the packets will be dropped.

Optional Commands

There are two other commands that you should configure on your BRI interface: the `dialer load-threshold` command and the `dialer idle-timeout` command.

The `dialer load-threshold` command tells the BRI interface when to bring up the second B channel. The option is from 1 to 255, where 255 tells the BRI to bring up the second B channel only when the first channel is 100 percent loaded. The second option for that command is in, out, or either. This calculates the actual load on the interface either on outbound traffic, inbound traffic, or combined. The default is outbound.

The `dialer idle-timeout` command specifies the number of seconds before a call is disconnected after the last interesting traffic is sent. The default is 120 seconds.

```
RouterA(config-if)#dialer load-threshold 125 either
RouterA(config-if)#dialer idle-timeout 180
```

The `dialer load-threshold 125` tells the BRI interface to bring up the second B channel if either the inbound or outbound traffic load is 50 percent. The `dialer idle-timeout 180` changes the default disconnect time from 120 to 180 seconds.

DDR with Access Lists

You can use access lists to be more specific about what is, or is not interesting traffic. In the preceding example you just set the dialer list to allow any IP traffic to bring up the line. That's great if you're testing, but it can defeat the purpose of why you use a DDR line in the first place. You can use extended access lists to set the restriction, for instance, to only e-mail or Telnet.

Here's how you define the dialer list to use an access list:

```
804A(config)#dialer-list 1 list 110
804A(config)#access-list 110 permit tcp any any eq smtp
804A(config)#access-list 110 permit tcp any any eq telnet
804A(config)#int bri0
804A(config-if)#dialer-group 1
```

I configured the `dialer-list` command to look at an access list. This doesn't have to be IP—it can be used with any protocol. Create your list, then apply it to the BRI interface with the `dialer-group` command.

Exam Essentials

Know the commands for PPP encapsulation. You can use the `encapsulation ppp` command on a serial interface to change from HDLC to PPP encapsulation. Also, you can further configure authentication using the `ppp authentication` command.

Know the commands for Frame Relay encapsulation. You can use the `encapsulation frame-relay` command on a serial interface to change the encapsulation to Frame Relay. Additionally, you will need to configure DLCI information, LMI and encapsulation types if they will differ from the default, and potentially subinterfaces if you will have multiple PVCs per physical interface.

Understand the five basis dialer map steps for configuring DDR. The five steps are as follows:

1. Dialer
2. Map
3. Protocol
4. Next hop
5. Dial string

Review Questions

1. How is EIGRP implemented on a router?

   A. `ip router eigrp` *as*

   B. `router ip eigrp` *as*

   C. `router eigrp` *process-id*

   D. `router eigrp` *as*

2. Which of the following commands will display a backup configuration?

   A. `sh running-config`

   B. `show startup-config`

   C. `show version`

   D. `show backup-config`

3. Which command will show you whether a DTE or DCE cable is plugged into Serial 0?

   A. `sh int s0`

   B. `sh int serial 0`

   C. `sho controllers s 0`

   D. `sho controllers s0`

4. Which command will copy the IOS to a backup host on your network?

   A. `transfer IOS to 172.16.10.1`

   B. `copy run start`

   C. `copy tftp flash`

   D. `copy start tftp`

   E. `copy flash tftp`

5. Which command will copy a router configuration stored on a TFTP host to the router's NVRAM?

   A. `transfer IOS to 172.16.10.1`

   B. `copy run start`

   C. `copy tftp startup`

   D. `copy tftp run`

   E. `copy flash tftp`

6. If you configure the following access list:

```
access-list 110 deny 10.1.1.128 0.0.0.63 eq smtp
access-list 110 deny any any eq 23
int ethernet 0
ip access-group 110 out
```

What will the result of this access list be?

A. E-mail and Telnet will be allowed out E0.

B. E-mail and Telnet will be allowed in E0.

C. Everything but e-mail and Telnet will be allowed out E0.

D. No IP traffic will be allowed out E0.

7. Which of the following series of commands will restrict Telnet access to the router?

A. Lab_A(config)#**access-list 10 permit 172.16.1.1**
Lab_A(config)#**line con 0**
Lab_A(config-line)#**ip access-group 10 in**

B. Lab_A(config)#**access-list 10 permit 172.16.1.1**
Lab_A(config)#**line vty 0 4**
Lab_A(config-line)#**access-class 10 out**

C. Lab_A(config)#**access-list 10 permit 172.16.1.1**
Lab_A(config)#**line vty 0 4**
Lab_A(config-line)#**access-class 10 in**

D. Lab_A(config)#**access-list 10 permit 172.16.1.1**
Lab_A(config)#**line vty 0 4**
Lab_A(config-line)#**ip access-group 10 in**

8. What is the default encapsulation type for Frame Relay in a Cisco router?

A. HDLC

B. IEFT

C. Cisco

D. PPP

E. Ansi

F. Q933i

9. Which of the following are the five basic steps to set up a dialer map command string?

   A. Dial-string, dialer, map, protocol, next-hop

   B. Dialer, dial-string, map, protocol, next hop

   C. Dialer, map, protocol, next hop, dial string

   D. Dialer, map, next-hop, protocol, dial-string

10. Which of the following are valid PPP authentication methods? (Choose two options.)

   A. LCP

   B. PAP

   C. CHAP

   D. MD5

Answers to Review Questions

1. **D.** The command `router eigrp` followed by the autonomous system number is used to implement EIGRP. Process numbers are not used by EIGRP. All of the other command options have radically incorrect command syntax.

2. **B.** The `show startup-config` command will display the configuration that will be loaded the next time the router is booted.

3. **C.** The `show controllers serial 0` command will show you whether either a DTE or DCE cable is connected to the interface.

4. **E.** To copy the IOS to a backup host, which is stored in flash memory by default, use the `copy flash tftp` command.

5. **C.** To copy a configuration of a router stored on a TFTP host to a router's NVRAM, use the `copy tftp startup-config` command.

6. **D.** If you add an access list to an interface and you do not have at least one permit statement, then you will effectively shut down the interface because of the implicit **deny any** at the end of every list.

7. **C.** Telnet access to the router is restricted by using either a standard or extended IP access list to the VTY lines on the router. The command `access-class` is used to apply the access list to the VTY lines.

8. **C.** If you just type from interface configuration mode, `encapsulation frame-relay`, the encapsulation type will be Cisco.

9. **C.** The five basic Dialer Map steps that you must be aware of are:
   1. Dialer
   2. Map
   3. Protocol
   4. Next hop
   5. Dial string

10. **B, C.** PAP and CHAP are valid authentication methods available to PPP authentication.

Chapter

3

Troubleshooting

CISCO CCNA EXAM OBJECTIVES COVERED IN THIS CHAPTER:

✓ **3.1 Utilize the OSI model as a guide for systematic network troubleshooting**

✓ **3.2 Perform LAN and VLAN troubleshooting**

✓ **3.3 Troubleshoot routing protocols**

✓ **3.4 Troubleshoot IP addressing and host configuration**

✓ **3.5 Troubleshoot a device as part of a working network**

✓ **3.6 Troubleshoot an access list**

✓ **3.7 Perform simple WAN troubleshooting**

When networks first came into being, computers could typically communicate only with computers from the same manufacturer. For example, companies ran either a complete DECnet solution or an IBM solution—not both together. In the late 1970s, the International Organization for Standardization (ISO) created the Open Systems Interconnection (OSI) reference model to break this barrier.

3.1 Utilize the OSI Model as a Guide for Systematic Network Troubleshooting

When networks first came into being, computers could typically communicate only with computers from the same manufacturer. For example, companies ran either a complete DECnet solution or an IBM solution—not both together. In the late 1970s, the International Organization for Standardization (ISO) created the Open Systems Interconnection (OSI) reference model to break this barrier.

The OSI model was meant to help vendors create interoperable network devices and software in the form of protocols so that different vendor networks could work with each other. Like world peace, it'll probably never happen completely, but it's still a great goal.

The OSI model is the primary architectural model for networks. It describes how data and network information are communicated from an application on one computer, through the network media, to an application on another computer. The OSI reference model breaks this approach into layers.

In this section, we will look at the OSI layered approach and it's practical implications on real-world networks—the five steps of data encapsulation. Understanding the five steps of data encapsulation is crucial in real-world troubleshooting.

The Layered Approach

A *reference model* is a conceptual blueprint of how communications should take place. It addresses all the processes required for effective communication and divides these processes into logical groupings called *layers*. When a communication system is designed in this manner, it's known as *layered architecture*.

Think of it like this: you and some friends want to start a company. One of the first things you'd do is sit down and think through what tasks must be done, who will do them, what order they will be done in, and how they relate to each other. Ultimately, you might group these tasks into departments. Let's say you decide to have an order-taking department, an inventory department, and a shipping department. Each of your departments has its own unique tasks, keeping its staff members busy and requiring them to focus on only their own duties.

In this scenario, I'm using departments as a metaphor for the layers in a communication system. For things to run smoothly, the staff of each department has to trust and rely heavily upon the others to do their jobs and competently handle their unique responsibilities. In your planning sessions, you should probably take notes, recording the entire process to facilitate later discussions about standards of operation that will serve as your business blueprint, or reference model.

Okay, once your business is launched, your department heads, armed with the part of the blueprint that relates to their department, will need to develop practical methods to implement their assigned tasks. These practical methods, or *protocols*, will need to be compiled into a standard operating procedures manual and followed closely. Each of the various procedures in your manual will have been included for different reasons and have varying degrees of importance and implementation. If you form a partnership or acquire another company, it will be imperative for its business protocols—its business blueprint—to match yours (or at least be compatible with it).

 The seven layers of the OSI model are discussed in detail in Chapter 4, "Technology."

Similarly, software developers can use a reference model to understand computer communication processes and see what types of functions need to be accomplished on any one layer. If they are developing a protocol for a certain layer, all they need to concern themselves with is the specific layer's functions, not those of any other layer. Another layer and protocol will handle the other functions. The technical term for this idea is *binding*. The communication processes that are related to each other are bound, or grouped together, at a particular layer.

Advantages of Reference Models

The OSI is hierarchical, and the benefits and advantages of this type of model can apply to any layered model. The primary purpose of all models, especially the OSI model, is to allow different vendors' networks to interoperate.

Advantages of using the OSI layered model include, but are not limited to, the following:

- Allows multiple-vendor development through standardization of network components
- Allows various types of network hardware and software to communicate
- Prevents changes in one layer from affecting other layers, so it does not hamper development

The implications of layered models have significant impact on troubleshooting scenarios. Since changes in one layer do not affect other layers, if you can successfully identify which layer of a layered model is causing the problem, you can safely rule out the components of other layers (assuming you only have one problem, which is not always the case!). For example, if you know you have a TCP tuning problem (Layer 4), you can rule out Ethernet configuration (Layer 2) and IP addressing (Layer 3). This allows you to focus on the real problem and not waste time addressing layers that are already working and are not contributing to the problem. Layered models contribute directly to problem isolation in troubleshooting scenarios.

Next I will explain how the layered OSI model applies in network communications. This process is called *data encapsulation.*

Data Encapsulation

When a host transmits data across a network to another device, the data goes through encapsulation: it is wrapped with protocol information at each layer of the OSI model. Each layer communicates only with its peer layer on the receiving device.

To communicate and exchange information, each layer uses Protocol Data Units (PDUs). These hold the control information attached to the data at each layer of the model. They are usually attached to the header in front of the data field, but they can also be in the trailer, or end, of it.

Each PDU is attached to the data by encapsulating it at each layer of the OSI model, and each has a specific name depending on the information provided in each header. This PDU information is only read by the peer layer on the receiving device. After it's read, it's stripped off, and the data is then handed to the next layer up.

Figure 3.1 shows the PDUs and how they attach control information to each layer. This figure demonstrates how the upper-layer user data is converted for transmission on the network. The data stream is then handed down to the Transport layer, which sets up a virtual circuit to the receiving device by sending over a synch packet. The data stream is then broken up into smaller pieces, and a Transport layer header (a PDU) is created and attached to the header of the data field; now the piece of data is called a *segment.* Each segment is sequenced so the data stream can be put back together on the receiving side exactly as it was transmitted.

FIGURE 3.1   Data encapsulation

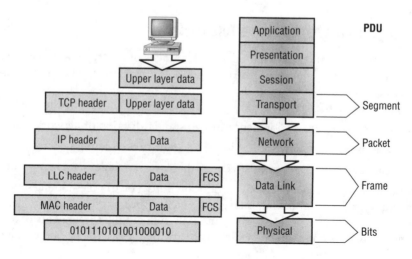

Each segment is then handed to the Network layer for network addressing and routing through the internetwork. Logical addressing (for example, Internet Protocol [IP]) is used to get each segment to the correct network. The Network layer protocol adds a control header to the segment handed down from the Transport layer, and what you have at this point is called a *packet* or *datagram*. Remember that the Transport and Network layers work together to rebuild a data stream on a receiving host, but it's not part of their work to place their PDUs on a local network segment—which is the only way to get the information to a router or host.

It's the Data Link layer that's responsible for taking packets from the Network layer and placing them on the network medium (cable or wireless). The Data Link layer encapsulates each packet in a frame, and the frame's header carries the hardware address of the source and destination hosts. If the destination device is on a remote network, then the frame is sent to a router to be routed through an internetwork. Once it gets to the destination network, a new frame is used to get the packet to the destination host.

To put this frame on the network, you must first put it into a digital signal. Since a frame is really a logical group of 1s and 0s, the Physical layer is responsible for encoding these digits into a digital signal, which is read by devices on the same local network. The receiving devices synchronize on the digital signal and extract (decode) the ones and zeros from the digital signal. At this point, the devices build the frames, run a cyclic redundancy check (CRC), and then check their answer against the answer in the frame's frame check sequence (FCS) field. If it matches, the packet is pulled from the frame, and what's left of the frame is discarded. This process is called *de-encapsulation*. The packet is handed to the Network layer, where the address is checked. If the address matches, the segment is pulled from the packet, and what's left of the packet is discarded. The segment is processed at the Transport layer, which rebuilds the data stream and acknowledges to the transmitting station that it received each piece. It then happily hands the data stream to the upper-layer application.

To summarize, at a transmitting device, the data encapsulation method works like this:

1. User information is converted to data for transmission on the network.

2. Data is converted to segments and a reliable connection is set up between the transmitting and receiving hosts.

3. Segments are converted to packets or datagrams, and a logical address is placed in the header so that each packet can be routed through an internetwork.

4. Packets or datagrams are converted to frames for transmission on the local network. Hardware (Ethernet) addresses are used to uniquely identify hosts on a local network segment.

5. Frames are converted to bits, and a digital encoding and clocking scheme is used.

The receiving device will follow these steps in reverse order to de-encapsulate the user information.

In real-world troubleshooting scenarios, understanding these steps of data encapsulation is probably the most important skill that derives from the OSI layered model. In many problem situations, you end up looking at packet traces or *sniffer traces* as they are often called. Sniffer is actually one of many tools called protocol analyzers that can capture frames from a wire and display them. These tools are able to analyze the headers on the PDUs, and display the frame, packet, segment, and often data headers. However, they don't always *explain* the headers, and thus a clear understanding of data encapsulation is required to understand the information they present.

Exam Essentials

Remember that the OSI model is a layered approach.   Functions are divided into layers, and the layers are bound together. This allows layers to operate transparently to each other; that is, changes in one layer should not impact other layers.

Know the steps of data encapsulation.   User information is encapsulated to data, data to segments, segments to packets or datagrams, packets or datagrams to frames, and frames to bits.

3.2 Perform LAN and VLAN Troubleshooting

When troubleshooting a VLAN environment you will use a variety of techniques. Remember that each VLAN is a separate subnet, and that all communications between VLANS must be routed. Therefore, troubleshooting communications between VLANS is the same as trouble-shooting any other routing issue between subnets (we'll cover troubleshooting IP addressing and routing shortly). Validation of trunking protocols (ISL, 802.1q) and Spanning Tree Protocol (STP) configurations is also required (these are covered in Chapters 2 and 4). Initially, you will probably end up looking at which VLANs are configured on a switch, and which ports are in those VLANs. Mapping which ports are in which VLANs will almost always be the starting point for troubleshooting LAN/VLAN issues.

On a Catalyst 1900, you can verify VLAN configuration with the `show vlan` command (`sh vlan` for short):

```
1900#sh vlan

VLAN Name              Status     Ports
-------------------------------------
1    default           Enabled    1-12, AUI, A, B
2    sales             Enabled
3    marketing         Enabled
4    mis               Enabled
1002 fddi-default      Suspended
1003 token-ring-defau  Suspended
1004 fddinet-default   Suspended
1005 trnet-default     Suspended
-------------------------------------
[output cut]
```

On a Catalyst 2950, you must examine the contents of the VLAN database. To see the VLAN database, use the `show vlan` command or the `show vlan brief` command:

Switch#**sh vlan brief**

VLAN	Name	Status	Ports
1	default	active	Fa0/1, Fa0/2, Fa0/3, Fa0/4 Fa0/7, Fa0/8, Fa0/9, Fa0/10 Fa0/11, Fa0/12
2	Marketing	active	
3	Accounting	active	
4	Shipping	active	
21	VLAN0021	active	
22	VLAN0022	active	
51	VLAN0051	active	
52	VLAN0052	active	
1002	fddi-default	active	
1003	token-ring-default	active	
1004	fddinet-default	active	
1005	trnet-default	active	

Switch#

Remember that VLAN Trunk Protocol (VTP) can dynamically make changes to the VLAN configuration on a switch if it is enabled. You can check the status of VTP with the `show vtp` command:

```
SwitchA#sh vtp ?
  counters  VTP statistics
  status    VTP domain status

SwitchA#sh vtp status
VTP Version                     : 2
Configuration Revision          : 1
Maximum VLANs supported locally : 64
Number of existing VLANs        : 7
VTP Operating Mode              : Server
VTP Domain Name                 : routersim
VTP Pruning Mode                : Disabled
VTP V2 Mode                     : Disabled
VTP Traps Generation            : Disabled
```

```
MD5 digest                      : 0x4C 0x60 0xA6 0x5D 0xD7 0x41 0x8C 0x37
Configuration last modified by 172.16.10.1 at 3-1-94 06:40:09
Local updater ID is 172.16.10.1 on interface Vl1 (lowest numbered VLAN interface
found)
```

Exam Essentials

Know the commands to find which VLANs are configured on a switch   Use the show vlan command on the Catalyst 1900 to see the configured VLANs, or use the same command on the Catalyst 2950 to examine the contents of the VLAN database.

Know the implications of VTP   Changes to VLAN configurations can propagate between switches; your VTP mode must be transparent if you do not want your switches to participate in VTP.

3.3 Troubleshoot Routing Protocols

Troubleshooting routing protocols and issues is, in many ways, one of the most fundamental skills you are expected to develop as a CCNA. After all, if routers don't route, what else really matters? In this section, we will look at a few general commands to troubleshoot routing protocols, and then take a closer look at each of the four routing protocols covered by the CCNA exam.

It's important to verify your configurations once you've completed them, or at least once you *think* you've completed them. The same commands are used to troubleshoot routing protocols that are used to verify them. These commands tell you if the router is, well, routing. The following list includes the commands you can use to verify the routed and routing protocols configured on your Cisco routers.

The show ip route command   This command is one of the most frequently used commands; it displays the current contents of the routing table.

```
Lab_A#sh ip route
[output cut]
Gateway of last resort is not set
D    192.168.30.0/24 [90/2172416] via 192.168.20.2,00:04:36, Serial0/0
C    192.168.10.0/24 is directly connected, FastEthernet0/0
D    192.168.40.0/24 [90/2681856] via 192.168.20.2,00:04:36, Serial0/0
C    192.168.20.0/24 is directly connected, Serial0/0
D    192.168.50.0/24 [90/2707456] via 192.168.20.2,00:04:35, Serial0/0
Lab_A#
```

The `show protocols` **command** This command is useful because it displays all the routed protocols and the interfaces upon which the protocol is enabled.

```
Lab_B#sh protocol
Global values:
  Internet Protocol routing is enabled
FastEthernet0 is up, line protocol is up
  Internet address is 192.168.30.1/24
Serial0/0 is up, line protocol is up
  Internet address is 192.168.20.2/24
Serial0/1 is up, line protocol is up
  Internet address is 192.168.40.1/24
Lab_B#
```

This output shows the IP address of the FastEthernet 0/0, Serial 0/0, and Serial 0/1 interfaces of the Lab_B router. If IPX or AppleTalk were configured on the router, those network addresses would've appeared as well.

The `show ip protocol` **command** The `show ip protocol` command shows you the routing protocols that are configured on your router. If you look at the following output, you can see that both Routing Information Protocol (RIP) and Interior Gateway Routing Protocol (IGRP) are running on the router, but that only IGRP appears in the routing table because of its lower administrative distance (AD).

The `show ip protocols` command also displays the timers used in the routing protocol. Now take a look in the next section of output; you can see that RIP is sending updates every 30 seconds—the default. Further down, you'll notice that RIP is routing for all directly connected networks, and the two neighbors it found are 192.168.40.2 and 192.168.20.1.

```
Lab_B#sh ip protocols
Routing Protocol is "rip"
  Sending updates every 30 seconds, next due in 6 seconds
  Invalid after 180 seconds, hold down 180, flushed after
  240
  Outgoing update filter list for all interfaces is
  Incoming update filter list for all interfaces is
  Redistributing: rip
  Default version control: send version 1, receive any
  version
    Interface        Send  Recv   Key-chain
    FastEthernet0     1     1 2
    Serial0/0         1     1 2
    Serial0/1         1     1 2
```

```
Routing for Networks:
  192.168.10.0
  192.168.20.0
  192.168.30.0
Routing Information Sources:
  Gateway          Distance     Last Update
  192.168.40.2        120       00:00:21
  192.168.20.1        120       00:00:23
Distance: (default is 120)
Routing Protocol is "igrp 10"
  Sending updates every 90 seconds, next due in 42 seconds
  Invalid after 270 seconds, hold down 280, flushed after
  630
  Outgoing update filter list for all interfaces is
  Incoming update filter list for all interfaces is
  Default networks flagged in outgoing updates
  Default networks accepted from incoming updates
  IGRP metric weight K1=1, K2=0, K3=1, K4=0, K5=0
  IGRP maximum hopcount 100
  IGRP maximum metric variance 1
  Redistributing: eigrp 10, igrp 10
  Routing for Networks:
    192.168.10.0
    192.168.20.0
    192.168.30.0
  Routing Information Sources:
    Gateway          Distance     Last Update
    192.168.40.2        100       00:00:47
    192.168.20.1        100       00:01:18
  Distance: (default is 100)
```

The information included in the show ip protocols command includes the autonomous system (AS), routing timers, networks being advertised, gateways, and AD (100).

You can use these commands on all IP routing protocols; basically, regardless of which routing protocol you are running, these can and should be used. What's next? Now I'll talk about some specific commands you can use with individual routing protocols to further troubleshoot their operation. These commands, including their associated debug commands, are specific to the routing protocols mentioned. I'll begin with Routing Information Protocol (RIP) and then look at Interior Gateway Routing Protocol (IGRP), Enhanced Interior Gateway Routing Protocol (EIGRP), and Open Shortest Path First (OSPF).

Troubleshooting RIP

Occasionally, the commands we just discussed will not be sufficient to figure out what is happening. When you need to look more thoroughly at what RIP is doing, you can use debug commands to monitor RIP events on the router.

The debug ip rip command sends information about routing updates as they are sent and received by the router to the console session. If you are telnetted into the router, you'll need to use the terminal monitor command to be able to receive the output from the debug commands.

In the following output, you can see that RIP is both sent and received on Serial 0/0 and Serial 0/1 interfaces. This is a sweet troubleshooting tool! The metric is the hop count.

```
Lab_B#debug ip rip
RIP protocol debugging is on
Lab_B#
07:12:56: RIP: received v1 update from 192.168.40.2 on
  Serial0/1
07:12:56:       192.168.50.0 in 1 hops
07:12:56: RIP: received v1 update from 192.168.20.1 on
  Serial0/0
07:12:56:       192.168.10.0 in 1 hops
```

In the preceding debug output, notice the route updates received on the Lab_B serial 0/0 and serial 0/1 interfaces. These are from routers Lab_A and Lab_C, respectively. What's important to nail here is that split-horizon rules stop the Lab_A and Lab_C routers from advertising back routes that they learned from Lab_B. This means that only network 192.168.50.0 is being advertised from Lab_C, and 192.168.10.0 is being advertised to Lab_B from Lab_A. Here is another debug.

```
07:12:58: RIP: sending v1 update to 255.255.255.255 via
  FastEthernet0/0 (192.168.30.1)
07:12:58:       subnet 192.168.50.0, metric 1
07:12:58:       subnet 192.168.40.0, metric 1
07:12:58:       subnet 192.168.20.0, metric 1
07:12:58:       subnet 192.168.10.0, metric 1
07:12:58: RIP: sending v1 update to 255.255.255.255 via
  Serial0/0 (172.16.20.2)
07:12:58:       subnet 192.168,50.0, metric 1
07:12:58:       subnet 192.168.40.0, metric 1
07:12:58:       subnet 192.168.30.0, metric 1
07:12:58: RIP: sending v1 update to 255.255.255.255 via
  Serial0/1 (172.16.40.1)
07:12:58:       subnet 192.168.30.0, metric 1
07:12:58:       subnet 192.168.20.0, metric 1
07:12:58:       subnet 192.168.10.0, metric 1
```

In the preceding output, split-horizon rules only allow networks 192.168.30.0, 40, and 50 to be advertised to Lab_A. Router Lab_B will not advertise the 192.168.10.0 network back to the Lab_A router, nor 192.168.50.0 back to Lab_C. Let's close down the debugger.

If the metric of a route shows 16, this is a route poison, and the route being advertised is unreachable.

```
Lab_B#undebug all
All possible debugging has been turned off
Lab_B#
```

To turn off debugging, use the undebug all or the no debug all command. You can also use the un all shortcut command.

Troubleshooting IGRP

With the debug ip igrp command, there are two options, events and transactions, as shown in this output:

```
Lab_B#debug ip igrp ?
  events         IGRP protocol events
  transactions  IGRP protocol transactions
```

The difference between these commands is explained in the following sections.

The *Debug IP IGRP Events* Command

The debug ip igrp events command is a summary of the IGRP routing information that is running on the network. The following router output shows the source and destination of each update as well as the number of routers in each update. Information about individual routes isn't something you'll get with this command.

```
Lab_B#debug ip igrp events
IGRP event debugging is on
07:13:50: IGRP: received request from 192.168.40.2 on
  Serial0/1
07:13:50: IGRP: sending update to 192.168.40.2 via Serial1
  (192.168.40.1)
07:13:51: IGRP: Update contains 3 interior, 0 system, and
  0 exterior routes.
```

```
07:13:51: IGRP: Total routes in update: 3
07:13:51: IGRP: received update from 192.168.40.2 on
  Serial0/1
07:13:51: IGRP: Update contains 1 interior, 0 system, and
  0 exterior routes.
07:13:51: IGRP: Total routes in update: 1
```

You can turn the command off with the undebug or undebug all command.

```
Lab_B#un all
All possible debugging has been turned off
```

The *Debug IP IGRP Transactions* Command

The debug ip igrp transactions command shows message requests from neighbor routers asking for an update and the broadcasts sent from your router toward that neighbor router.

In the following output, a request was received from a neighbor router on network 192.168.40.2 to Serial 0/1 of Router Lab_B, which responded with an update packet:

```
Lab_B#debug ip igrp transactions
IGRP protocol debugging is on
07:14:05: IGRP: received request from 192.168.40.2 on
  Serial1
07:14:05: IGRP: sending update to 192.168.40.2 via Serial1
  (172.16.40.1)
07:14:05:        subnet 192.168.30.0, metric=1100
07:14:05:        subnet 8192.16.20.0, metric=158250
07:14:05:        subnet 192.168.10.0, metric=158350
07:14:06: IGRP: received update from 192.168.40.2 on
  Serial1
07:14:06:        subnet 192.168.50.0, metric 8576 (neighbor
  1100)
```

You can turn off the command with the undebug all command (un all for short).

```
Lab_B#un all
All possible debugging has been turned off
```

Troubleshooting EIGRP

You can use several commands on a router to help you troubleshoot and verify the EIGRP configuration. Table 3.1 contains all of the commands that are used in conjunction with verifying EIGRP operation, and it offers a brief description of what each command does.

TABLE 3.1   EIGRP Troubleshooting Commands

Command	Description/Function
show ip route	Shows the entire routing table
show ip eigrp route	Shows only EIGRP entries in the routing table
show ip eigrp neighbor	Shows all EIGRP neighbors
show ip egrp topology	Shows entries in the EIGRP topology table

Since we have already looked at the show ip route command, let's take a look at the other two show commands commonly used to troubleshoot EIGRP. First, familiarize yourself with show ip eigrp neighbor:

```
Lab_C#show ip eigrp neighbor
H   Address Interface   Hold Uptime    SRTT  RTO  Q  Seq Type
                        (sec)          (ms)       Cnt Num
0   192.168.40.1 Se0      12 00:13:24    26   200  0  7
```

Let me break this down for you:

- H indicates the order in which the neighbors were discovered.
- The Hold time indicates how long this router will wait for a Hello packet to arrive from a specific neighbor.
- The Uptime indicates how long the neighborship has been established.
- The SRTT field is the smooth round-trip timer, which indicates the time a round trip takes from this router to its neighbor and back. You use this value to determine how long to wait after a multicast for a reply from this neighbor. If a reply isn't received in time, the router switches to using unicasts in an attempt to complete the communication. The time between multicast attempts is specified by...
- The RTO field, which stands for Retransmission Time Out, is itself based upon the SRTT values.
- The Q value indicates whether there are any outstanding messages in the queue—consistently large values would indicate a problem.
- The Seq field indicates the sequence number of the last update from that neighbor—which is used to maintain synchronization and avoid duplicate or out-of-sequence processing of messages.

Okay—it's all good. Now let's see what's in the `show ip eigrp topology` command:

```
Lab_C#show ip eigrp topology
Codes: P - Passive, A - Active, U - Update, Q - Query, R - Reply,
       r - reply Status, s - sia Status
P 192.168.40.0/24, 1 successors, FD is 2169856
        via Connected, Serial0
P 192.168.50.0/24, 1 successors, FD is 281600
        via Connected, Ethernet0
P 192.168.10.0/24, 1 successors, FD is 2707456
        via 192.168.40.1 (2707456/2195456), Serial0/0
P 192.168.30.0/24, 1 successors, FD is 2172416
        via 192.168.40.1 (2172416/28160), Serial0/0
P 192.168.20.0/24, 1 successors, FD is 2681856
        via 192.168.40.1 (2681856/2169856), Serial0/0
Lab_C#
```

Notice that every route is preceded by a P. This means that the route is in the passive state, which is good. Routes in the active state indicate that the router has lost its path to this network and is searching for a replacement. Each entry also indicates the feasible distance, or FD, to each remote network plus the next-hop neighbor through which packets will travel to this destination. Each entry also has two numbers in parentheses—for example, (2681856/2169856). The first number indicates the feasible distance, and the second indicates the advertised distance to a remote network.

Troubleshooting OSPF

There are several ways to verify and troubleshoot proper OSPF configuration and operation; I'll show you the OSPF `show` commands you need to know about to do this. They include

- `show ip ospf`
- `show ip ospf database`
- `show ip ospf interface`
- `show ip ospf neighbor`

In this section, not only will we look at these commands, but we'll also take another look at the `show ip protocols` command to see how it stacks up in OSPF.

The *show ip ospf* command

You can use the `show ip ospf` command to display OSPF information for one or all OSPF processes running on the router. Information contained therein includes the Router ID, area information, SPF (Shortest Path First) statistics, and Link State Advertisement (LSA) timer information. Let's check out the output:

```
Lab_A#sho ip ospf
Routing Process "ospf 132" with ID 192.168.20.1
 Supports only single TOS(TOS0) routes
 Supports opaque LSA
 SPF schedule delay 5 secs, Hold time between two SPFs 10 secs
 Minimum LSA interval 5 secs. Minimum LSA arrival 1 secs
 Number of external LSA 0. Checksum Sum 0x000000
 Number of opaque AS LSA 0. Checksum Sum 0x000000
 Number of DCbitless external and opaque AS LSA 0
 Number of DoNotAge external and opaque AS LSA 0
 Number of areas in this router is 1. 1 normal 0 stub 0 nssa
 External flood list length 0
    Area BACKBONE(0)
        Number of interfaces in this area is 2
        Area has no authentication
        SPF algorithm executed 5 times
        Area ranges are
        Number of LSA 3. Checksum Sum 0x020E9A
        Number of opaque link LSA 0. Checksum Sum 0x000000
        Number of DCbitless LSA 0
        Number of indication LSA 0
        Number of DoNotAge LSA 0
        Flood list length 0
```

Notice the RID of 192.168.20.1, which is the highest IP address in the router. Now let's take a look at the OSPF database.

The *show ip ospf database* Command

The information displayed by the show ip ospf database command indicates the number of links and the neighboring router's ID. The output is broken down by area. Here's a sample output:

```
Lab_A#sh ip ospf database

        OSPF Router with ID (192.168.20.1) (Process ID 132)

            Router Link States (Area 0)
```

```
Link ID         ADV Router      Age     Seq#      Checksum Link count
192.168.20.1    192.168.20.1    648     0x80000003 0x005E2B 3
192.168.40.1    192.168.40.1    351     0x80000003 0x00E32F 5
192.168.40.2    192.168.40.2    192     0x80000003 0x00CD40 3
Lab_A#
```

The router output shows the link ID (remember that an interface is also a link) and the Router ID of the router on that link.

The *show ip ospf interface* Command

The `show ip ospf interface` command displays all interface-related OSPF information. Data is displayed about OSPF information for all interfaces or for specified interfaces. The information included here is shown in this list:

- The interface IP address
- The area assignment
- The Process ID
- Router ID
- Network type
- Cost
- Priority
- Designated router/backup designated router (DR/BDR) (if applicable)
- Timer intervals
- Adjacent neighbor information

Here's the output from the same router:

```
Lab_A#show ip ospf interface
Serial0/0 is up, line protocol is up
  Internet Address 192.168.20.1/24, Area 0
  Process ID 132, Router ID 192.168.20.1, Network Type POINT_TO_POINT, Cost: 64
  Transmit Delay is 1 sec, State POINT_TO_POINT,
  Timer intervals configured, Hello 10, Dead 40, Wait 40, Retransmit 5
    Hello due in 00:00:06
  Index 2/2, flood queue length 0
  Next 0x0(0)/0x0(0)
  Last flood scan length is 1, maximum is 1
  Last flood scan time is 0 msec, maximum is 0 msec
  Neighbor Count is 1, Adjacent neighbor count is 1
    Adjacent with neighbor 192.168.40.1
```

```
  Suppress hello for 0 neighbor(s)
FastEthernet0/0 is up, line protocol is up
  Internet Address 192.168.10.1/24, Area 0
  Process ID 132, Router ID 192.168.20.1, Network Type BROADCAST, Cost: 10
  Transmit Delay is 1 sec, State DR, Priority 1
  Designated Router (ID) 192.168.20.1, Interface address 192.168.10.1
  No backup designated router on this network
  Timer intervals configured, Hello 10, Dead 40, Wait 40, Retransmit 5
    Hello due in 00:00:04
  Index 1/1, flood queue length 0
  Next 0x0(0)/0x0(0)
--More--
```

The *show ip ospf neighbor* Command

The show ip ospf neighbor command is super useful because it summarizes the pertinent OSPF information regarding neighbors and the adjacency state. If a DR or BDR exists, that information will also be displayed. Here's a sample:

```
Lab_A#sh ip ospf neighbor

Neighbor ID   Pri  State      Dead Time   Address       Interface
192.168.40.1   1   FULL/  -   00:00:30    192.168.20.2  Serial0/0
Lab_A#
```

The *show ip protocols* Command

Finally, here is another look at the show ip protocols command. As I've mentioned before, this command is useful no matter what routing protocol you're running, as long as it can be configured on your router. It provides an excellent overview of the actual operation of all currently running protocols.

Check out the output from this OSPF router:

```
Lab_A#sh ip protocols
Routing Protocol is "ospf 132"
  Outgoing update filter list for all interfaces is not set
  Incoming update filter list for all interfaces is not set
  Router ID 192.168.20.1
  Number of areas in this router is 1. 1 normal 0 stub 0 nssa
  Maximum path: 4
  Routing for Networks:
    192.168.10.1 0.0.0.0 area 0
    192.168.20.1 0.0.0.0 area 0
```

```
Routing Information Sources:
   Gateway         Distance      Last Update
   192.168.40.1        110       00:05:56
   192.168.40.2        110       00:05:56
   192.168.20.1        110       00:05:56
Distance: (default is 110)
```

Lab_A#

Based upon this output, you can determine the OSPF Process ID, the OSPF Router ID, the type of OSPF area, networks and areas configured for OSPF, and the OSPF Router IDs of neighbors—that's a lot. Read: efficient!

Exam Essentials

Remember how to verify RIP routing.   `show ip route` provides you with the contents of the routing table. An R on the left side of the table indicates a RIP-found route. The `debug ip rip` command shows you RIP updates being sent and received on your router. If you see a route with a metric of 16, that route is considered down.

Remember how to verify IGRP routing.   `show ip route` shows you the routing table, and an I on the left side of the table indicates an IGRP-found route. The `[100/123456]` indicates the administrative distance—100 is for IGRP, the composite metric. The composite metric is determined by bandwidth and delay of the line, by default.

Know how to verify EIGRP operation.   You can verify EIGRP operation using the commands `show ip eigrp neighbour` and `show ip eigrp topology`.

Be able to verify operation of OSPF.   There are many `show` commands that provide useful details on OSPF. You should be completely familiar with the output of each of the following: `show ip ospf`, `show ip ospf database`, `show ip ospf interface`, `show ip ospf neighbor`, and `show ip protocols`.

3.4 Troubleshoot IP Addressing and Host Configuration

There are a number of skills involved in troubleshooting IP addressing and configuration issues. Therefore, you must really have a strong understanding of IP addressing and validation techniques in order to understand the specifics of this requirement. We will start by looking at a fundamental skill—converting between binary, decimal, and hexadecimal numbers. Then we'll discuss some specific techniques you can use to troubleshoot IP addressing, and finally I'll show you some basic commands for validating IP configuration.

Binary to Decimal and Hexadecimal Conversion

Anyone who has spent much time in networking has probably collected half a dozen or so "tricks" to avoid using binary or hexadecimal numbers (hey, I used one when we covered IP addressing!). However, when you really have to understand why something is not working, you must know the differences between a binary, decimal, and hexadecimal number, and how to convert from one format into the other. There are going to be times when you have to look at the ones and zeros to see what is going on, especially when you are troubleshooting, say, subnet mask problems (Are they really in the same subnet? and Do they agree on the broadcast address?) or wildcard masking problems (Am I really allowing the addresses I think I am?).

So first, we're going to start with binary numbering. It's pretty simple really. The digits used are limited to either a 1(one) or a 0 (zero), with each digit being called one bit (short for *binary digit*). Typically, you count either four or eight bits together, with these being referred to as a *nibble* or a *byte*, respectively.

What interests us in binary numbering is the value represented in a decimal format—the typical decimal format is the base 10 number scheme we've all used since kindergarten. The binary numbers are placed in a value spot; starting at the right and moving left, with each spot having double the value of the previous spot.

Here are the decimal values of each bit location in a nibble and in a byte. Remember, a nibble is four bits and a byte is eight bits.

Nibble values

8 4 2 1

Byte values

128 64 32 16 8 4 2 1

What all this means is that if a one digit (1) is placed in a value spot, then the nibble or byte takes on that decimal value and adds it to any other value spots that have a one. And if a zero (0) is placed in a bit spot, then you don't count that value.

Let me clarify things—if you have a 1 placed in each spot of your nibble, you would then add up 8 + 4 + 2 + 1, which would give you a maximum value of 15. Another example for your nibble values would be 1010, which means the 8 bit is turned on, as is the 2 bit, which equals a decimal value of 10. If you have a nibble binary value of 0110, then your decimal value would be 6, because the 4 and 2 bits are turned on.

But the byte values can add up to a value that's significantly higher than 15. Here's how: if you counted every bit as a one (1), then the byte binary value would look like this (remember, 8 bits equal a byte):

11111111

You would then count up every bit spot because each is turned on:

128 + 64 + 32 + 16 + 8 + 4 + 2 + 1 = 255

This demonstrates the maximum value of a byte.

There are plenty of other decimal values that a binary number can equal. Let's work through a couple examples. Here's the first:

10010110

Which bits are on? The 128, 16, 4, and 2 bits are on, so we'll just add them up: 128 + 16 + 4 + 2 = 150.

Here's the next example:

01101100

Again, which bits are on? The 64, 32, 8, and 4 bits are on, so we just need to add them up: 64 + 32 + 8 + 4 = 108.

And finally,

11101000

Which bits are on now? As you can see, the 128, 64, 32 and 8 bits are on—just add the values up as you did before: 128 + 64 + 32 + 8 = 232.

Table 3.2 is a table you should memorize (it is used for subnet masking).

TABLE 3.2   Binary to Decimal Memorization Chart

Binary Value	Decimal Value
10000000	128
11000000	192
11100000	224
11110000	240
11111000	248
11111100	252
11111110	254
11111111	255

Hexadecimal addressing is completely different than binary or decimal—it's converted by reading nibbles not bytes. By using nibbles, you can convert them to hex pretty easily. First, make sure you understand that the hexadecimal addressing scheme uses only the numbers 0 through 9. Since the numbers 10, 11, 12, and so on can't be used because they are two digits, the letters A, B, C, D, E, and F are used to represent 10, 11, 12, 13, 14, and 15, respectively.

Table 3.3 shows both the binary value and decimal value for each hexadecimal digit.

TABLE 3.3 Hex to Binary to Decimal Chart

Hexadecimal Value	Binary Value	Decimal Value
0	0000	0
1	0001	1
2	0010	2
3	0011	3
4	0100	4
5	0101	5
6	0110	6
7	0111	7
8	1000	8
9	1001	9
A	1010	10
B	1011	11
C	1100	12
D	1101	13
E	1110	14
F	1111	15

Did you notice that the first 10 hexadecimal digits (0–9) are the same value as the decimal values? If not, look again. This handy fact makes those values super easy to convert.

So suppose you have something like this: 0x6A. (Sometimes Cisco likes to put 0x in front of characters so that you know that they are a hex value; these two characters don't have any other special meaning.) What are the binary and decimal values? All you have to remember is that each hex character is one nibble and two hex characters together make a byte. To figure out the binary value, you need to convert the hex characters into two nibbles and then put these two together into a byte. For instance, 6 = 0110, and A (which is 10 in hex) is 1010, so the complete byte would be 01101010.

To convert from binary to hex, just take the byte and break it into nibbles. Here's what I mean:

Say you have the binary number 01010101. First, break it into nibbles—0101 and 0101. In this case the value of each nibble is 5 since the 1 and 4 bits are on. This makes the hex answer 55. Why? Because we're converting a whole byte. And in decimal format, the binary number is 01101010, which converts to 64 + 32 + 8 + 2 = 106.

Here's another binary number. Take a stab at the conversion on your own.

11001100

Your answer should be 1100 = 12 and 1100 = 12, (therefore it's converted to CC in hex). The decimal conversion answer should then be 128 + 64 + 8 + 4 = 204.

One more example, and then we've got to move on into IP addressing. Suppose you had the following binary number:

10110101

The hex answer is 1011 = 11 (B in hex) and 0101 = 5 (5 in hex), so the answer is B5. The decimal equivalent is 128 + 32 + 16 + 4 + 1 = 181.

Troubleshooting IP Addressing

Troubleshooting IP addressing is obviously an important section because trouble always happens—it's just a matter of time! And you must be able to determine and fix a problem on an IP network whether you're at work or at home. This section teaches you the "Cisco way" of troubleshooting IP addressing.

Four Steps to Troubleshooting IP Addressing

Let's go over the troubleshooting steps that Cisco uses first. These are pretty simple, but important nonetheless. Pretend you're at a customer host and they're complaining that their host cannot communicate to a server, which just happens to be on a remote network. Here are the four troubleshooting steps Cisco recommends:

1. Open a DOS window and ping 127.0.0.1. This is the diagnostic or loopback address, and if you get a successful ping, your IP stack is considered initialized. If it fails, then you have an IP stack failure and need to reinstall TCP/IP on the host.

2. From the DOS window, ping the IP address of the local host. If that's successful, then your Network Interface Card (NIC) is functioning. If it fails, then you have a problem with the NIC. This doesn't mean that a cable is plugged into the NIC, only that the IP stack on the host can communicate to the NIC.

3. From the DOS window, ping the default gateway (router). If the ping works, it means that the NIC is plugged into the network and can communicate on the local network. It also means that the default router is responding and is configured with the proper IP address on its local interface. If it fails, then you have a local physical network problem that could be happening anywhere from the NIC to the router.

4. If steps 1 through 3 were successful, try to ping the remote server. If that works, then you know that you have IP communication between the local host and the remote server. You also know that the remote physical network is working.

If the user still can't communicate with the server after steps 1 through 4 are successful, then you probably have some type of name resolution problem and need to check your Domain Name Server (DNS) settings. But if the ping to the remote server fails, then you know you have some type of remote physical network problem, and you'll need to go to the server and work through steps 1 through 3 until you find the snag.

Once you've gone through all these steps, what do you do if you find a problem? How do you go about fixing an IP address configuration error? Let's move on and discuss how to determine the IP address problems and how to fix them.

Determining IP Host Address Problems

It's common for a host, router, or other network device to be configured with the wrong IP address, subnet mask, or default gateway. Because this happens way too often, I'm going to teach you how to both determine and fix IP address configuration errors.

Once you've worked through the four basic steps of troubleshooting and determined that you have a problem, you obviously need to find and fix it. It really helps to draw out the network and IP addressing scheme, unless you're lucky and that's already been done; if it has, go buy a lottery ticket! Though this should be done, it rarely is, and even if it has been done, it's usually outdated or inaccurate. In most cases, you'll probably just have to bite the bullet and start from scratch.

Once you have your network accurately drawn out, including the IP addressing scheme, you need to verify each host's IP address, mask, and default gateway address to determine the problem (I'm assuming you don't have a physical problem, or if you did, you've already fixed it).

Let's check out the example illustrated in Figure 3.2. Here a user in the Sales department calls and tells you that they can't get to ServerA in the Marketing department. You ask if they can get to ServerB in the Marketing department, but they don't know because they don't have rights to log on to that server. What do you do?

FIGURE 3.2   IP Address Problem 1

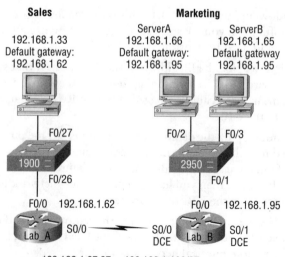

You ask the client to go through the four troubleshooting steps that you just learned about. Steps 1 through 3 work, but step 4 fails. By looking at the figure, can you determine the problem? Look for clues in the network drawing. First, the wide area network (WAN) link between the Lab_A router and the Lab_B router shows the mask as a /27. You should already know this mask is 255.255.255.224 and then you should be able to determine that all networks are using this mask. The network address is 192.168.1.0. What are your valid subnets and hosts? 256 – 224 = 32, so this makes your subnets 32, 64, 96, 128, and so on. So, by looking at the figure, you can see that the Sales department is using subnet 32, the WAN link is using subnet 96, and the Marketing department is using subnet 64.

Now you've got to determine what the valid host ranges are for each subnet. You should be able to determine the subnet address, broadcast addresses, and valid host ranges. The valid hosts for the Sales LAN are 33 through 62—the broadcast address is 63 because the next subnet is 64, right? For the Marketing LAN, the valid hosts are 65 through 94 (broadcast 95), and for the WAN link, 97 through 126 (broadcast 127). By looking at the figure, you can determine that the default gateway on the Lab_B router is incorrect. That address is the broadcast address of the 64 subnet, so there's no way it could be a valid host.

Did you get all that? Maybe you should try another one, just to make sure. Figure 3.3 has a network problem. A user in the Sales LAN can't get to ServerB. You have the user run through the four basic troubleshooting steps and find that the host can communicate to the local network, but not to the remote network. Find and define the IP addressing problem.

FIGURE 3.3   IP Address Problem 2

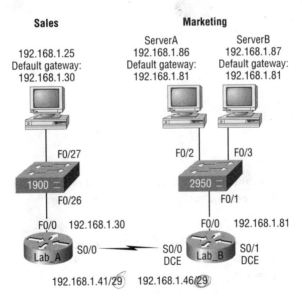

If you use the same steps used to solve the last problem, you can see first that the WAN link again provides the subnet mask to use—/29 or 255.255.255.248. You need to determine what the valid subnets, broadcast addresses, and valid host ranges are to solve this problem.

The 248 mask is a block size of 8 (256 − 248 = 8), so the subnets both start and increment in multiples of 8. By looking at the figure, you can see that the Sales LAN is in the 24 subnet, the WAN is in the 40 subnet, and the Marketing LAN is in the 80 subnet. Can you see the problem yet? The valid host range for the Sales LAN is 25 through 30, and the configuration appears correct. The valid host range for the WAN link is 41 through 46, and this also appears correct. The valid host range for the 80 subnet is 81 through 86, with a broadcast address of 87 because the next subnet is 88. ServerB has been configured with the broadcast address of the subnet.

Checking Network Connectivity

You can use the `ping` and `traceroute` commands to test connectivity to remote devices, and both of them can be used with many protocols, not just IP.

Using the *ping* Command

So far, you've seen many examples of pinging devices to test IP connectivity and name resolution using the DNS server. To see all the different protocols that you can use with `ping`, use the `ping ?` command like this:

```
Todd2509#ping ?
  WORD       Ping destination address or hostname
  apollo     Apollo echo
  appletalk  Appletalk echo
  clns       CLNS echo
  decnet     DECnet echo
  ip         IP echo
  ipx        Novell/IPX echo
  srb        srb echo
  tag        Tag encapsulated IP echo
  vines      Vines echo
  xns        XNS echo
  <cr>
```

The `ping` output displays the minimum, average, and maximum times it takes for a Ping packet to find a specified system and return. Here's another example:

```
Todd2509#ping todd2509
Translating "todd2509"...domain server (192.168.0.70)[OK]
Type escape sequence to abort.
Sending 5, 100-byte ICMP Echos to 192.168.0.121, timeout
  is 2 seconds:
!!!!!
```

```
Success rate is 100 percent (5/5), round-trip min/avg/max
  = 32/32/32 ms
Todd2509#
```

You can see that the DNS server was used to resolve the name, and the device was pinged in 32ms (milliseconds).

> The ping command can be used in user and privileged mode, but not in configuration mode.

Using the *traceroute* Command

Traceroute (the `traceroute` command, or `trace` for short) shows the path a packet takes to get to a remote device. To see the protocols that you can use with `traceroute`, use the `traceroute ?` command, like this:

```
Todd2509#traceroute ?
  WORD         Trace route to destination address or
               hostname
  appletalk    AppleTalk Trace
  clns         ISO CLNS Trace
  ip           IP Trace
  ipx          IPX Trace
  oldvines     Vines Trace (Cisco)
  vines        Vines Trace (Banyan)
  <cr>
```

The `trace` command shows the hop or hops that a packet traverses on its way to a remote device. Here's an example:

```
Todd2509#trace 2501b
Type escape sequence to abort.
Tracing the route to 2501b.lammle.com (172.16.10.2)

  1 2501b.lammle.com (172.16.10.2) 16 msec *  16 msec
Todd2509#
```

You can see that the packet went through only one hop to find the destination.

> Do not get confused on the exam. You can't use the `tracert` command—it's a Windows command. For a router, use the `traceroute` command!

Exam Essentials

Understand when you would use the `ping` command.   Packet Internet Groper (Ping) uses ICMP echo requests and ICMP echo replies to verify an active IP address on a network.

Remember how to ping a valid host ID.   You can ping an IP address from a router's user mode or privileged mode, but not from configuration mode. You must ping a valid address, like 1.1.1.1. Examples of invalid addresses are 192.168.10.0, 192.168.10.255, and 192.168.10.256.

3.5 Troubleshoot a Device as Part of a Working Network

Troubleshooting one device is difficult, but the problems are compounded when you trouble-shoot multiple devices. When you have multiple Cisco devices connected in a working network, you can use a few tricks and techniques between devices to help isolate and solve problems.

In this section, we will look at the following three troubleshooting tools that, well, only make sense when you have more than one device!

- Cisco Discovery Protocol (CDP)
- Name Resolution
- Telnet

The Cisco Discovery Protocol (CDP)

CDP is a proprietary protocol designed by Cisco to help administrators collect information about both locally attached and remote devices. By using CDP, you can gather hardware and protocol information about neighbor devices—majorly useful info for troubleshooting and doc-umenting the network!

Getting CDP Timers and Holdtime Information

The `show cdp` command (`sh cdp` for short) provides you with information about two CDP global parameters that can be configured on Cisco devices:

- The CDP timer specifies how often CDP packets are transmitted to all active interfaces
- CDP holdtime is the amount of time that the device will hold packets received from neighbor devices.

The output on a router looks like this:

```
Router#sh cdp
Global CDP information:
        Sending CDP packets every 60 seconds
```

```
          Sending a holdtime value of 180 seconds
Router#
```

Use the global commands cdp holdtime and cdp timer to configure the CDP holdtime and timer on a router:

```
Router#config t
Enter configuration commands, one per line.  End with
  CNTL/Z.
Router(config)#cdp ?
  holdtime  Specify the holdtime (in sec) to be sent in
            packets
  timer     Specify the rate at which CDP packets are
            sent (in sec)
  run

Router(config)#cdp timer 90
Router(config)#cdp holdtime 240
Router(config)#^Z
```

You can turn off CDP completely with the no cdp run command from the global configuration mode of a router. To turn CDP on or off on an interface, use the no cdp enable and cdp enable commands. Be patient—I'll work through these with you in a second.

Gathering Neighbor Information

The show cdp neighbor command (sh cdp nei for short) delivers information about directly connected devices. It's important to remember that CDP packets aren't passed through a Cisco switch, and that you only see what's directly attached. So this means that if your router is connected to a switch, you won't see any of the devices hooked up to that switch.

The following output shows the show cdp neighbor command used on a Cisco 2509 router:

```
Todd2509#sh cdp nei
Capability Codes: R - Router, T - Trans Bridge,
  B - Source Route Bridge, S - Switch, H - Host,
  I - IGMP, r - Repeater
Device ID  Local Intrfce Holdtme Capability Platform Port ID
1900Switch    Eth 0       238     T S        1900     2
2500B         Ser 0       138     R          2500     Ser 0
Todd2509#
```

Okay—connected directly to the 2509 router are a switch with a hostname of 1900Switch and a 2500 router with a hostname of 2500B. Notice that no devices connected to the 1900Switch and the 2500B router show up in the CDP table on the 2509 router. All you get to see are directly connected devices.

Table 3.4 summarizes the information displayed by the show cdp neighbor command for each device.

TABLE 3.4 Output of the show cdp neighbor Command

Field	Description
Device ID	The hostname of the device directly connected.
Local Interface	The port or interface on which you are receiving the CDP packet.
Holdtime	The amount of time the router will hold the information before discarding it if no more CDP packets are received.
Capability	The neighbor's capability, such as router, switch, or repeater. The capability codes are listed at the top of the command output.
Platform	The type of Cisco device. In the above output, a Cisco 2509, Cisco 2511, and Catalyst 5000 are attached to the switch. The 2509 only sees the switch and the 2501 router connected through its Serial 0 interfac.
Port ID	The neighbor device's port or interface on which the CDP packets are broadcast.

Another command that'll deliver the goods on neighbor information is the show cdp neighbor detail command (show cdp nei de for short). You can run this command on both routers and switches, and it displays detailed information about each device connected to the device on which you're running the command. Check out this router output to see an example of this:

```
Todd2509#sh cdp neighbor detail
-------------------------
Device ID: 1900Switch
Entry address(es):
  IP address: 0.0.0.0
Platform: cisco 1900,  Capabilities: Trans-Bridge Switch
Interface: Ethernet0,  Port ID (outgoing port): 2
Holdtime : 166 sec
Version :
V9.00

-------------------------
Device ID: 2501B
Entry address(es):
```

```
    IP address: 172.16.10.2
Platform: cisco 2500,  Capabilities: Router
Interface: Serial0,  Port ID (outgoing port): Serial0
Holdtime : 154 sec
Version :
Cisco Internetwork Operating System Software
IOS (tm) 3000 Software (IGS-J-L), Version 11.1(5),
   RELEASE SOFTWARE (fc1)Copyright (c) 1986-1996 by cisco
   Systems, Inc.Compiled Mon 05-Aug-03 11:48 by mkamson
Todd2509#
```

What are you being shown here? Well first, you're given the hostname and IP address of all directly connected devices. In addition to the same information displayed by the show cdp neighbor command (see Table 3.4), the show cdp neighbor detail command also gives you the IOS version of the neighbor device.

The show cdp entry * command displays the same information as the show cdp neighbor details command. Here's an example of the router output using the show cdp entry * command:

```
Todd2509#sh cdp entry *
-------------------------
Device ID: 1900Switch
Entry address(es):
   IP address: 0.0.0.0
Platform: cisco 1900,  Capabilities: Trans-Bridge Switch
Interface: Ethernet0,  Port ID (outgoing port): 2
Holdtime : 223 sec
Version :
V9.00
-------------------------
Device ID: 2501B
Entry address(es):
   IP address: 172.16.10.2
Platform: cisco 2500,  Capabilities: Router
Interface: Serial0,  Port ID (outgoing port): Serial0
Holdtime : 151 sec
Version :
Cisco Internetwork Operating System Software
IOS (tm) 3000 Software (IGS-J-L), Version 11.1(5),
   RELEASE SOFTWARE (fc1)Copyright (c) 1986-1996 by cisco
   Systems, Inc.Compiled Mon 05-Aug-03 11:48 by mkamson
Todd2509#
```

Gathering Interface Traffic Information

The show cdp traffic command displays information about interface traffic, including the number of CDP packets sent and received and the errors with CDP.

The following output shows the show cdp traffic command used on the 2509 router.

```
Todd2509#sh cdp traffic
CDP counters:
        Packets output: 13, Input: 8
        Hdr syntax: 0, Chksum error: 0, Encaps failed: 0
        No memory: 0, Invalid packet: 0, Fragmented: 0
Todd2509#
```

This is not really the most important information you can gather from a router, but it does show how many CDP packets are sent and received on a device.

Gathering Port and Interface Information

The show cdp interface command (sh cdp inter for short) gives you the CDP status on router interfaces or switch ports.

And as I said earlier, you can turn off CDP completely on a router by using the no cdp run command. But did you know that you can also turn off CDP on a per interface basis with the no cdp enable command? You can. You enable a port with the cdp enable command. All ports and interfaces default to cdp enable.

On a router, the show cdp interface command displays information about each interface using CDP, including the encapsulation on the line, the timer, and the holdtime for each interface. Here's an example of this command's output on the 2509 router:

```
Todd2509#sh cdp interface
Ethernet0 is up, line protocol is up
  Encapsulation ARPA
  Sending CDP packets every 60 seconds
  Holdtime is 180 seconds
Serial0 is administratively down, line protocol is down
  Encapsulation HDLC
  Sending CDP packets every 60 seconds
  Holdtime is 180 seconds
Serial1 is administratively down, line protocol is down
  Encapsulation HDLC
  Sending CDP packets every 60 seconds
  Holdtime is 180 seconds
```

To turn off CDP on one interface on a router, use the no cdp enable command from interface configuration mode:

```
Todd2509#config t
Enter configuration commands, one per line.  End with
  CNTL/Z.
Router(config)#int s0
Router(config-if)#no cdp enable
Router(config-if)#^Z
```

Verify the change with the show cdp interface command:

```
Todd2509#sh cdp int
Ethernet0 is up, line protocol is up
  Encapsulation ARPA
  Sending CDP packets every 60 seconds
  Holdtime is 180 seconds
Serial1 is administratively down, line protocol is down
  Encapsulation HDLC
  Sending CDP packets every 60 seconds
  Holdtime is 180 seconds
Todd2509#
```

Notice above that serial 0 isn't listed in the router output. To get that, you'd have to perform a cdp enable on Serial 0. It would then show up in the output.

Name Resolution

Have you memorized every IP address in your enterprise? What if you have 5,000 routers? Think you can memorize those? Hostnames and DNS can greatly simplify troubleshooting by allowing you to access devices based on names rather than IP addresses. It is much easier to ping la than to try and remember the IP address of the LA router. In order to use a hostname rather than an IP address to connect to a remote device, the device that you are using to make the connection must be able to translate the hostname to an IP address.

There are two ways to resolve hostnames to IP addresses: building a host table on each router or building a Domain Name System (DNS) server, which is kind of like a dynamic host table.

Building a Host Table

A *host table* provides name resolution on the router that it was built upon only. The command to build a host table on a router is

```
ip host name tcp_port_number ip_address
```

The default is TCP port number 23, but you can create a session using Telnet with a different TCP port number if you want. You can also assign up to eight IP addresses to a hostname.

Here's an example of configuring a host table with two entries to resolve the names for the 2501B router and the switch:

```
Todd2509#config t
Enter configuration commands, one per line.  End with
  CNTL/Z.
Todd2509(config)#ip host ?
  WORD  Name of host

Todd2509(config)#ip host 2501B ?
  <0-65535>  Default telnet port number
  A.B.C.D    Host IP address (maximum of 8)

Todd2509(config)#ip host 2501B 172.16.10.2 ?
  A.B.C.D  Host IP address (maximum of 8)
  <cr>
Todd2509(config)#ip host 2501B 172.16.10.2
Todd2509(config)#ip host 1900Switch 192.168.0.148
Todd2509(config)#^Z
```

And to see the newly built host table, just use the show hosts command:

```
Todd2509#sh hosts
Default domain is not set
Name/address lookup uses domain service
Name servers are 255.255.255.255

Host            Flags      Age Type  Address(es)
2501B           (perm, OK) 0   IP    172.16.10.2
1900Switch      (perm, OK) 0   IP    192.168.0.148
Todd2509#
```

You can see the two hostnames plus their associated IP addresses in this output. The perm in the Flags column means that the entry is manually configured. If it said temp, it would be an entry that was resolved by DNS.

To verify that the host table resolves names, try typing the hostnames at a router prompt. Remember that if you don't specify the command, the router assumes you want to telnet. In the following example, I used the hostnames to telnet into the remote devices, then pressed Ctrl+Shift+6 and then X to return to the main console of the Todd2509 router:

```
Todd2509#2501b
Trying 2501B (172.16.10.2)... Open
```

```
User Access Verification

Password:
2501B>
Todd2509#[Ctrl+Shift+6, then x]
Todd2509#1900switch
Trying 1900switch (192.168.0.148)... Open

Catalyst 1900 Management Console
Copyright (c) Cisco Systems, Inc.  1993-1999
All rights reserved.
Enterprise Edition Software
Ethernet Address:       00-B0-64-75-6B-C0

PCA Number:             73-3122-04
PCA Serial Number:      FAB040131E2
Model Number:           WS-C1912-A
System Serial Number:   FAB0401U0JQ
Power Supply S/N:       PHI033108SD
PCB Serial Number:      FAB040131E2,73-3122-04
-------------------------------------------------

1 user(s) now active on Management Console.

        User Interface Menu

    [M] Menus
    [K] Command Line

Enter Selection:[Ctrl+Shift+6, then x]
Todd2509#
```

I successfully used the host table to create a session to two devices, and used the names to telnet into both devices. Notice that the entries in the show sessions output below now display the hostnames and IP addresses instead of just the IP addresses.

```
Todd2509#sh sess
Conn Host          Address         Byte  Idle Conn Name
   1 1900switch    192.168.0.148     0     0 switch
*  2 2501b         172.16.10.2       0     0 2501b
Todd2509#
```

If you want to remove a hostname from the table, just use the `no ip host` command like this:

```
RouterA(config)#no ip host routerb
```

The problem with the host table method is that you would need to create a host table on each router to be able to resolve names. And if you have a whole bunch of routers and want to resolve names, using DNS is a much better choice!

Using DNS to Resolve Names

So if you have a lot of devices and don't want to create a host table in each device, you can use a DNS server to resolve hostnames.

Any time a Cisco device receives a command it doesn't understand, it tries to resolve it through DNS by default. Watch what happens when I type the special command **todd** at a Cisco router prompt:

```
Todd2509#todd
Translating "todd"...domain server (255.255.255.255)
% Unknown command or computer name, or unable to find
  computer address
Todd2509#
```

It doesn't know my name or what command I am trying to type, so it tries to resolve this through DNS. This is really annoying for two reasons: first, because it doesn't know my name (grin), and second, because I need to hang out and wait for the name lookup to time out. You can get around this nasty little habit and prevent a time-consuming DNS lookup by using the `no ip domain-lookup` command on your router from global configuration mode.

If you have a DNS server on your network, you need to add a few commands to make DNS name resolution work:

- The first command is `ip domain-lookup`, and it's turned on by default. It only needs to be entered if you previously turned it off (with the `no ip domain-lookup` command).

- The second command is `ip name-server`. This sets the IP address of the DNS server. You can enter the IP addresses of up to six servers.

- The last command is `ip domain-name`. Although this command is optional, it really should be set. It appends the domain name to the hostname you type in. Since DNS uses a fully qualified domain name (FQDN) system, you must have a full DNS name, in the form `domain.com`.

Here's an example that uses these three commands:

```
Todd2509#config t
Enter configuration commands, one per line.  End with
  CNTL/Z.
Todd2509(config)#ip domain-lookup
Todd2509(config)#ip name-server ?
  A.B.C.D  Domain server IP address (maximum of 6)
```

```
Todd2509(config)#ip name-server 192.168.0.70
Todd2509(config)#ip domain-name lammle.com
Todd2509(config)#^Z
Todd2509#
```

After the DNS configurations are set, you can test the DNS server by using a hostname to ping or telnet a device, like this:

```
Todd2509#ping 2501b
Translating "2501b"...domain server (192.168.0.70) [OK]
Type escape sequence to abort.
Sending 5, 100-byte ICMP Echos to 172.16.10.2, timeout is
  2 seconds:
!!!!!
Success rate is 100 percent (5/5), round-trip min/avg/max
  = 28/31/32 ms
```

Notice that the router uses the DNS server to resolve the name.

After a name is resolved using DNS, use the show hosts command to see that the device cached this information in the host table:

```
Todd2509#sh hosts
Default domain is lammle.com
Name/address lookup uses domain service
Name servers are 192.168.0.70
```

Host	Flags	Age	Type	Address(es)
2501b.lammle.com	(temp, OK)	0	IP	172.16.10.2
1900switch	(perm, OK)	0	IP	192.168.0.148

```
Todd2509#
```

The entry that was resolved is shown as temp, but the 1900 switch device is still perm, meaning it's a static entry. Notice that the hostname is a full domain name. If I hadn't used the ip domain-name lammle.com command, I would have needed to type in ping 2501b.lammle.com, which is a pain.

Telnet

Telnet is probably the most fundamental troubleshooting tool you will use. After all, you are probably not going to run from device to device in a routed network to check out problems. You are going to telnet from device to device and use the troubleshooting commands included in this chapter to check out the operation of devices.

Telnet is a virtual terminal protocol that uses the TCP/IP protocol suite; it allows you to make connections to remote devices, gather information, and run programs.

After your routers and switches are configured, you can use the Telnet program to reconfigure and/or check up on your routers and switches without using a console cable. You run the Telnet program by typing **telnet** at any command prompt (DOS or Cisco). You have to have VTY passwords set on the routers for this to work.

Remember—when you are working on reachability issues with remote devices, you can't use CDP to gather information about routers and switches that aren't directly connected to your device. However, you can use the Telnet application to connect to your neighbor devices, then run CDP on those remote devices to get the skinny on them, and eventually reach those remote routers and switches. You can issue the telnet command from any router prompt, like this:

```
Todd2509#telnet 172.16.10.2
Trying 172.16.10.2 ... Open

Password required, but none set

[Connection to 172.16.10.2 closed by foreign host]
Todd2509#
```

Oops! Ummm, I guess I didn't set my passwords—how embarrassing! Note to self (and you)—the VTY ports on a router are configured as login, meaning we have to either set the VTY passwords, or use the no login command.

On a Cisco router, you don't need to use the telnet command, you can just type in an IP address from a command prompt, and the router will assume that you want to telnet to the device. Here's how that looks:

```
Todd2509#172.16.10.2
Trying 172.16.10.2 ... Open

Password required, but none set

[Connection to 172.16.10.2 closed by foreign host]
Todd2509#
```

Okay—at this point, it would be a great idea to set those VTY passwords on the router you want to telnet into. Here's what I did on the remote router:

```
2501B#config t
Enter configuration commands, one per line.  End with
  CNTL/Z.
2501B(config)#line vty 0 4
2501B(config-line)#login
2501B(config-line)#password todd
2501B(config-line)#^Z
```

```
2501B#
%SYS-5-CONFIG_I: Configured from console by console
```

Now, let's try this again—here, I'm connecting to the router from the 2509's console:

```
Todd2509#172.16.10.2
Trying 172.16.10.2 ... Open

User Access Verification

Password:
2501B>
```

Remember that the VTY password is the user mode password, not the enable mode password. Watch what happens when I try to go into privileged mode after telnetting into router 2501B:

```
2501B>en
% No password set
2501B>
```

It says "no way!" This is a really good security feature. Why? Because you don't want bad guys telnetting into your device and being able to just type the enable command to get into privileged mode, now do you? Nope! You've got to set your enable mode password or enable secret password to use Telnet to configure remote devices.

Telnetting into Multiple Devices Simultaneously

Sometimes when working on a complicated problem, you want to see what multiple devices are seeing. For example, you may want to do a show ip route command on several routers to see if a route is propagating correctly or not. If you telnet to a router or switch, you can end the connection by typing **exit** at any time, but what if you want to keep your connection to a remote device but still come back to your original router console? To do that, you can press the Ctrl+Shift+6 key combination, release it, and then press X.

Here's an example of connecting to multiple devices from my Todd2509 router console:

```
Todd2509#telnet 172.16.10.2
Trying 172.16.10.2 ... Open

User Access Verification

Password:
2501B>[Cntl+Shift+6, then x]
Todd2509#
```

In this example, I telnetted to the 2501B router, then typed the password to enter user mode. I then pressed Ctrl+Shift+6 and then X, but you can't see that because it doesn't show on the screen output. Notice my command prompt is now back at the Todd2509 router.

You can also telnet into a Catalyst 1900 switch, but to get away with that, you must set the enable mode password level 15 or the enable secret password on the switch before you can gain access via the Telnet application.

In the following example, I telnetted into a 1900 switch that responded by giving me the console output of the switch:

```
Todd2509#telnet 192.168.0.148
Trying 192.168.0.148 ... Open


Catalyst 1900 Management Console
Copyright (c) Cisco Systems, Inc.  1993-1999
All rights reserved.
Enterprise Edition Software
Ethernet Address:        00-B0-64-75-6B-C0

PCA Number:              73-3122-04
PCA Serial Number:       FAB040131E2
Model Number:            WS-C1912-A
System Serial Number:    FAB0401U0JQ
Power Supply S/N:        PHI033108SD
PCB Serial Number:       FAB040131E2,73-3122-04
-------------------------------------------------


1 user(s) now active on Management Console.


        User Interface Menu

   [M] Menus
   [K] Command Line


Enter Selection:
```

At this point, I pressed Ctrl+Shift+6, then X, which took me back to my Todd2509 router console.

```
Todd2509#
```

Checking Telnet Connections

In the heat of a problem, you may end up with many telnet sessions open. To see the connections made from your router to a remote device, use the show sessions command.

```
Todd2509#sh sessions
Conn Host          Address       Byte Idle Conn Name
   1 172.16.10.2    172.16.10.2    0    0  172.16.10.2
*  2 192.168.0.148 192.168.0.148  0    0  192.168.0.148
Todd2509#
```

See that asterisk (*) next to connection 2? It means that session 2 was your last session. You can return to your last session by pressing Enter twice. You can also return to any session by typing the number of the connection and pressing Enter twice.

Checking Telnet Users

When you are working on a problem, you will probably want to know who else is working on it. After all, you don't want someone else to change something on a router you are trouble-shooting without knowing about it! You can list all active consoles and VTY ports in use on your router with the show users command:

```
Todd2509#sh users
    Line     User    Host(s)        Idle Location
*   0 con 0           172.16.10.2    00:07:52
                      192.168.0.148  00:07:18
```

In the command's output, the con represents the local console. In this example, the console is connected to two remote IP addresses, or in other words, two devices.

In the next example, I typed show users on the 2501B router that the Todd2509 router had telnetted into:

```
2501B>sh users
    Line     User    Host(s)        Idle Location
    0 con 0           idle           9
*   2 vty 0
```

This output shows that the console is active and that VTY port 2 is being used. The asterisk represents the current terminal session user.

Closing Telnet Sessions

You can end Telnet sessions a few different ways—typing exit or disconnect is probably the easiest and quickest.

To end a session from a remote device, use the exit command:

```
Todd2509#[Enter] and again [Enter]
[Resuming connection 2 to 192.168.0.148 ... ]


1900Switch>exit


[Connection to 192.168.0.148 closed by foreign host]
Todd2509#
```

Since the 1900Switch was my last session, I just pressed Enter twice to return to that session. To end a session from a local device, use the disconnect command:

```
Todd2509#disconnect ?
  <1-2>  The number of an active network connection
  WORD   The name of an active network connection
  <cr>


Todd2509#disconnect 1
Closing connection to 172.16.10.2 [confirm]
Todd2509#
```

In this example, I used the session number 1 because that was the connection to the 2501B router that I wanted to end. As I said, you can use the show sessions command to see the connection number.

If you want to end a session of a device attached to your router through Telnet, you should check and see if any devices are attached to your router first. Use the show users command to get that information, like this:

```
2501B#sh users
    Line     User     Host(s)       Idle Location
*  0 con 0            idle          0
   1 aux 0            idle          0
   2 vty 0            idle          0 172.16.10.1
```

This output shows that VTY 0 has IP address 172.16.10.1 connected. That's the Todd2509 router.

To clear the connection, use the clear line # command:

```
2501B#clear line 2
[confirm]
 [OK]
```

Then verify that the user has been disconnected with the **show users** command:

```
2501B#sh users
    Line      User     Host(s)       Idle Location
*   0 con 0            idle          0
    1 aux 0            idle          1

2501B#
```

This output confirms that the line has been cleared.

Exam Essentials

Understand when you would use CDP.   Cisco Discovery Protocol can be used to help you document and troubleshoot your network.

Remember the output from the show cdp neighbors command.   The show cdp neighbors command provides the following information: device ID, local interface, holdtime, capability, platform, and port ID.

Understand how to telnet into a router, keep your connection, but return to your originating console.   If you telnet to a router or switch, you can end the connection by typing **exit** at any time. However, if you want to keep your connection to a remote device but still come back to your original router console, you can press the Ctrl+Shift+6 key combination, release it, and then press X.

Remember the command to verify your Telnet sessions.   The command show sessions will provide you with all the sessions your router has to other routers.

Remember how to build a static host table on a router.   By using the global configuration mode command ip host *host_name ip_address*, you can build a static host table on your router.

Remember how to verify your host table on a router.   You can verify the host table with the show hosts command.

3.6 Troubleshoot an Access List

When working on a problem, be sure to eliminate the possibility of an access list blocking traffic. It is a crucial troubleshooting skill to be able to quickly view both the contents of access lists, and where they are applied.

Table 3.5 shows the commands that you can use to view the configuration and application of access lists on a router:

TABLE 3.5 Access-List Commands

Command	Effect
show access-list	Displays all access lists and their parameters configured on the router. This command does not show you which interface the list is set on.
show access-list 110	Shows only the parameters for the access list 110. This command does not show you the interface the list is set on.
show ip access-list	Shows only the IP access lists configured on the router.
show ip interface	Shows which interfaces have access lists set.
show running-config	Shows the access lists and which interfaces have access lists set.

You should already be familiar with the show running-config command; let's now focus on some access list–specific commands. The show access-list command lists all access lists on the router, regardless of whether they're applied to an interface:

```
Acme#show access-list
Standard IP access list 10
    deny    172.16.40.0, wildcard bits 0.0.0.255
    permit any
Standard IP access list BlockSales
    deny    172.16.40.0, wildcard bits 0.0.0.255
    permit any
Extended IP access list 110
    deny tcp any host 172.16.30.5 eq ftp
    deny tcp any host 172.16.30.5 eq telnet
    permit ip any any
Acme#
```

A few things to note here... First, notice that both numbered and named access lists appear on this list. Second, notice that even though I entered actual numbers for TCP ports in access list 110 when the access list was created, the show command gives me the protocol names rather than TCP ports for readability (hey, not everyone has them all memorized!). With this information in hand, you are ready to look and see if these access lists are applied to interfaces.

Okay—here's the output of the show ip interface command:

```
Acme#show ip interface el
Ethernet1 is up, line protocol is up
  Internet address is 172.16.30.1/24
  Broadcast address is 255.255.255.255
  Address determined by non-volatile memory
  MTU is 1500 bytes
  Helper address is not set
  Directed broadcast forwarding is disabled
  Outgoing access list is BlockSales
  Inbound access list is not set
  Proxy ARP is enabled
  Security level is default
  Split horizon is enabled
  ICMP redirects are always sent
  ICMP unreachables are always sent
  ICMP mask replies are never sent
  IP fast switching is disabled
  IP fast switching on the same interface is disabled
  IP Null turbo vector
  IP multicast fast switching is disabled
  IP multicast distributed fast switching is disabled
  Router Discovery is disabled
  IP output packet accounting is disabled
  IP access violation accounting is disabled
  TCP/IP header compression is disabled
  RTP/IP header compression is disabled
  Probe proxy name replies are disabled
  Policy routing is disabled
  Network address translation is disabled
  Web Cache Redirect is disabled
  BGP Policy Mapping is disabled
Acme#
```

Be sure and notice the bold line that indicates that the outgoing list on this interface is BlockSales, but the inbound access list isn't set.

Exam Essentials

Remember the command to verify an access list on an interface.   To see whether an access list is set on an interface and in which direction it is filtering, use the show ip interface command.

This command will not show you the contents of the access list, merely which access lists are applied on the interface.

Remember the command to verify the access lists configuration. To see the configured access lists on your router, use the `show access-list` command. This command will not show you which interfaces have an access list set.

3.7 Performing Simple WAN Troubleshooting

In this section, I will show you some of the troubleshooting commands specific to WAN protocols. We will look at commands used to validate and troubleshoot Point-to-Point Protocol (PPP), Frame Relay, and Integrated Services Digital Network (ISDN).

Troubleshooting PPP

If you have PPP encapsulation enabled, here's an example of how you would verify that it's up and running with the `show interface` command:

```
RouterA#show int s0
Serial0 is up, line protocol is up
 Hardware is HD64570
 Internet address is 172.16.20.1/24
 MTU 1500 bytes, BW 1544 Kbit, DLY 20000 usec, rely
  255/255, load 1/255
 Encapsulation PPP, loopback not set, keepalive set (10 sec)
 LCP Open
 Listen: IPXCP
 Open: IPCP, CDPCP, ATCP
[output cut]
```

Notice that the sixth line lists encapsulation as PPP and the seventh tells you that the link control protocol (LCP) is open. Remember that LCP's job is to build and maintain connections. The ninth line tells us that Internet Protocol Control Protocol (IPCP), Cisco Discovery Protocol Control Protocol (CDPCP), and the AppleTalk Control Protocol (ATCP) are open. This shows the Internet Protocol (IP), Cisco Discovery Protocol (CDP), and AppleTalk support from Network Control Protocol (NCP) layer in PPP. The eighth line reports that we're listening for Internetwork Packet Exchange Control Protocol (IPXCP).

You can verify the PPP authentication configuration by using the `debug ppp authentication` command.

Troubleshooting Frame Relay

As you know, frame relay is, well, a bit more complex than High-Level Data Link Control (HDLC) protocol or the Point-to-Point Protocol (PPP). You have to understand the technology, and there are many commands on the router you can use to ensure that various parts of Frame Relay are functioning. Since most Frame Relay networks are not privately owned, you will likely be working on Frame Relay problems while on the telephone with your service provider.

There are several commands frequently used to check the status of your interfaces and permanent virtual circuits (PVCs) once you have had Frame Relay encapsulation set up and running. These commands will prove useful when you are working with the service provider to isolate exactly what is working and what is not. Here are some of the commands you will be using:

```
RouterA>sho frame ?
  ip       show frame relay IP statistics
  lmi      show frame relay lmi statistics
  map      Frame-Relay map table
  pvc      show frame relay pvc statistics
  route    show frame relay route
  traffic  Frame-Relay protocol statistics
```

Let's take a look at the most frequently used commands and the information they provide.

The *show frame relay lmi* Command

The show frame relay lmi command (abbreviated sh frame lmi) gives you the Local Management Interface (LMI) traffic statistics exchanged between the local router and the Frame Relay switch:

```
Router#sh frame lmi

LMI Statistics for interface Serial0 (Frame Relay DTE)
LMI TYPE = CISCO
   Invalid Unnumbered info 0      Invalid Prot Disc 0
   Invalid dummy Call Ref 0       Invalid Msg Type 0
   Invalid Status Message 0       Invalid Lock Shift 0
   Invalid Information ID 0        Invalid Report IE Len 0
   Invalid Report Request 0       Invalid Keep IE Len 0
   Num Status Enq. Sent 0         Num Status msgs Rcvd 0
   Num Update Status Rcvd 0       Num Status Timeouts 0
Router#
```

The router output from the show frame relay lmi command tells you about any LMI, as well as the LMI type.

The *show frame pvc* Command

The show frame pvc command lists all configured PVCs and Data Link Connection Identifiers (DLCI) numbers. It provides the status of each PVC connection and traffic statistics. It also gives you the number of Backward-Explicit Congestion Notification (BECN) and Forward-Explicit Congestion Notification (FECN) packets received on the router:

```
RouterA#sho frame pvc

PVC Statistics for interface Serial0 (Frame Relay DTE)

DLCI = 16,DLCI USAGE = LOCAL,PVC STATUS =ACTIVE,
INTERFACE = Serial0.1
 input pkts 50977876    output pkts 41822892
  in bytes 3137403144
 out bytes 3408047602    dropped pkts 5
  in FECN pkts 0
 in BECN pkts 0      out FECN pkts 0      out BECN pkts 0
 in DE pkts 9393      out DE pkts 0
 pvc create time 7w3d, last time pvc status changed 7w3d

DLCI = 18,DLCI USAGE =LOCAL,PVC STATUS =ACTIVE,
INTERFACE = Serial0.3
 input pkts 30572401    output pkts 31139837
  in bytes 1797291100
 out bytes 3227181474    dropped pkts 5
  in FECN pkts 0
 in BECN pkts 0      out FECN pkts 0      out BECN pkts 0
 in DE pkts 28      out DE pkts 0
 pvc create time 7w3d, last time pvc status changed 7w3d
```

To see information about only PVC 16, you can type the command **show frame relay pvc 16**.

The *show interface* Command

You can also use the show interface command to check for LMI traffic. This command displays information about encapsulation as well as Layer-2 and Layer-3 information.

The LMI DLCI, as shown in the following output, is used to define the type of LMI being used. If it's 1023, it's Cisco's default LMI type. If the LMI DLCI is zero, then it's the ANSI LMI type. If the LMI DLCI is anything other then 0 or 1023, call your provider—they have a definite problem!

```
RouterA#sho int s0
Serial0 is up, line protocol is up
```

```
Hardware is HD64570
MTU 1500 bytes, BW 1544 Kbit, DLY 20000 usec, rely
 255/255, load 2/255
Encapsulation FRAME-RELAY, loopback not set, keepalive
 set (10 sec)
LMI enq sent 451751,LMI stat recvd 451750,LMI upd recvd
 164,DTE LMI up
LMI enq recvd 0, LMI stat sent 0, LMI upd sent 0
LMI DLCI 1023 LMI type is CISCO frame relay DTE
Broadcast queue 0/64, broadcasts sent/dropped 0/0,
 interface broadcasts 839294
```

The show interface command displays line, protocol, DLCI, and LMI information.

The *show frame map* Command

The show frame map command displays the Network layer–to–DLCI mappings:

```
RouterB#show frame map
Serial0 (up): ipx 20.0007.7842.3575 dlci 16(0x10,0x400),
              dynamic, broadcast,, status defined, active
Serial0 (up): ip 172.16.20.1 dlci 16(0x10,0x400),
              dynamic, broadcast,, status defined, active
Serial1 (up): ipx 40.0007.7842.153a dlci 17(0x11,0x410),
              dynamic, broadcast,, status defined, active
Serial1 (up): ip 172.16.40.2 dlci 17(0x11,0x410),
              dynamic, broadcast,, status defined, active
```

Notice that the serial interface has two mappings, one for IP and one for IPX. Also, notice that the Network layer addresses were resolved with the dynamic protocol Inverse ARP (IARP). After the DLCI number is listed, you can see some numbers in parentheses. Notice the first number is 0x10. That's the hex equivalent for the DLCI number 16, used on Serial 0. The 0x11 is the hex for DLCI 17 used on Serial 1. The second numbers, 0x400 and 0x410, are the DLCI numbers configured in the Frame Relay frame. They're different because of the way the bits are spread out in the frame.

The *debug frame lmi* Command

The debug frame lmi command shows output on the router consoles by default. The information from this command allows you to verify and troubleshoot the Frame Relay connection by helping you to determine whether the router and switch are exchanging the correct LMI information:

```
Router#debug frame-relay lmi
Serial3/1(in): Status, myseq 214
```

```
RT IE 1, length 1, type 0
KA IE 3, length 2, yourseq 214, myseq 214
PVC IE 0x7 , length 0x6 , dlci 130, status 0x2 , bw 0
Serial3/1(out): StEnq, myseq 215, yourseen 214, DTE up
datagramstart = 0x1959DF4, datagramsize = 13
FR encap = 0xFCF10309
00 75 01 01 01 03 02 D7 D6

Serial3/1(in): Status, myseq 215
RT IE 1, length 1, type 1
KA IE 3, length 2, yourseq 215, myseq 215
Serial3/1(out): StEnq, myseq 216, yourseen 215, DTE up
datagramstart = 0x1959DF4, datagramsize = 13
FR encap = 0xFCF10309
00 75 01 01 01 03 02 D8 D7
```

Troubleshooting ISDN

One frequent use of ISDN is as a backup to another WAN connection, such as Frame Relay. When the Frame Relay link goes down, the ISDN automatically establishes a connection. The technology that provides this backup connectivity is called dial-on-demand routing (DDR), and you need to be prepared for it. Some of these commands have been covered before, others are specific to ISDN and DDR.

Table 3.6 shows commands that can be used to verify legacy DDR and ISDN.

T A B L E 3 . 6   DDR and ISDN Troubleshooting Commands

Command	Description
ping and telnet	Great IP tools for any network. However, your interesting traffic restriction must dictate that Ping and Telnet are acceptable as interesting traffic in order to bring up a link. Once a link is up, you can ping or telnet to your remote router regardless of your interesting traffic lists.
show dialer	Gives good information about your dialer diagnostic information and shows the number of times the dialer string has been reached, the idle-timeout values of each B channel, the length of the call, and the name of the router to which the interface is connected.

TABLE 3.6 DDR and ISDN Troubleshooting Commands *(continued)*

Command	Description
show isdn active	Shows the number called and whether a call is in progress.
show isdn status	A good command to use before trying to dial. Shows if your service profile identifiers (SPIDs) are valid and if you are connected to and communicating with Layers 1 through 3 information to the provider's switch.
show ip route	Shows all routes the router knows about.
debug isdn q921	Used to see Layer-2 information only.
debug isdn q931	Used to see Layer-3 information, including call setup and teardown.
debug dialer	Gives you call-setup and teardown activity.
isdn disconnect int bri0	Clears the interface and drops the connection. Performing a shutdown on the interface can give you the same results.

Exam Essentials

Remember the commands for troubleshooting Frame Relay. The show frame relay lmi command will give you the LMI traffic statistics exchanged between the local router and the Frame Relay switch. The show frame pvc command will list all configured PVCs and DLCI numbers.

Remember the commands for troubleshooting PPP and ISDN. In addition to standard show interface and IP troubleshooting tools, there are debug and show commands specific to each technology.

Review Questions

1. Protocol data units (PDUs) at the Network layer of the OSI are called what?
   A. Transport
   B. Frames
   C. Packets
   D. Segments

2. Segmentation of a data stream happens at which layer of the OSI model?
   A. Physical
   B. Data Link
   C. Network
   D. Transport

3. Which of the following is not an advantage of a layered model?
   A. Allows multiple-vendor development through standardization of network components
   B. Allows various types of network hardware and software to communicate
   C. Allows changes to occur in all layers without having to change just one layer
   D. Prevents changes in one layer from affecting other layers so that it does not hamper development

4. When data is encapsulated, which is the correct order?
   A. Data, frame, packet, segment, bit
   B. Segment, data, packet, frame, bit
   C. Data, segment, packet, frame, bit
   D. Data, segment, frame, packet, bit

5. Which Cisco IOS command can you use to see the IP routing table?
   A. `sh ip config`
   B. `sh ip arp`
   C. `sh ip route`
   D. `sh ip table`

6. You type **debug ip rip** on your router console and see that 172.16.10.0 is being advertised with a metric of 16. What does this mean?

    A. The route is 16 hops away.

    B. The route has a delay of 16 microseconds.

    C. The route is inaccessible.

    D. The route is queued at 16 messages a second.

7. Which of the following commands can be used to learn the number of EIGRP packets sent and received?

    A. `show ip eigrp mail`

    B. `show ip eigrp sent`

    C. `show ip eigrp traffic`

    D. `show ip eigrp data`

    E. `show ip eigrp counters`

8. Which command will show you the hostname resolved to the IP address on a router?

    A. `sh router`

    B. `sho hosts`

    C. `sh ip hosts`

    D. `sho name resolution`

9. What router command allows you to determine whether an IP access list is enabled on a particular interface?

    A. `show ip port`

    B. `show access-list`

    C. `show ip interface`

    D. `show access-list interface`

10. Which command can you use to list all configured PVCs and DLCIs?

    A. `show frame-relay pvc`

    B. `show frame-relay`

    C. `show frame-relay lmi`

    D. `show pvc`

Answers to Review Questions

1.   C.   PDUs are used to define data at each layer of the OSI model. PDUs at the Network layer are called packets.

2.   D.   The Transport layer receives large data streams from the upper layers and breaks these up into smaller pieces called segments.

3.   C.   The largest advantage of a layered model is that it can allow application developers to change the aspects of a program in just one layer of the layer model's specifications.

4.   C.   The encapsulation method is data, segment, packet, frame, bit.

5.   C.   You use the `sh ip route` command to view the contents of the IP routing table.

6.   C.   You cannot have 16 hops on a RIP network by default. If you receive a route advertised with a metric of 16, this means it is inaccessible.

7.   C.   The `show ip eigrp traffic` command shows the sent and received packets. The other commands are not real commands that can be used on a router.

8.   B.   The command to see the host table, which resolves hostnames to IP addresses, is `show host` or `show hosts`.

9.   C.   Only the `show ip interface` command tells you which ports have access lists applied. `show access-lists` will not show you which interfaces have an access list applied. The other two commands are not actual commands.

10.   A.   The `show frame-relay pvc` command will show the PVCs configured and the associated DLCI numbers.

Chapter

4

Technology

CISCO CCNA EXAM OBJECTIVES COVERED IN THIS CHAPTER:

- ✓ 4.1 Describe network communications using layered models
- ✓ 4.2 Describe the Spanning Tree process
- ✓ 4.3 Compare and contrast key characteristics of LAN environments
- ✓ 4.4 Evaluate the characteristics of routing protocols
- ✓ 4.5 Evaluate TCP/IP communication process and its associated protocols
- ✓ 4.6 Describe the components of network devices
- ✓ 4.7 Evaluate rules for packet control
- ✓ 4.8 Evaluate key characteristics of WANs

Technology is a core component of the CCNA exam. You will be expected to not only implement and troubleshoot, but also to understand underlying technologies. Once again, we will cover all aspects of the CCNA exam in looking at technology. We will begin with OSI, cover Ethernet LAN and Layer 3 routing technologies, cover TCP/IP, and finish up with ACLs and WANs. Let's get started!

4.1 Describe Network Communications Using Layered Models

We are primarily concerned with two layered models for the CCNA exam. One is the Cisco three-layer hierarchical model. The second is the industry-standard seven-layer OSI model. Each has an important place in networking; one is not a replacement for the other. Let's take a closer look at the details of each.

The Cisco Three-Layer Hierarchical Model

Most of us were exposed to hierarchy early in life. Anyone with older siblings learned what it was like to be at the bottom of the hierarchy. Regardless of where you first discovered hierarchy, today most of us experience it in many aspects of our lives. It is hierarchy that helps us understand where things belong, how things fit together, and what functions belong at which levels. Hierarchy brings order and understandability to otherwise complex models. If you want a pay raise, for instance, hierarchy dictates that you ask your boss, not your subordinate; your superior is the person whose role it is to grant (or deny) your request. So basically, understanding hierarchy helps you discern where you should go to get what you need.

Hierarchy has many of the same benefits in network design that it does in other areas of life. When used properly, it makes networks more predictable. It helps you define which areas should perform certain functions. Likewise, you can use tools such as access lists at certain levels in hierarchical networks and avoid them at others.

Let's face it, large networks can be extremely complicated, with multiple protocols, detailed configurations, and diverse technologies. Hierarchy helps summarize a complex collection of details into an understandable model. Then, as you need specific configurations, the model dictates the appropriate manner in which to apply them.

The Cisco hierarchical model can help you design, implement, and maintain a scalable, reliable, and cost-effective hierarchical internetwork. Cisco defines three layers of hierarchy, as shown in Figure 4.1, each of which has specific functions.

FIGURE 4.1   The Cisco hierarchical model

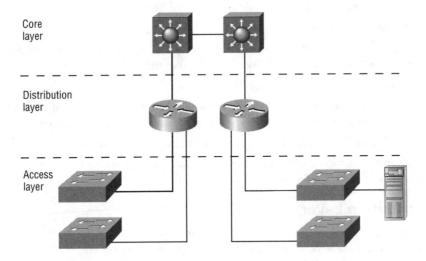

The following are the three layers and their typical functions:

- The core layer acts as a backbone.

- The distribution layer performs routing.

- The access layer performs switching.

Each layer has specific responsibilities. Remember, however, that the three layers are logical and are not necessarily physical devices. For instance, consider the OSI model, another logical hierarchy that we'll discuss later in this section. Its seven layers describe functions but not necessarily protocols. Sometimes a protocol maps to more than one layer of the OSI model, and sometimes multiple protocols communicate within a single layer. In the same way, when you build physical implementations of hierarchical networks, you may have many devices in a single layer, or you might have a single device performing functions at two layers. This is why I say that the definition of the layers is logical, not physical.

Now, let's take a closer look at each of the layers of the hierarchical model.

The Core Layer

The *core layer* is literally the core of the network. At the top of the hierarchy, the core layer is responsible for transporting large amounts of traffic both reliably and quickly. The only purpose of the network's core layer is to switch traffic as fast as possible. The traffic transported across the core is common to a majority of users. However, remember that user data is processed at the distribution layer, which forwards the requests to the core if needed.

A failure in the core is a very big deal—*every user* can be affected. Therefore, fault tolerance at this layer is necessary. The core is likely to see large volumes of traffic, so speed and latency are also driving concerns. Now that you know the function of the core, you should consider some design specifics. Let's start with some things you don't want to do:

- Don't do anything to slow down traffic. This includes using access lists, routing between virtual local area networks (VLANs), and packet filtering.

- Don't support workgroup access here.

- Avoid expanding the core when the internetwork grows (i.e., adding routers). If performance becomes an issue in the core, give preference to upgrades over expansion.

Now here are the things you *do* want to do:

- Design the core for high reliability. Consider data-link technologies that facilitate both speed and redundancy like FDDI, Fast Ethernet (with redundant links), or even ATM.

- Design with speed in mind. The core should have very little latency.

- Select routing protocols with lower convergence times. Fast and redundant data-link connectivity is no help if your routing tables are shot!

The Distribution Layer

The *distribution layer* is sometimes referred to as the workgroup layer, and it is the communication point between the access layer and the core. The primary functions of the distribution layer are to provide routing, filtering, and WAN access and to determine how packets can access the core, if they need to. The distribution layer must determine the fastest way that network service requests are handled—for example, how a file request is forwarded to a server. After the distribution layer determines the best path, it forwards the request to the core layer if necessary. The core layer then quickly transports the request to the correct service.

The distribution layer is the place to implement policies for the network. Here you can exercise considerable flexibility in defining network operation. Here are several actions that you should generally perform at the distribution layer:

- Routing.

- Perform packet filtering and queuing and implement tools such as access lists.

- Implement security and network policies, including address translation and firewalls.

- Redistribute between routing protocols, including static routing.

- Perform routing between VLANs and other workgroup support functions.

- Define broadcast and multicast domains.

Things you should avoid doing at the distribution layer are limited to those functions that exclusively belong to one of the other layers.

The Access Layer

The *access layer* (sometimes referred to as the desktop layer) controls user and workgroup access to internetwork resources. The network resources most users need will be available locally. The distribution layer handles any traffic for remote services. The following are some of the functions you should perform at the access layer:

- Access control and policies, continued from distribution layer.

- Creation of separate collision domains (segmentation).

- Workgroup connectivity into the distribution layer

Technologies such as dial-on-demand routing (DDR) and Ethernet switching are frequently seen in the access layer. Static routing (instead of dynamic routing protocols) is seen here as well.

As already noted, three separate levels does not imply three separate routers. You could encounter fewer, or more. Remember, this is a *layered* approach.

The OSI Reference Model

The OSI reference model was created in the late 1970s, and the main reason the International Organization for Standardization (ISO) released the OSI model was so different vendor networks could work (communicate) with each other. One of the greatest functions of the OSI specifications is that they assist in data transfer between disparate hosts; this means, for example, that you can use them to transfer data between a Unix host and a PC or a Mac.

The OSI isn't a physical model, though. Rather, it's a set of guidelines that application developers can use to create and implement applications that run on a network. It also provides a framework for creating and implementing networking standards, devices, and internetworking schemes.

The OSI has seven different layers, which are divided into two groups. The top three layers define how the applications within the end stations communicate with each other and with users. The bottom four layers define how data is transmitted end-to-end. Figure 4.2 shows the three upper layers and their functions; Figure 4.3 shows the four lower layers and their functions.

FIGURE 4.2   The upper layers

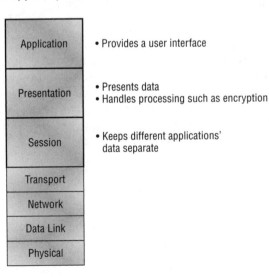

When you study Figure 4.2, you can see that the user interfaces with the computer at the Application layer, and also that the upper layers are responsible for applications communicating between hosts. Remember that none of the upper layers know anything about networking or network addresses. That's the responsibility of the four bottom layers.

In Figure 4.3 you can see that the four bottom layers define how data is transferred through a physical wire or through switches and routers. These bottom layers also determine how to rebuild a data stream from a transmitting host to a destination host's application.

FIGURE 4.3   The lower layers

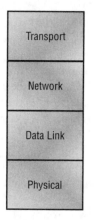

Transport	• Provides reliable or unreliable delivery • Performs error correction before retransmit
Network	• Provides logical addressing, which routers use for path determination
Data Link	• Combines packets into bytes and bytes into frames • Provides access to media using MAC address • Performs error detection not correction
Physical	• Moves bits between devices • Specifies voltage, wire speed, and pin-out of cables

The following is a list of network devices that operate at all seven layers of the OSI model:

- Network management stations (NMS).

- Web and application servers.

- Gateways (not default gateways). Gateways are translators that work at all seven layers of the OSI model.

- Network hosts.

Basically, the ISO is pretty much the Emily Post of the network protocol world. Just like Ms. Post, who wrote the book setting the standards—or protocols—for human social interaction, the ISO developed the OSI reference model as the precedent and guide for an open network protocol set. The OSI reference model not only defines the etiquette of communication models, it remains the most popular means by which you can compare protocol suites.

The OSI reference model has the following seven layers:

- Application layer

- Presentation layer

- Session layer

- Transport layer

- Network layer

- Data Link layer
- Physical layer

Figure 4.4 shows the functions defined at each layer of the OSI model. With this in hand, you're now ready to explore each layer's function in detail.

FIGURE 4.4   Layer functions

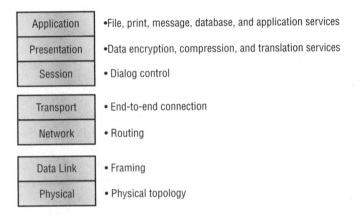

Application	•File, print, message, database, and application services
Presentation	•Data encryption, compression, and translation services
Session	• Dialog control
Transport	• End-to-end connection
Network	• Routing
Data Link	• Framing
Physical	• Physical topology

The Application Layer

The Application layer of the OSI model marks the spot where users actually communicate with the computer. The Application layer actually only comes into play when network access will eventually be required. For instance, take the case of Internet Explorer (IE). You could uninstall every trace of networking components from a system—such as TCP/IP, network interface card (NIC), and so on—and still use IE to view a local HTML document without any problems. It is only when you specify that you would like to view an HTML document that must be retrieved using HTTP, or a file structure that must be retrieved using FTP, that IE attempts to access the Application layer. Even at this point, the Application layer acts as an interface between the actual application process, which is not part of the layered structure at all, and the next layer down, offering services that allow the application to send information down through the protocol stack. That is to say, IE is not in the Application layer, but it interfaces with Application layer protocols when it is dealing with remote resources.

This layer is also responsible for identifying and establishing the availability of the intended communication partner and determining if sufficient resources for the intended communication exist.

These tasks are important because computer applications sometimes require more than just desktop resources. Often, they'll unite communicating components from more than one network application. Things like performing file transfers and sending e-mail, as well as enabling remote access, managing network activities and client/server processes, and locating information are prime examples. Many network applications provide services that allow you to communicate over enterprise networks, but for present and future internetworking, these communication needs are beginning to fall short; such needs are quickly developing to reach beyond the limits of current physical networking. As a result, today, transactions and information exchanges between organizations are expanding to include internetworking applications like the following:

- World Wide Web (WWW)
- E-mail gateways
- Electronic data interchange (EDI)
- File Transfer Protocol (FTP)
- Voice over IP (VoIP)

The Presentation Layer

The Presentation layer gets its name from its purpose: it presents data to the Application layer and is responsible for translating data and formatting code.

This layer essentially functions as a translator and provides coding and conversion functions. A successful data-transfer technique involves adapting the data into a standard format before it is transmitted. Computers are configured to receive this generically formatted data and then convert the data back into its native format for actual reading (for example, EBCDIC to ASCII). By providing translation services, the Presentation layer ensures that data transferred from the Application layer of one system can be read by the Application layer of another.

The OSI has protocol standards that define how standard data should be formatted. Tasks like data compression, decompression, encryption, and decryption are associated with this layer. Some Presentation layer standards are involved in multimedia operations too. The following direct graphic and visual image presentation:

- PICT
- TIFF
- JPEG
- MIDI
- MPEG
- QuickTime
- RTF

The Session Layer

The Session layer is responsible for setting up, managing, and then tearing down sessions between Presentation layer entities. This layer also controls dialog between devices, or nodes. It coordinates communication between systems and serves to organize their communication by offering three different modes: simplex, half-duplex, and full-duplex. To sum up, the Session layer basically keeps different applications' data separate from other applications' data.

The following are some examples of Session layer protocols and interfaces (according to Cisco):

- Network File System (NFS)

- Structured Query Language (SQL)

- Remote Procedure Call (RPC)

- X Window

- AppleTalk Session Protocol (ASP)

- Digital Network Architecture Session Control Protocol (DNA SCP)

The Transport Layer

The Transport layer segments and reassembles data into a data stream. Services located in the Transport layer both segment and reassemble data from upper-layer applications and unite it onto the same data stream. They provide end-to-end data transport services and can establish a logical connection between the sending host and destination host on an internetwork.

Some of you are probably familiar with the Transmission Control Protocol (TCP) and the User Datagram Protocol (UDP) already. If so, you know that both work at the Transport layer, and that TCP is a reliable service whereas UDP is not. This means that application developers have more options because they have a choice between the two protocols when they are working with TCP/IP.

The Transport layer is responsible for providing mechanisms for multiplexing upper-layer applications, establishing sessions, and tearing down virtual circuits. It also hides details of any network-dependent information from the higher layers by providing transparent data transfer. We will look at four components that are frequently implemented at the transport layer. They are:

- Flow control

- Connection-oriented communication

- Windowing

- Acknowledgments

Flow Control

Data integrity is ensured at the Transport layer by maintaining flow control and by allowing users to request reliable data transport between systems. *Flow control* prevents a sending host on one side of the connection from overflowing the buffers in the receiving host—an event that can result in lost data. Reliable data transport employs a connection-oriented communications session between systems and the protocols involved ensure that the following are achieved:

- The segments delivered are acknowledged back to the sender upon their receipt.

- Any segments not acknowledged are retransmitted.

- Segments are sequenced back into their proper order upon arrival at their destination.

- A manageable data flow is maintained in order to avoid congestion, overloading, and data loss.

Connection-Oriented Communication

In reliable transport operation, one device first establishes a connection-oriented session with its peer system. This is called a call setup, or a three-way handshake. Data is then transferred, and when the transfer completes, a call termination takes place to tear down the virtual circuit.

Figure 4.5 depicts a typical reliable session taking place between sending and receiving systems. Both hosts' application programs begin by notifying their individual operating systems that a connection is about to be initiated. The two operating systems communicate by sending messages over the network that confirm that the transfer is approved and that both sides are ready for it to take place. Once all this required synchronization takes place, a connection is fully established and the data transfer begins.

FIGURE 4.5   Establishing a connection-oriented session

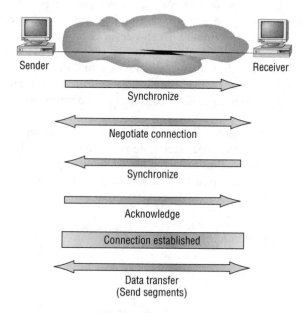

While the information is being transferred between hosts, the two machines periodically check in with each other, communicating through their protocol software to ensure that all is going well and that the data is being received properly.

Let me sum up the steps in the connection-oriented session—the three-way handshake—pictured in Figure 4.5:

- The first "connection agreement" segment requests synchronization.

- The second and third segments acknowledge the request and establish connection parameters—the rules—between hosts. The receiver's sequencing requests to be synchronized here, as well, so that a bidirectional connection can be formed.

- The final segment is also an acknowledgment. It notifies the destination host that the connection agreement has been accepted and that the actual connection has been established. Data transfer can now begin.

Sounds pretty simple, but things don't always flow so smoothly. Sometimes during a transfer, congestion can occur because a high-speed computer is generating data traffic a lot faster than the network can handle the transfer. A bunch of computers simultaneously sending datagrams through a single gateway or destination can also botch things up nicely. In the latter case, a gateway or destination can become congested even though no single source is causing the problem. In either case, the problem is basically akin to a freeway bottleneck—too much traffic for too small a capacity. It's not usually one car that's the problem; there are simply too many cars on that freeway.

Okay, so what happens when a machine receives a flood of datagrams too quickly for it to process? It stores them in a memory section called a *buffer*. But this buffering action can only solve the problem if the datagrams are part of a small burst. If they aren't, and the datagram deluge continues, a device's memory will eventually be exhausted, its flood capacity will be exceeded, and it will react by discarding any additional datagrams that arrive.

No huge worries here, though. Because of the transport function, network flood control systems actually work quite well. Instead of dumping resources and allowing data to be lost, the transport can issue a "not ready" indicator to the sender, or source, of the flood (as shown in Figure 4.6). This mechanism works kind of like a stop light, signaling the sending device to stop transmitting segment traffic to its overwhelmed peer. After the peer receiver processes the segments already in its memory reservoir—its buffer—it sends out a "ready" transport indicator. When the machine waiting to transmit the rest of its datagrams receives this "go" indictor, it resumes its transmission.

In fundamental, reliable, connection-oriented data transfer, datagrams are delivered to the receiving host in exactly the same sequence they're transmitted—and the transmission fails if this order is breached! If any data segments are lost, duplicated, or damaged along the way, a failure will transmit. This problem is solved by having the receiving host acknowledge that it has received every data segment.

FIGURE 4.6   Transmitting segments with flow control

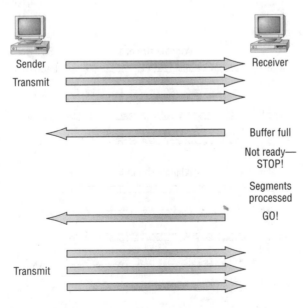

Windowing

Ideally, data throughput happens quickly and efficiently. And as you can imagine, it would be slow if the transmitting machine had to wait for an acknowledgment, which we'll discuss in a moment, after sending each segment. But because there's time available *after* the sender transmits the data segment and *before* it finishes processing acknowledgments from the receiving machine, the sender uses the break as an opportunity to transmit more data. The quantity of data segments (measured in bytes) the transmitting machine is allowed to send without receiving an acknowledgment for them is called a *window*.

Windows are used to control the amount in outstanding, unacknowledged data segments.

So the size of the window controls how much information is transferred from one end to the other. Whereas some protocols quantify information by observing the number of packets, TCP/IP measures it by counting the number of bytes.

As you can see in Figure 4.7, there are two window sizes—one set to 1, and one set to 3. When you've configured a window size of 1, the sending machine waits for an acknowledgment for each data segment it transmits before it transmits another. If you've configured a window size of 3, it's allowed to transmit three data segments before it must receive an acknowledgment. In this simplified example, both the sending and receiving machines are workstations. However, reality is rarely that simple; most often, acknowledgments and packets commingle as they travel over the network and pass through routers.

FIGURE 4.7   Windowing

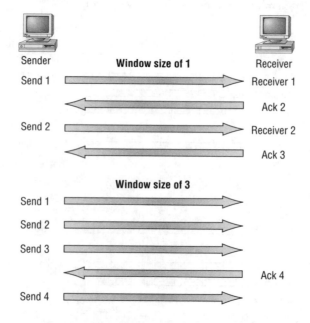

Acknowledgments

Reliable data delivery ensures the integrity of a stream of data sent from one machine to the other through a fully functional data link. It guarantees that the data won't be duplicated or lost. This is achieved through something called *positive acknowledgment with retransmission*—a technique that requires the receiving machine to communicate with the transmitting source by sending an acknowledgment message back when it receives data. The sender documents each segment it sends and waits for this acknowledgment before it sends the next segment. When it sends a segment, the transmitting machine starts a timer and retransmits if it expires before an acknowledgment is returned from the receiving end.

In Figure 4.8, the sending machine transmits segments 1, 2, and 3. The receiving node acknowledges it has received them by requesting segment 4. When it receives the acknowledgment, the sender then transmits segments 4, 5, and 6. If segment 5 doesn't make it to the destination, the receiving node acknowledges that event with a request for the segment to be resent. The sending machine will then resend the lost segment and wait for an acknowledgment, which it must receive in order to move on to the transmission of segment 7.

F I G U R E   4 . 8   Transport layer reliable delivery

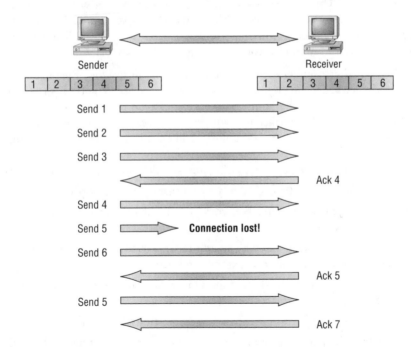

The Network Layer

The Network layer (also called Layer 3) manages device addressing, tracks the location of devices on the network, and determines the best way to move data, which means that the Network layer must transport traffic between devices that aren't locally attached. Routers (Layer 3 devices) are specified at the Network layer and provide the routing services within an internetwork.

It happens like this:

1. First, when the router interface receives a packet, the destination IP address is checked. If the packet isn't destined for that particular router, it will look up the destination network address in the routing table.

2. Once the router chooses an exit interface, the router sends the packet to that interface to be framed and sent out on the local network.

3. Then, if the router can't find an entry for the packet's destination network in the routing table, it drops the packet.

Two types of packets are used at the Network layer: data and route updates.

Data packets   Transport user data through the internetwork. Protocols used to support data traffic are called *routed protocols*; examples of routed protocols are IP and IPX. You learned about IP addressing in Chapter 2, "Implementing and Operation," and Chapter 3, "Troubleshooting."

Route update packets   Update neighboring routers about the networks connected to all routers within the internetwork. Protocols that send route update packets are called *routing protocols*; examples of some common ones are RIP, EIGRP, and OSPF. Route update packets are used to help build and maintain routing tables on each router.

As I mentioned earlier, routers break up broadcast domains, which means that by default, broadcasts aren't forwarded through a router. Do you remember why this is a good thing? Routers also break up collision domains, but you can also do that using Layer 2 (Data Link layer) switches. Because each interface in a router represents a separate network, it must be assigned unique network identification numbers, and each host on the network connected to that router must use the same network number.

Here are some points about Layer 3 routing you should really commit to memory:

- Routers, by default, will not forward any broadcast or multicast packets.

- Routers use the logical address in a Network layer header to determine the next hop router to forward the packet to.

- Routers can use access lists, created by an administrator, to control security on the types of packets that are allowed to enter or exit an interface.

- Routers can provide Layer 2 bridging functions if they need to and can simultaneously route through the same interface.

- Layer 3 devices (routers in this case) provide connections between VLANs.

- Routers can provide quality of service (QoS) for specific types of network traffic.

The Data Link Layer

The Data Link layer of the OSI model provides the physical transmission of the data and handles error notification, network topology, and flow control. This means the Data Link layer will ensure that messages are delivered to the proper device on a LAN using hardware addresses, and translates messages from the Network layer into bits for the Physical layer to transmit.

The Data Link layer formats the message into pieces, each called a *data frame*, and adds a customized header containing the hardware destination and source address. This added information forms a sort of capsule that surrounds the original message in much the same way that the engines, navigational devices, and other tools were attached to the lunar modules of the Apollo project. These various pieces of equipment were useful only during certain stages of space flight and were stripped off the module and discarded when their designated stage was complete. Data traveling through networks is similar.

Figure 4.9 shows the Data Link layer with the Ethernet and IEEE specifications. When you check it out, notice that the IEEE 802.2 standard is used in conjunction with and adds functionality to the other IEEE standards.

FIGURE 4.9   Data Link layer

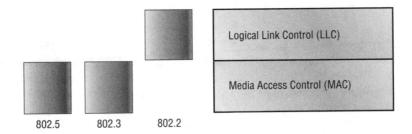

It's important for you to understand that routers, which work at the Network layer, don't care at all about where a particular host is located. They're only concerned about where networks are located, and the best way to reach them—including remote ones. Routers are totally obsessed when it comes to networks. And for once, this is a good thing! It's the Data Link layer that's responsible for the actual unique identification of each device that resides on a local network.

For a host to send packets to individual hosts and between routers, the Data Link layer uses *hardware addressing* (as opposed to network or logical addressing). Each time a packet is sent between routers it's framed with control information at the Data Link layer, but that information is stripped off at the receiving router and only the original packet is left completely intact. This framing of the packet continues for each hop until the packet is finally delivered to the correct receiving host. It's really important to understand that the packet itself is never altered along the route; it's only encapsulated with the type of control information required for it to be properly passed on to the different media types.

The IEEE Ethernet Data Link layer has two sublayers:

Media Access Control (MAC) 802.3   This defines how packets are placed on the media. *Contention media access* (one form of media access that is used by Ethernet) is "first come/first served" access where everyone competes for the same bandwidth—hence the name. Physical addressing is defined here, as well as *logical topologies*. What's a logical topology? It's the signal path through a physical topology. Line discipline, error notification (not correction), ordered delivery of frames, and optional flow control can also be used at this sublayer.

Logical Link Control (LLC) 802.2   This sublayer is responsible for identifying Network layer protocols and then encapsulating them. An LLC header tells the Data Link layer what to do with a packet once a frame is received. It works like this: a host receives a frame and looks in the LLC header and finds out that the packet is destined for, say, the IP protocol at the Network layer. The LLC can also provide flow control and sequencing of control bits.

Data-link layer devices

Switches and bridges both work at the Data Link layer and filter the network using hardware (MAC) addresses. Layer 2 switching is considered hardware-based bridging because it uses specialized hardware called an application-specific integrated circuit (ASIC). ASICs can run up to gigabit speeds with very low latency rates.

Latency is the time measured from when a frame enters a port to the time it exits.

Bridges and switches read each frame as it passes through the network. The Layer 2 device then puts the source hardware address in a filter table and keeps track of which port the frame was received on. This information (logged in the bridge's or switch's filter table) is what helps the machine determine the location of the specific sending device.

The real estate business is all about location, location, location, and it's the same way for both Layer 2 and 3 devices. Though both need to be able to negotiate the network, it's crucial to remember that they're concerned with very different parts of it. Primarily, routers, or Layer-3 machines, need to locate specific networks, whereas Layer 2 machines (switches and bridges) need to locate specific devices. So, networks are to routers as individual devices are to switches and bridges. And routing tables that "map" the internetwork are for routers, as filter tables that "map" individual devices are for switches and bridges.

After a filter table is built on the Layer 2 device, it will only forward frames to the segment where the destination hardware address is located. If the destination device is on the same segment as the frame, the Layer 2 device will block the frame from going to any other segments. If the destination is on a different segment, the frame can only be transmitted to that segment. This is called *transparent bridging*.

When a switch interface receives a frame with a destination hardware address that isn't found in the device's filter table, it will forward the frame to all connected segments. If the unknown device that was sent the "mystery frame" replies to this forwarding action, the switch updates its filter table regarding that device's location. But if the destination address of the transmitting frame is a broadcast address, the switch forwards all broadcasts to every connected segment by default.

All devices that the broadcast is forwarded to are considered to be in the same broadcast domain. This can be a problem; Layer 2 devices propagate Layer 2 broadcast storms that choke performance, and the only way to stop a broadcast storm from propagating through an internetwork is with a Layer 3 device—a router.

Using switches for Layer 2 segmentation

The biggest benefit of using switches instead of hubs in your internetwork is that each switch port is actually its own collision domain. (Conversely, a hub creates one large collision domain.) But even armed with a switch, you still can't break up broadcast domains. Neither switches nor bridges will do that. Typically, they'll simply forward all broadcasts instead.

Another benefit of LAN switching over hub-centered implementations is that each device on every segment plugged into a switch can transmit simultaneously—as long as there is only one host on each port and the hub isn't plugged into the switch port, which is another benefit of each switch port being its own collision domain. As you might have guessed, hubs only allow one device per segment to communicate at a time.

Each network segment connected to the switch must have the same type of devices attached. This means that you can connect an Ethernet hub into a switch port and then connect multiple Ethernet hosts into the hub, but you can't mix Token Ring hosts in with the Ethernet gang on the same segment. Mixing hosts in this manner is called *media translation*, and Cisco says you've just got to have a router around if you need to provide this service. Although I have found this not to be true in reality, remember, we're studying for the CCNA exam here, right?

The Physical Layer

Finally arriving at the bottom, we find that the Physical layer does two things: it sends bits and receives bits. Bits come only in values of 1 or 0—a Morse code with numerical values. The Physical layer communicates directly with the various types of actual communication media. Different kinds of media represent these bit values in different ways. Some use audio tones, while others employ *state transitions*—changes in voltage from high to low and low to high. Each type of media needs specific protocols to describe the proper bit patterns to be used, how data is encoded into media signals, and the various qualities of the physical media's attachment interface.

Physical layer in the WAN

The Physical layer specifies the electrical, mechanical, procedural, and functional requirements for activating, maintaining, and deactivating a physical link between end systems. This layer is also where you identify the interface between the data terminal equipment (DTE) and the data communication equipment (DCE). (Some old phone company employees still call DCE data circuit–terminating equipment.) The DCE is usually located at the service provider, while the DTE is the attached device. The services available to the DTE are most often accessed via a modem or channel service unit/data service unit (CSU/DSU).

Physical layer in the LAN

The Physical layer's connectors and different physical topologies are defined by the OSI as standards, allowing disparate systems to communicate. The CCNA exam is only interested in the IEEE Ethernet standards.

Of the Ethernet devices at the physical layer, the only one we are concerned with is the hub. A *hub* is really a multiple-port repeater. A repeater receives a digital signal, reamplifies or regenerates that signal, and then forwards it out all active ports without looking at any data. An active hub does the same thing. Any digital signal received from a segment on a hub port is regenerated or reamplified and transmitted out all ports on the hub. This means all devices plugged into a hub are in the same collision domain as well as in the same broadcast domain.

Hubs, like repeaters, don't actually examine any of the traffic as it enters and is then transmitted out to the other parts of the physical media. Every device connected to the hub, or hubs, must listen to see if a device transmits. A *physical star network*—where the hub is a central device and cables extend in all directions out from it—is the type of topology a hub creates. Visually, the design really does resemble a star, whereas Ethernet networks run a logical bus topology, meaning that the signal has to run from one end of the network to the other.

Exam Essentials

Remember the three layers in the Cisco three-layer model. The three layers in the Cisco hierarchical model are the core, distribution, and access layers.

Remember the seven layers of the OSI model. You must remember the seven layers of the OSI model and what function each layer provides. The Application, Presentation, and Session layers are upper layers and are responsible for communicating between a user interface and an application. The Transport layer provides segmentation, sequencing, and virtual circuits. The Network layer provides logical network addressing and routing through an internetwork. The Data Link layer provides framing and places data on the network medium. The Physical layer takes ones and zeros and encodes them into a digital signal that it can transmit on the network segment.

Remember the difference between connection-oriented and connectionless network services. Connection-oriented uses acknowledgments and flow control to create a reliable session. More overhead is used than in a connectionless network service. Connectionless services are used to send data with no acknowledgments or flow control. This is considered unreliable.

4.2 Describe the Spanning Tree Process

Back before it was purchased and renamed Compaq, a company called Digital Equipment Corporation (DEC) created the original version of Spanning Tree Protocol (STP). The IEEE later created its own version of STP called 802.1D. All Cisco switches run the IEEE 802.1D version of STP, which isn't compatible with the DEC version.

STP's main task is to stop network loops from occurring on your Layer 2 network (bridges or switches). It vigilantly monitors the network to find all links, making sure that no loops occur by shutting down any redundant ones. STP uses the spanning-tree algorithm (STA) to first create a topology database, then search out and destroy redundant links. With STP running, frames will only be forwarded on the premium, STP-picked links.

Spanning-Tree Terms

Before I get into describing the details of how STP works in the network, you need to understand some basic ideas and terms and how they relate within the Layer 2 switched network:

STP   Spanning Tree Protocol (STP) is a bridge protocol that uses the STA to find redundant links dynamically and create a spanning-tree topology database. Bridges exchange Bridge Protocol Data Unit (BPDU) messages with other bridges to detect loops, and then remove them by shutting down selected bridge interfaces.

Root bridge   The root bridge is the bridge with the best bridge ID. With STP, the key is for all the switches in the network to elect a root bridge that becomes the focal point in the network. All other decisions in the network—like which port is to be blocked and which port is to be put in forwarding mode—are made from the perspective of this root bridge.

BPDU   All the switches exchange information to use in the selection of the root switch, as well as for subsequent configuration of the network. Each switch compares the parameters in the BPDU that they send to one neighbor with the one that they receive from another neighbor.

Bridge ID   This is how STP keeps track of all the switches in the network. The bridge ID is determined by a combination of the bridge priority (32,768 by default on all Cisco switches) and the base MAC address. The lowest bridge ID becomes the root bridge in the network.

Nonroot bridge   All bridges that are not the root bridge. These exchange BPDUs with all bridges and update the STP topology database on all switches, preventing loops and providing a measure of defense against link failures.

Root port   Always the link directly connected to the root bridge, or the shortest path to the root bridge. If more than one link connects to the root bridge, then a port cost is determined by checking the bandwidth of each link. The lowest cost port becomes the root port.

Designated port   Either a root port or a port that has been determined as having the best (lower) cost—a designated port will be marked as a forwarding port.

Port cost   Determined when multiple links are used between two switches and none are root ports. The cost of a link is determined by the bandwidth of a link.

Nondesignated port   Port with a higher cost than the designated port that will be put in blocking mode—a nondesignated port is not a forwarding port.

Forwarding port   Port that forwards frames.

Blocked port   Port that will not forward frames in order to prevent loops. However, a blocked port will always listen to frames.

Spanning-Tree Operations

As I've said before, STP's job is to find all links in the network and shut down any redundant ones, thereby preventing network loops from occurring. STP does this by first electing a root bridge that will preside over network topology decisions. Those decisions include determining which "roads" are the best ones for frames to travel on normally, and which ones should be reserved as backup routes if one of the primary "roads" fail.

Things tend to go a lot more smoothly when you don't have more than one person making a navigational decision, and so there can only be one root bridge in any given network. I'll discuss the root bridge election process more completely in the next section.

Selecting the Root Bridge

The bridge ID is used to elect the root bridge in the network as well as to determine the root port. This ID is 8 bytes long and includes both the priority and the MAC address of the device. The default priority on all devices running the IEEE STP version is 32,768.

To determine the root bridge, the priorities of the bridge and the MAC address are combined. If two switches or bridges happen to have the same priority value, then the MAC address becomes the tiebreaker for figuring out which one has the lowest (best) ID. It's like this: if two switches—I'll name them A and B—both use the default priority of 32,768, then the MAC address will be used instead. If switch A's MAC address is 0000.0c00.1111 and switch B's MAC address is 0000.0c00.2222, then switch A would become the root bridge. Just remember that the lower value is the better one when it comes to electing a root bridge.

BPDUs are sent every 2 seconds, by default, out all active ports on a bridge/switch, and the bridge with the lowest (best) bridge ID is elected the root bridge. You can change the bridge's ID so that it will become a root bridge automatically. Being able to do that is important in a large switched network—it ensures that the best paths are chosen.

Changing STP parameters is beyond the scope of this book, but it's covered in the Sybex *CCNP®: Building Cisco Multilayer Switched Networks Study Guide* (Sybex, 2004).

Selecting the Designated Port

If more than one link is connected to the root port, then port cost becomes the factor used to determine which port will be the root port. So, to determine the port or ports that will be used to communicate with the root bridge, you must first figure out the path's cost. The STP cost is an accumulated total path cost based on the available bandwidth of each of the links. Table 4.1 shows the typical costs associated with various Ethernet networks.

TABLE 4.1   Typical Costs of Different Ethernet Networks

Speed	New IEEE Cost	Original IEEE Cost
10Gbps	2	1
1Gbps	4	1

TABLE 4.1   Typical Costs of Different Ethernet Networks *(continued)*

Speed	New IEEE Cost	Original IEEE Cost
100Mbps	19	10
10Mbps	100	100

The IEEE 802.1D specification has recently been revised to handle the new higher-speed links. The IEEE 802.1D specification assigns a default port cost value to each port based on bandwidth.

Spanning-Tree Port States

The ports on a bridge or switch running STP can transition through five different modes:

Blocking   A blocked port won't forward frames; it just listens to BPDUs. All ports are in blocking state by default when the switch is powered up. The purpose of the blocking state is to prevent the use of looped paths.

Listening   The port listens to BPDUs to make sure no loops occur on the network before passing data frames. A port in listening state prepares to forward data frames without populating the MAC address table.

Learning   The switch port listens to BPDUs and learns all the paths in the switched network. A port in learning state populates the MAC address table but doesn't forward data frames.

Forwarding   The port sends and receives all data frames on the bridged port.

Disabled   A port in the disabled state does not participate in the frame forwarding or STP. A port in the disabled state is virtually nonoperational.

Switch ports are most often in either the blocking or forwarding state. A forwarding port is one that has been determined to have the lowest (best) cost to the root bridge. But when and if the network experiences a topology change (because of a failed link or because someone adds in a new switch), you'll find the ports on a switch in listening and learning state.

As I said, blocking ports is a strategy for preventing network loops. Once a switch determines the best path to the root bridge, then all other ports will be in blocking mode. Blocked ports can still receive BPDUs—they just don't send out any frames.

If a switch determines that a blocked port should now be the designated port, it will go into listening mode and check all BPDUs it receives to make sure that it won't create a loop once the port goes to forwarding mode—nice!

Convergence

Convergence occurs when bridges and switches have transitioned to either the forwarding or blocking modes. No data is forwarded during this time. Before data can be forwarded again, all devices must be updated. Convergence is important to make sure all devices have the same database, but it does cost you some time. It usually takes 50 seconds to go from blocking to forwarding mode, and I don't recommend changing the default STP timers. (But you can adjust those timers if necessary.)

Exam Essentials

Understand the states of STP.   The purpose of the blocking state is to prevent the use of looped paths. A port in listening state prepares to forward data frames without populating the MAC address table. A port in learning state populates the MAC address table but doesn't forward data frames. The forwarding port sends and receives all data frames on the bridged port. Lastly, a port in the disabled state is virtually nonoperational.

Understand the main purpose of the spanning tree in a switched LAN.   The main purpose of STP is to prevent switching loops in a network with redundant switched paths.

4.3 Compare and Contrast Key Characteristics of LAN Environments

There have been several popular LAN technologies in the past, but the one that has emerged dominant has been Ethernet. Although technologies such as Token Ring are still available, they are not experiencing the development or expansion that Ethernet is. If there is a new kid on the block, though, it has to be wireless technologies. In this section, we will first discuss Ethernet networking, and then move on to cover LAN switching as it applies to Ethernet LANs. Finally, we will take a quick look at some of the newest wireless LANs.

For purposes of preparing for the CCNA exam, we will confine our discussion to Ethernet and wireless LANs.

Ethernet Networking

Ethernet is a contention media access method that allows all hosts on a network to share the same bandwidth of a link. Ethernet is popular because it's readily scalable, which means that it's comparatively easy to integrate new technologies, like FastEthernet and Gigabit Ethernet, into an existing network infrastructure. It's also relatively simple to implement in the first place, and with it, troubleshooting is reasonably straightforward. Ethernet uses both Data Link and Physical layer specifications, and this section of the chapter will give you both the Data Link and Physical layer information you need to effectively implement, troubleshoot, and maintain an Ethernet network.

Ethernet networking uses Carrier Sense Multiple Access with Collision Detect (CSMA/CD), a protocol that helps devices share the bandwidth evenly without having two devices transmit at the same time on the network medium. CSMA/CD was created to overcome the problem of those collisions that occur when packets are transmitted simultaneously from different nodes. And trust me, good collision management is crucial, because when a node transmits in a CSMA/CD network, all the other nodes on the network receive and examine that transmission. Only bridges and routers can effectively prevent a transmission from propagating throughout the entire network!

So, how does the CSMA/CD protocol work? Like this: when a host wants to transmit over the network, it first checks for the presence of a digital signal on the wire. If all is clear (no other host is transmitting), the host will then proceed with its transmission. But it doesn't stop there. The transmitting host constantly monitors the wire to make sure no other hosts begin transmitting. If the host detects another signal on the wire, it sends out an extended jam signal that causes all nodes on the segment to stop sending data (think, busy signal). The nodes respond to that jam signal by waiting a while before attempting to transmit again. Backoff algorithms determine when the colliding stations can retransmit. If collisions keep occurring after 15 tries, the nodes attempting to transmit will then time out. Pretty clean!

The effects of having a CSMA/CD network sustaining heavy collisions include the following:

- Delay
- Low throughput
- Congestion

Backoff on an 802.3 network is the retransmission delay that's enforced when a collision occurs.

Half- and Full-Duplex Ethernet

Half-duplex Ethernet is defined in the original 802.3 Ethernet and Cisco says you only use one wire pair with a digital signal running in both directions on the wire. It also uses the CSMA/CD protocol to help prevent collisions and to permit retransmitting if a collision does occur. If a hub is attached to a switch, it must operate in half-duplex mode because the end stations must be able to detect collisions. Half-duplex Ethernet—typically 10BaseT—is only about 30 to 40 percent efficient as Cisco sees it, because a large 10BaseT network will usually only give you 3- to 4Mbps—at most.

Full-duplex Ethernet uses two pairs of wires, instead of one wire pair like half duplex. Also, full duplex uses a point-to-point connection between the transmitter of the transmitting device and the receiver of the receiving device, which means that with full-duplex data transfer, you get a faster data transfer compared to half duplex. And because the transmitted data is sent on a different set of wires than the received data, no collisions occur—sweet!

The reason you don't need to worry about collisions is because now Full-duplex Ethernet is like a freeway with multiple lanes instead of the single-lane road provided by half duplex. Full-duplex Ethernet is supposed to offer 100 percent efficiency in both directions; this means you can get 20Mbps with a 10Mbps Ethernet running full duplex, or 200Mbps for FastEthernet—woohoo! But this rate is something known as an *aggregate rate*, which translates into "You're supposed to get" 100 percent efficiency. No guarantees in networking, as in life.

Full-duplex Ethernet can be used in three situations:

- With a connection from a switch to a host
- With a connection from a switch to a switch
- With a connection from a host to a host using a crossover cable

Full-duplex Ethernet requires a point-to-point connection when only two nodes are present.

Now, if it's capable of all that speed, why won't it deliver? Well, when a Full-duplex Ethernet port is powered on, it first connects to the remote end, and then it negotiates with the other end of the FastEthernet link. This is called an *auto-detect mechanism*. This mechanism first decides on the exchange capability, which means it checks to see if it can run at 10 or 100Mbps. It then checks to see if it can run full duplex, and if it can't, it will run half duplex.

Remember that half-duplex Ethernet shares a collision domain and provides a lower effective throughput than Full-duplex Ethernet, which typically has a private collision domain and a higher effective throughput.

Ethernet at the Data Link Layer

Ethernet at the Data Link layer is responsible for Ethernet addressing, commonly referred to as hardware addressing or MAC addressing. Ethernet is also responsible for framing packets received from the Network layer and preparing them for transmission on the local network through the Ethernet contention media access method.

Ethernet Addressing

Here's where we get into how Ethernet addressing uses the MAC address burned into every Ethernet NIC. The MAC, or hardware address, is a 48-bit (6 byte) address written in a hexadecimal format.

Figure 4.10 shows the 48-bit MAC addresses and how the bits are divided.

FIGURE 4.10   Ethernet addressing using MAC addresses

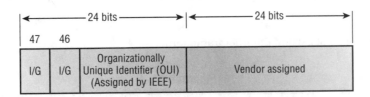

The organizationally unique identifier (OUI) is assigned by the IEEE to an organization. It's composed of 24 bits, or 3 bytes. The organization, in turn, assigns a globally administered address (24 bits, or 3 bytes) that is unique (supposedly—again, no guarantees) to every adapter they manufacture. Look closely at the figure. The high-order bit is the Individual/Group (I/G) bit. When it has a value of 0, you can assume the address is actually the MAC address of a device and may well appear in the source portion of the MAC header. When it is a 1, you can assume that the address represents either a broadcast or multicast address in Ethernet, or a broadcast or functional address in Token Ring and FDDI (who really knows about FDDI?). The next bit is the Global/Local (G/L) bit (also known as U/L, where U means Universal). When set to 0, this bit represents a globally administered address (as by the IEEE). When the bit is a 1, it represents an administratively locally governed address (as in DECnet). The low-order 24 bits of an Ethernet address represent a *locally* (if anything) administered or manufacturer assigned code. This portion commonly starts with 24 zeros (0s) for the first card made and continues in order until there are 24 ones (1s) for the last (16,777,216th) card made. You'll actually find that many manufacturers use these same 6 hex digits as the last 6 characters of their serial number on the same card.

Ethernet Frames

The Data Link layer is responsible for combining bits into bytes and bytes into frames. Frames are used at the Data Link layer to encapsulate packets handed down from the Network layer for transmission on a type of media access. There are three types of media access methods: contention (Ethernet), token passing (Token Ring and FDDI), and polling (IBM Mainframes and 100VG-AnyLAN).

100VG-AnyLAN is a twisted-pair technology that was the first 100Mbps LAN. However, because it was incompatible with Ethernet signaling techniques (it used a demand priority access method), it wasn't very popular, and is now essentially dead.

The function of Ethernet frames is to pass data between hosts using a group of bits known as a *MAC frame format*. This provides error detection from a cyclic redundancy check (CRC). But remember—this is error detection, not error correction.

There are several ways to create Ethernet frames. Each way is called a frame type or frame format, and has a unique name. The 802.3 frames and the Ethernet_II frame formats are shown in Figure 4.11.

FIGURE 4.11 802.3 and Ethernet frame formats

Ethernet_II

Preamble 8 bytes	DA 6 bytes	SA 6 bytes	Type 2 bytes	Data	FCS 4 bytes

802.3_Ethernet

Preamble 8 bytes	DA 6 bytes	SA 6 bytes	Length 2 bytes	Data	FCS

Encapsulating a frame within a different type of frame is called *tunneling*.

The following points detail the different fields in the 802.3 and Ethernet_II frame types.

Preamble An alternating 1,0 pattern provides a 5MHz clock at the start of each packet, which allows the receiving devices to lock the incoming bit stream.

Start Frame Delimiter (SFD)/Synch The SDF/Synch is in the last octet of the eight octet preamble. The SFD is 10101011, where the last pair of ones (1s) allows the receivers to come into the alternating 1,0 pattern somewhere in the middle and still synch up and detect the beginning of the data.

Destination Address (DA) This transmits a 48-bit value using the least significant bit (LSB) first. Receiving stations use the DA to determine if an incoming packet is addressed to a particular node. The DA can be an individual address or a broadcast or multicast MAC address. Remember that a broadcast is all 1s (or Fs in hex) and is sent to all devices, but a multicast is only sent to a similar subset of nodes on a network.

Hex is short for *hexadecimal*, which is a numbering system that uses the first 6 letters of the alphabet (A through F) to extend beyond the available 10 digits in the decimal system. Hexadecimal has a total of 16 digits.

Source Address (SA)   The SA is a 48-bit MAC address used to identify the transmitting device, and it uses the LSB first. Broadcast and multicast address formats are illegal within the SA field.

Length or Type field   802.3 uses a Length field, but the Ethernet frame uses a Type field to identify the Network layer protocol. 802.3 cannot identify the upper-layer protocol and must be used with a proprietary LAN—IPX, for example.

Data   This is a packet sent down to the Data Link layer from the Network layer. The size can vary from 64 to 1500 bytes.

Frame Check Sequence (FCS)   FCS is a field at the end of the frame that's used to store the CRC.

Let's hang out here for a minute and take a good look at some frames caught on our trusty protocol analyzer (a protocol analyzer is a tool that allows you to capture and view packets on the wire, such as Sniffer). You can see that the following frame has only three fields: a Destination, a Source, and a Type field. This is an Ethernet_II frame. Notice that the type field is IP, or 08-00 in hexadecimal.

```
Destination:    00:60:f5:00:1f:27
Source:         00:60:f5:00:1f:2c
Protocol Type: 08-00 IP
```

The next frame has the same fields, so it must be an Ethernet_II frame too. I included this one so that you could see that the frame can carry more than just IP—it can also carry IPX, or 81-37. Did you notice that this frame was a broadcast? You can tell because the destination hardware address is all 1s in binary, or all Fs in hexadecimal.

```
Destination:    ff:ff:ff:ff:ff:ff Ethernet Broadcast
Source:         02:07:01:22:de:a4
Protocol Type: 81-37 NetWare
```

Now, pay special attention to the Length field in the next frame. This must be an 802.3 frame. The problem with this frame is this: how do you know which protocol this packet is going to be handed to at the Network layer? It doesn't specify in the frame, so it must be IPX. Why? Because when Novell created the 802.3 frame type (before the IEEE did—they called it 802.3 Raw), they were pretty much the only LAN server out there. So, Novell was assuming that if you're running a LAN, it must be IPX, and so they didn't include any Network layer protocol field information in the 802.3 frame.

```
Flags:          0x80 802.3
Status:         0x00
Packet Length: 64
Timestamp:      12:45:45.192000 06/26/1998
Destination:    ff:ff:ff:ff:ff:ff Ethernet Broadcast
Source:         08:00:11:07:57:28
Length:         34
```

Since the 802.3 Ethernet frame cannot by itself identify the upper-layer (Network) protocol, it obviously needs some help. The IEEE defined the 802.2 LLC specifications to provide this function and more. Figure 4.12 shows the IEEE 802.3 with LLC (802.2) and the Subnetwork Access Protocol (SNAP) frame types.

FIGURE 4.12 802.2 and SNAP

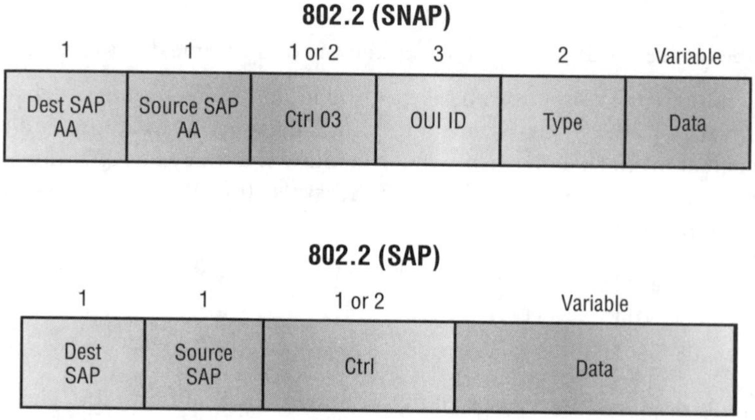

802.2 (SNAP)

1	1	1 or 2	3	2	Variable
Dest SAP AA	Source SAP AA	Ctrl 03	OUI ID	Type	Data

802.2 (SAP)

1	1	1 or 2	Variable
Dest SAP	Source SAP	Ctrl	Data

Figure 4.12 shows how the LLC header information is added to the data portion of the frame. Now, let's take a look at an 802.2 frame and SNAP captured from our protocol analyzer.

The following is an 802.2 frame captured with a protocol analyzer. You can see that the first frame has a Length field, so it's probably an 802.3, right? Maybe. Look again. It also has a Destination SAP (DSAP) and a Source SAP (SSAP), so it's not an 802.3. Therefore, it has to be an 802.2 frame. (Remember—an 802.2 frame is an 802.3 frame with the LLC information in the data field of the header so that you know what the upper-layer protocol is.)

```
Flags:          0x80 802.3
Status:         0x02 Truncated
Packet Length:64
Slice Length:  51
Timestamp:      12:42:00.592000 03/26/1998
Destination:    ff:ff:ff:ff:ff:ff Ethernet Broadcast
Source:         00:80:c7:a8:f0:3d
LLC Length:     37
Dest. SAP:      0xe0 NetWare
Source SAP:     0xe0 NetWare Individual LLC
  SublayerManagement Function
Command:        0x03 Unnumbered Information
```

The SNAP frame has its own protocol field to identify the upper-layer protocol. This is really a way to allow an Ethernet_II Ether-Type field to be used in an 802.3 frame. Even though the following network trace shows a protocol field, it is really an Ethernet_II type (Ether-Type) field.

```
Flags:          0x80 802.3
Status:         0x00
Packet Length:78
Timestamp:      09:32:48.264000 01/04/2000
802.3 Header
Destination:    09:00:07:FF:FF:FF AT Ph 2 Broadcast
Source:         00:00:86:10:C1:6F
LLC Length:     60
802.2 Logical Link Control (LLC) Header
Dest. SAP:      0xAA SNAP
Source SAP:     0xAA SNAP
Command:        0x03 Unnumbered Information
Protocol:       0x080007809B AppleTalk
```

You can identify a SNAP frame because the DSAP and SSAP fields are always hexadecimal AA, and the Command field is always 3. This frame type was created because not all protocols worked well with the 802.3 Ethernet frame, which doesn't have an Ether-Type field. To allow the proprietary protocols created by application developers to be used in the LLC frame, the IEEE defined the SNAP format that uses the exact same codes as Ethernet II. Up until about 1997 or so, the SNAP frame was on its way out of the corporate market. However, the new 802.11 wireless LAN specification uses an Ethernet SNAP field to identify the Network layer protocol. Cisco also still uses a SNAP frame with their proprietary protocol, the Cisco Discovery Protocol (CDP).

Ethernet at the Physical Layer

Ethernet was first implemented by a group called DIX (Digital, Intel, and Xerox). They created and implemented the first Ethernet LAN specification, which the IEEE used to create the IEEE 802.3 Committee. This was a 10Mbps network that ran on coax, and then eventually twisted-pair, and fiber physical media.

The IEEE extended the 802.3 Committee to three new committees known as 802.3u (FastEthernet) and 802.3ab (Gigabit Ethernet on Category 5) and 802.3ae (10Gbps over fiber and coax). These are all specified on twisted-pair and fiber physical media.

Figure 4.13 shows the IEEE 802.3 and original Ethernet Physical layer specifications.

FIGURE 4.13 Ethernet Physical layer specifications

Data Link (MAC layer)		802.3							
Physical	Ethernet	10Base2	10Base5	10BaseT	10BaseF	100BaseTX	100BaseFX	100BaseT4

When designing your LAN, it's really important to understand the different types of Ethernet media available to you. Sure, it would certainly be great to run Gigabit Ethernet to each desktop and 10Gbps between switches, and although this might happen one day, justifying the cost of that network today really is pretty unreasonable. But if you mix and match the different types of Ethernet media methods available today, you can come up with a cost-effective network solution that works great.

The Electronic Industries Association and the newer Telecommunications Industry Alliance (EIA/TIA) is the standards body that creates the Physical layer specifications for Ethernet. The EIA/TIA specifies that Ethernet uses a registered jack (RJ) connector with a 4 5 wiring sequence on unshielded twisted-pair (UTP) cabling (RJ-45). However, the industry is moving toward calling this just an 8-pin modular connector.

Here are the original IEEE 802.3 standards:

10Base2 10Mbps, baseband technology, up to 185 meters in length. The 10 means 10Mbps, Base means baseband technology, and the 2 means almost 200 meters. 10Base2 is also known as *thinnet* and it can support up to 30 workstations on a single segment. It uses a physical and logical bus with Attachment Unit Interface (AUI) connectors.

 NOTE 10Base2 Ethernet cards use BNC (which stands for either British Naval Connector, Bayonet Neill Concelman, or Bayonet Nut Connector) and T-Connectors to connect to a network.

10Base5 10Base5 stands for 10Mbps, baseband technology, and up to 500 meters in length. This is also known as *thicknet*, and it uses a physical and logical bus with AUI connectors. The total distance could be up to 2500 meters with repeaters and include 1024 users across all segments.

10BaseT 10BaseT stands for 10Mbps using Category 3 unshielded twisted-pair (UTP) wiring. Unlike the 10Base2 and 10Base5 networks, each device must connect into a hub or switch, and you can only have one host per segment or wire. 10BaseT uses an RJ-45 (8-pin modular) connector with a physical star topology and a logical bus.

Each of the 802.3 standards defines an AUI, which allows a one-bit-at-a-time transfer to the Physical layer from the Data Link media access method. This allows the MAC to remain constant but means the Physical layer can support any existing and new technologies. The original AUI interface was a 15-pin connector, which allowed a transceiver (transmitter/receiver) that provided a 15-pin–to–twisted-pair conversion.

The thing is, the AUI interface cannot support 100Mbps Ethernet because of the high frequencies involved. So 100BaseT needed a new interface, and the 802.3u specifications created one called the Media Independent Interface (MII), which provides 100Mbps throughput. The MII uses a *nibble*, defined as 4 bits. Gigabit Ethernet uses a Gigabit Media Independent Interface (GMII) and is 8 bits at a time.

802.3u (FastEthernet) is compatible with 802.3 Ethernet because they both share the same physical characteristics. FastEthernet and Ethernet use the same maximum transmission unit (MTU), same MAC mechanisms, and preserve the frame format that is used by 10BaseT Ethernet. Basically, FastEthernet is just based on an extension of the IEEE 802.3 specification, except that it offers a speed increase of 10 times that of 10BaseT.

Here are the expanded IEEE Ethernet 802.3 standards:

100BaseTX   Uses EIA/TIA Category 5, 6, or 7 UTP two-pair wiring. 100BaseTX allows one user per segment, each segment can be up to 100 meters long. 100BaseTX uses an RJ-45connector with a physical star topology and a logical bus.

100BaseFX   Uses fiber cabling 62.5/125-micron multimode fiber. 100BaseFX is a Point-to-point topology; each run can be up to 412 meters long. 100BaseFX uses an ST or SC connector.

1000BaseCX   Uses a copper twisted-pair called twinax (a balanced coaxial pair) that can only run up to 25 meters.

1000BaseT   Uses Category 5, four-pair UTP wiring up to 100 meters long.

1000BaseSX   Uses MMF (multi-mode fiber) using 62.5 and 50-micron core; uses an 850-nanometer laser and can go up to 220m with 62.5-micron, and 550m with 50-micron.

1000BaseLX   A single-mode fiber that uses a 9-micron core, a 1300-nanometer laser, and can go from 3km up to 10km.

Now that we have looked at the fundamental technologies of Ethernet and framing, let's go on to look at the technologies involved with implementing Ethernet. Next, we will discuss LAN switching and how it has changed Ethernet implementation and efficiency.

LAN Switching

First, we're going to go back in time a bit and take a look at the condition of networks before switches came to be, and then look at how switches have helped segment the corporate LAN.

Before LAN switching, a typical network design looked like the network in Figure 4.14.

FIGURE 4.14   Before switching

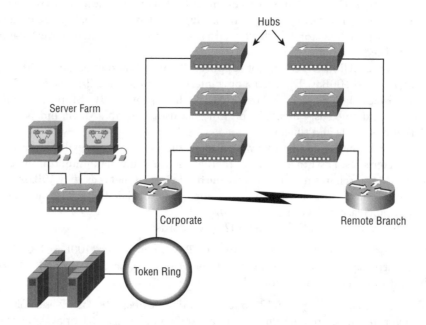

The design in Figure 4.14 was called a *collapsed backbone* because all hosts would need to go to the corporate backbone to reach any network services—both LAN and mainframe.

Going back even further, before networks like the one shown in Figure 4.14 had physical segmentation devices like routers and hubs, there was the mainframe network. This network included the mainframe (IBM, Honeywell, Sperry, DEC, etc.), controllers, and dumb terminals that connected into the controller. Any remote sites were connected to the mainframe with bridges.

When the PC began its rise to stardom, the mainframe was connected to the Ethernet or to a Token Ring LAN where the servers were installed. These servers were usually OS/2 or LAN Manager because this was "pre-NT." Each floor of a building ran either coax or twisted-pair wiring to the corporate backbone and was then connected to a router. PCs ran an emulating software program that allowed them to connect to the mainframe services, giving those PCs the ability to access services from the mainframe and LAN simultaneously. Eventually the PC became robust enough to allow application developers to port applications more effectively than they ever could have before—this advance markedly reduced networking prices and enabled businesses to grow at a much faster rate.

When Novell became more popular in the late 1980s and early 1990s, OS/2 and LAN Manager servers were by and large replaced with Novell NetWare services. This made the Ethernet network even more popular, because that's what Novell 3.*x* servers used to communicate with client/server software.

So that's the story of how the network in Figure 4.14 came into being. There was only one problem with this—the corporate backbone grew and grew, and as it grew, network services became slower. A big reason for this was that, at the same time this huge burst in growth was taking place. LAN services needed even faster service, and the network was becoming totally saturated. Everyone was dumping the Macs and dumb terminals used for the mainframe service in favor of those slick new PCs so that they could more easily connect to the corporate backbone and network services.

All this was taking place before the Internet's momentous popularity (Al Gore was still inventing it?), so everyone in the company needed to access the corporate network's services. Why? Because without the Internet, all network services were internal—exclusive to the company network. The Internet created a screaming need to segment that one humongous and plodding corporate network that was connected with sluggish old routers. At first, Cisco just created faster routers (no doubt about that), but more segmentation was needed, especially on the Ethernet LANs. The invention of FastEthernet was a very good and helpful thing too, but it didn't address that network segmentation need at all.

However, devices called *bridges* did, and they were first used in the network to break up collision domains. But bridges were sorely limited by the number of ports and other network services they could provide, and that's when Layer 2 *switches* came to the rescue. These switches saved the day by breaking up collision domains on every port, and switches could provide hundreds of them! This early, switched LAN looked like the network pictured in Figure 4.15:

FIGURE 4.15   The first switched LAN

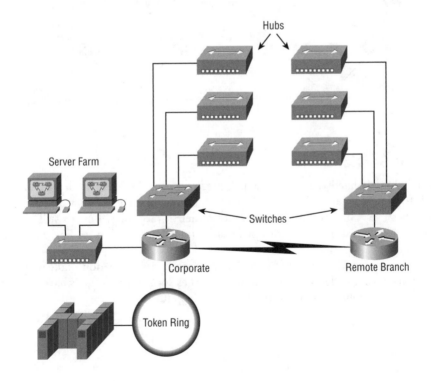

Each hub was placed into a switch port, an innovation that vastly improved the network. Now, instead of each building being crammed into the same collision domain, each hub became its own separate collision domain. But there was a catch—switch ports were still very new, and as a result, unbelievably expensive. Because of that, simply adding a switch into each floor of the building just wasn't going to happen—at least, not yet. Thanks to whomever you choose to thank for these things, the price has dropped dramatically, so now, having every one of your users plugged into a switch port is both good and feasible.

So there it is—if you're going to create a network design and implement it, including switching services is a must. A typical contemporary network design would look something like Figure 4.16, which shows a complete switched network design and implementation.

"But I still see a router in there," you say! Yes, it's not a mirage—there *is* a router in there. But its job has changed. Instead of performing physical segmentation, it now creates and handles logical segmentation. Those logical segments are called VLANs.

FIGURE 4.16 The typical switched network design

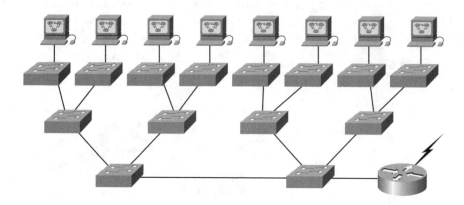

Switching Services

Layer 2 switching is hardware based, which means it uses the MAC address from the host's NIC cards to filter the network. Unlike bridges that use software to create and manage a filter table, switches use ASICs to build and maintain their filter tables. But it's still okay to think of a Layer 2 switch as a multiport bridge because their basic reason for being is the same: to break up collision domains.

Layer 2 switches and bridges are faster than routers because they don't take up time looking at the Network layer header information. Instead, they look at the frame's hardware addresses before they decide to either forward the frame or drop it.

Switches create private dedicated domains and don't share bandwidth like a hub would. Figure 4.17 shows five hosts connected to a switch—all running 10Mbps half duplex to the server:

FIGURE 4.17   Switches create private domains

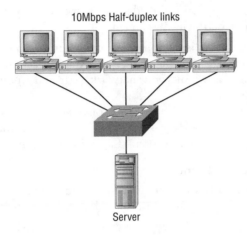

10Mbps Half-duplex links

Server

And unlike a hub, each host has 10Mbps dedicated communication to the server. Layer 2 switching provides the following:

- Hardware-based bridging (MAC)
- Wire speed
- Low latency reduced contention
- Low cost

What makes Layer 2 switching so efficient is that no modification to the data packet takes place. The device only reads the frame encapsulating the packet, which makes the switching process considerably faster and less error-prone than routing processes are.

And if you use Layer 2 switching for both workgroup connectivity and network segmentation (breaking up collision domains), you can create a flatter network design with more network segments than you can with traditional 10BaseT shared networks.

Plus, Layer 2 switching increases bandwidth for each user because, again, each connection (interface) into the switch is its own collision domain. This feature makes it possible for you to connect multiple devices to each interface.

Limitations of Layer 2 Switching

Since we commonly stick Layer 2 switching into the same category as bridged networks, we also tend to think it has the same hang-ups and issues that bridged networks do. Keep in mind that bridges are good and helpful things if you design the network correctly, keeping their features as well as their limitations in mind. And to design well with bridges, keep these two most important considerations in mind:

- You absolutely must break up the collision domains correctly.

- The right way to create a functional bridged network is to make sure that its users spend 80 percent of their time on the local segment.

Bridged networks break up collision domains, but remember, that network is still one large broadcast domain. Both Layer 2 switches and bridges don't break up broadcast domains by default—something that not only limits your network's size and growth potential, but can also reduce its overall performance.

Broadcasts and multicasts, along with the slow convergence time of spanning trees, can give you some major grief as your network grows. These are the big reasons why Layer 2 switches and bridges cannot completely replace routers (Layer 3 devices) in the internetwork.

Bridging versus LAN Switching

It's true—Layer 2 switches really are pretty much just bridges that give us a bunch more ports, but there are some important differences you should always keep in mind:

- Bridges are software based, while switches are hardware based because they use ASIC chips to help make filtering decisions.

- A switch is basically a multiport bridge.

- Bridges can only have one spanning-tree instance per bridge, while switches can have many.

- Switches have a higher number of ports than most bridges.

- Both bridges and switches forward Layer 2 broadcasts.

- Bridges and switches learn MAC addresses by examining the source address of each frame received.

- Both bridges and switches make forwarding decisions based on Layer 2 addresses.

Three Switch Functions at Layer 2

There are three distinct functions of Layer 2 switching (you need to remember these!):

Address learning   Layer 2 switches and bridges remember the source hardware address of each frame received on an interface, and they enter this information into a MAC database called a forward/filter table.

Forward/filter decisions   When a frame is received on an interface, the switch looks at the destination hardware address and finds the exit interface in the MAC database. The frame is only forwarded out the specified destination port.

Loop avoidance   If multiple connections between switches are created for redundancy purposes, network loops can occur. STP is used to stop network loops while still permitting redundancy.

LAN Switch Types

LAN switch types decide how a frame is handled when it's received on a switch port. Latency—the time it takes for a frame to be sent out an exit port once the switch receives the frame—depends on the chosen switching mode. There are three switching modes: cut-through, Fragment Free, and store-and-forward.

Figure 4.18 delimits the different points where the switching mode takes place in the frame.

FIGURE 4.18   Different switching modes within a frame

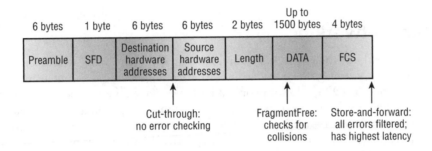

Okay—it's time to talk about these three switching modes in more detail.

Cut-Through (Real Time)

With the cut-through switching method, the LAN switch copies only the destination address (the first six bytes following the preamble) onto its onboard buffers. That done, it looks up the hardware destination address in the MAC switching table, determines the outgoing interface, and proceeds to forward the frame toward its destination.

A cut-through switch really helps reduce latency because it begins to forward the frame as soon as it reads the destination address and determines the outgoing interface. And after it determines the destination port, the following frames are immediately forwarded out through it.

With some switches, you get an extra super-cool feature: the flexibility to perform cut-through switching on a per-port basis until a user-defined error threshold is reached. At the point that threshold is attained, the ports automatically change over to store-and-forward mode, so they will stop forwarding the errors. And, when the error rate on the port falls back below the threshold, the port automatically changes back to cut-through mode.

FragmentFree (Modified Cut-Through)

FragmentFree is a modified form of cut-through switching in which the switch waits for the collision window (64 bytes) to pass before forwarding. This is because if a packet has an error, it almost always occurs within the first 64 bytes. So, in this mode, each frame will be checked into the data field to make sure no fragmentation has occurred.

FragmentFree mode provides better error checking than the cut-through mode with practically no increase in latency. It's the default switching method for the Catalyst 1900 switches.

Store-and-Forward

Store-and-forward switching is Cisco's primary LAN switching method. When in store-and-forward, the LAN switch copies the entire frame onto its onboard buffers and then computes the CRC. Because it copies the entire frame, latency through the switch varies depending on the frame length.

The frame is discarded if it contains a CRC error—if it's too short (less than 64 bytes including the CRC), or if it's too long (more than 1518 bytes including the CRC). If the frame doesn't contain any errors, the LAN switch looks up the destination hardware address in its forwarding or switching table to find the correct outgoing interface. When it does, out goes the frame toward its destination.

Wireless Networking

No book on this subject today would be complete without mentioning wireless networking. That's because two years ago, it just wasn't all that common to find people using this technology. Remember, in 1996, a lot of people didn't even have an e-mail address. Oh yeah—sure, some did, but now everyone does, and the same thing is happening in the wireless world. That's because wireless networking is just way too convenient not to use. I'm betting that some of you reading this probably have a wireless network at home. If not, you probably do at work. I do! For this reason, I'm now going to go over the various types of wireless networks as well as their speeds and distance limitations.

Narrowband Wireless LANs   Narrowband radio does as its name suggests—it keeps the radio signal frequency as narrow as possible while still being able to pass the information along. The problem of interference is avoided by directing different users onto different channel frequencies. The distance you get is decent, but the speeds available today just aren't adequate enough for corporate users. Plus, you've also got to have proprietary equipment to run it on, as well as buy a Federal Communications Commission (FCC) license to run the frequency at each site!

Personal Communication Services (PCS)   Personal Communication Service (PCS) includes a whole bunch of mobile, portable, and auxiliary communications services for individuals and businesses. The FCC roughly defined PCS as mobile and fixed communications options for both individuals and businesses that can be incorporated with various kinds of competing networks. Narrowband or broadband PCS is what's used today.

Narrowband PCS   Again as the name implies, the narrowband PCS flavor requires a smaller serving size of the spectrum than broadband PCS does. With licenses for narrowband PCS, you get to access services like two-way paging and/or text-based messaging. Think about people with PDAs, keyboard attachments, and so on getting and sending wireless e-mail—these subscribers are able to do this via microwave signals. With narrowband PCS you can also access cool services like wireless telemetry—the monitoring of mobile or stationary equipment remotely. When the energy company remotely monitors your utility meters, commonly known as automatic meter reading (AMR), they accomplish this using this technology.

Broadband PCS   Broadband PCS is used for a many kinds of wireless services—both mobile and fixed radio. The mobile broadband set includes both the voice and advanced two-way data features usually available to us via small, mobile, multifunction devices like digital camera/cell phones, and so on. In the industry, these services are commonly referred to as Mobile Telephone Services and Mobile Data Services. Sources of these services include companies that rule huge amounts of the broadband PCS spectrum like AT&T Wireless, Verizon, and Sprint PCS.

Satellite   With satellite services, the speed you get is sweet—it's up to around 1Mbps upload and 2Mpbs download! But there's an annoying delay when connecting, so it doesn't work very well when you're dealing with bursty traffic. The good news is that speeds are increasing, but even so, they just can't compete with what you get via wireless LANs. The real upside to using a satellite-based network is that its geographic coverage area can be huge.

Infrared Wireless LANs   Here we have pretty much the opposite of satellite service. This technology works really well handling short, bursty traffic in the Personal Area Network (PAN) sector. These speeds are increasing too, but the available range is still very short. It's commonly used for laptop-to-laptop and laptop-to/PDA transfers. The speed range we usually get is anywhere from 115Kbps to 4Mbps, but a new specification called Very Fast Infrared (VFIR) says we'll see speeds up to 16Mbps in the future—we'll see!

Spread Spectrum Wireless LANs   Your typical wireless LANs (WLANs) uses something called *spread spectrum*. This is a wideband radio frequency technique that the military came up with that's both reliable, and secure (that's debatable). The most popular WLAN in use today is 802.11b, which runs up to 11Mbps, but the new 802.11g specifications can bump that figure up to around 22Mbps and more, depending on who made your equipment. Plus, the new 802.11a lives in the 5Ghz range and can run bandwidth around 50Mbps—and it's pledging over 100Mbps in the near future! But the distance is still less than what you get with the 802.11b and 802.11g 2.4Ghz range models (which is about 300 feet or so). So basically, you usually find 802.11b/g used indoors, and 802.11a in the shorter outdoor market where more bandwidth is needed. Remember, the market is still young and who knows what the future holds for these up and coming WLANs.

Exam Essentials

Know the four Ethernet frame types and the difference between them.   Ethernet_II has a type field, 802.3 has a length field, 802.2 has DSAPs and SSAPs, and SNAP has its own protocol field.

Understand how the cut-through LAN switch method works.   When the switch is in this mode, it waits only for the destination hardware address to be received before it looks up the address in the MAC filter table.

Know the three LAN switch methods and their functions.   The three LAN switch methods are cut-through, FragmentFree (also known as modified cut-through) and store-and-forward. Store-and-forward offers error checking; cut-through and FragmentFree offer lower latency.

Understand how the FragmentFree LAN switch method works.   The FragmentFree LAN switch method checks the first 64 bytes of a frame before forwarding it for fragmentation.

Understand how the store-and-forward LAN switch method works.   Store-and-forward first receives the complete data frame on the switch's buffer, then a CRC is run, and then the switch looks up the destination address in the MAC filter table.

4.4 Evaluate the Characteristics of Routing Protocols

All routing protocols have one task in common, that is, they are required to update the routing tables on routers across the internetwork. Whether static or dynamic, distance vector or link state, or even hybrid, routing protocols are required to make entries in the routing table. Let's take a deeper look at how the routing table is used once it is created by the individual routing protocols.

 NOTE See Section 1.3, "Select an appropriate routing protocol based on user requirements," in this book, for more detailed information on different routing protocols.

The process of an IP packet being routed across an internetwork is fairly simple and doesn't change, regardless of the size of network you have. For an example, we'll use Figure 4.19 to describe step by step what happens when Host A wants to communicate with Host B on a different network.

FIGURE 4.19 IP routing example using two hosts and one router

In this example, a user on Host A pings Host B's IP address. Routing doesn't get simpler than this, but it still involves a lot of steps. This entire process is dependent on the routing table being filled by some routing protocol in a large internetwork. Let's work through the routing steps:

1. Internet Control Message Protocol (ICMP) creates an echo request payload (which is just the alphabet in the data field).

2. ICMP hands that payload to IP, which then creates a packet. At a minimum, this packet contains an IP source address, IP destination address, and a protocol field with 01h. All that tells the receiving host to whom it should hand the payload when the destination is reached—in this example, ICMP.

3. Once the packet is created, IP works with the Address Resolution Protocol (ARP) to determine whether the destination IP address is on the local network or a remote one.

4. Since ARP and IP determine this is a remote request, the packet needs to be sent to the default gateway so that the packet can be routed to the remote network. The Registry in Windows is parsed to find the configured default gateway.

5. The default gateway of host 172.16.10.2 (Host_A) is configured to 172.16.10.1. To be able to send this packet to the default gateway, the hardware address of the router's interface Ethernet 0 (configured with the IP address of 172.16.10.1) must be known. Why? So the packet can be handed down to the Data Link layer, framed, and sent to the router's interface connected to the 172.16.10.0 network. Hosts communicate only via hardware addresses on the local LAN. It is important to understand that in order to communicate to Host_B, Host_A must send the packets to the MAC address of the default gateway on the local network.

6. Host A's ARP cache is checked to see if the IP address of the default gateway has already been resolved to a hardware address:

   - If it has, the packet is then free to be handed to the Data Link layer for framing. (The hardware destination address is also handed down with that packet.)

   - If the hardware address isn't already in the ARP cache of the host, an ARP broadcast is sent out onto the local network to search for the hardware address of 172.16.10.1. The router responds to the request and provides the hardware address of Ethernet 0, and the host caches this address. The router also caches the hardware address of Host A in the ARP cache.

7. Once the packet and destination hardware address are handed to the Data Link layer, the LAN driver is used to provide media access via the type of LAN being used (in this example, Ethernet). A frame is then generated, encapsulating the packet with control information. Within that frame are the hardware destination and source addresses, plus an Ether-Type field that describes the Network layer protocol that handed the packet to the Data Link layer—in this case, IP. At the end of the frame is an FCS field that houses the answer to the CRC.

8. Once the frame is completed, it's handed down to the Physical layer to be put on the physical medium (in this example, the twisted-pair wire) one bit at a time.

9. Every device in the collision domain receives these bits and builds the frame. They each run a CRC and check the answer in the FCS field. If the answers don't match, the frame is discarded. If the CRC matches (which, in this example, is the router's interface Ethernet 0), then the hardware destination address is checked to see if it matches too. If it's a match, then the Ether-Type field is checked to find the protocol used at the Network layer.

10. The packet is pulled from the frame, and the frame is discarded. The packet is handed to the protocol listed in the Ether-Type field—it's given to IP.

11. IP receives the packet and checks the IP destination address. Since the packet's destination address doesn't match any of the addresses configured on the receiving router, the router will look up the destination IP network address in its routing table.

12. The routing table must have an entry for the network 172.16.20.0, or the packet will be discarded immediately and an ICMP message will be sent back to the originating device with a "destination network unavailable" message.

13. If the router does find an entry for the destination network in its table, the packet is switched to the exit interface—in this example, interface Ethernet 1.

14. The router packet-switches the packet to the Ethernet 1 buffer.

15. The Ethernet 1 buffer needs to know the hardware address of the destination host and first checks the ARP cache. If the hardware address of Host B has already been resolved, then the packet and the hardware address are handed down to the Data Link layer to be resolved.

16. If the hardware address has not already been resolved, the router sends an ARP request looking for the hardware address of 172.16.20.2.

17. Host B responds with its hardware address, and the packet and destination hardware address are both sent to the Data Link layer for framing.

18. The Data Link layer creates a frame with the destination and source hardware address, Ether-Type field, and FCS field at the end of the frame. The frame is handed to the Physical layer to be sent out on the physical medium one bit at a time.

19. Host B receives the frame and immediately runs a CRC. If the answer matches what's in the FCS field, the hardware destination address is then checked. If the host finds a match, the Ether-Type field is then checked to determine the protocol the packet should be handed to at the Network layer—IP, in this example.

20. At the Network layer, IP receives the packet and checks the IP destination address. Since there's finally a match made, the protocol field is checked to find out whom the payload should be given to.

21. The payload is handed to ICMP, which understands that this is an echo request. ICMP responds to this by immediately discarding the packet and generating a new payload as an echo reply.

22. A packet is then created including the source and destination address, protocol field, and payload. The destination device is now Host A.

23. ARP then checks to see whether the destination IP address is a device on the local LAN or on a remote network. Since the destination device is on a remote network, the packet needs to be sent to the default gateway.

24. The default gateway IP address is found in the Registry of the Windows device, and the ARP cache is checked to see if the hardware address has already been resolved from an IP address.

25. Once the hardware address of the default gateway is found, the packet and destination hardware address are handed down to the Data Link layer for framing.

26. The Data Link layer frames the packet of information and includes the following in the header:

   - The destination and source hardware address
   - Ether-Type field with IP in it
   - FCS field with the CRC answer in tow

27. The frame is now handed down to the Physical layer to be sent out over the network medium one bit at a time.

28. The router's Ethernet 1 interface receives the bits and builds a frame. The CRC is run, and the FCS field is checked to make sure the answers match.

29. Once the CRC is found to be okay, the hardware destination address is checked. Since the router's interface is a match, the packet is pulled from the frame and the Ether-Type field is checked to see what protocol at the Network layer the packet should be delivered to.

30. The protocol is determined to be IP, so it gets the packet. IP runs a CRC check on the IP header first, and then checks the destination IP address. (Note: IP does not run a complete CRC like the Data Link layer—it only checks the header for errors.) Since the IP destination address doesn't match any of the router's interfaces, the routing table is checked to see whether it has a route to 172.16.10.0. If it doesn't have a route over to the destination network, the packet will be discarded immediately. (This is the source point of confusion for a lot of administrators—when a ping fails, most people think the packet never reached the destination host. But as we see here, that's not *always* the case! All it takes is for just one of the remote routers to be lacking a route back to the originating host's network and POOF! The packet is dropped on the *return trip*, not on its way to the host.)

31. But the router does know how to get to network 172.16.10.0—the exit interface is Ethernet 0—so the packet is switched to interface Ethernet 0.

32. The router checks the ARP cache to determine if the hardware address for 172.16.10.2 has already been resolved.

33. Since the hardware address to 172.16.10.2 is already cached from the originating trip to Host B, the hardware address and packet are handed to the Data Link layer.

34. The Data Link layer builds a frame with the destination hardware address and source hardware address, and then puts IP in the Ether-Type field. A CRC is run on the frame, and the answer is placed in the FCS field.

35. The frame is then handed to the Physical layer to be sent out onto the local network 1 bit at a time.

36. The destination host receives the frame, runs a CRC, checks the destination hardware address, and looks in the Ether-Type field to find who to hand the packet to.

37. IP is the designated receiver, and after the packet is handed to IP at the Network layer, it checks the protocol field for further direction. IP finds instructions to give the payload to ICMP, and ICMP determines the packet to be an ICMP echo reply.

38. ICMP acknowledges it has received the reply by sending an exclamation point (!) to the user interface. ICMP then attempts to send four more echo requests to the destination host.

You've just experienced 38 easy steps to understanding IP routing. The key point I want to make here is that if you had a much larger network, the process would be the *same*. In a really big internetwork, the packet just goes through more hops before it finds the destination host.

A very important point to remember is that when you check the ARP table on Host A, it will show the MAC address for Host B as the MAC address of the local router's Ethernet port (default gateway). This is because frames can't be placed on remote networks, only local networks, and packets destined for remote networks must go to the default gateway.

Exam Essentials

Understand the basic IP routing process.   You need to remember that the frame changes at each hop, but that the packet is never changed or manipulated in any way until it reaches the destination device. Also know when to use certain protocols during the process.

4.5 Evaluate TCP/IP Communication Process and Its Associated Protocols

TCP/IP is based on the Department of Defense (DoD) model, which pre-dates the OSI model. It is basically a condensed version of the OSI model—it's composed of four, instead of seven, layers:

- Process/Application layer
- Host-to-Host layer
- Internet layer
- Network Access layer

Figure 4.20 shows a comparison of the DoD model and the OSI reference model. As you can see, the two are similar in concept, but each has a different number of layers with different names.

FIGURE 4.20   The DoD and OSI models

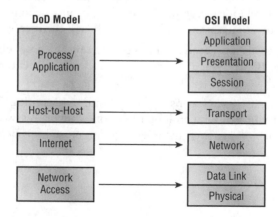

When we talk about the different protocols in the IP stack, the layers of the OSI and DoD models are interchangeable. In other words, the Internet layer and the Network layer describe the same thing, as do the Host-to-Host layer and the Transport layer.

A vast array of protocols combine at the DoD model's Process/Application layer to integrate the various activities and duties spanning the focus of the OSI's corresponding top three layers (Application, Presentation, and Session). We'll be looking closely at these protocols in the next part of this chapter. The Process/Application layer defines protocols for node-to-node application communication and also controls user-interface specifications.

The Host-to-Host layer parallels the functions of the OSI's Transport layer, defining protocols for setting up the level of transmission service for applications. It tackles issues like creating reliable end-to-end communication and ensuring the error-free delivery of data. It handles packet sequencing and maintains data integrity.

The Internet layer corresponds to the OSI's Network layer, designating the protocols relating to the logical transmission of packets over the entire network. It takes care of the addressing of hosts by giving them an IP address, and it handles the routing of packets among multiple networks.

At the bottom of the DoD model, the Network Access layer monitors the data-exchange between the host and the network. The equivalent of the Data Link and Physical layers of the OSI model, the Network Access layer oversees hardware addressing and defines protocols for the physical transmission of data.

Although the DoD and OSI models are alike in design and concept and have similar functions in similar places, *how* those functions occur is different. Figure 4.21 shows the TCP/IP suite and how its protocols relate to the DoD model layers.

FIGURE 4.21   The TCP/IP suite

DoD Model

Process/ Application	Telnet	FTP	LPD	SNMP
	TFTP	SMTP	NFS	X Window

Host-to-Host	TCP	UDP

Internet	ICMP	ARP	RARP
	IP		

Network Access	Ethernet	Fast Ethernet	Token Ring	FDDI

In the following sections, we will look at the different layers in more detail, starting with the protocols of the Process/Application layer.

The Process/Application Layer Protocols

In this section, I'll describe the different applications and services typically used in IP networks. The different protocols and applications covered in this section include the following:

- Telnet
- FTP
- TFTP
- NFS
- SMTP
- LPD
- X Window
- SNMP
- DNS
- DHCP/BootP

Telnet

Telnet is the chameleon of protocols—its specialty is terminal emulation. It allows a user on a remote client machine, called the Telnet client, to access the resources of another machine, the Telnet server. Telnet achieves this by pulling a fast one on the Telnet server and making the client machine appear as though it were a terminal directly attached to the local network. This projection is actually a software image—a virtual terminal that can interact with the chosen remote host.

These emulated terminals are of the text-mode type and can execute refined procedures like displaying menus that give users the opportunity to choose options from them and access the applications on the duped server. Users begin a Telnet session by running the Telnet client software and then logging into the Telnet server.

The name *Telnet* comes from "telephone network," which is how most Telnet sessions used to occur.

File Transfer Protocol (FTP)

File Transfer Protocol (FTP) is the protocol that actually lets us transfer files, and it can accomplish this between any two machines that are using it. But FTP isn't just a protocol; it's also a program. Operating as a protocol, FTP is used by applications. As a program, it's employed by users to perform file tasks by hand. FTP also allows you to access both directories and files and it can accomplish certain types of directory operations, like relocating directories into different ones. FTP teams up with Telnet to transparently log you into the FTP server and then provide you with the ability to transfer files.

Accessing a host through FTP is only the first step, though. Users must then be subjected to an authentication login that's probably secured with passwords and usernames implemented by system administrators to restrict access. But you can get around this somewhat by adopting the username "anonymous"—though what you'll gain access to will be limited.

Even when employed by users manually as a program, FTP's functions are limited to listing and manipulating directories, typing file contents, and copying files between hosts. It can't execute remote files as programs.

Trivial File Transfer Protocol (TFTP)

Trivial File Transfer Protocol (TFTP) is the stripped-down, stock version of FTP, but it's the protocol of choice if you know exactly what you want and where to find it. It doesn't give you the abundance of functions that FTP does, though. TFTP has no directory-browsing abilities; it can do nothing but send and receive files. This compact little protocol also skimps in the data department, sending much smaller blocks of data than FTP, and there's no authentication as with FTP, so it's insecure. Few sites support it because of the inherent security risks.

Network File System (NFS)

Network File System (NFS) is a jewel of a protocol specializing in file sharing. It allows two different types of file systems to interoperate. It works like this: suppose the NFS server software is running on an NT server, and the NFS client software is running on a Unix host. NFS allows for a portion of the RAM on the NT server to transparently store Unix files, which can, in turn, be used by Unix users. Even though the NT file system and Unix file system are unlike—they have different case sensitivity, filename lengths, security, and so on—both Unix users and NT users can access that same file with their normal file systems, in their normal way.

Simple Mail Transfer Protocol (SMTP)

Simple Mail Transfer Protocol (SMTP), answering our ubiquitous call to e-mail, uses a spooled, or queued, method of mail delivery. Once a message has been sent to a destination, the message is spooled to a device—usually a disk. The server software at the destination posts a vigil, regularly checking this queue for messages. When it detects them, it proceeds to deliver them to their destination. SMTP is used to send mail; POP3 is used to receive mail.

Line Printer Daemon (LPD)

The Line Printer Daemon (LPD) protocol is designed for printer sharing. The LPD, along with the LPR (Line Printer) program, allows print jobs to be spooled and sent to the network's printers using TCP/IP.

X Window

Designed for client-server operations, X Window defines a protocol for writing client/server applications based on a graphical user interface (GUI). The idea is to allow a program, called a client, to run on one computer and have it display things through a window server on another computer.

Simple Network Management Protocol (SNMP)

Simple Network Management Protocol (SNMP) collects and manipulates this valuable network information. It gathers data by polling the devices on the network from a management station at fixed or random intervals, requiring them to disclose certain information. When all is well, SNMP receives something called a *baseline*—a report delimiting the operational traits of a healthy network. This protocol can also stand as a watchdog over the network, quickly notifying managers of any sudden turn of events. These network watchdogs are called *agents*, and when aberrations occur, agents send an alert called a *trap* to the management station.

Domain Name Service (DNS)

Domain Name Service (DNS) resolves host names, specifically Internet names, like www.routersim.com. You don't have to use DNS; you can just type in the IP address of any device you want to communicate with. An IP address identifies hosts on a network and the Internet as well. However, DNS was designed to make our lives easier. Think about this: what would happen if you wanted to move your web page to a different service provider? The IP address would change and no one would know what the new one was. DNS allows you to use a domain name to specify an IP address. You can change the IP address as often as you want, and no one will know the difference.

DNS is used to resolve a fully qualified domain name (FQDN)—for example, www.lammle.com or todd.lammle.com. An FQDN is a hierarchy that can logically locate a system based on its domain identifier.

If you want to resolve the name "todd," you either must type in the FQDN of todd.lammle.com or have a device like a PC or router add the suffix for you. For example, on a Cisco router, you can use the command ip domain-name lammle.com to append each request with the lammle.com domain. If you don't do that, you'll have to type in the FQDN to get DNS to resolve the name.

Dynamic Host Configuration Protocol (DHCP)/Bootstrap Protocol (BootP)

Dynamic Host Configuration Protocol (DHCP) gives IP addresses to hosts. It allows easier administration and works well in small-to-even-very-large network environments. All types of hardware can be used as a DHCP server, including a Cisco router.

DHCP differs from BootP in that BootP gives an IP address to a host, but the host's hardware address must be entered manually in a BootP table. You can think of DHCP as a dynamic BootP. But there is a lot of information a DHCP server can provide to a host when the host is requesting an IP address from the DHCP server. Here's a list of the information a DHCP server can provide:

- IP address
- Subnet mask
- Domain name
- Default gateway (routers)
- DNS
- WINS information

A DHCP server can give us even more information than this, but the items in that list are the most common.

The Host-to-Host Layer Protocols

The main purpose of the Host-to-Host layer is to shield the upper-layer applications from the complexities of the network. This layer says to the upper layer, "Just give me your data stream, with any instructions, and I'll begin the process of getting your information ready to send."

The following sections describe the two protocols at this layer:

- Transmission Control Protocol (TCP)
- User Datagram Protocol (UDP)

In addition, we'll look at some of the key host-to-host protocol concepts, and well as the port numbers.

Transmission Control Protocol (TCP)

TCP takes large blocks of information from an application and breaks them into segments. It numbers and sequences each segment so that the destination's TCP can put the segments back into the order that the application intended. After these segments are sent, TCP (on the transmitting host) waits for an acknowledgment of the receiving end's TCP virtual circuit session, retransmitting those that aren't acknowledged.

Before a transmitting host starts to send segments down the model, the sender's TCP contacts the destination's TCP to establish a connection. What is created is known as a *virtual circuit*. This type of communication is called *connection-oriented*. During this initial handshake, the two TCP layers also agree on the amount of information that's going to be sent before the recipient's TCP sends back an acknowledgment. With everything agreed upon in advance, the path is paved for reliable communication to take place.

TCP is a full-duplex, connection-oriented, reliable, and accurate protocol, but establishing all these terms and conditions, in addition to error checking, is no small task. TCP is very complicated and, not surprisingly, costly in terms of network overhead. And since today's networks are much more reliable than those of yore, this added reliability is often unnecessary.

TCP Segment Format

Since the upper layers just send a data stream to the protocols in the Transport layers, I'll demonstrate how TCP segments a data stream and prepares it for the Internet layer. The Internet layer then routes the segments as packets through an internetwork. The segments are handed to the receiving host's Host-to-Host layer protocol, which rebuilds the data stream to hand to the upper-layer applications or protocols.

Figure 4.22 shows the TCP segment format and the different fields within the TCP header.

FIGURE 4.22 TCP segment format

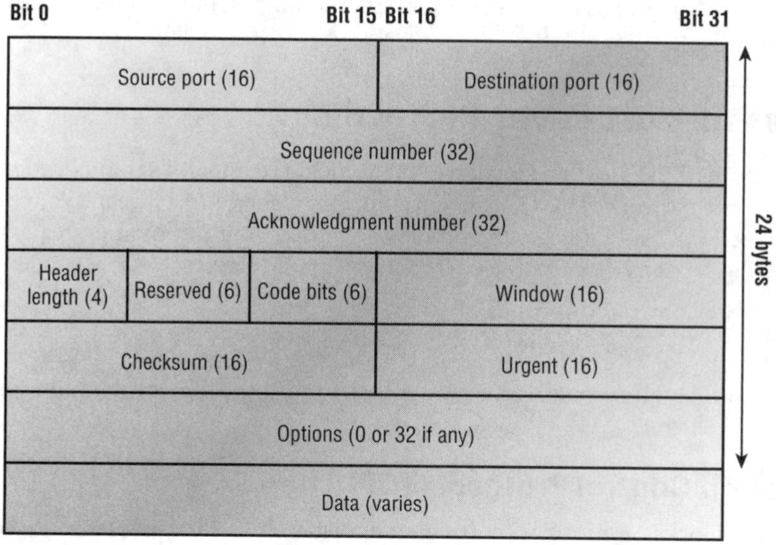

The TCP header is 20 bytes long, or up to 24 bytes with options. You need to understand what each field in the TCP segment is. The TCP segment contains the following fields:

Source port The port number of the application on the host sending the data. (Port numbers will be explained a little later in this section.)

Destination port The port number of the application requested on the destination host.

Sequence number This puts the data back in the correct order or retransmits missing or damaged data, a process that is called *sequencing*.

Acknowledgment number This defines which TCP octet is expected next.

Header Length (HELN) The number of 32-bit words in the TCP Header. This indicates where the data begins. The TCP header (even one including options) is an integral number of 32 bits long.

Reserved   Always set to zero.

Code bits   Control functions used to set up and terminate a session.

Window   The window size the sender is willing to accept, in octets.

Checksum   The CRC, because TCP doesn't trust the lower layers and checks everything. The CRC checks the header and data fields.

Urgent   This field is only valid if the Urgent pointer in the code bits is set. If so, this value indicates the offset from the current sequence number, in octets, where the first segment of nonurgent data begins.

Option   The option field may be 0 or a multiple of 32 bits, if any. What this means is that no options have to be present (option size of 0). However, if any options are used that do not cause the option field to total a multiple of 32 bits, you must use 0s as padding to make sure the data begins on a 32-bit boundary.

Data   Handed down to TCP at the Transport layer, which includes the upper-layer headers.

Let's take a look at a TCP segment copied from a network analyzer:

```
TCP - Transport Control Protocol
  Source Port:      5973
  Destination Port: 23
  Sequence Number:  1456389907
  Ack Number:       1242056456
  Offset:           5
  Reserved:         %000000
  Code:             %011000
      Ack is valid
      Push Request
  Window:           61320
  Checksum:         0x61a6
  Urgent Pointer:   0
  No TCP Options
  TCP Data Area:
  vL.5.+.5.+.5.+.5  76 4c 19 35 11 2b 19 35 11 2b 19 35 11
    2b 19 35 +. 11 2b 19
Frame Check Sequence: 0x0d00000f
```

Did you notice that everything I talked about above is in the segment? As you can see from the number of fields in the header, TCP creates a lot of overhead. Application developers may opt for efficiency over reliability to save overhead, and so, UDP was also defined at the Transport layer as an alternative.

User Datagram Protocol (UDP)

If you were to compare UDP with TCP, you'd find that UDP is basically the scaled-down economy model that's sometimes referred to as a *thin protocol*. Like a thin person on a park bench, a thin protocol doesn't take up a lot of room—or in this case, much bandwidth on a network.

UDP doesn't offer all the bells and whistles of TCP, but it does do a fabulous job of transporting information that doesn't require reliable delivery—and it does so using far fewer network resources.

There are some situations where it would definitely be wise for developers to opt for UDP rather than TCP. Remember the watchdog SNMP up there at the Process/Application layer? SNMP monitors the network, sending intermittent messages and a fairly steady flow of status updates and alerts, especially when it is running on a large network. The cost in overhead to establish, maintain, and close a TCP connection for each one of those little messages would reduce what would be an otherwise healthy, efficient network to a dammed-up bog in no time!

Another circumstance calling for UDP over TCP is when reliability is already handled at the Process/Application layer. NFS handles its own reliability issues, making the use of TCP both impractical and redundant. But ultimately, it's up to the application developer who decides whether to use UDP or TCP, not the user who wants to transfer data faster.

UDP does *not* sequence the segments and does not care in which order the segments arrive at the destination. But after that, UDP sends the segments off and forgets about them. It doesn't follow through, check up on them, or even allow for an acknowledgment of safe arrival—complete abandonment. Because of this, it's referred to as an unreliable protocol. This does not mean that UDP is ineffective, only that it doesn't handle issues of reliability.

Further, UDP doesn't create a virtual circuit, nor does it contact the destination before delivering information to it. Because of this, it's also considered a connectionless protocol. Since UDP assumes that the application will use its own reliability method, it doesn't use any. This gives an application developer a choice when running the IP stack: they can choose TCP for reliability or UDP for faster transfers.

UDP Segment Format

Figure 4.23 clearly illustrates UDP's markedly low overhead as compared to TCP's hungry usage. Look at the figure carefully—can you see that UDP doesn't use windowing or provide for acknowledgments represented within it?

FIGURE 4.23   UDP segment

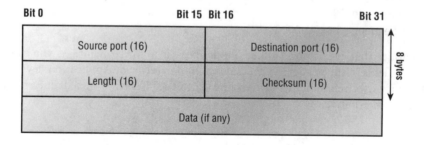

It's important for you to understand what each field in the UDP segment is. The UDP segment contains the following fields:

Source port   Port number of the application on the host sending the data.

Destination port   Port number of the application requested on the destination host.

Length of the segment   Length of UDP header and UDP data.

CRC   Checksum of both the UDP header and UDP data fields.

Data   Upper-layer data.

UDP, like TCP, doesn't trust the lower layers and runs its own CRC. Remember that the FCS is the field that houses the CRC, which is why you can see the FCS information.

The following shows a UDP segment caught on a network analyzer:

```
UDP - User Datagram Protocol
  Source Port:      1085
  Destination Port: 5136
  Length:           41
  Checksum:         0x7a3c
  UDP Data Area:
  ..Z.............  00 01 5a 96 00 01 00 00 00 00 00 11 00
    00 00
  ...C..2...._C._C  2e 03 00 43 02 1e 32 0a 00 0a 00 80 43
    00 80
Frame Check Sequence: 0x00000000
```

Notice that low overhead! Try to find the sequence number, acknowledgment number, and window size in the UDP segment. You can't (I hope) because they just aren't there!

Key Concepts of Host-to-Host Protocols

Since you've seen both a connection-oriented (TCP) and connectionless (UDP) protocol in action, it would be good to summarize them here. Table 4.2 highlights some of the key concepts that you should keep in mind regarding these two protocols. You should memorize this table.

TABLE 4.2   Key Features of TCP and UDP

TCP	UDP
Sequenced	Unsequenced
Reliable	Unreliable

TABLE 4.2 Key Features of TCP and UDP *(continued)*

TCP	UDP
Connection-oriented	Connectionless
Virtual circuit	Low overhead
Acknowledgments	No acknowledgment
Windowing flow control	No windowing or flow control

A telephone analogy could really help you understand how TCP works. Most of us know that before you speak to someone on a phone, you must first establish a connection with that other person—wherever they are. This is like a virtual circuit with the TCP protocol. If you were giving someone important information during your conversation, you might say, "You know?" or ask, "Did you get that?" Saying something like this is a lot like a TCP acknowledgment—it's designed to get you verification. From time to time (especially on cell phones), people also ask, "Are you still there?" They end their conversations with a "Goodbye" of some kind, putting closure on the phone call. TCP also performs these types of functions.

Alternately, using UDP is like sending a postcard. To do that, you don't need to contact the other party first. You simply write your message, address the postcard, and mail it. This is analogous to UDP's connectionless orientation. Since the message on the postcard is probably not a matter of life or death, you don't need an acknowledgment of its receipt. Similarly, UDP does not involve acknowledgments.

Port Numbers

TCP and UDP must use port numbers to communicate with the upper layers, because they're what keeps track of different conversations crossing the network simultaneously. Originating-source port numbers are dynamically assigned by the source host and will equal some number starting at 1024. 1023 and below are defined in RFC 3232, which discusses what are called well-known port numbers.

Virtual circuits that don't use an application with a well-known port number are assigned port numbers randomly from a specific range instead. These port numbers identify the source and destination application or process in the TCP segment.

Figure 4.24 illustrates how both TCP and UDP use port numbers to identify well-known applications.

FIGURE 4.24   Port numbers for TCP and UDP

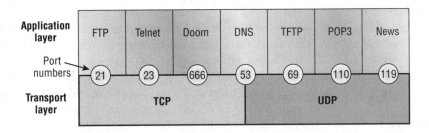

The different port numbers that can be used are explained next:

- Numbers below 1024 are considered well-known port numbers and are defined in RFC 3232.

- Numbers 1024 and above are used by the upper layers to set up sessions with other hosts, and by TCP to use as source and destination addresses in the TCP segment.

In the following sections we'll take a look at an analyzer output showing a TCP session.

TCP Session: Source Port

The following listing shows a TCP session captured with Etherpeek protocol analyzer software:

```
TCP - Transport Control Protocol
  Source Port:      5973
  Destination Port: 23
  Sequence Number:  1456389907
  Ack Number:       1242056456
  Offset:           5
  Reserved:         %000000
  Code:             %011000
        Ack is valid
        Push Request
  Window:           61320
  Checksum:         0x61a6
  Urgent Pointer:   0
  No TCP Options
  TCP Data Area:
  vL.5.+.5.+.5.+.5  76 4c 19 35 11 2b 19 35 11 2b 19 35 11
    2b 19 35 +. 11 2b 19
Frame Check Sequence: 0x0d00000f
```

Notice that the source host makes up the source port; in this case it is 5973. The destination port is 23, which is used to tell the receiving host the purpose of the intended connection (Telnet).

By looking at this session, you can see that the source host makes up the source port. But why does the source make up a port number? To differentiate between sessions with different hosts, my friend. How else would a server know where information is coming from if it didn't have a different number from a sending host? TCP and the upper layers don't use hardware and logical addresses to understand the sending host's address like the Data Link and Network layer protocols do. Instead, they use port numbers. And it's easy to imagine the receiving host getting thoroughly confused if all the hosts used the same port number to get to FTP!

TCP Session: Destination Port

Now, you'll sometimes look at an analyzer and see that only the source port is above 1024 and the destination port is a well-known port, as shown in the following Etherpeek trace:

```
TCP - Transport Control Protocol
 Source Port:        1144
 Destination Port: 80 World Wide Web HTTP
 Sequence Number:  9356570
 Ack Number:        0
 Offset:            7
 Reserved:          %000000
 Code:              %000010
       Synch Sequence
 Window:            8192
 Checksum:          0x57E7
 Urgent Pointer:    0
 TCP Options:
  Option Type: 2 Maximum Segment Size
    Length:    4
    MSS:       536
  Option Type: 1 No Operation
  Option Type: 1 No Operation
  Option Type: 4
    Length:    2
    Opt Value:
 No More HTTP Data
Frame Check Sequence: 0x43697363
```

As expected, the source port is over 1024, but the destination port is 80, or HTTP service. The server, or receiving host, will change the destination port if it needs to.

In the preceding trace, a "syn" packet is being sent to the destination device. This is visible in the Code section (Etherpeek represents it as Synch). The syn sequence is what's telling the remote destination device that it wants to create a session.

TCP Session: Syn Packet Acknowledgment

The next trace shows an acknowledgment to the syn packet:

```
TCP - Transport Control Protocol
  Source Port:       80 World Wide Web HTTP
  Destination Port: 1144
  Sequence Number:   2873580788
  Ack Number:        9356571
  Offset:            6
  Reserved:          %000000
  Code:              %010010
      Ack is valid
      Synch Sequence
  Window:            8576
  Checksum:          0x5F85
  Urgent Pointer:    0
  TCP Options:
    Option Type: 2 Maximum Segment Size
      Length:    4
      MSS:       1460
  No More HTTP Data
Frame Check Sequence: 0x6E203132
```

Notice the *Ack is valid*, which means that the source port was accepted and the device agreed to create a virtual circuit with the originating host.

And here again, you can see that the response from the server shows the source is 80 and the destination is the 1144 sent from the originating host—all's well.

The Internet Layer Protocols

In the DoD model, there are two main reasons for the Internet layer's existence: routing, and providing a single network interface to the upper layers.

None of the other upper- or lower-layer protocols have any functions relating to routing—that complex and important task belongs entirely to the Internet layer. The Internet layer's second duty is to provide a single network interface to the upper-layer protocols. Without this layer, application programmers would need to write "hooks" into every one of their applications for each different Network Access protocol. This would not only be a pain in the neck, but it would lead to different versions of each application—one for Ethernet, another one for Token Ring, and so on. To prevent this, IP provides one single network interface for the upper-layer protocols. That accomplished, it's then the job of IP and the various Network Access protocols to get along and work together.

All network roads don't lead to Rome—they lead to IP. And all the other protocols at this layer, as well as all those in the upper layers, use it. Never forget that. Let me say it again: all paths through the DoD model go through IP. The following sections describe the protocols at the Internet layer:

- Internet Protocol (IP)
- Internet Control Message Protocol (ICMP)
- Address Resolution Protocol (ARP)
- Reverse Address Resolution Protocol (RARP)

Internet Protocol (IP)

IP essentially is the Internet layer. The other protocols found here merely exist to support it. IP holds the big picture and could be said to "see all," in that it's aware of all the interconnected networks. It has this ability because all the machines on the network have a software, or logical, address called an IP address.

IP looks at each packet's address. Then, using a routing table, it decides where a packet is to be sent next, choosing the best path. The protocols of the Network Access layer at the bottom of the DoD model don't possess IP's enlightened scope of the entire network; they deal only with physical links (local networks).

Identifying devices on networks requires answering these two questions: Which network is it on? and What is its ID on that network? The first answer is the software address, or logical address (the correct street). The second answer is the hardware address (the correct mailbox). All hosts on a network have a logical ID called an IP address. This is the software, or logical, address and contains valuable encoded information, which greatly simplifies the complex task of routing. (Please note that IP is discussed in RFC 791.)

IP receives segments from the Host-to-Host layer and fragments them into datagrams (packets) if necessary. IP then reassembles datagrams back into segments on the receiving side. Each datagram is assigned the IP address of the sender and of the recipient. Each router (Layer 3 device) that receives a datagram makes routing decisions based on the packet's destination IP address.

Figure 4.25 shows an IP header. This will give you an idea of what the IP protocol has to go through every time user data is sent from the upper layers and is to be sent to a remote network.

FIGURE 4.25   IP header

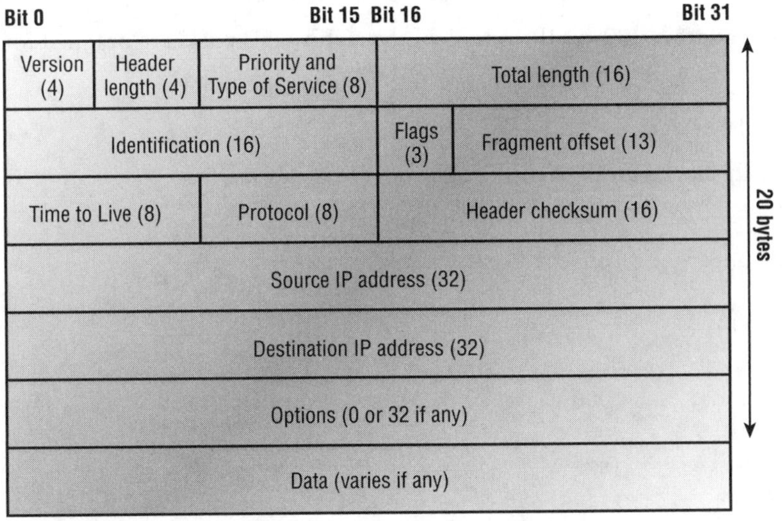

The following fields make up the IP header:

Version   IP version number.

Header Length (HLEN)   Header length in 32-bit words.

Type of Service (ToS) with IP Precedence Bits   Type of Service tells how the datagram should be handled. The first three bits are the priority bits.

Total length   Length of the packet including header and data.

Identification   Unique IP packet value.

Flags   Specifies whether fragmentation should occur.

Fragment offset   Provides fragmentation and reassembly if the packet is too large to put in a frame. It also allows different MTUs on the Internet.

Time to live (TTL)   The TTL is set into a packet when it is originally generated. If it doesn't get to where it wants to go before the TTL expires, boom—it's gone. This stops IP packets from continuously circling the network looking for a home.

Protocol   This is the port of the upper-layer protocol (TCP is port 6 or UDP is port 17 [hex]). This allows IP to know which Transport layer protocol to pass the packet too.

Header checksum   This means that this CRC is run on the IP header only.

Source IP address   32-bit IP address of the sending station.

Destination IP address   32-bit IP address of the station this packet is destined for.

Options   Used for network testing, debugging, security, and more.

Data   Upper-layer data.

Here's a snapshot of an IP packet caught on a network analyzer (notice that all the header information just discussed appears here):

```
IP Header - Internet Protocol Datagram
  Version:                4
  Header Length:          5
  Precedence:             0
  Type of Service:        %000
  Unused:                 %00
  Total Length:           187
  Identifier:             22486
  Fragmentation Flags:    %010 Do Not Fragment
  Fragment Offset:        0
  Time To Live:           60
  IP Type:                0x06 TCP
  Header Checksum:        0xd031
  Source IP Address:      10.7.1.30
  Dest. IP Address:       10.7.1.10
No Internet Datagram Options
```

Can you distinguish the logical, or IP, addresses in this header?

The Type field—it's typically a Protocol field, but this analyzer sees it as an IP Type field—is important. If the header didn't carry the protocol information for the next layer, IP wouldn't know what to do with the data carried in the packet. The example above tells IP to hand the segment to TCP.

Figure 4.26 demonstrates how the Network layer sees the protocols at the Transport layer when it needs to hand a packet to the upper-layer protocols.

FIGURE 4.26   The Protocol field in an IP header

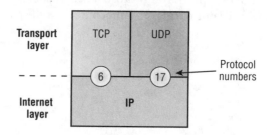

In this example, the Protocol field tells IP to send the data to either TCP port 6 or UDP port 17 (both hex addresses). But it will only be UDP or TCP if the data is part of a data stream headed for an upper-layer service or application. It could just as easily be destined for ICMP, ARP, or some other type of Network layer protocol.

Table 4.3 is a list of some other popular protocols that can be specified in the Protocol field.

TABLE 4.3   Possible Protocols Found in the Protocol Field of an IP Header

Protocol	Protocol Number
ICMP	1
IGRP	9
EIGRP	88
OSPF	89
IPv6	41
GRE	47
IPX in IP	111
Layer-2 tunnel (L2TP)	115

Internet Control Message Protocol (ICMP)

ICMP works at the Network layer and is used by IP for many different services. ICMP is a management protocol and messaging service provider for IP. Its messages are carried as IP datagrams. RFC 1256 is an annex to ICMP, which affords hosts' extended capability in discovering routes to gateways.

Periodically, router advertisements are announced over the network, reporting IP addresses for the router's network interfaces. Hosts listen for these network infomercials to acquire route information. A router solicitation is a request for immediate advertisements and may be sent by a host when it starts up.

NOTE   RFC 792 references ICMP and describes how ICMP must be implemented by all TCP/IP hosts.

The following are some common events and messages that ICMP relates to:

Destination Unreachable   If a router can't send an IP datagram any further, it uses ICMP to send a message back to the sender, advising it of the situation. For example, if a router receives a packet destined for a network that the router doesn't know about, it will send an ICMP Destination Unreachable message back to the sending station.

Buffer Full   If a router's memory buffer for receiving incoming datagrams is full, it will use ICMP to send out this message until the congestion abates.

Hops   Each IP datagram is allotted a certain number of routers, called hops, to pass through. If it reaches its limit of hops before arriving at its destination, the last router to receive that datagram deletes it. The executioner router then uses ICMP to send an obituary message, informing the sending machine of the demise of its datagram.

Ping   Ping (Packet Internet Groper) uses ICMP echo messages to check the physical and logical connectivity of machines on an internetwork.

Traceroute   Traceroute uses the TTL field and receives progressive ICMP timeouts to discover the path a packet takes as it traverses an internetwork.

Both Ping and Traceroute (also just called Trace; Microsoft Windows uses tracert) allow you to verify address configurations in your internetwork.

The following data is from a network analyzer catching an ICMP echo request:

```
Flags:          0x00
 Status:         0x00
 Packet Length: 78
 Timestamp:      14:04:25.967000 05/06/2002
Ethernet Header
 Destination: 00:a0:24:6e:0f:a8
 Source:        00:80:c7:a8:f0:3d
 Ether-Type:   08-00 IP
IP Header - Internet Protocol Datagram
 Version:             4
 Header Length:       5
 Precedence:          0
 Type of Service:    %000
 Unused:             %00
 Total Length:       60
 Identifier:         56325
 Fragmentation Flags: %000
```

```
Fragment Offset:       0
Time To Live:          32
IP Type:               0x01 ICMP
Header Checksum:       0x2df0
Source IP Address:     100.100.100.2
Dest. IP Address:      100.100.100.1
No Internet Datagram Options
ICMP - Internet Control Messages Protocol
 ICMP Type:            8 Echo Request
 Code:                 0
 Checksum:             0x395c
 Identifier:           0x0300
 Sequence Number: 4352
 ICMP Data Area:
 abcdefghijklmnop   61 62 63 64 65 66 67 68 69 6a 6b 6c 6d
 qrstuvwabcdefghi   71 72 73 74 75 76 77 61 62 63 64 65 66
Frame Check Sequence: 0x00000000
```

Notice anything unusual? Did you catch the fact that even though ICMP works at the Internet (Network) layer, it still uses IP to do the Ping request? The Type field in the IP header is 0x01, which specifies ICMP

The Ping program just uses the alphabet in the data portion of the packet as a payload, 100 bytes by default.

If you remember reading about the Data Link layer and the different frame types earlier in this chapter, you should be able to look at the preceding trace and tell what type of Ethernet frame this is. The only fields are destination hardware address, source hardware address, and Ether-Type. The only frame that uses an Ether-Type field exclusively is an Ethernet_II frame. (SNAP uses an Ether-Type field also, but only within an 802.2 LLC field, which isn't present in the frame.)

Address Resolution Protocol (ARP)

ARP finds the hardware address of a host from a known IP address. Here's how it works: when IP has a datagram to send, it must inform a Network Access protocol, such as Ethernet or Token Ring, of the destination's hardware address on the local network. (It has already been informed by upper-layer protocols of the destination's IP address.) If IP doesn't find the destination host's hardware address in the ARP cache, it uses ARP to find this information.

As IP's detective, ARP interrogates the local network by sending out a broadcast asking the machine with the specified IP address to reply with its hardware address. So basically, ARP translates the software (IP) address into a hardware address—for example, the destination machine's Ethernet board address—and from it, deduces its whereabouts on LAN by broadcasting for this address. Figure 4.27 shows how an ARP looks to a local network:

FIGURE 4.27   Local ARP broadcast

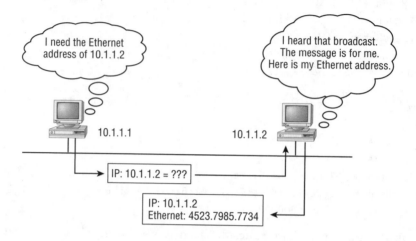

 ARP resolves IP addresses to Ethernet (MAC) addresses.

The following trace shows an ARP broadcast. Notice that the destination hardware address is unknown, and is all Fs in hex (all 1s in binary) and a hardware address broadcast:

```
Flags:          0x00
Status:         0x00
Packet Length:  64
Timestamp:      09:17:29.574000 01/04/2002
Ethernet Header
Destination:    FF:FF:FF:FF:FF:FF Ethernet Broadcast
Source:         00:A0:24:48:60:A5
Protocol Type:  0x0806 IP ARP
ARP - Address Resolution Protocol
Hardware:                  1 Ethernet (10Mb)
Protocol:                  0x0800 IP
Hardware Address Length:   6
```

```
Protocol Address Length: 4
Operation:              1 ARP Request
Sender Hardware Address: 00:A0:24:48:60:A5
Sender Internet Address: 172.16.10.3
Target Hardware Address: 00:00:00:00:00:00 (ignored)
Target Internet Address: 172.16.10.10
Extra bytes (Padding):
    ............... 0A 0A 0A 0A 0A 0A 0A 0A 0A 0A 0A 0A 0A
    0A 0A 0A 0A 0A
Frame Check Sequence: 0x00000000
```

Reverse Address Resolution Protocol (RARP)

When an IP machine happens to be a diskless machine, it has no way of initially knowing its IP address—but it does know its MAC address. RARP discovers the identity of the IP address for a diskless machine by sending out a packet that includes its MAC address and a request for the IP address assigned to that MAC address. A designated machine, called a RARP server, responds with the answer, and the identity crisis is over. RARP uses the information it does know about the machine's MAC address to learn its IP address and complete the machine's ID portrait.

 RARP resolves Ethernet (MAC) addresses to IP addresses.

Exam Essentials

Know the Process/Application layer protocols.   Telnet is a terminal emulation protocol and it allows you to log into a remote host and run programs. File Transfer Protocol (FTP) is a connection-oriented service that allows you to transfer files. Trivial FTP (TFTP) is a connectionless file transfer program. Simple Mail Transfer Protocol (SMTP) is a send-mail program.

Know the Host-to-Host layer protocols.   Transmission Control Protocol (TCP) is a connection-oriented protocol that provides reliable network service by using acknowledgments and flow control. User Datagram Protocol (UDP) is a connectionless protocol that provides low overhead and is considered unreliable.

Know the Internet layer protocols.   Internet Protocol (IP) is a connectionless protocol that provides network address and routing through an internetwork. Address Resolution Protocol (ARP) finds a hardware address from a known IP address. Reverse ARP (RARP) finds an IP address from a known hardware address. Internet Control Message Protocol (ICMP) provides diagnostics and unreachable messages.

4.6 Describe the Components of Network Devices

In order to configure and troubleshoot a Cisco internetwork, you need to know the major components of Cisco routers and understand what each one does. Table 4.4 describes the major Cisco router components:

TABLE 4.4   Cisco Router Components

Component	Description
Bootstrap	Stored in the microcode of the ROM, the bootstrap is used to bring a router up during initialization. It will boot the router and then load the IOS.
POST (power-on-self-test)	Stored in the microcode of the ROM, the POST is used to check the basic functionality of the router hardware and determines which interfaces are present.
ROM monitor	Stored in the microcode of the ROM, the ROM monitor is used for manufacturing, testing, and troubleshooting
Mini-IOS	Called the RXBOOT or bootloader by Cisco, the mini-IOS is a small IOS in ROM that can be used to bring up an interface and load a Cisco IOS into flash memory. The mini-IOS can also perform a few other maintenance operations.
RAM (random access memory)	Used to hold packet buffers, ARP cache, routing tables, and also the software and data structures that allow the router to function. running-config is stored in RAM, and the IOS can also be run from RAM in some routers.
ROM (read-only memory)	Used to start and maintain the router.
Flash memory	Used on the router to hold the Cisco IOS. Flash memory is not erased when the router is reloaded. It is an EEPROM created by Intel.
NVRAM (nonvolatile RAM)	Used to hold the router and switch configuration. NVRAM is not erased when the router or switch is reloaded.
Configuration register	Used to control how the router boots up. This value can be seen with the show version command and typically is 0x2102, which tells the router to load the IOS from flash memory.

When a router boots up, it performs a series of steps, called the *boot sequence*, to test the hardware and load the necessary software. The boot sequence consists of the following steps:

1. The router performs a POST. The POST tests the hardware to verify that all components of the device are operational and present.

2. The bootstrap looks for and loads the Cisco IOS software. By default, the IOS software is loaded from flash memory in all Cisco routers.

3. The IOS software looks for a valid configuration file stored in NVRAM. This file is called `startup-config` and is only there if an administrator copies the `running-config` file into NVRAM.

4. If a `startup-config` file is in NVRAM, the router will load and run this file. The router is now operational. If a `startup-config` file is not in NVRAM, the router will start the setup mode configuration upon bootup.

Exam Essentials

Know the different components on a Cisco router.   You need to know the difference between RAM, ROM, NVRAM, and Flash types of memory. Also, understand that the configuration register is used to control router bootup.

4.7 Evaluate Rules for Packet Control

When considering Cisco routers, there is really only one rule for packet control, and that rule is an access control list or ACL. As you know, ACLs are used extensively by IOS for many functions beyond packet control. However, they are the main tool used to control packets in an internetwork.

An *access list* is essentially a list of conditions that categorize packets. Such a list can be really helpful when you need to exercise control over network traffic—it would be your tool of choice for decision-making in these situations.

One of the most common and easy-to-understand uses of access lists is for filtering unwanted packets when you are implementing security policies. You can set them up to make very specific decisions about regulating traffic patterns so that they'll only allow certain hosts to access WWW resources on the Internet while restricting others. With the right combination of access lists, network managers arm themselves with the power to enforce nearly any security policy they can invent.

Access lists can even be used in other situations that don't necessarily involve blocking packets. You can use them to control which networks will or won't be advertised by dynamic routing protocols. Creating or scripting the access list uses the same syntax or format regardless of application. The difference here is simply how you apply them—to a routing protocol instead of an interface. When you apply an access list like this, it's called a *distribute list*, and it doesn't stop routing advertisements, it just controls their content. You can also use access lists to categorize packets for queuing or QoS type services, and for controlling which types of traffic can activate an expensive ISDN link.

> The CCNA focuses on using access lists as packet filters, so that's what we're going to zero in on too!

Creating access lists is really a lot like programming a series of if-then statements—if a given condition is met, then a given action is taken. If the specific condition isn't met, nothing happens, and the next statement is evaluated. Access lists statements are basically packet filters that packets are compared against, categorized by, and acted upon accordingly. Once the lists are built, they can be applied to either inbound or outbound traffic on any interface. Applying an access list causes the router to analyze every packet crossing that interface in the specified direction and take the appropriate action.

There are a few important rules a packet follows when it's being compared with an access list:

- It's always compared with each line of the access list in sequential order; that is, it'll always start with the first line of the access list, then go to line 2, then line 3, and so on.

- It's compared with lines of the access list only until a match is made. Once the packet matches the condition on a line of the access list, the packet is acted upon, and no further comparisons take place.

- There is an implicit "deny" at the end of each access list—this means that if a packet doesn't match the condition on any of the lines in the access list, the packet will be discarded.

Each of these rules has some powerful implications when you are filtering IP packets with access lists, so keep in mind that creating effective access lists truly takes some practice.

Exam Essentials

Understand the relationship between access lists and packet control.   Access lists can be used to filter or drop packets in order to control who has access to resources such as VTY, or to determine what networks are advertised by dynamic routing protocols.

Understand the term "implicit deny."   At the end of every access list is an implicit deny. What this means is that if a packet does not match any of the lines in the access list, then it will be discarded. Also, if you have nothing but deny statements in your list, then the list will not permit any packets.

4.8 Evaluate Key Characteristics of WANs

So, what is it that makes something a WAN instead of a LAN? Distance is the first idea that comes to mind, but these days, wireless LANs can cover some serious turf! So, is it bandwidth? Here again, really big pipes can be had for a price in many places, so that's not it either. Well, what then? Perhaps one of the best ways to tell a WAN from a LAN is that you generally own a LAN infrastructure, but you generally lease your WAN infrastructure from a service provider. While modern technologies will blur even this definition, it applies well in the context of the CCNA. I've already talked about a data link that you usually own (Ethernet), but now we're going to take a look at the data links you most often don't own, but instead lease from a service provider.

Key to understanding WAN technologies is being familiar with the different WAN terms and connection types often used by service providers to join your networks together. So I'll begin by going over these with you.

Defining WAN Terms

It would be a good idea to understand the following terms that service providers commonly use before ordering a WAN service type:

CPE   Or customer premises equipment, is, (surprise!) equipment that's owned by the subscriber and located on the subscriber's premises.

Demarcation point   Marks the spot that the service provider's responsibility ends and the CPE begins. It's generally a device in a telecommunications closet owned and installed by the telco. The customer is responsible for installing cable (extended demarc) from this box to the CPE—usually in the form of a CSU/DSU or ISDN interface.

Local loop   This connects the demarc to the closest switching office, called a central office (CO).

Central office (CO)   This point connects the customers to the provider's switching network. A CO is sometimes referred to as a point of presence (POP).

Toll network   These are trunk lines inside a WAN provider's network. The toll network is a collection of switches and facilities.

Make sure you fully dial these terms in—they're critical to understanding WAN technologies!

WAN Connection Types

Figure 4.28 shows the different WAN connection types that can be used to connect your LANs together over a DCE network.

FIGURE 4.28 WAN connection types

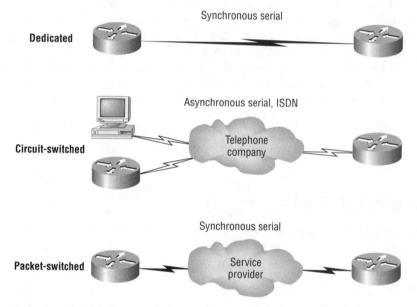

Here's a description of the different WAN connection types:

Leased lines Typically, these are referred to as a point-to-point connection or dedicated connection. A leased line is a preestablished WAN communications path from the CPE, through the DCE switch, to the CPE of the remote site; this allows DTE networks to communicate at any time with no setup procedures before transmitting data. If you're rolling in dough, it's really the best choice. It uses synchronous serial lines up to 45Mbps. HDLC and PPP encapsulations are frequently used on leased lines.

Circuit switching When you hear circuit switching, think phone call. The big advantage is cost—you only pay for the time you actually use. No data can transfer before an end-to-end connection is established. Circuit switching uses dial-up modems or ISDN and is used for low-bandwidth data transfers.

Packet switching This is a WAN switching method that allows you to share bandwidth with other companies to save money. Think of packet switching as a network that's designed to look like a leased line (always available), yet it costs more like circuit switching (pay for what you use). Think I'm making this up? I'm not, but there is a downside—if you need to transfer data constantly, forget about this option. Just get yourself a leased line. This will only work well if your data transfers are bursty in nature. Frame Relay and X.25 are packet-switching technologies. Speeds can range from 56Kbps to T3 (45Mbps).

WAN Protocols

Many WAN protocols have been developed. Some have even been deployed, and a few have seen huge deployments. Following is a look at some of the most popular WAN protocols:

Frame Relay   A packet-switched technology that emerged in the early 1990s, Frame Relay is a Data Link and Physical layer specification that provides high performance. Frame Relay is a successor to X.25, except that much of the technology in X.25 used to compensate for physical errors (noisy lines) has been eliminated. Frame Relay can be more cost-effective than point-to-point links, and can typically run at speeds of 64Kbps up to 45Mbps (T3). Frame Relay provides features for dynamic bandwidth allocation and congestion control.

LAPB   Link Access Procedure, Balanced (LAPB) was created to be a connection-oriented protocol at the Data Link layer for use with X.25. It can also be used as a simple Data Link transport. LAPB causes a huge amount of overhead because of its strict timeout and windowing techniques.

HDLC   High-Level Data Link Control (HDLC) was derived from Synchronous Data Link Control (SDLC), which was created by IBM as a Data Link connection protocol. HDLC is a connection-oriented protocol at the Data Link layer, but it has very little overhead compared to LAPB. HDLC wasn't intended to encapsulate multiple Network layer protocols across the same link. The HDLC header carries no identification of the type of protocol being carried inside the HDLC encapsulation. Because of this, each vendor that uses HDLC has their own way of identifying the Network layer protocol, which means that each vendor's HDLC is proprietary for their equipment.

PPP   Point-to-Point Protocol (PPP) is an industry-standard protocol. Because all multi-protocol versions of HDLC are proprietary, you can use PPP to create point-to-point links between different vendors' equipment. It uses a NCP field in the Data Link header to identify the Network layer protocol. It allows authentication and multilink connections and can be run over asynchronous and synchronous links.

ATM   Asynchronous Transfer Mode (ATM) was created for time-sensitive traffic; it provides simultaneous transmission of voice, video, and data. ATM uses cells instead of packets that are a fixed 53-bytes long. It also uses isochronous clocking (external clocking) to help the data move faster.

Exam Essentials

Know the differences between leased lines, circuit switching, and packet switching.   A leased line is a dedicated connection, a circuit-switched connection is like a phone call and can be on or off, and packet switching is essentially a connection that looks like a leased line but is priced more like a circuit-switched connection.

Understand the different WAN protocols.   Pay particular attention to HDLC, Frame Relay, and PPP. HDLC is the default encapsulation on Cisco routers; PPP provides an industry-standard way of encapsulating multiple routed protocols across a link and must be used when connecting equipment from multiple vendors. Frame Relay is a packet-switched technology that can offer cost advantages over leased lines but has more complex configuration options.

Review Questions

1. Which of the following are Presentation layer protocols? Select all that apply.
   A. TFTP
   B. IP
   C. RTF
   D. QuickTime
   E. MIDI

2. Which two statements about a reliable connection-oriented data transfer are true?
   A. Receiving hosts acknowledge receipt of data.
   B. When buffers are full, packets are discarded and are not retransmitted.
   C. Windowing is used to provide flow control and unacknowledged data segments.
   D. If the transmitting host's timer expires before receipt of an acknowledgment, the transmitting host drops the virtual circuit.

3. If you use either Telnet or FTP, which is the highest layer you are using to transmit data?
   A. Application
   B. Presentation
   C. Session
   D. Transport

4. The DoD model (also called the TCP/IP stack) has four layers. Which layer is the Network layer from the OSI model equivalent to on the DoD model?
   A. Application
   B. Host-to-Host
   C. Internet
   D. Network Access

5. You want to install a wireless network in your corporate office and need good speed, but you only need a range of no more than about 250 feet. Which of the following wireless technologies should you install?
   A. Narrowband
   B. Narrowband PCS
   C. Broadband PCS
   D. Infrared
   E. Spread Spectrum

6. Which layer of the OSI provides translation of data?

    A. Application

    B. Presentation

    C. Session

    D. Transport

    E. Data Link

7. Which of the following are true? (Choose two.)

    A. TCP is connection-oriented but doesn't use flow control.

    B. IP is not necessary on all hosts that use TCP.

    C. ICMP must be implemented by all TCP/IP hosts.

    D. ARP is used to find a hardware address from a known IP address.

8. Which LAN switch method is also known as a modified version of cut-through?

    A. Cut-throughout

    B. FragmentFree

    C. Store-and-forward

    D. Store-and-release

9. Which of the following are true regarding store-and-forward? (Select all that apply.)

    A. The latency time varies with frame size.

    B. The latency time is constant.

    C. The frame is transmitted only after the complete frame is received.

    D. The frame is transmitted as soon as the header of the frame is read.

10. What could happen on a network if no loop avoidance schemes are put in place? (Choose two options.)

    A. Faster convergence times

    B. Broadcast storms

    C. Multiple frame copies

    D. IP routing will cause flapping on a serial link.

Answers to Review Questions

1. C, D, E. The Presentation layer defines many protocols; RTF, QuickTime, and MIDI are correct answers. IP is a Network layer protocol; TFTP is an Application layer protocol.

2. A, C. When a virtual circuit is created, windowing is used for flow control and acknowledgment of data.

3. A. Both FTP and Telnet use TCP at the Transport layer; however, they both are Application layer protocols, so the Application layer is the best answer for this question.

4. C. The four layers of the DoD model are Application/Process, Host-to-Host, Internet, and Network Access. The Internet layer is equivalent to the Network layer of the OSI model.

5. E. Spread Spectrum LANs typically can run up to 11Mbps for about 300 feet depending on the environment, although the speeds are increasing to 20Mbps or higher.

6. B. The only layer of the OSI model that can actually change data is the Presentation layer.

7. C, D. ICMP must be implemented by all TCP/IP hosts, and ARP is used to find a hardware address from a known IP address. TCP always requires IP, and TCP always uses flow control.

8. B. The modified version of cut-through is called FragmentFree. This technology essentially delays forwarding of the frame until the collision window has passed, resulting in fewer errors. Store-and-forward operates differently. There is no such thing as cut-throughout or store-and-release.

9. A, C. Store-and-forward latency (delay) will always vary because the complete frame must be received before the frame is transmitted back out the switch.

10. B, C. Broadcast storms and multiple frame copies are typically found in a network that has multiple links to remote locations without some type of loop-avoidance scheme.

Index

Note to the reader: Throughout this index **boldfaced** page numbers indicate primary discussions of a topic. *Italicized* page numbers indicate illustrations.

E